# IN THE WEEKLY PARASHAH

The classical interpretations of major topics and themes in the Torah

by
Yehuda Nachshoni

translated from the Hebrew by
Shmuel Himelstein

FIRST EDITION
First Impression . . . October, 1988

Published and Distributed by
MESORAH PUBLICATIONS, Ltd.
Brooklyn, New York 11232

Distributed in Israel by
MESORAH MAFITZIM / J. GROSSMAN
Rechov Harav Uziel 117
Jerusalem, Israel

Distributed in Europe by
J. LEHMANN HEBREW BOOKSELLERS
20 Cambridge Terrace
Gateshead, Tyne and Wear
England NE8 1RP

THE ARTSCROLL JUDAICA CLASSICS®
STUDIES IN THE WEEKLY PARASHAH
Vol I: Bereishis
© Copyright 1988, by MESORAH PUBLICATIONS, Ltd.
4401 Second Avenue / Brooklyn, N.Y. 11232 / (718) 921-9000

No part of this book may be reproduced
in any form without **written** permission from the copyright holder,
except by a reviewer who wishes to quote brief passages in connection with a review
written for inclusion in magazines or newspapers.

THE RIGHTS OF THE COPYRIGHT HOLDER WILL BE STRICTLY ENFORCED.

ISBN:
0-89906-933-9 (hard cover)
0-89906-934-7 (paperback)

Typography by CompuScribe at ArtScroll Studios, Ltd.
4401 Second Avenue / Brooklyn, N.Y. 11232 / (718) 921-9000
Printed in the United States of America by Noble Book Press Corp.
Bound by Sefercraft, Quality Bookbinders, Ltd. Brooklyn, N.Y.

❧ Publisher's Preface

Since Rabbi Yehudah Nachshoni's writings on the *parashah* first appeared many years ago in a magazine, its respectful audience grew and grew. Here was something new and different, yet something as firmly rooted in the tradition of Torah scholarship as the classic commentators from which it drew and upon which it shed such dazzling light. In each weekly reading, he chose topics, usually the most difficult ones, and illuminated them with the primary rays of the major commentators, spanning hundreds of years. The range of his knowledge was breathtaking; no less so was his ability to distill the main lines of thought from among scores and often hundreds of books, and show where they converged and where they differed.

The years went by, and he received requests from all sides that his work be collected in book form. Refining his material and adding to it, Rabbi Nachshoni acceded to these requests with *Hagus BaParshios HaMikra*, or *Studies in the Weekly Parashah*. To two generations of his "students," his work was known simply as "Nachshoni," and has gone through several printings.

As people to whom "Nachshoni" has been a valued teacher over the years, we consider it a great privilege to present this seminal work in English for the first time. We have no doubt that this brilliant scholar and teacher will soon acquire a new and devoted audience in his "new" language, an audience that will rival in enthusiasm the one he has long had in the original.

We are grateful to Shmuel Blitz, director of ArtScroll/Jerusalem, who shepherded the translation and editing through every stage of production. His absolute devotion to quality shows in every facet of the book. We are also grateful to Shmuel Himelstein who translated and to Rabbi Avie Gold who edited and prepared the manuscript for publication.

It is our sincere hope that this and the following volumes of "Nachshoni" will bring a new and broader understanding of the Torah to thousands of readers in the English-speaking world. Surely that will be the most meaningful memorial that can be erected to the memory of this great scholar and teacher.

Cheshvan 5749   Rabbi Meir Zlotowitz
October 1988   Rabbi Nosson Scherman

ও§ Author's Preface to the Hebrew Edition

This book is being published for the first time in its present form, but it is not new in terms of thought and research in the chapters of our Torah, as God has enabled me to understand them. For many years I published my inquiries into the Torah in various publications. This work was well received by rabbis, Torah scholars, and students of Scripture. Many have urged me to continue my work and to publish in book form what I have done up to now. Once it became possible for me to do so, I acceded to their request. In those who have assisted me, I perceived Heavenly assistance, so I set aside my reluctance in deference to His will and that of my good friends, who felt that the public would benefit from this volume.

※ ※ ※

What is the nature of this work?

It would seem at first glance that it contains nothing new, yet it is *entirely* new. It is not new because the vast majority of the commentary is found in the books of the *Rishonim* and *Acharonim*, the classic early and later commentators of all the generations. I have added my own thoughts, which God has granted me. It would appear that what I have written is but a drop in the ocean of the hundreds and even thousands of books that have illuminated the *parashah* throughout the generations. But the novelty of this book is that this wealth of information and commentary has been distilled and re-distilled, but without changing the minutest part of their essential intention. Rather, the many commentaries have been broken down to their main lines of thought. Such a task involves a backbreaking effort of research and gathering, editing so that much is captured in as few words as possible, and the concentration of hundreds of thoughts and opinions into small segments that can be woven together into a large book that will be original in its content and nature.

It should be known that for every explanation that appears in the book I sometimes omitted dozens more, because it seemed to me that one captured the central meaning of the particular topic as I understood it. This goal required research and investigation into all the books of commentary, exposition, homiletics, and Kabbalah, so that I could produce a book that more or less includes them all. I believe that this work, which concentrates not on a particular saying or idea, but on entire chapters of the Torah, is original and unique in the range of commentary on the Torah. Primarily, it is not a linguistic commentary, but one that follows the spirit of the Torah according to how our generation can comprehend it. It is for the reader to determine whether this manner of preparation suits his needs: If the reader chooses to recognize the uniqueness of the book, well and good. If there are those who ask, "What is new about it?" — this massive effort is more than wisdom, it is an enhancement of the knowledge that God has granted me.

As a matter of principle, I have not used any commentator who is not rooted in our tradition; not only because of my negative attitude toward any commentary that was not written with a sincere desire to study Torah for its own sake, but because I have not found anything of value in their works that does not appear in the classic commentators that preceded them. Sometimes this lack of originality is masked by the author's use of language or style that makes old material appear new. But scrupulously insisting on content, I have found their central enlightening theme in the works of our earlier or later commentators, until I frequently wondered whether these supposedly original authors were familiar with the sources and simply plagiarized and poured the thoughts of others into their own vessels. Or perhaps they did not know, and thought that these old ideas of theirs were truly new. In their creations I did not find any flashes of lightning or true novella that were not said before them, except for matters that contradicted or criticized the principles of the Torah — and such ideas certainly have no place in this book.

Another facet of this book that I consider new is that all kinds of Torah commentary — from the plain meaning to the esoteric — come together in this book and are treated with equal regard, until one cannot detect a distinction between them, in their relative value or even in how they elucidate the *parashah*. The Torah is like a hammer that smashes a rock; it has seventy facets. Of course, most of the book deals with the simple meaning, because I have taken into consideration the comprehension of most students and scholars, and because books on the simple meaning are far more numerous than the others. Regarding the respective quality of the different kinds of commentaries, I take no position, and I include them all, whatever directions they take. One of the new goals of the book is to make the point that all seventy facets are of equal validity.

I hope to God that my book will be favorably received. Great and worthy people have praised it. It has been used regularly by outstanding Torah figures from all camps. I have taken their suggestions seriously and have incorporated many of them into the book, generally without mentioning them by name, because I did not want the book to be stamped as one sided or as representative of a particular philosophical perspective. To our distress, it is well known that we are very splintered, even in how we explain the Torah. I wanted this to be a book of explanation and inquiry without preconceptions. I presented it for review to qualified Torah authorities before I had it published; took their suggestions under consideration, and did what they asked of me. It would add to the book's prestige were I to publicize their names, but I did not ask their permission to do so.

※ ※ ※

I dedicate this book to the sacred memory of

אאמו״ר הרה״ג ר׳ חיים יהושע הי״ד בן אסתר לאה

והרה״ח ר׳ אברהם דוד רזמיבש ממרגרטן־גרויסוורדיין,

אמי מורתי שרה בת גיניא

והרה״ג ר׳ מאיר צבי סג״ל ממיידאן הי״ד

ולכל בני המשפחה שנספו בשואה,

שחנכוני לתורה וליהדות במאמצים עצומים.

וכן לנשמותיהם של חמי ר׳ משה ברוממר ז״ל מברגסס,

ואשתו נעכא לבית הוויער הי״ד

May this book be an eternal light to the luminous memory of my nephew

חיים יהושע הי״ד בן אחי ר׳ מאיר צבי נחשוני־רזמיבש,

ואמו רבקה תחי׳ מבני ברק

who fell in the defense of *Eretz Yisrael* in the Yom Kippur War, on 22 Tishrei, 5734, on the Egyptian side of the Suez Canal. He had a brilliant mind and was a Torah scholar of great potential from whom great accomplishments were expected, but who fell when he was only twenty-three years old.

תנצב״ה

I express my appreciation to the anonymous benefactor who encouraged me and provided the funds for the Hebrew edition of this book, on the condition that his name not be mentioned. A person's wish is his honor. For his exalted deeds, may He who knows all thoughts repay him from His treasure of good.

Yehudah Nachshoni
(Razmivash)

↭ Table of Contents

Bereishis
    I. He Told His People the Power of His Deeds 1
    II. Man in the Image of God 7
    III. He Who Increases Knowledge Increases Pain 14

Noach
    I. The Separation Between Man and Beast 20
    II. The First Covenant Between Hashem and Creation 27
    III. I Will Not Again Curse 34
    IV. The Failure of Civilization 41

Lech Lecha
    I. Avraham Avinu's Origin 48
    II. Because of Pure Belief 55
    III. The Pronouncement of the Exile and the Redemption 62
    IV. The Holy Sign of the Covenant 71

Vayeira
    I. Why Did Hashem Appear? 78
    II. S'dom and the Pilegesh in Giv'ah 85
    III. The Fear of God Prevents Sin 92
    IV. The Influence of the Akeidah on Our People's Life 99

Chayei Sarah
    I. Avraham Buys the Cave of Machpelah 108
    II. The Beauty of the Speech of our Forefathers' Servants 114
    III. The Torah of Kindness on Her Tongue 120
    IV. Hashem Determines One's Wife 127

Toldos
    I. An Eternal Struggle Between Yaakov and Esav 135
    II. The Sale of the Birthright 143
    III. Forerunners for the Hatred of Israel 150
    IV. This Is from Hashem 158

Vayeitzei

    I. Who Is Rich? He Who Is Satisfied with His Lot   164
    II. The Modesty of the Mothers   170
    III. The Sources of Work Ethics   176
    IV. A "Double" Theft from Lavan's House   182

Vayishlach

    I. Lesson of the Meeting Between Yaakov and Esav   190
    II. A Nation Which Dwells Alone   197
    III. Not by Might Nor by Power   202
    IV. Punishment According to Justice and Halachah   209

Vayeishev

    I. Brotherly Hatred as a Factor in the Exile to Egypt   216
    II. "Come and See the Works of Elokim"   223
    III. Who Sold Yosef to Egypt?   229
    IV. "For I Know All Thoughts"   235

Mikeitz

    I. Miracles and Natural Events in Man's Actions   245
    II. Yosef Interprets Dreams   252
    III. The Purpose of the False Allegations and Punishments   260

Vayigash

    I. Yosef Reveals Himself to His Brothers   267
    II. The First "Ghetto" in Jewish History   274
    III. The Wagons Which Yosef Sent   282
    IV. Going Down to Egyptian Exile   288

Vayechi

    I. Rejection of the Firstborn Cult   295
    II. Do Not Bury Me in Egypt   301
    III. To Whom Was Yaakov's Will Told?   308
    IV. Blessing or Prophecy?   313

STUDIES IN THE WEEKLY PARASHAH

הגות בפרשיות התורה

ספר בראשית
Bereishis

Bereishis – בראשית

I.

He Told His People the Power of His Deeds

R' Yitzchak said, "Since the Torah is a book of laws, it should have begun with 'this month shall be to you the first of months' (Shemos 12:2), for that was the first mitzvah given to Israel as a nation. Why, then, did it begin with the narrative of creation? The reason is in order to establish that Hashem is sovereign over the entire universe; this is in accordance with the verse (Tehillim 111:6), 'He declared to His people the power of His works, in order to give them the heritage of the nations.' Now if the other nations of the world accuse Israel of banditry for seizing the lands of the Seven Nations of Canaan, Israel will answer them: 'The entire universe belongs to Hashem. He created it and gave it to whomever He deemed fit. It was His desire to give it to the Canaanites at first, and it was then His desire to take it from them and to cede it to us'" (adapted from Rashi's introductory comment on the first verse in Bereishis).

We will explain what *Chazal* meant when they made this remarkable statement in the name of R' Yitzchak, but first it would be proper to mention a historical reason for the order of the *parashiyos* in the Torah. Let us also stress at the very beginning of our study of the Torah that *Eretz Yisrael* belongs to our nation by right, and that its conquest by Yehoshua and those who came after him was justified both historically and legally. Before that however, let us identify the 'R' Yitzchak' with whom *Rashi* begins his commentary on the Torah.

People are accustomed to say that R' Yitzchak was *Rashi's* father. This view is also found in *Divrei David* by *Taz*, quoting an old manuscript of commentary on *Rashi* that he had seen in his youth.

In *Nachal Kedumim*, *Chida* brings the same statement in the name of an anonymous source, but notes that this teaching is to be found in *Chazal*, its source being *Yalkut Shimoni* on *Parashas Bereishis*. This, though, must be a scribal error, because the statement in *Yalkut Shimoni* is in *Parashas Bo*, *Remez* 187, quoting *Midrash Tanchuma*.

This same view is also cited in a number of other places, although with minor differences. In *Bereishis Rabbah* 1 it is cited in the name of R' Yehoshua of Sichnin quoting R' Levi. In *Midrash Shir HaShirim* it is found in the name of R' Yannai, and in *Zohar Parashas Bo* in the name of R' Yitzchak.

We should note *Rashi's* description of the New Moon as the first *mitzvah* given to all does not appear in any of the texts we cited. It appears that this must be *Rashi's* own explanation of R' Yitzchak's question, just as the concluding words, "that the (other) nations of the world should not say to Israel..." are *Rashi's* own addition.

Tosafos and other *rishonim* are surprised at *Rashi's* description of the New Moon as the first *mitzvah* in the Torah, for is it not preceded by the *mitzvos* of *bris milah* and *gid hanasheh* (not to eat the sciatic nerve in the hindquarters of cattle)? They answer that *Rashi* refers to it as the first *mitzvah* that was commanded to the Jewish community as a whole. But this doesn't answer the question entirely, because if we consider the *mitzvos* that came before the giving of the Torah, we will see that *bris milah* too was given to the entire Jewish community that existed at that time, namely the family of Avraham.

∽§ Seeing and Hearing

Perhaps we can add another meaning to R' Yitzchak's question as to why the Torah didn't begin with "This month..." *Ramban*, in his commentary on the Torah, wonders how one could imagine that the Torah would not begin with *Bereishis*, when, after all, the story of creation is the basis for our faith that the world has not been in existence for all eternity, but was created *yesh mei'ayin* — "substance out of nothingness." *Ikarim* (1:11) also considers the order of the *parashiyos* as a basic introduction to the Torah. First, the Torah proclaims that Hashem is the Prime Cause of all of creation, and then it tells us that man was chosen and that he is superior to the other creatures. Following this, we are told how Hashem transmitted His words to man, that being the basis for our belief in prophecy and in the Torah's Divine origin. Afterwards, the Torah implants in us the fear of punishment for our wrongdoings, teaches us the ways of repentance, and instructs us about other principles of our faith. Thus the obvious question is: Can it be that *Chazal* really preferred the *parashah* of "This month . . ." over all the other principles which we find in the Torah until that point, to the extent that they asked why the Torah didn't start with that *parashah*?

After studying this matter, though, perhaps we can say that *Chazal's* question does not refer exclusively to the New Moon by itself as the first public *mitzvah*, but rather to the entire narrative of *yetzias Mitzrayim* — the Exodus — for its place in the Torah and in Jewish thought is loftier, perhaps, than the creation of the world. In the first of the *Aseres HaDibros* — the Ten Commandments — the Torah mentions *yetzias Mitzrayim* as the basis for our belief in the Oneness of Hashem and of Hashem's rule over all of creation, as it states there (*Shemos* 20:2), "I am Hashem your God, who took you out of the Land of Egypt." This element has been discussed extensively by both *rishonim* and *acharonim*. R' Yehudah Halevi, in his *Kuzari* 1:25, says to the king of the Khazars:

> [The Ten Commandments] do not commence, "the God of the Heavens and the earth," nor "My Creator and your Creator," but Hashem began His words to Israel with "I am Hashem your God, who took you out," and not, "the Creator of the world and your Creator." So too, when you asked me about my faith I answered you what I am obligated to do as are all of the congregation of Israel, which was made clear to them at this event that they themselves saw, and this was then followed by the ongoing tradition, which is as valid as if it had been seen."

The commentators on *Kuzari* have two different explanations of his above words:

R' Yehudah Muscato, in his *Kol Yehudah*, explains that the *Kuzari* means that the Torah mentioned *yetzias Mitzrayim* because that was what Israel saw with their own eyes, while as to the Creation, they had only heard about it from their forefathers. Thus Hashem chose a conclusive sign to make them recognize His Godliness, a fact which they had learned from their own experience, by both seeing and hearing.

R' Sa'adiah Gaon, in his *Emunos VeDeos* 3, also praises proof that was actually *seen*, but then adds that "the tradition is as trustworthy as something which one has observed with his own eyes." Similarly,

Ramban in *Parashas Va'eschanan* on the verse (*Devarim* 4:9), "Only guard yourself ... that your eyes saw," says:

> As the Torah came to us from the Omnipotent through our ears which heard and through our eyes which saw, without any intermediary, we will reject anyone who disagrees or casts doubts ... And that is as it is said, "And also in you (i.e., Moshe) will they believe forever," for when we transmit the matter (the Revelation at Sinai) to our children, they will know that this was true without a doubt, as if all the generations had seen it.
>
> What this means is that the miracle of *yetzias Mitzrayim* proves the truth of the creation of the world, with all of these events verifying one another.

Using this assumption, *Sha'arei Simchah* links the end of the Torah to the beginning, "for all the signs and the miracles which Moshe did before the eyes of all Israel" prove and verify the sanctity of our faith that "In the beginning, Hashem created." And the fact that we saw testifies to the tradition, as we noted in *Kuzari* above.

✊ Bereishis as Against Yetzias Mitzrayim

R' Yisrael Halevi, in his *Otzar Nechmad* on *Kuzari*, gives another interpretation of the latter's words. According to him, what *Kuzari* wished to say was that when the Torah mentions *yetzias Mitzrayim* in the first Commandment, it is to stress the fact that the Jewish people are a chosen nation, and that only they are linked to the Torah. The reason why the Ten Commandments did not mention that Hashem is the God of the Heavens and the earth but rather, "I am Hashem, your God who took you out of the Land of Egypt," was because Hashem wanted to prevent the other nations from claiming (*Malachi* 2:10), "Have we not all one father? Has not one God created us? Why do we deal treacherously every man against his brother?" What *Kuzari* meant in his statement, "what I am obligated to do as are all of the congregation of Israel," was to stress the principle of the difference between Israel and the other nations, which is personified by *yetzias Mitzrayim* and *not* by the Creation.

It would seem that *Otzar Nechmad's* explanation is verified by a statement of R' Yehudah Halevi, at the beginning of *Kuzari*. There the Jew mentions to the king of the Khazars: "The God of Avraham, Yitzchak and Yaakov, who took *Bnei Yisrael* out of Egypt," which arouses the surprised king to ask, "Why does he not say that Hashem created the Heavens and the earth?"

Other commentators on the Torah and on *hashkafah* also stress the preeminence of the miracle of *yetzias Mitzrayim* over the Creation. *Ikarim* (3:26) says that the miracle of *yetzias Mitzrayim* includes within itself the act of creation, as in the words of the *Shacharis* prayer, "He who each day renews the act of creation continually." Part of this continuous creation is that Hashem constantly supervises His creatures, and especially Israel.

Ibn Ezra on *Parashas Yisro* also addresses the question of R' Yehudah Halevi as to why the Torah links God's sovereignty to *yetzias Mitzrayim*. The reason is that in *yetzias Mitzrayim* the principle of the Creation is also stressed, and *yetzias Mitzrayim* includes the wonders that everyone saw at the time. In addition, our obligation to observe the *mitzvos* is tied to the fact that we were freed from slavery. *Ramban*, too, says:

> It states, "who took you out of the Land of Egypt," because the fact that they were taken out of there indicates the existence and will (of Hashem), for they left there with His knowledge and at His direction. (The Exodus) also alludes to the Creation, for if the universe were eternal, nothing of its nature could change (i.e., no miracles would have occurred). This then shows His ability, and His ability shows His Unity.

Rabbenu Bachya on the Torah also spells out the advantage of *yetzias Mitzrayim* over the Creation, and so do other commentators. (The Magid of Dubno, in his *Ohel Yaakov*, also gives this explanation.)

What emerges from all the above is that the *parashah* of *yetzias Mitzrayim* is of greater importance in implanting in us faith and in instilling in us the values of Judaism and its fundamentals than is the act of Creation, for *yetzias Mitzrayim* includes in itself: (a) the Creation, (b) the chosenness of Israel, (c) *hashgachah pratis* (Divine providence) over the world, and (d) the evidence obtained by seeing.

Thus we can understand why R' Yitzchak wondered why the Torah didn't begin with this *parashah*, which is the introduction to the *Aseres HaDibros*.

It may even be that when *Rashi* refers to "the first *mitzvah* that Israel was commanded," he means the *Aseres HaDibros*. In any event, it is definitely possible to attribute this meaning to the words of *Chazal* when they say that, "The Torah should not have begun but from 'this month is unto you.'" It is not that *Chazal* denigrated the value of the historical section of the Torah as compared to the *mitzvos* and *halachos*, but, on the contrary, they felt that the Torah should have begun with *yetzias Mitzrayim* because the preeminent historical facts, the choice of

Israel and its ties to the Torah, emerge from the Exodus. This is preferable to the story of the Creation, which is the general history of mankind, in terms of "the God of Heaven and earth."

⇜§ Miracles and Nature Are All One

Now, R' Yitzchak's answer is most appropriate. By beginning as it does, the Torah meant to stress the ties between the people of Israel and *Eretz Yisrael*, just as, in the first of the *Aseres HaDibros*, it wanted to stress the ties between Israel and the Torah. This emphasis belongs at the very beginning of the Torah, because the *mitzvos* of the Torah are bound inextricably to the Land of the Torah. And this is what *Maharal* of Prague writes in his *Gur Aryeh* on the Torah, regarding R' Yitzchak:

> And if you say that it is still difficult: What connection is there between the giving of the Land to Israel and the *mitzvos* of the Torah, that this should be written in the Torah? That is not difficult, because most of the Torah's *mitzvos* are dependent on the Land, for the *terumos* and *maasros* and the building of the *Beis HaBechirah* (i.e., the *Beis haMikdash*) depend on the Land. And if the Land does not belong to Israel, these *mitzvos* cannot be observed at all, for regarding all of these it states, "and you shall inherit it and dwell in it." The (other) nations may claim, "You are bandits and did not inherit the Land, but received it through theft." (*Ramban* too wrote that all the *mitzvos* of the Torah are the laws of "the God of the Land," namely that all the *mitzvos* belong specifically to the Land.) And therefore it had to be written in the Torah, that the Land came to Israel by right, for He created it and gave it.

Very interesting and of actual application is the explanation on the statement of R' Yitzchak, of *Chasam Sofer*, in his *d'rashos* for *Simchas Torah*. He explains that the grievance of the other nations stems primarily from their mistaken belief that Israel can be saved only through miraculous means and not by natural means. They therefore claim we are bandits for having "conquered" the land; namely by using force to conquer the Land, we have committed "ideological theft," for everything that happens to us must be miraculous, such as *yetzias Mitzrayim*. The Torah therefore began with *Bereishis*, to show that there is no difference between miraculous and natural means, and what Israel acquires and conquers according to the command of Hashem by natural means and by the use of conquest is ours, as if we had acquired it by miraculous means. The Land is ours, and we have the right to conquer it always, for (*Tehillim* 111:6), "He revealed to His people the power of His deeds, to give them the heritage of nations."

II.
Man in the Image of God

The description of the creation of man in the Torah gives rise to a number of difficulties which are dealt with by the commentators: The very form נַעֲשֶׂה — "let us make" — gives heretics an opening to question the unity of Hashem. So too is there need to understand בְּצַלְמֵנוּ כִּדְמוּתֵנוּ — "in *our* image, after *our* likeness."

Rambam, Akeidah and others explain the expression "let us make" as an invitation to have the upper beings (the angels) and lower beings (the creatures on earth) involved in the creation of man. After Hashem created the upper and lower beings, the need was felt for a creature that would link lower beings with the upper world, so that the lower beings would be able to exist. That is the essence of man. He was created from the lower beings, dust from the earth, but the life spirit in him comes from the upper beings, as it states, "and He breathed into his nostrils the breath of life."

Chazal in *Midrash Rabbah* 5 tell us:

> When the Holy One, Blessed be He, created man, He consulted with the ministering angels and said to them, "If I create him from the upper beings, he will live and not die, and if from the lower beings, he will die and not live. I will therefore create him from the upper and lower beings, so that if he lives he will die, and if he dies he will live."

This saying of *Chazal* gives a most penetrating description of man's character and nature. His personality is composed of the two contradictory elements of life and death, of the upper beings and the lower beings, and it is thus that he can fulfill his role as the central pillar joining the two worlds.

R' Samson Raphael Hirsch also discusses what the Torah means when it stresses the importance of man. His name is given to him even before he is created — "let us make *Adam* — a man" — and that is unlike any other creature. According to R' Samson Raphael Hirsch, the word *Adam* is not derived from *adamah* — the earth — but the other

BEREISHIS — BEREISHIS / 7

way around. The earth is called *adamah* because of *Adam* — man — who was created from it. The word *Adam* is derived from the word *hadom* — a footstool — because man serves as the footstool to Hashem's throne. Hashem uses the plural נַעֲשֶׂה in the creation of man just as a king uses the royal plural to stress that all of his actions are on behalf of the community and for the good of the community. The phrase "let us make" stresses that what is about to be created will be for the good of all of creation. Hashem is preparing a ruler over His creatures in the form of *Adam*, who will answer the desires of the creatures below to give them a master in this world.

R' Eliezer Ashkenazi, in his *Ma'asei Hashem*, takes this idea further. When Hashem said, "Let us make," He was not only informing His creatures, but was also issuing them a command. He was warning the lower beings not to diverge from their assigned task of serving all of man's needs. That is also the meaning of the verse, "which Hashem created to do" — Hashem created all His creatures to do whatever man needs of them.

~§ The Greater Is to Consult with the Lesser

According to *Chazal* in a number of places in *Shas* and in the *Midrash*, the phrase "let us make" is used in the *plural* to teach man that a greater person should always consult with lesser people before making decisions, just as Hashem consulted with the angels before creating man. *Chazal* place the highest value on the need to consult, for the Torah was even willing to leave room for heretics who might claim that there are two gods, *chas veshalom*, as long as the Torah could carry this essential message. It is not for nothing that *Chazal* said, states R' Heschel of Cracow, that "whoever is conceited is as if he serves idolatry." This is very logical: A person who is conceited will not perceive "let us make" in the context of modest behavior and consultation with inferiors, for that is not the way he acts. He therefore will interpret "let us make" to imply two gods, *chas veshalom*. This means that either a person learns the lessons of this *parashah*, or he is an idolater who concurs with the views of heretics.

Nachalas Yosef has a beautiful explanation of the essential nature of this consultation. Hashem intends to make man the ruler over His creations, and it is only proper that He consult with those whom man will rule. *Chazal* learned from the fact that it states, "See, Hashem has called in the name of Bezalel . . .", that one does not appoint a leader of a community without consulting with the community (*Berachos* 55). Similarly, before appointing a ruler over the lower world, Hashem consulted with the community over whom man would rule. And that is why it states, "let us make man."

A number of the *rishonim* explain the phrase "let us make" as meaning that Hashem wanted to stress that He himself wanted to deal with the creation of man, and that He would contribute His own unique part — man's spirit and soul. Only on the first day did Hashem create *yesh mei'ayin* — substance out of nothingness. From that point on, whatever creatures were made, were formed from the existing substance. Only in the creation of man did Hashem contribute something essential and original, a part of Himself, as it were.

The phrase "let us make," says *Ramban*, was also an invitation to the earth to be a partner with Hashem in the creation of man, so that it, together with Hashem, should compose his essence. Abarbanel and Ibn Ezra also use this type of approach. Man had to be created from new elements, in which Hashem contributed man's spirit, while the earth gave his physical side. In this statement of "let us make," Hashem stresses that He Himself is part of man's creation, and that man is made in the mold of the One Above.

Malbim expands on the idea of the involvement of all creatures as a prologue to the creation of man. The creation developed and ascended in stages. The lowest level — of inanimate objects such as rocks, etc. — is part of the earth. The plants grow up above this, with grass above herbs and trees above grass. The larger the thing, the greater the preparation needed for it. Herbs grow by themselves, while grass grows only after it has been sown and the tree after it has been planted, and all of these are rooted in the soil. Above them are animals, which walk above the earth, and above them is man, whose roots are in the upper worlds, and who turns to these roots. The characteristics of the inanimate objects are to be found in plants, the characteristics of plants in animals, and the characteristics of animals in man. Physically, inanimate objects are stronger than plants, plants are stronger than animals, and man is the weakest of all, but man surpasses all spiritually, and it is through his spiritual qualities that he raises all the others to the heights. *Malbim* quotes in this regard the definition of Abarbanel, that all of creation comes from Hashem and returns to Hashem through the ladder of man, who raises up everything to its roots.

Man was created last — says the Magid of Dubno — so that all the powers of the other creatures would be included in him. The Torah said regarding the creation of man "let us make," because all the powers of the other creatures are embodied in him. *Zohar* says this clearly in *Parashas Pinchas*, and this is how it puts it: " 'And Hashem said, "Let us make man." ' After He completed His work, each species by itself, He said to them, 'This creature of Mine will be a partner of all the others.'"

It is said in the name of the Gaon of Vilna, that each creature has its own good *middah* — quality — through which it lives, as *Chazal* tell us that even had the Torah not been given, we could have learned modesty from the cat, (the prohibition of) theft from the ant, valor from the lion, and fervor from an eagle. Hashem said to His creatures, "let us make a man," in the sense of, "Give of your good qualities, and from them man will be created, to include within himself all the exalted qualities and characteristics."

Another idea is brought in the name of *Yismach Moshe*. Not only did Hashem include His creatures in His consultation, but He included man himself. Man too must improve himself and develop his spiritual dimensions, so that he will fulfill his task in the world. Hashem calls to man and says to him: "Let us together make the man within you. I will create man, while you *are to complete him* by Torah and good deeds, and this way we will all be partners in the creature known as man."

܀§ To Whom Will You Compare Me?

The first chapter in *Rambam's Moreh Nevuchim* — *Guide to the Perplexed* — is devoted entirely to explaining difficulties in the Torah with the phrases "let us make man in our image, in our likeness," and "in the image of God He created him." If we read it literally, man was created in the image of God, implying, *chas veshalom*, that Hashem has a form and image. *Rambam* discusses at length the terms involved, and concludes that בְּצַלְמֵנוּ — "in our image" — refers to *intellectual* understanding, by which man is superior to any creature, while כִּדְמוּתֵנוּ — "in our likeness" — is a term which is used metaphorically to compare one's *characteristics*, and he brings a number of verses to corroborate this. The word דְּמוּת in this context refers to certain characteristics which are being compared (wickedness, valor, etc.). In our case, דְּמוּת is meant to compare man to Hashem — just as Hashem is the ruler in the world on High, man is the ruler of this world, etc.

Those who interpret *Moreh Nevuchim*, such as Abarbanel and Crescas, expand on *Rambam's* words, which are often difficult to understand. But *Rambam* repeats this concept more clearly in his *Yad HaChazakah, Hil. Yesodei HaTorah* 4:5, where he says:

> The soul of each person is his form, which Hashem gave him, and the superior intellect within the soul of man is the form of man ... It is of this form that the Torah states, "Let us make man in our form, in our likeness," i.e., that he will have a form which knows

and understands opinions, which is not physical, just as the angels, who have a form without physical shape, so that man resembles them. And this does not refer to the form which is visible to the eyes such as the mouth, brow and cheeks, and the other parts of the body, which are referred to as תּוֹאַר ("appearance"). And this spirit is not the one found in all living creatures, with which they eat and drink, give birth and feel and think, but *the intellect*, which is *the form* of the soul, and the Torah is referring to the form of the soul when it says, "in our form, in our likeness." And this form is often referred to as נֶפֶשׁ and רוּחַ.

Ibn Ezra, like *Rambam*, rejects any possibility of Hashem having a physical form in any way. "Heaven forbid to apply תּוֹאַר to Hashem. After all, it states, 'To whom can you compare Me that I be equal?'" According to him, the Torah spoke in language which man can understand when it stated "in His image," just as the Torah applies parts of the body to inanimate objects, such as "the mouth of the earth," or "the hand of the Jordan," where these references are purely allegorical. The same is true for "in His image," where there is no attempt at a physical comparison. The comparison may lie in the fact that man is a microcosm that is an epitome of the worlds above him. Or the comparison may refer to man's soul, which is eternal.

As opposed to these commentators, *Rashi* (in our editions) explains, that "in His image" is meant as a total comparison, just as *Rashi* says clearly later: "In the image of God," means that "he is in the form of his Maker." This explanation is in keeping with the references to the appearance of the *Shechinah* on many occasions in the form of a man.

Kli Yakar has a very fine interpretation on this point, stating that even though we cannot, *chas veshalom*, imply that Hashem has a form, when He appears before man He appears as a man, as, for example, when he appeared at Sinai as a mighty man, and when He appeared to Yechezkel as a man.

These appearances, says R' Yosef Bechor Shor, are in accordance with man's comprehension. Thus we find that *Chazal* tell us that a person who sees a vision sees it in accordance with his senses and comprehension.

Rabbenu Bachya also says that Hashem speaks to people in language they understand, so that they have the possibility of comprehending Him according to their own perceptions. After they understand and comprehend this and advance in their perceptions, they realize that whatever they had thought they had understood was only metaphorical, and that no person with his human perceptions can understand Hashem.

R' Yosef Leib Bloch, in *Shiurei Da'as*, volume 2, has a unique approach. According to him, the word בְּצַלְמֵנוּ means the description of one's limbs and their forms, while כִּדְמוּתֵנוּ refers to one's feelings and spiritual powers. Even though this explanation is very bold in applying the forms of limbs to the forces on High, the author permits himself to explain it this way based on a kabbalistic principle, that whatever is to be found in man is to be found in the sources of Creation, based on their Divine element.

Every feeling and power which appears in man exists in all the other worlds in a spiritual form. The spiritual form of man is like the form of Divine conduct, even though the differences between them are the differences between Heaven and earth. When the Torah talks of the hand of Hashem or the eyes of Hashem, it does so because at the source these are also descriptive names of the forces above. There is no doubt that our צֶלֶם and דְּמוּת are totally different from the צֶלֶם and דְּמוּת above, and nevertheless they parallel these forces, in the forms which emerged in the lower world.

◆§ In Our Image, in Our Likeness

S'forno explains the Divine צֶלֶם and דְּמוּת, to which man is compared, as referring to the power of choice. Man resembles the angels in that he can know and recognize, but he does not resemble them in that he has free will, which they do not. On the other hand, he resembles Hashem in that he has free will, but does not resemble Him in His desires, because Hashem's desires are always for the good. That is the reason the Torah states כִּדְמוּתֵנוּ ("like our form") and not בִּדְמוּתֵנוּ ("in our form"). What the Torah wishes to say is that man is somewhat like the form Above in some respects. "In the image of God" means, according to *S'forno*, in the image of the creatures above, who have a special status because of their intelligence and understanding. Judges are referred to in the Torah as *elohim* because of their status. When a person is born, he has not reached that status, but his image is that of God, and he is meant to achieve that status. He can ascend, but he is also liable to fall into the deep abyss, as it states (*Tehillim* 49:21), "Man that is in honor, and does not understand, is like the beasts that perish."

There are also *acharonim* who hold that "in the image of God" refers to man's free will, when he is not forced to act purely by his nature. The fact that Hashem knows what a person will do, says *Meshech Chochmah*, does not disturb his free will. How these two are reconciled is the secret of *tzimtzum*, that Hashem, as it were, limits His place to allow man the power to choose, even with Hashem's great and comprehensive knowledge.

HaD'rash VeHaIyun uses this to explain a verse in *Koheles*(3:19), וּמוֹתַר הָאָדָם מִן הַבְּהֵמָה אָיִן, which is normally translated as, "Man is no better than a beast." *HaD'rash VeHaIyun*, though, explains it as follows: "And what is superior in man over the beast is אָיִן (i.e., 'no')." Man is above the beast in that he can say *no* and restrain his impulses. Every creature acts in accordance with its natural tendencies and is a slave to its passions, but man can control his natural tendencies, and from that point of view he resembles his Creator. That is the "image of God" that is part of his essence.

Abarbanel explains the word צֶלֶם as if it comes from the root צל — shade or a shadow. Just as a shadow is intimately linked with matter, man's intellect is linked with his body. This combination of body and soul characterizes the nature of man, and this is what the Torah meant when it stated, "let *us* make a man." The latter summons, according to *Ramban* and Abarbanel, is addressed to the earth itself. Man consists of both the spiritual and the earthly. His spirituality extends down from the Divine, while his corporeal self derives from the earth. This is the meaning of "in our image and in our form."

The Chassidic works see the image of Hashem in man as something tangible, which can be seen with the eye. The great Chassidic leaders would look at a man's forehead and recognize his nature and deeds. The major part of man, says *Baal Shem Tov*, is his צֶלֶם. *Zohar* states in *Parashas Vayeshev* that no animal tramples a man until he appears to it as an animal. A man who loses his צֶלֶם loses his being. The word אָדָם in *gematria* is מָה. *Chazal* say: "Who is a simpleton? One who loses that which (מַה) he is given, namely that he loses the man within himself, which is his image of God."

R' Simcha Zisl of Kelm goes along the same lines in a letter to his son in *Or Rashaz*: "Each type of creature has its own תּוֹאַר (figure), because each species has its own special purpose, and its appearance indicates its purpose. Man has his own special תּוֹאַר, because he was created in the form of Hashem, to understand and gain knowledge. If he is missing this understanding and logic, he is an animal in the form of man, and his sin is too great to bear, because he offends the צֶלֶם."

◆§ A Garment for Divine Ideas

The interpretation of R' Samson Raphael Hirsch is penetrating and beautiful. בְּצַלְמֵנוּ refers to the outer garment and physical form. If

Hashem's attributes of mercy, truth, justice and holiness are given a physical form, they will adopt the garments that Hashem gave to man. It is through this that the image of Hashem is revealed in the world. כִּדְמוּתֵנוּ — man must attempt to resemble (יִדְמֶה) Hashem. This resemblance is expressed in a negative form, that there should be nothing in man's heart which contradicts the Divine attributes. One cannot be equal to Hashem, but man is commanded to resemble Him as much as possible. This means, first of all, that there should be nothing in his heart which is in opposition to *the Divine vision*. The meaning of "we will make" is that Hashem, as it were, says, "We will make for ourselves a representative in Our garb, who will be worthy and capable of resembling Us."

R' Hirsch notes the *kedushah* that the Torah requires applies not only to man's spirit, but also to his body. The Torah repeats a number of times: "He created man in His form," to stress that man's body with its inclinations and powers was created in the form of Hashem. The sanctity of man's body and the preservation of his Divine צֶלֶם are a firm foundation for his ethical purification and a condition for every spiritual virtue.

Chazal in *Megillah* 9 tell us that King Ptolemy placed seventy-two Sages in separate rooms to translate the Torah into Greek, and that all translated the word as "I will make" rather than "Let us make," so as not to give the heretics any room for distortion. But by doing that, they also left out the spiritual and ethical content that our rabbis found in these words.

III.
He Who Increases Knowledge Increases Pain

The question of good and evil is a basic one among the commentators, in regard to the punishment decreed upon Adam after the sin of the Tree of Knowledge. *Rambam* discusses this question at length in *Moreh Nevuchim* 1:2. He brings the question of a certain Torah Sage who asked how it is possible that before his sin Adam was like the other creatures, without any intelligence or thought, and that it appears that only after the sin were his eyes first opened to know the difference between good and evil.

Rambam gives an interesting answer. Before the sin, Adam, who was blessed with superior understanding, did not know the concepts of *good and evil*, but only those of *truth and falsehood*. These two types of concepts are not identical. Truth and falsehood are eternal and Divine values, while good and evil are transient values, and their source stems from man's *evaluation*.

Before the sin, Adam did not feel, objectively, that there was anything wrong with being naked. After the sin, he moved toward a subjective and imaginative evaluation, as we see in "the tree was good to eat and pleasant to the eyes." He exchanged the concepts of truth and falsehood for those of good and evil. Only then did he open his eyes to "know" that he was naked. The Torah does not say "to see" that he was naked, but "to know." His *seeing* had not changed. What had changed was his *evaluation* and his "knowledge." What had appeared to him before to be obvious, in terms of *the truth*, had now become *evil*, based on his feelings and imagination. This knowledge of good and evil was thus man's falling from his previous level and his exchange of eternal values for transitory values. Adam was not able to understand the basic change which had occurred in his evaluation, but Hashem knew that he had descended from a spiritual level to a human one.

This basic view of *Rambam* is to be found in many different types of Torah commentaries and Chassidic works, who explain and stress that our *human evaluation* is a move away from the supreme recognition of truth and falsehood, and that it is a result of the fall of Adam after the sin. The stress on *shame* in man is a sign that his conscience is bothering him, for animal feelings have now penetrated into him. Before he was infected by eating of the Tree of Knowledge, man was separate from his physical senses, and it follows that he did not know to be ashamed of his being.

Adam, says *Or HaChayim*, did not attach importance to any special organ of his body over any other organ, because he was free of the senses which differentiate between one organ and another. Abraham too said to his servant, "Place your hand under my thigh," because he too was at the same level as Adam before the sin, where, we are told, "they were not ashamed." The feeling of shame testifies to a *physical feeling*, which stems from the animal element in us.

S'forno states that before his sin Adam did not seek physical pleasures, and all his pleasures were directed at doing the will of his Creator. In his perception, all essential matters occupied the same degree of importance. To him, marital relations were like eating; his genital organ was no different from any other. It was the snake which was the first to arouse the power of imagination in man, as a counterforce to that of comprehending Hashem. Suddenly Adam and Eve noticed the differences between the different organs, and they therefore hastened to cover the organ which now appeared to them to be ugly and detestable.

The other commentators follow in the footsteps of *Rambam*, each in his own way. An extraordinary interpretation is to be found in *Kli Chemdah* on the Torah. *Rashi* on the verse "they knew they were naked" states: "They had one *mitzvah* (to perform) and they stripped themselves of it." This refers to the commandment not to eat of the Tree of Knowledge, which they had just violated. A number of *rishonim* wonder at *Rashi*, because they already had another *mitzvah* they had been given earlier — to be fruitful and multiply. *Kli Chemdah* answers that *Rashi* too was referring to the *mitzvah* to be fruitful and multiply. Until that time, this concept had been one of a *mitzvah*, but now it was changed to lust. In other words, Adam exchanged the concepts of truth and falsehood for those of good and evil. He exchanged Hashem's command to a physical feeling, in accordance with *Rambam's* explanation.

ৼ§ Content and Dress

Man's dress is a result of his sin. It is a mark of Cain which proclaims to all that he has descended to the lowest level. A penetrating analogy on this is to be found in *Tzemach Tzaddik*. A certain minister committed a terrible sin against his king, and was punished by having to wear an iron chain through his nose. After the minister died, his sons too wore such a chain, as it was already a tradition in the family. But they made their chains of gold and silver. A certain wise man, who knew the reason for the first chain, said to them: "Fools! What value is there in the fact that you have such decorated chains? It is the very chain in itself which makes the wearer detestable and proclaims the reason for his wearing it." The same is true, says *Tzemach Tzaddik*, for people who wear the latest fashions. The person boasts of his finery, when the very wearing of clothes is a sign of our disgrace. Clothes are but the mark of Cain in man, who turned away from his Divine association and chose instead his physical pleasures. What then do fashions accomplish, when they are but fig leaves which man uses to cover his fall?

Abarbanel and *Akeidah* also see the birth of fashion as taking place at the instant that Adam ate of the Tree of Knowledge. Then he opened his eyes to search for pleasure and renown, but all that he found at the time were fig leaves.

Abarbanel expands on this idea to other forms of luxury and to man's turning aside from the natural way, a way which he regards as the purpose of creation. He sees the sin of Adam as the beginning of man's fall into the abyss. The children of Adam also symbolize the twisted path of corrupting the essence of creation, and their names show this. Cain — קַיִן — comes from the same root as קִנְיָן — acquisition — and symbolizes the lust for wealth and land. Abel — הֶבֶל — is at a higher level, but his name too testifies that all his work is in vain (הֶבֶל — vanity). Only the third son, Seth — שֵׁת — symbolizes the healthy principle upon which the world rests (מְשׁוּתֵת). This principle means rooting oneself in nature, as it is, which Abarbanel sees as the salvation of mankind. The fig leaf with which Adam covered himself represented a partition between man and his Creator, or between man's superiority and his animal side.

Malbim clarifies this idea succinctly. Man himself was created with a body and soul, where the body is meant to be the clothing of the soul, yet man comes and puts clothes on this clothing, making his body into something of content in its own right. This action brought about a blurring between content and clothing, and to a separation between the body and soul.

Along these lines, R' Levi Yitzchak of Berdichev explains the verse, "and the eyes of both of them were opened," in the sense of a package coming apart. The unity and harmony between the body and soul was lost, with one no longer having a connection with the other. The body appeared in the guise of content, which itself needs clothing, as we saw in *Malbim's* explanation.

The Tzaddik of Sanz, *Divrei Chaim*, expands on this idea. According to him, clothing and content refer to action and thought. There is a constant debate between those who preserve the traditions and actions of the *mitzvos*, and those who are opposed to the value of actions. Many people claim that ethical thought is enough in itself, and that there is no need to do *mitzvos*. It appears that Adam was the first to err in this debate. The snake persuaded him that there was no need for practical *mitzvos*. Only after he had listened to the snake and perceived the consequences was he able to conclude that without the clothing of a *mitzvah* he was totally naked and had no ethical existence of his own.

That is also the approach used by R' Isaac Breuer in his *Moriah*. He does not quote the Tzaddik of Sanz, and may not have seen his work, but all Torah works flow from the same source. According to R' Isaac Breuer, Adam erred in thinking that justice and ethics are possible without the spirit of Hashem. After he fell, though, it became clear to him that justice and ethics are valid only when they are commandments of Hashem and His words. "Did He tell you, O man, what is good?" (*Micha* 6:8) — Do you want to understand what is good ethically? It is only "what Hashem demands of you."

According to Adam's assessment, the Tree of Knowledge was good. "The tree was good to eat and pleasant to the eyes and a tree to be desired," and yet in spite of this Adam was punished for eating it, because Hashem had told him not to eat it. It is what Hashem commands which is the *absolute good*. That and nothing else.

↘ Free Will and Forced Action

Ramban and, following him, Rabbenu Bachya and other scholars hold that *it was with this sin* that man acquired free will, and that was a fall from his previous level. Before that, he carried out all his actions like the ministering angels. Rabbenu Bachya also adds that even though Adam had no free will, he still deviated from Hashem's *mitzvah*, because sometimes even angels stray from the proper path. (See Rabbenu Bachya on the verse, "and the woman saw that it was good.") *Ramban* on *Bereishis* 2:9 says this more clearly when he states, "for Adam would do by his nature what was proper to do, as the Heavens and all their hosts do."

This view was the cause of innumerable comments by later commentators. R' Chaim of Volozhin, in his *Nefesh HaChaim* 1:6, explains this beautifully. According to him, Adam had free will even before the sin, but evil was not part of him himself, but was something outside of him. As someone with free will, Adam could enter into evil, just as he could have walked into a fire, knowing clearly that it was fire. After the sin, though, the *yetzer hara* entered into him, and became part of him, so that now it entices man from within himself. Now it is much harder for man to choose, because now he has to recognize that it is not he that speaks, but his *yetzer hara* which is enticing him.

R' Eliyahu Dessler expands on the difference between free will where a person knows that it is an outside force that is enticing him, and free will based on the error that a person thinks it is he himself doing the speaking. The second is infinitely harder to resist.

Another explanation of the change that took place after the sin is given by R' Eliezer Ashkenazi in his *Ma'asei Hashem*. Man is indeed created with free will, but at the same time he needs the spiritual strengthening that comes about from habit, so that he should not fall into the trap that sometimes awaits a person who relies too heavily on his intellect alone. Avraham was able to recognize the existence of Hashem by his intellect alone, but other people are led astray by their intellect, if it is not preceded by faith (*emunah*). Hashem wanted to accustom Adam to His existence, so that his *emunah* would become firm within himself and he would not be led astray, but Adam scorned the conventional approach and chose to use only his intellect. Relying on one's intellect alone is a very difficult and convoluted path to follow, and one can easily err in differentiating between good and bad. That, though, was the test that Adam chose for himself.

Man has two choices, says R' Isaac Breuer. Either his decisions are derived from Hashem and he remains complete as a worker who is faithful to his employer, or he revolts against Him and places the crown of sovereignty on his own head. Adam chose sovereignty (*Moriah*, p. 46).

And when Adam chose that, he chose death, because only eternal values are eternal, while the values of mortal are transitory. Therefore, the day that he exchanged the concepts of truth and falsehood for those of good and evil, death was decreed upon him.

According to *Michtav Me'Eliyahu*, death was not a punishment, but a result of man's choice, as in *Yirmiyahu* 2:19: "Your own wickedness shall correct you."

Man sought to understand that which was above his comprehension, and found death. He thought he would find redemption for his soul, and found himself slave to his passions. Only then did he open his eyes and realize that he was more naked than he had ever been before.

BEREISHIS — BEREISHIS / 19

Noach – נח

I.
The Separation Between Man and Beast

Among the many changes that took place in the world after the Flood, of special interest to us are the fundamental changes which took place between man and beast. Before the Flood, man was promised control over animals, as it states (*Bereishis* 1:26), "and let them have dominion over the fish of the sea, and over the fowl of the air, and over the cattle, and over all the earth, and over every creeping thing that creeps upon the earth." After the Flood, there was no longer any promise by Hashem of man exercising *control* over the animals. Instead, Hashem promised that He would put *fear* of man in the animals, as He said to Noach (*Bereishis* 9:2), "And the fear of you and the dread of you shall be upon every beast of the earth, and upon every fowl of the air, upon all that moves upon the earth, and upon all the fish of the sea; into your hand are they delivered."

Another fundamental change, which is even more noticeable than the first, is that before the Flood man was forbidden to eat meat, as Hashem said to Adam (*Bereishis* 1:29), "Behold, I have given you every herb bearing seed, which is upon the face of all the earth, and every tree, in which is the fruit of a tree yielding seed; to you it shall be for food. And to every beast of the earth, and to every fowl of the air, and to every thing that creeps upon the earth, in which there is life, I have given every green herb for food." After the Flood, though, Noach was permitted to eat meat, as it states (*Bereishis* 9:3), "Every moving thing that lives shall be meat for you; even as the green herb have I given you all things."

Chazal in *Sanhedrin* 59 mention this fundamental change and comment:

R' Yehudah said in the name of Rav: "Adam was not permitted to eat meat, as it states, 'To you it shall be for food; and to every beast on earth,' and not the beast of the earth to you. And even though it states, 'And let them have dominion over the fish of the sea, and over the fowl of the air, and over the cattle, and over all the earth, and over every creeping thing that creeps upon the earth,' that only referred to having them work."

There is an argument between *Tosafos* and the other commentators on this. According to *Tosafos* in *Sanhedrin* 56, Adam was only forbidden to kill an animal and eat its flesh, but he was permitted to eat the flesh of an animal that had died of other causes. *Rashi* too, in *Parashas Bereishis*, on the verse, "Behold, I have given you every herb bearing seed," comments, "Man was not permitted to kill any creature and eat its flesh."

Other commentators ask basic questions on these words of *Tosafos*. *Lev Aryeh* on the Torah has a very interesting question and answer. We are told in *Sanhedrin* 59 that R' Yehudah ben Tema says that the angels roasted meat for Adam in the Garden of Eden. The *gemara* then asks what the source was for this meat, and answers that the flesh came down from heaven. *Lev Aryeh* asks: If Adam was permitted to eat the flesh of dead animals, then there is no room for the *gemara's* question about the source of the meat, for could this not refer to the meat of an animal which had died by itself? He answers this beautifully: This happened before Adam's sin, and at that time there was no death in the world, so no animal would have died.

In any event, after the Flood the relationship between man and beast changed to the extent that man was now permitted to kill creatures and eat them. According to *Ramban* and other commentators, there were already qualitative changes even before the Flood in what man and the animals were permitted to eat. These commentators argue with *Rashi*, who lumps man and beast together and says that before the Flood they all ate fruit and herbs. According to the other commentators, this was not so. Man was permitted every herb bearing seed and every tree, while the animals and fowl were permitted to eat only green herbs and not the fruit of trees. But that difference between man and beast was far less than the one that went into effect after the Flood, when man was permitted to eat the flesh of animals.

Many commentators attempt to explain this innovation. *Revid HaZahav* quotes *Avudraham* that the reason we recite the *shehakol* blessing on meat rather than a בְּרָכָה specifying *borei chayas ha'aretz* (creator of the beasts of the earth) is because the main purpose of animals was not meant to be to serve as food for man. It is thus necessary to find a suitable explanation for the fact that the purpose of Creation changed after the Flood, just as we must seek to understand why man's *fear* was put in the animals, as opposed to the control that he had over them before the Flood.

~§ The Fear of Man in Animals

Chazal in *Shabbos* 151 give us a vivid example of the animals' fear of man:

> R' Shimon ben Elazar said: "A live, one-day-old child does not need to be protected from a weasel or from rats, while a dead Og, king of Bashan, must be protected from a weasel and rats, as it states, 'And the fear of you and the dread of you shall be upon every beast of the earth.' As long as a person is alive, fear of him is to be found among the creatures, and when he dies, fear of him is annulled."

In the end, *Chazal* conclude that that only applies to a person who preserves his *tzelem Elokim* — his image of Hashem. If a person does not preserve it but acts like an animal, then animals have no fear of him.

Akeidah dwells on this at length in our *parashah*, and uses this to explain the reason why man was permitted to eat meat after the Flood. Man is only human when he fulfills his spiritual function in the world and preserves his *tzelem Elokim*. If, however, he follows his animalistic urges, the other creatures no longer fear him, and he is torn to pieces by them according to the natural principle of the Creation whereby the strong rules the weak — and most animals are stronger than man.

There is a hint at this in *Chazal*, when they say that no animal prevails over a human until he appears to it as an animal. So too do we see: "It is not the wild ass that kills, but sin kills." Thus, with regard to the Flood, where all creatures had corrupted their ways and had sinned, nature itself arose to destroy them, and only Noach and his family were saved. At that time, as man was at such a low level, he was not permitted to eat meat. This prohibition was only revoked after the Flood.

The animals' fear of man, according to *Akeidah*, is a result of the Flood. It was then that morals were improved in the world, and man again attained his status of *tzelem Elokim*, who imposed his fear on the other creatures. *Tur*, though, explains this fear in a simple manner. In the Ark, the animals became used to man, and no longer had any fear of him. Thus, after the Flood Hashem promised Noach that the animals would once again fear man.

Oznayim LaTorah explains the promise as Hashem reassuring man. The animals of prey left the Ark and would gradually regain their desire and power to capture prey once more. Noach and his sons were thus afraid: What did Hashem do to us when He told us to bring these into the Ark — to have us raise animals that will later injure us? Thus Hashem reassured them and said to them: "Do not fear. They will fear you, and not you them. Even the animals of prey will flee from you to the far forests, and will not be near human settlements."

Other commentators see the need for Hashem to impose the fear of man on animals as a result of the fact that the flesh of animals was now permitted to be eaten. *Kli Yakar* explains that after Hashem gave man permission to kill animals, there was concern that the ox might not allow itself to be led to the slaughter and might rise up against the man coming to kill it. The Torah thus promised, "And the fear of you and the dread of you shall be upon every beast of the earth." The animals will not oppose their fate, but will accept it submissively.

Malbim says that after the Flood, animals too were permitted to eat meat, just as man was permitted to do. Man therefore feared that the animals might eat him as well. Man therefore needed an additional blessing that the animals would fear him and would not eat him as food.

Avnei Shoham holds that as Adam did not eat meat, the animals left him alone. From Noach on, though, humans began to hunt animals, and as a result the animals began harming humans. Thus there was need for a blessing from Hashem to protect man from animals. This explanation resembles that of *Kli Yakar* above.

Avnei Shoham also give another explanation. *Ramban* in *Parashas Bechukosai*, in explaining the verse (*Vayikra* 26:6), "and I will rid evil beasts out of the land," says that when the world was first created, before man sinned, he was not prey to wild animals. Only after Adam's sin was it decreed that he could become their prey. Thus the promise given to Adam before his sin that he would rule over the animals was not enough, because after the sin the animals had permission to attack humans. There was thus need for another blessing so that animals who are predisposed to attack their prey should nevertheless fear man.

◆§ The Deep Division Between Man and Beast

R' Samson Raphael Hirsch sees the new development after the Flood as a deep and fundamental division between man and beast. Before the Flood, man was meant to rule the world, whereas after the

Flood man must protect himself and improve himself. Before the Flood, says R' Hirsch, there was a division between man and the animals. Man was given the different grains and legumes to eat as well as fruit, while the animals ate the herbs and grasses of the field. It appears that good and healthful vegetarian food was available in abundance everywhere, because the earth's climate was different from today's. Evidence of this can be seen in the remnants of tropical fruits discovered in the far north. Only after the Flood was man permitted to kill and eat animals, for the Flood had transformed the nature of the earth. This we see in *Bereishis* 6:13, "I will destroy them with the earth" (here taken to mean "I will destroy them as well as the earth" — trans.). Once meat became permissible, the only prohibition that was left was *eiver min ha'chai* — eating flesh taken from an animal while it was still alive.

At first, R' Hirsch continues, man was made ruler over all of Creation. The Torah stated this when it said (*Bereishis* 1:28), "Fill the earth and subdue it ..." Here man was not given the license to destroy any animals, but merely to impose discipline upon them.

At the outset, man's relationship to the earth was one of closeness and protection, "to work it and preserve it." This relationship changed totally after the Flood. From then on, man was required to guard himself and his life. Instead of closeness, he was told (*Bereishis* 9:2), "And the fear of you and the dread of you shall be upon every beast of the earth." From that point on, animals would run away in fear of man, and would keep out of his way. Man's role from then on has not been to rule the land and perfect it, but to perfect and return to himself the status he deserves. The return to that state will occur after all the souls are purified in the End of Days.

When man's life changed, he was given different food. It is logical to associate this with the drastic shortening of man's lifespan. What would take a lifespan of seven or eight hundred years now had to be completed in seventy or eighty years. This speeded-up development required man to eat meat. Man changed and the climate changed. In his previous strong state, he was forbidden to eat meat, but from the Flood on, meat became necessary for man.

According to *Tur*, only after the Flood did man develop an urge to eat meat. Until then, he had no such urge. *Tur* explains in *Parashas Bereishis* that after Hashem gave man the fruit of the tree, and the animals the grass and herbs of the field, it states, "and it was so." This means that man had no urge to eat meat. He regarded killing an animal as no different than killing another man. Otherwise, man could not live with that command.

At first, says R' Bunim of Pshischa, there wasn't even a concept of food, until Hashem said, "for you it shall be to eat." But that only applied to those things that Hashem specified. As meat was not mentioned, it remained unfit for food, and there was no need to prohibit it. Only afterwards, with Noach, when Hashem said (*Bereishis* 9:3), "Every moving thing that lives shall be food for you," was meat included in the concept of food, and the urge to eat meat was created. This will also explain the meaning of the verse in *Parashas Bereishis* that the animals were permitted to eat herbs and grasses, but not fruit (see *Ramban*). At first glance, this seems strange. What do we mean that the animals were "permitted"? Are animals then commanded to do anything or to refrain from doing anything? What it means, though, is that Hashem implanted in the animals' nature that they would only eat herbs and grasses. Fruit was not considered as food for them and they felt no desire to eat it, until Hashem changed the nature of man and the animals.

↞§ The Reason for the Change and its Purpose

Ramban in *Parashas Bereishis* dwells on the reason for the change which occurred in the relationship between man and the animals after the Flood. He explains the prohibition of eating meat before the Flood as follows: There are certain common elements between man and animals in which man is no better than they, and therefore he is not permitted to kill them and eat their meat:

> Those creatures which have the ability to move (i.e., animals) have a certain superiority in their soul, in which they resemble a rational soul (i.e., man). They (too) have a choice in what is good for them and concerning their food. And they flee from pain and death. And the verse says (*Koheles* 3:21), "Who knows the spirit of man that goes upward, and the spirit of the beast that goes downward to the earth?"

If we follow *Ramban's* reasoning, the question that then arises is why meat was permitted after the Flood. *Ramban* answers this elsewhere, where he states that as it was Noach who saved all the animal species from destruction, he was given permission to slaughter animals and eat them.

Or HaChayim, as *Ramban*, finds three similar reasons why meat was permitted to man after the Flood: (a) It was through Noach that Hashem enabled the survival of the different species of animals. Without Noach, there would be no animals. Therefore Noach earned the right to partake of animals for his food. (b) Noach worked hard in the Ark on behalf of the animals, and a verse states (*Tehillim* 128:2), "You shall eat the labor of your hands." (c) It was by means of the sacrifice that Noach brought that Hashem was "appeased" and swore not to destroy all flesh, etc. Therefore Hashem permitted him to eat the fruits of his endeavors. *Chizkuni* too gives that same reason.

Torah Temimah quotes a *Midrash Aggadah* on the Torah that Noach was permitted to eat meat because he brought a sacrifice, and in any event all will eventually die. On the other hand, before Adam's sin, there was no death in the world.

Abarbanel, though, explains that the permission to eat meat was by necessity, and for man's health. Hashem gave Adam *Gan Eden* to live in, where the best trees and fruits grew, as we read (*Bereishis* 2:9), "And Hashem God made every tree that is pleasant to the sight and good for food grow out of the ground." But when Noach and his sons left the Ark, they had nothing to eat, for the vegetation had been destroyed in the Flood. If they would have to wait until they planted a crop and harvested it, they would have starved to death. Therefore Hashem permitted them to eat meat.

Tzror HaMor says that it was because of the weaknesses of the generations after the Flood that Hashem permitted them to eat meat, something which had not been permitted to Adam. *Malbim* too follows in his footsteps and says that in Adam's day people's bodies were strong and the fruits had not yet been corrupted, so that they sustained man just like meat. After the Flood, though, people's bodies were weaker and fruit lost its strength. The climate was changed, with heat and cold being created. It was also decreed that man would be dispersed to the farthermost points of the world, and therefore meat became essential for his health and existence.

There are many more explanations in all four manners of Torah interpretation — *p'shat, remez, d'rush, sod* (פרד״ס) — as to why the generations after the Flood did need meat. Those who study using *remez* and *sod* see in this a stage in raising up creatures to a higher level through man. *Domem* — inanimate objects — are raised up by *tzome'ach* — vegetation. *Tzome'ach* is in turn raised up by *chai* — animals; and *chai* is raised up by man.

In any event, the principles involving the world are different after the Flood than they were before it, when the world had first been created. It was only after the Flood that the fundamental difference between man and the animals developed, and they became enemies.

II.
The First Covenant Between Hashem and Creation

After the Flood, Hashem made His *first* covenant with man, that from then on He would never wipe out mankind. The sign of this covenant is the rainbow, as it states (*Bereishis* 9:13), "I have set My rainbow in the cloud, and it shall be as a sign of a covenant between Me and the earth."

According to R' Samson Raphael Hirsch, this sign is meant to remind mankind of the covenant, just as there are other signs, such as *tefillin*, *Shabbos* and *bris milah*, which are unique to the Jewish people. The rainbow in the clouds reminds us that there is a covenant between Hashem and man, not to have mankind destroyed again.

According to R' Hirsch, there is nothing forcing us to say that rainbows were first created after the Flood, with a change taking place in nature, for *Chazal* in *Avos* 5 list the rainbow as one of the ten things created at twilight before the first *Shabbos* of Creation. The change that took place was that from the Flood on the rainbow became a sign, just as this is true with other natural phenomena. For example, we see that Hashem showed Avraham the stars and said to him, "so will be your seed." At a later time, the new moon would become a sign of the renewal of Israel. Here too, "I have set My rainbow (at the time of Creation) in the cloud," and from now on "it shall be as a sign of a covenant." This explanation is also brought in *Radak* quoting *Midrash Rabbah*, but our version of the Midrash does not contain it.

Ri of Barcelona, in his commentary on *Sefer Yetzirah*, also states,

> There are those who err and say that the rainbow was created in the days of Noach, but that is not so, because it was created *Erev Shabbos* (i.e., of Creation) at twilight, for there is nothing new under the sun. Only later did it become a sign and token, in the days of Noach. When it states, "I have set My rainbow in the cloud," it means earlier, whereas it became a sign of the covenant only from then on.

Among the *rishonim*, *Ramban* too explains the verses in that fashion. The rainbow is not a supernatural sign, because we know that if we put a glass of water in the sunlight, we will also see the colors of the rainbow. What then is the sign when the rainbow appears? What is new about it after the Flood is that from now on the rainbow, which was created in the six days of Creation, will be a sign and witness for the existence of mankind and its continued presence in the world. Before the Flood, the rainbow was nothing but a natural phenomenon, without any special significance.

Akeidah too explains this in similar fashion, even though there are some differences in his interpretation. According to him, the rainbow in itself signifies the eternity of creation. The appearance of the rainbow when the skies are not completely covered by clouds is a hint to us that the rain we receive is beneficial to us, and not harmful. After the Flood, it is only possible to have a situation where (*Amos* 4:7), "I will rain on one place and on another place I will not rain," but not a flood that will wipe out the world. Retribution for sin will from now on be like the rainbow in the cloud. It is not that the rainbow was created after the Flood, but it was then that Hashem informed the world that His anger would only be like the rainbow. "It shall be as a sign of a covenant between Me and the earth." It will not only be a sign and witness, as *Ramban* says, but it will serve as evidence that the danger of total destruction to mankind has been removed. Hashem's retribution for sin will now be like the rainbow, which only appears if the sky is clear in at least one place.

As opposed to these interpretations, *Ma'asei Hashem* holds that the sign of the rainbow is not one with a positive message for mankind, as *Ramban* or *Akeidah* explain, but is a reminder to it that it has sinned and deserves to be destroyed, had it not been for the fact that Hashem had taken an oath not to destroy all of mankind. When the rainbow appears, it is meant to arouse man to mend his deeds and to know that, based on his deeds, he deserves to be destroyed. It is not the existence of the rainbow that is a sign, but its appearance. The Torah does not say, "I have set My rainbow in the cloud as a sign." Instead, it says, "it shall be as a sign," namely that it must serve that purpose. Nor does it say "to remind Me," but "to remember" (*Bereishis* 9:16). It is not I, Hashem, that must remember, but you who must grasp its significance.

Ma'asei Hashem also explains the verse (*Bereishis* 9:14), "And it shall come to pass, when I bring a cloud over the earth," in a spiritual sense. When Hashem's *midas ha'din* — attribute of strict justice — becomes predominant because of man's evil deeds, then, "the rainbow will be seen in the cloud," to remind mankind of its duties to Hashem. This explanation is in keeping with the statement of *Chazal* in a number of places, that the rainbow is a sign of the spiritual decline of the generation. Thus, in the days of R' Shimon bar Yochai the rainbow never appeared, because in his days there was no need for the reminder implicit in the rainbow.

Yet, in spite of man's sins, Hashem will remember His covenant. He only makes us aware that we have sinned, so that we can know and improve our ways, but He will not destroy mankind totally. According to R' Samson Raphael Hirsch, this promise is also included in the rainbow. A rainbow is a single clear ray which has been broken down into seven colors. R' Hirsch sees this as symbolic of the variety in mankind, from the darkest to the lightest color. "All the different shades of mankind — from the most spiritual, who radiates his spirituality, to the most material person, in whom Hashem's light glimmers but faintly — are joined together in life."

⊷§ A Supernatural Phenomenon

Ibn Ezra maintains that the rainbow was created after the Flood. He says, " 'I have set My rainbow in the cloud' means now, and it does not mean, as the *gaon* (i.e., *Ramban*) says, that it was there from the beginning." As to the Greek scholars whom *Ramban* quotes, who hold that the rainbow is created by the heat of the sun, Ibn Ezra says, "If we believe their words, we can say that the sun became stronger after the Flood, and from then on it has produced rainbows."

Maharal of Prague, in his *Gur Aryeh* on *Rashi*, also holds this view, but he ties together the effect and the cause and says: "The increased light of the sun after the Flood prevents the coming of a new flood. Before the Flood, the light of the sun was not strong enough to create a rainbow, and therefore the Flood was possible." According to him, there is no need to say that the sun's heat increased after the Flood. All that happened was that the various coverings and partitions, which had screened out the full force of the heat, were removed. *Maharal* is very concise in his words, and does not explain why this should prevent another flood.

Ran says that before the Flood the clouds were much thicker, and did not permit the rays of the sun to penetrate through to the earth. Thus, even if there was a rainbow, it was high up beyond the clouds, which blocked it off so that it could not be seen on earth. In those days, the rainfall was very heavy, with all the water in the clouds falling as rain. That was why it was possible for a flood to come. Afterwards Hashem took pity on mankind, and made the clouds much less dense, thus allowing the sun's rays to penetrate through them. Since that time, the clouds have not contained enough water to cause destruction to the world.

Abarbanel is not content with that explanation. According to him, today, too, we cannot tell whether rainbows are in the sky or in the clouds. They were and have always been caused by moisture in the air. The difference is that before Hashem swore not to destroy mankind, a tremendous amount of water vapor would rise from the earth and form thick, heavy clouds, and the sun was not strong enough to melt or dry up all of that moisture. That was why rainbows could not be seen in either the sky or the clouds. After the Flood, though, Hashem decreased the water vapor rising from the earth to the sky, so that the sun was now able to dry out the moisture, and the rainbow became visible. As to the statement by *Chazal* in *Avos* that the rainbow was created at twilight on Friday evening, this indicates that the capacity of the sun to produce rainbows out of vapor already existed at the time of creation. But this capacity was not realized until the special conditions that followed the Flood were created. The same holds true with the other things which were created at twilight on Friday, where all were created potentially, and only later were transformed from potential to reality. These included, among others, the ram that was sacrificed in place of Yitzchak, the mouth of Bilaam's donkey, and others. Thus the decrease in moisture after the Flood enabled the rainbow to be seen.

R' Mordechai Yaffe, in his *Levush HaOrah*, says the same thing, with minor changes. Not every cloud creates a rainbow. Before the Flood, all the clouds were of the type which did not produce rainbows. After the Flood, there were changes in the clouds, and some now appeared which did produce rainbows. Such clouds appear when Hashem wants to let us know of His anger, yet at the same time to remind us of His covenant.

Other commentators also state that there were changes in nature after the Flood, and nature was modified to ensure man's survival. *Meleches Machsheves* says that until the Flood the sun's rays did not reflect back into the atmosphere, but were absorbed by the earth, whereas the water vapor that arose from the earth then deposited tremendous amounts of water on the earth. Only after the Flood did the sun's rays begin reflecting back into the atmosphere, where they lead to the formation of water, which then rains on the earth.

Malbim, too, holds Creation became more refined after the Flood. Before the Flood, everything was coarse and unrefined. And this applied to people as well as clouds. Then, the clouds were thick and filled with devastating amounts of water. The appearance of the rainbow is a sign of the refinement that took place in Creation. This applied to people and clouds, and thus there will no longer be any flood to destroy the world.

HaKesav VeHaKabalah takes the opposite view. He too holds that

Creation changed after the Flood, but for the worse rather than for the better. He says that there are many hints in *Chazal* that when the world was first created, it was not the same as our present world. According to the Midrash (*Bereishis* 34), there was no need at that time to sow except once each forty years. Grain remained unspoiled for extended periods of time because of the purity of the air. One of the Sages who had a headache exclaimed: "See what the generation of the Flood did to us!" So too did *Chazal* say (in the Midrash ch. 14) that once every forty years vapor would come up from the ground and would water the land for forty years. If those were the climactic conditions, where rain did not fall more than once every forty years, and where (as the Midrash continues) it took forty years for a full revolution of the sun, then there were no natural conditions for the formation of a rainbow. Only after the Flood was nature changed to the way it is today, and only then were the conditions created for the appearance of a rainbow.

The change in nature, for the good or for bad, resulted in a change in man's nature. Since then, says *S'forno*, man's disposition has changed, and he is no longer able to overcome his evil impulse. As a result, Hashem had to diminish His attribute of strict justice — *midas ha'din* — as the Midrash says on the verse (*Bereishis* 9:16),

> "And the rainbow shall be in the cloud; and I will look upon it, that I may remember the everlasting covenant between Hashem" — that is Hashem's *midas ha'din* (attribute of strict justice) in the Heavens above; "and every living creature" — that is Hashem's *midas ha'din* on the earth below. That above is harsh, while that below is weak.

The rainbow is the witness of the change which occurred in Creation and in the climate, and a sign that Hashem takes into account the weakness which descended upon the earth.

According to the verses themselves, the rainbow is a combination of justice and mercy. On the one hand, it reminds us of mankind's sins and the punishment which it suffered for them, whereas on the other hand it signifies the promise not to destroy mankind. This combination of justice and mercy is a reflection of the exalted light of Hashem, which too includes justice and mercy. It is not for nothing that the *rishonim* such as *Akeidah* and others quote the prophet *Yechezkel* (1:28), "As the appearance of the rainbow that is in the cloud in the day of rain, so was the appearance of the brightness. This was the appearance of the likeness of the glory of Hashem." Also see *Chazal* on *Berachos* 59.

And not only the commentators on the Torah, but *Chazal* themselves in *Midrash Rabbah* (*Bereishis* 35) say: " 'My rainbow' (קַשְׁתִּי) — My likeness (קִישׁוּתִי), that which resembles Me." *Eitz Yosef* and *Matnas Kehunah*, in their commentaries on the Midrash, state, "This is something which resembles Me, as it states, 'the rainbow which is in the cloud.'" The Midrash then asks: "Can this be?" (i.e., can anything be compared to Hashem?) The Midrash answers: "This is as the peel to the fruit" (the rainbow in comparison to Hashem's image is as the peel to the fruit). We thus see that *Chazal* already regarded the rainbow as the appearance of Hashem's image. So too does the *gemara* say in *Berachos*: "One who sees a rainbow must fall on his face," and it is obvious that it is because of the above reason.

⊸§ The Righteous Man and the Rainbow

R' Gedalyah of Lintz, one of the disciples of the *Besht*, says that the rainbow in the cloud represents the defects that one sees in the *tzaddik* because of the sins of the generation, as in the verse (*Yeshayahu* 53:5), "He was wounded (מְחוֹלָל) because of our transgressions." The *tzaddik* is profaned (becomes חוּלִין) because of our sins, so that he can protect the generation, "and that is the rainbow in the cloud" (*T'shu'as Chen*). This Chassidic idea is original, but we already find in *Chazal* the connection between the rainbow and the *tzaddik*. In a number of places in the *Zohar* and in other sources, *Chazal* praise R' Shimon bar Yochai for the fact that "the rainbow was never seen in his days." In *Kesubos* 77 we are even told that when R' Yehoshua ben Levi came to *Gan Eden*, Eliyahu proclaimed: "Make way for the son of Levi!" R' Yehoshua ben Levi was then asked: "Was the rainbow seen in your days?" When he answered, "Yes," they said to him: " You are not the son of Levi" (i.e., that Eliyahu was announcing).

Kli Yakar uses these words of *Chazal* to dispute the views of the *rishonim* we brought above, that after the Flood the clouds became thinner, for if so, how did they become thicker again in the days of R' Shimon bar Yochai, when no rainbow was seen? Based on this question, he has an interesting *chiddush* on *Chazal's* words. It is not that there were no rainbows in R' Shimon bar Yochai's days, but the people in his time had no need to look at the rainbow. Until his time, those who used to sin would always look to the Heavens in fear, seeking for a rainbow that would show that in spite of their sins the world would not be destroyed. In the days of R' Shimon bar Yochai, though, people were all tranquil and assured. There were no sinners, and thus the generation did not need the rainbow to calm it down. In addition, the people trusted that the righteousness of R' Shimon bar Yochai would save the world.

Rashi explains the verse (*Bereishis* 9:14), "And it shall come to pass, when I bring a cloud over the earth," to mean "when I have a thought to bring about darkness and destruction." Where does *Rashi* get the idea to explain the verse in a spiritual rather than in the simple material sense? Couldn't the Torah be referring to regular clouds? However, says *Kli Yakar*, *Rashi* understood that the Torah was not referring to regular clouds, because not every cloud has a rainbow. *Rashi* therefore explained that the Torah was referring to a generation which is totally guilty, and which has no righteous people to protect it, for then a rainbow must appear to remind and inform the people that Hashem has sworn not to destroy His world.

Chazal say that "Whoever looks at the rainbow has no regard for the honor of his Maker." One who looks at the rainbow shows that he feels guilty, and does not have a clear conscience. In the generation of R' Shimon bar Yochai people had clear consciences, and they did not look at the clouds.

This explanation is very interesting. Many commentators discuss the meaning of these words of *Chazal* on R' Shimon bar Yochai, and give various explanations. *Ramo* in *Toras HaOlah* gives a very sharp answer. No rainbow appeared in the time of R' Shimon bar Yochai because when the Jews do Hashem's will, He gives them rain on Tuesday nights, as *Chazal* explain the verse, "I will give your rain at their appointed season." And as that is night time, one cannot see any rainbow. (See *She'elos u'Teshuvos Maharasham* 124, where he rules that even if one sees a rainbow at night he must recite the blessing. *Midrash Talpios* says that in the year 5430 (1670 C.E.) a rainbow appeared at night.)

Chazal mention two generations that did not see the rainbow: that of Chizkiyahu and that of R' Shimon bar Yochai. (It is a custom for children in Israel to carry bows on *Lag BaOmer*. There are some who wish to say that this commemorates the battles of Bar Kochba. It is, however, more reasonable to assume that it is meant to commemorate R' Shimon bar Yochai, in whose generation no rainbows were seen — note that in Hebrew the words "bow" and "rainbow" are the same — קֶשֶׁת.)

III.
I Will Not Again Curse

The verses in this *parashah* are the cause for much discussion among various commentators. They pause at such expressions as "And Hashem smelled the sweet savor;" or "And Hashem said to His heart," which are cases of anthropomorphism (attributing human characteristics to Hashem). They also ponder the meaning of Hashem's decision not to bring a flood on the world any more (*Bereishis* 8:21), giving as His reason, "because the impulse of man's heart is evil from his youth," when that was exactly Hashem's reason for bringing the Flood in the first place (*Bereishis* 6:5): "Because the impulse of the thoughts of his heart is evil all the day."

Many commentators on the Torah also question the meaning of the verse, "because the impulse of man's heart is evil from his youth." Also surprising is the repeated promise that there will not be another flood (*Bereishis* 8:21): "I will not again curse the ground;" "And I will not again smite every living thing;" and (*Bereishis* 9:11) "neither shall all flesh be cut off any more by the waters of a flood." And later we are told (*Bereishis* 9:15), "And there will not be another flood to destroy the earth."

Another verse which needs to be explained is (*Bereishis* 8:22), "While the earth remains, seedtime and harvest, and cold and heat, and summer and winter." Nor is the end of this verse, "and day and night will not cease," readily explained. Does this mean that day and night did cease during the Flood? After all, there is no hint at this anywhere in the Torah.

◈ And Hashem Said to His Heart

Ibn Ezra says:

> Heaven forbid that Hashem should smell or eat, even though it states (*Devarim* 32:38), "Who ate the fat of their sacrifices." Rather, the meaning is that He accepted the burnt offering and He found it favorable before Him, as a person who smells an aroma which is pleasing."

As to the verse, "Hashem said to His heart," Ibn Ezra explains that

Hashem first thought of the matter, and afterwards revealed it to Noach, who was a prophet.

Rambam in *Moreh Nevuchim* (1:29) also says, "Whatever Hashem wanted (to do) but did not reveal to a prophet at the time that that event took place is referred to as 'to His heart.'" *Rambam's* interpretation is in accordance with that of Ibn Ezra, but *Rambam* does not explain when and to which prophet Hashem revealed the fact that there would never be another flood.

S'forno too follows this route, and explains that Hashem waited until Noach and his sons had accepted His commandments and had made a covenant with Him, before revealing to them that He would never again bring such a flood upon the world.

Ramban's interpretation is somewhat different. According to him, Hashem did not disclose to Noach that He was pleased with his sacrifices. It was only when Hashem commanded Moshe to write the Torah that He revealed that Noach's sacrifices had been favorably accepted. But *Ramban* does not explain why Hashem concealed this, even though Noach was a prophet. He evidently bases his explanation on the fact that the Torah does not tell us that Hashem did reveal this fact to Noach.

HaKesav VeHaKabalah has an original interpretation: Hashem said what He said to the heart of Noach, namely that He appeased him and placated him with words. Until that time, Noach was forbidden to have marital relations, and was distressed over the fact that the world was to be destroyed. Now Hashem promised him that there would never again be such a flood, and he could without fear begin repopulating the world.

Tiferes Yehonasan holds that at first Hashem did not express Himself openly, but only to the heart, because He was afraid that His creatures would again corrupt their ways if they heard that there would never again be such a flood. Only after Noach and his sons accepted upon themselves their *mitzvos*, and Hashem made His promise to them, did He tell them what He had already decided — namely that He would not bring another flood.

Akeidah is surprised at the change for the better in Hashem's relationship with man after the Flood. He asks: "If man's bad qualities brought about the Flood in the past, why should they not do so in the future? Does Hashem then play favorites?" In his answer, he discusses the differences which took place in human society after the Flood. From that time on, this event would never happen again, because fear of Hashem's punishment would dissuade people from acting as they had. Before the Flood, they did not believe that sin could bring about such a terrible punishment. Now that the few who remained alive saw what had happened to everyone and everything else, they knew enough to keep away from sin.

Besides this, there was a change in man himself. Until then, mankind was all unified and one, but now they were divided into three large groups — Shem, Ham and Yefet. The differences between the various groups will prevent them all from uniting, and thus there will be no single general sin for all of mankind, which was what brought about the Flood. What characterizes this new situation is the rainbow in the cloud. Rainbows only appear when one part of the sky is cloudy and another part is clear, with the sun shining. This hints at the division which took place in mankind, which would from then on leave its imprint on man's actions. Mankind will no longer be unified, and thus never again totally guilty.

The interpretation of R' Samson Raphael Hirsch is very interesting. According to him, the word "heart" (לֵב) is a term which is used metaphorically for the love of Hashem for His creatures, as in the verse (II Divrei HaYamim 7:16), "My eyes and My heart shall be there all the days." Hashem wants man to be happy, but because of man's sins, He does not implement His desires. That is the meaning of (Bereishis 6:7), "It grieved Him in His heart." After the Flood, the opposite occurred. "Hashem said to His heart," namely that all of Hashem's attributes of love and mercy stood, as it were before the Throne of Glory and pleaded in defense of the continued existence of mankind.

Very interesting is R' Hirsch's approach to all the anthropomorphisms in general. Not only is he not perturbed by those words which seem to imply that Hashem has bodily organs or senses, but he thinks that these verses have a positive effect, for he maintains that it is better to have Hashem referred to in human terms than to blur His nature and His relationship with man. R' Hirsch also justifies the view of Ra'avad, "the true Jewish scholar," and says that "faith in the nature of Hashem is more important than investigations that deny His bodily manifestations."

⇜ I Will Not Again Curse

Rashi explains the repetition of the phrase, "I will not again" ("... curse the earth;" "... smite every living thing"). According to him, this duplication is meant as a vow, in accordance with what Chazal tell us in Shevu'os 37: "One who says, 'Yes, yes,' or 'No, no' — that is a vow." Evidence that the repetition of the phrase is taken to be a vow can be seen in the verse (Yeshayahu 54:9), "for as I have sworn that the waters of Noach should no more go over the earth," even though there is no mention in the Torah of such an oath. Thus we see that the repetition of the promise is considered to be an oath.

The commentators on *Rashi* are surprised at the fact that he refers to *Chazal* in *Shevu'os*, because the *gemara* there does not mention the duplication of "... I will not again" at all, but deduces that Hashem gave an oath from the fact that He said twice, "there shall not be" ("... water as a flood to destroy the earth;" "... another flood to destroy all flesh").

The one who argues most ardently against *Rashi* is *Or HaChayim*, who concludes that *Rashi* must have had another version of the text of the *gemara* there. But *Or HaChayim* justifies our version. The repetition of "I will not again" comes as a promise not to curse even part of the earth, and not to punish just the animals without the earth itself being punished. As opposed to this, the repetition of "there shall not be ..." is the oath that Hashem took not to bring another flood.

Many of the commentators deal with this matter, each in his own way. (See the commentaries on *Rashi* by R' Eliyahu Mizrachi and *Maharal* of Prague.) But one who delves into the verses themselves finds that there are two oaths for everything. The Torah repeats the promise not to destroy all flesh (*Bereishis* 9:11 — "Neither shall all flesh be cut off any more by the waters of a flood, neither shall there be a flood any more to destroy the earth"). So too does it repeat the promise not to destroy the earth, in terms of "I will not again" and "there shall not be" ("neither shall there be a flood any more to destroy the earth"). It is thus logical to assume that these are not different versions of the *gemara*, but that there is a purposeful repetition that is intended to stress the oath about all living creatures and about the earth. *Rashi* mentions the oath in terms of "I will not again," while the other commentators quote "there shall not be," as the oath was given twice with these formulations for each body.

In *halachah*, *Rambam* rules (*Hil. Shevu'os* 6; see also *Yoreh De'ah* 237) that "Yes, yes" and "No, no" are considered oaths, but only provided that the person said them consecutively without a break in between. If, however, a person asked another to do something and he said, "I will not do it," and after the other pleaded he repeated, "I will not do it," that is not an oath. It is interesting that *Chazal* in *Tosefta* (8:4) say that such repetition is *darkei Emori* (i.e., a pagan custom). But *Gra* in his comments changes it to read, "it is not *darkei Emori*," because in our *parashah*, *Chazal* say that "no, no" is an oath, and Hashem swore not to bring a flood of this kind again.

This oath, as mentioned, came to calm Noach and to have him start again to build the world, without having to fear another flood which might destroy all living things. *Binah L'Itim*, too, explains Hashem's words and the way He encouraged Noach, along the same lines.

Chazal said on the verse: "'And it was very good' — this refers to the *yetzer hara* (evil inclination)." When then asked if the *yetzer hara* is good, they answered: "Had it not been for the *yetzer hara*, no man would build a house, or marry a woman, or have children or engage in trade." *Ramban* explains that while the *yetzer hara* does have a negative side, its right to exist derives from its positive contribution to the maintenance of the world. In ancient times, in the time of the *nefilim*, man did not use his *yetzer hara* in a positive way so as to improve the world, "because the impulse of man's heart is evil from his youth." He only used the *yetzer* for *ra* — evil. Then Hashem regretted that He had created man, for he had spoiled Creation and had turned it to act exactly contrary to what Hashem wanted. Then Noach left the Ark and offered sacrifices, and thought of rebuilding the world along the lines that Hashem had wanted. And after Hashem had "smelled the sweet savor" coming from refined mankind, He said to Himself, "I will not again curse the ground because of man, because the impulse of man's heart is evil from his youth." In other words, while man had been evil from the beginning of his development, he had now finally begun to use the "good" of his *yetzer* so as to perfect the world. Also, Hashem promised that "I will not again smite every living thing," for they too are perfected by man when he sacrifices them to Hashem. Thus the world returned to its original path, and now fulfills the task assigned to it. Now, by its own efforts, it will continue eternally.

From now on, says R' Yosef Bechor Shor, I will not destroy the grass on the earth, or the domesticated or wild animals. Now I will only punish the sinners, but Creation will develop according to the wants of the Creator, without any change.

The difference between what was before the Flood and what would be after it, says *Ha'amek Davar*, is that after the Flood man would have to engage much more in physical work, as work makes one forget to sin. The destruction came about because mankind had corrupted its ways with adultery and frivolity. Sin is linked to free time and an abundance of goods, without any effort or trouble. But from now on this would change (*Bereishis* 8:22): "While the earth remains, seedtime and harvest, and cold and heat, and summer and winter." There would be a natural change in Creation, which would require work and effort. "And day and night will not cease" — mankind would be so busy that it would no longer have the free time it had, and as a result it would stop sinning.

✥ The Impulse of Man's Heart Is Evil from His Youth

The following idea is developed beautifully in *Ma'asei Hashem*. Hashem is the one who comes to the defense of mankind when people err in their lives. "The impulse of man's heart is evil from his youth" — mankind was, as it were, just born, and is still in its diapers. That is the reason that it does childish things and is persuaded to sin. However in the future when mankind develops and matures, it will know how to act and will follow the proper path.

S'forno explains this in a similar fashion, where the change which occurred in Creation after the Flood was for its good. From that point on, man's nature and his understanding have been weaker than they were before the Flood. Man no longer has the intelligence to overcome the *yetzer* of his youth. Man is weak and is unable to oppose his lusts.

But *Or HaChayim* explains the verse literally. Hashem comes to the defense of man. There is a *halachah* in *Bava Kama* 39 that "an ox that has been trained to gore, should it gore someone, is not liable to the death penalty, for it says, 'if it gores,' and not 'if they make it gore.'" Man himself is not that blameworthy for his sins, for from his youth his *yetzer hara* has been egging him on.

Ramban explains this the opposite way. Sin only takes root in man until his youth (some say that the word מִנְּעָרָיו should be translated "in his youth" as if it were spelled בִּנְעָרָיו, a usage found elsewhere in *Tanach*). In his old age, man regrets the sins of his youth. Man should not be destroyed because of the sins of his youth. One should wait until he grows up and repents his sins.

R' Samson Raphael Hirsch has an interesting explanation. According to him, youth refers to the days when man is innocent and has dreams. His *yetzer* is not *ra* from his youth. In normal times, the number of adults desiring to sin exceeds the number of youths who wish to sin. But the youth are liable to commit the sins, because they have not become accustomed to submit to the yoke of *mitzvos* and of controlling themselves. In their search for "independence," they "shake off" (יְנַעֲרוּ — with the same root as נַעַר — a youth) this yoke from themselves. It is difficult to overcome this independence of one's desires: "The lack of mental maturity weaves the web of obstinacy, but this independence is the root of the future moral person."

According to R' Hirsch, the verse (*Bereishis* 8:21), "The impulse of man's heart is evil from his youth," is a parenthetical statement: "I will no longer curse the earth, even in a case where the impulse of man's heart is evil from his youth, something which is unusual under normal conditions. And even then I will not smite all living creatures, for 'all the days of the earth, cold and heat,' etc."

There would also be a change from now on in man's nature. Until the Flood, they would only sow grain once each forty years (*Bereishis Rabbah* 34). The seasons were all equal. The climate was the same throughout the world. It was possible to move swiftly from one end of the world to the other, as in the words of *Chazal*: "They would walk from one side of the world to the other in a short time." But it was the environment that caused the destruction, as *Chazal* indicate: "Who caused them to rebel against Me, was it not because they sowed but did not harvest; gave birth but did not bury?" From now on the climate would change dramatically. Differences in the climates and times would become evident throughout the world. Man would now be dependent on various natural phenomena, that would shorten his life span and even make him lose some of his pride. After the Flood people became different from one another. The division of the land into nations and continents eliminated the means of universal transportation. Young and fresh nations inherited the places of various ancient nations. This was a new era in man's development and education, and it was due to that development that man knew how to support himself, and to build his future on new foundations.

✑§ They Will Not Rest

The idea of R' Samson Raphael Hirsch of the changes in nature after the Flood is found in many commentators, both *rishonim* and *acharonim*. *S'forno* states that until the Flood, the sun traveled in a path which caused perpetual spring and sunshine. The creatures in the world were extremely large, and all lived very long lives. After the Flood, the natures of the heavenly hosts and of the creatures in the world changed. The year was divided into six seasons of two months each. This situation will continue until the damage caused at the time of the Flood is rectified, as it is written (*Yeshayahu* 66:22), "The new earth which I (i.e., Hashem) will make." Then there will be a general rectification of all principles, plants and animals, and they will again live much longer, just as before the Flood, as it says (*Bereishis* 65:20), "The youth of a hundred years will die, and the sinner of a hundred years will be cursed."

Chasam Sofer also explains the defect which occurred in the Creation in the period after the Flood. The people of the Generation of the Flood, says *Chasam Sofer*, sinned because they were bored and had nothing to do. They did not have to labor at planting crops and raising children.

Now the Holy One, Blessed be He, imposed on mankind the cares of the world. People now must sow and reap, and "they will not rest" — they will not yawn because of excessive boredom. They will therefore not sin. And indeed Noach immediately began to live according to the new order of things (*Bereishis* 9:20), "And Noach the man of the earth began and planted a vineyard."

There were three basic changes, says *Malbim*: (a) Until then, according to *Chazal*, they only had to sow once every forty years, now they had to work all the time; (b) until then, the sun circled the equator, and it was always warm and light, now there are six seasons of the year, with all the effects on man's nature and health; (c) from then on, people no longer had the opportunity to rest, and they would not be free to do whatever they wanted.

Ya'aros Dvash, though, explains the phrase "they shall not rest" as applying to the Heavenly hosts and the seasons of the year; there will be day and night, summer and winter, at the same time. In one place it will be day while in another it will be night. In one place it will be summer, and in another winter. This interpretation is brought by R' Yosef Shaul Nathanson in the name of R' Zerachyah Halevi. He uses this to explain the verse (*Bereishis* 1:5), "And it was evening and it was morning; one day." The full twenty-four-hour-day cycle is composed of both night and day together, for it is evening in one place and morning in another at the same time. This variation results in people developing differently, in accordance with the harmony of Creation. By this means, mankind loses its *unity*, and therefore all people cannot be grouped together for either a reward or punishment. That is what Hashem meant when He said, "I will not again curse the ground," but instead will bring about a change in the order of Creation which will force man to look toward the Heavens and to pray that Hashem should aid him and bless the work of his hands.

IV.
The Failure of Civilization

In telling the story of the Tower of Babel, the Torah wished to explain the reason why there are a multitude of languages, although Adam was born alone. This multiplicity of languages became essential, because mankind tried to exploit its unity until that time to ascend to the heavens, rather than to spread out on the earth. Hashem therefore mixed up the languages of people, whereupon they settled throughout the world and created heterogeneous cultures. This is the simple explanation, according to the commentators, of the story of the Tower of Babel in the Torah.

Chazal, though, go further than this interpretation. The utter rejection by the Torah of the actions of the builders of the Tower of Babel clearly implies that they intended nothing less than a rebellion against Heaven. And indeed *Chazal* in *Sanhedrin* 109 say that "all intended this as *avodah zarah* — idolatry." This is also stressed in the Midrash. *Chazal* only differ as to the nature and the purpose of the rebellion.

There are those who see in the actions of that generation nothing less than gross heresy, as (*Sanhedrin* 109), "We will beat Him with axes. We will go up and sit there. We will go up and fight Him. We will go up and worship idols there." Similarly, we are told (*Tanchuma* 58), "Either we or He," and (*Bereishis Rabbah* 38), "We will make an idol and place a sharp sword on its head."

Some commentators indicate that it was their fear of the Flood that led the Generation of the Separation to seek means to *defend* itself from a God who punishes the wicked (*Bereishis Rabbah* 38): "Come and let us make supports for the Heavens," and (*Yalkut Shimoni* 58:12): "It is not fair for Him to choose the upper regions for Himself and to give us the lower regions."

Other commentators perceive in this an *ideological* background and the beginnings of anti-Semitism. The builders of the Tower rebelled against the God of Avraham for having chosen *him*, and claimed that the choice was not warranted, because "Avraham is childless." (According to some commentators, they expressed this sorrowfully, and wanted to transfer Hashem's choice to themselves. According to others, they said this joyfully.)

A number of the *rishonim* interpret this section in the same spirit as *Chazal*. *Ramban* is astonished at those who explain the Torah according to *p'shat* — the literal meaning of the text — and who wish to explain this episode in a rational manner. He follows completely in the footsteps of *Zohar* and the kabbalists, who explain the actions of that generation as an attempt "to tear out the shoots" (i.e., to cut themselves off from Hashem). *Ramban* bases this on the verse which states (*Bereishis* 11:4), "And we will make ourselves a name," implying that they wanted to fashion themselves into dieties.

Rabbenu Bachya and others also bring the explanations of the kabbalists, as well as those of *Chazal*. *S'forno* even delves deeper into this explanation and says that they wanted to make Nimrod into a deity and to seat him in Heaven, so that he might supervise the entire world.

Some *acharonim* also follow this path. *HaKesav VeHaKabalah* explains the text beautifully in this fashion. He interprets the verse (*Bereishis* 11:4), "Come, let us build ourselves a city," in terms of "Come, let us set up for ourselves a guard, who will protect us, and will have his eyes open to help us." According to his explanation, they wanted to set up an idol to protect them from natural calamities. Other *acharonim* go even further, using *d'rush*. "And this is what made them begin to do (*Bereishis* 11:6)." They regarded themselves as those who had begun the Creation, and did not want to recognize that they were merely carrying on Hashem's Creation.

R' Dushinski expands on the ideas cited by *Chazal* that their rebellion was against the choosing of Avraham. According to him, they wanted to gather together all of Creation in one place, in order to suppress Avraham and his ideas, and indeed, "The Holy One, Blessed be He, did a kindness to Israel in that He spread them (i.e., Israel) among the nations." By spreading Israel throughout the world, Hashem ensured that they brought Torah to every place. The Generation of the Separation, however, wanted to encircle Avraham, so that he would not be able to escape them and go from one nation to another proclaiming the message of Hashem. In this, R' Dushinski echoes *Kuzari* (2:68), who says that the reason the Holy Tongue (Hebrew) is called עִבְרִית — *Ivris* — is because Avraham remained with the language of עֵבֶר — *Ever*, who was "the father of Peleg" (literally "separation"), for in the latter's times the earth was separated. In other words, the separation brought about that only Avraham remained with his native tongue, and was not dragged along by the current of others.

≈§ Separation is Better for the Wicked

Why was the Generation of the Flood, which was guilty of *theft*, destroyed, while the Generation of the Separation, which was guilty of *heresy*, not destroyed? *Chazal* in *Sanhedrin* 109 and in *Midrash Rabbah* give an interesting *hashkafah* answer. The Generation of the Separation was saved because of the *peace and unity* among them. Peace is so great that even when they worshiped *avodah zarah*, as it were, they could not be destroyed, as stated in the verse (*Hoshea* 4:17), "Ephraim is joined to idols: let him alone" (i.e., the fact that they are united is reason to leave them alone, in spite of their idol worship).

The Chassidic works stress that this was what Hashem meant when He said (*Bereishis* 11:6), "Behold, the people are one, and they all have one language; and they have begun to do this; and now nothing will restrain them, of that which they have planned to do." In other words, it was their power of being united which enabled them to sin as they did. Hashem therefore decreed that they should be spread about the earth. As *S'forno* explains it, if they had remained unified, it would have prevented them from ever arriving at the truth. A "spiritual" unity under the tyrannical rule of Nimrod would have made a lasting imprint on their bodies and souls. By separating them and by splitting them up into different blocs, it became possible for them to arrive at the proper path in the End of Days.

R' David Zvi Hoffmann too follows this direction and says that,

> As long as mankind distances itself further from Hashem, its division into different nations in different lands, to nations which hate and envy others, is better for it ... Only when all the nations unite to come under the wings of the God of truth, to do His will and to serve Him — only then will their unity be a blessing to them, and their unity will remain eternally.

Other commentators, such as Rabbenu Bachya, *Kli Yakar*, *Or HaChayim*, and others, do not see the generation's actions as involving a deliberately negative plan in the spiritual realm. They maintain that Hashem saw the very fact of their coming together as something contrary to His plans at the time of Creation. He commanded that man was to (*Bereishis* 1:28) "fill the earth," while they tried to concentrate all of mankind in a single place. According to these commentators, their dispersal was not a punishment, but Hashem's implementation of His overall scheme, as opposed to the shortsightedness of man.

Kli Yakar says that the Generation of the Separation thought that by coming together, they would bring about world peace, but Hashem knew man's heart, and knew that such a concentration would have to eventually bring about total annihilation. He therefore foiled their plans for their own good.

Ibn Ezra too explained that their intention was pragmatic and egotistical. This *parashah* comes to teach us that in the end, Hashem's plans are the ones which succeed. He wanted mankind to be spread throughout the world, because that would be good for the preservation of the world and would be beneficial for it spiritually as well. Physically, this would ensure that mankind would not be wiped out at a single blow, and spiritually, it would make it easier for people to learn about the true religion, because, with the great number and variety of religions, everyone will in the end realize that "Hashem is greater than all the gods" (see *S'forno*). By spreading them, Hashem finished the work of the Creation according to His will. (See *Ramban* on *Bereishis* 1:28, "and replenish the earth and subdue it," who says the same.)

Sefas Emes has an original view of the Generation of the Separation. He too discusses the question of *Chazal* as to why the Generation of the Flood was destroyed, while that of the Separation was merely spread out about the face of the earth. This question is especially acute as, according to *Chazal*, the latter were guilty of idolatry. He provides an answer which our generation will appreciate: According to him, the Generation of the Flood was only interested in materialism and the pleasures of the body, without any spiritual content. They thus deserved to perish. The Generation of the Separation, on the other hand, at least used their minds intelligently. Unfortunately, they did not couple their intelligence with faith. According to *Sefas Emes*, the Generation of the Flood, who acted like animals, did not deserve to live, but those of the Separation were on a higher level, for they did use their intelligence as human beings. All they were missing was the knowledge of Hashem, but they were at least "spiritual" in their true essence. They did not deserve to be destroyed, because there was still hope for them.

⋖§ Natural Explanations

In the *rishonim*, we find a number of *natural* explanations for the Tower of Babel, including some which hint at some of the most advanced of sciences, either of their times or even thereafter. According to Rabbenu Bachya, the Tower was meant to serve as a technical instrument to prevent fire from striking the earth, like the lightning rods of our time. This was a wise invention of the scientists of the time, who were afraid that Hashem might bring a "flood" of fire, just as He had brought one of water. Rabbenu Bachya continues that they planned to go up to the heavens, because they thought that people might not die there, and that way they would live for ever.

R' Yehonasan Eibeschutz in his *Tiferes Yehonasan* sees the Tower as a place from which they would be able to launch weapons ("missiles"), and as a way to settle on the moon, where they would find refuge from the natural calamities of the world.

Ha'amek Davar, following on the *rishonim*, says that the Generation of the Separation wanted to create a tyrannical regime, by which all men's deeds could be supervised. The Tower was meant to be a watchtower. "We will make us a name," namely people would be stationed that would supervise everyone's coming and going. "Lest we be scattered" — and then mankind would be unsupervised. But Hashem was concerned for man's welfare, and refused to allow all people to be treated like sheep. He therefore mixed up their languages, and "they ceased to build the city." Their plan was foiled, because there was no use for a watchtower when the people were scattered to the four corners of the earth.

Abarbanel explains at length that the sin of the Generation of the Separation was that they began to develop civilization, as opposed to the desire of Hashem that they should have a natural form of life, based on working the land and other natural tasks. According to him, civilization is the root of all sin:

> They wanted to put their hands and minds to perfect the tasks needed for building a city, which includes all types of tasks; and a tower within it, so that they could join together there and make themselves urban people rather than people of the field, thinking that it was a special assignment for them to have a state ... and violence and theft and murder, none of which existed when they were in the field.

Later he says that their worst sin was that they attempted to establish a regime in which each person would have private property, as opposed to the purpose of Creation:

> At the time, everything they had was owned by all equally, because no person had an inheritance or anything else private for his own use, because everything belonged to all ... When they began to build the city and the tower, they removed themselves from comradeship, and their possessions and inheritances became private. And they came to exchanging things and setting them aside, because of their desire for each to have his own things, saying: What is mine is mine and what is yours is yours, until because of this they separated from one another.

According to Abarbanel, *Chazal* refer to this development when they say, " 'When they traveled from the east' (קֶדֶם) — they moved away from the Ancient (קַדְמוֹן) of Days."

As to the question: If such a regime is forbidden and evil in Hashem's eyes, why didn't the Torah forbid it? Abarbanel answers:

> When Hashem saw that Adam and all his descendants had immersed themselves in all the lusts for luxury and had defiled themselves with them, He did not forbid His people ... but encouraged the Children of Israel to behave in those matters with justice and in a proper manner, not in a despicable manner.

In any event, the purpose of the world, according to him, is for it to be as it was before, before man ruined it by "progress" and by building the city and the tower.

46 / *The Failure of Civilization*

And indeed the ruination of mankind by making technology into a god is also seen in the words of *Chazal* in the *Midrash* that at the time of the Generation of the Separation, "If a man fell and died, no one would pay attention to it, whereas if a single brick fell they would sit and cry, exclaiming, 'When will there be another like it?'" Technology, which was created to serve mankind, appeared as a goal, upon whose altar man was to be sacrificed. And that was the failure of the Generation of the Separation.

⊷§ Unity only on a Spiritual Basis

One who delves into the verses sees that here the Torah stresses the principle that civilization cannot exist without Hashem's spirit. *Chazal's* words are penetrating when they say, "And all intended this to be *avodah zarah*." According to various explanations and commentaries regarding the Generation of the Separation, this was a *technical* act by man in order to either rebel, to defend himself, or to bypass Hashem's deeds.

This *parashah* should also be regarded as a prophesy for the future, indicating what awaits man from similar actions. Man's powers are limited, but he presumes to fulfill the role of God in creation. *Chazal* say that in regard to the people of the Generation of the Separation, neither their sin nor their punishment is spelled out, but the Torah does say clearly that they exclaimed: "Come, let us build a city and its top in the Heavens, and let us make us a name." Mankind has not desisted from that aim from that time until today, but the punishment for this is inherent in the actions themselves. The occurrence of "each man could not understand the language of his fellow" must necessarily result from the plan to build technology on *material* foundations in terms of "and they had brick for stone, and had slime for mortar." Neither can mankind succeed in achieving its goals by the artificial unity of "and the whole earth was of one language, and of one speech." Such unity can only arise on spiritual foundations: "On that day Hashem will be one and His name one." Until that time, it is better that man be divided, for this division prevents him at the least from having a single totalitarian, tyrannical government, and permits the existence of spiritual streams and of nations living side by side. Technology will not unite mankind, but will split it up and splinter it so it cannot be united, because "Hashem confounded all the languages of the earth, and from there Hashem scattered them on the face of all the earth." This then is the meaning of *Chazal* that neither the sin nor the punishment of the Generation of the Separation was spelled out, in accordance with the above.

Lech Lecha – לך לך

I.
Avraham Avinu's Origin

The place from which Avraham set out to the Promised Land and his birthplace are not clear, and the commentators differ about this. In the previous *parashah* we read (*Bereishis* 11:28): "And Haran died before his father Terach in the land of his birth, in Ur Kasdim." Thus we see that the birthplace of Avraham's family was Kasdim. Later we read (verse 29), "And Terach took Avram his son and Lot son of Haran son of his son, and Sarai his daughter-in-law the wife of Avram his son, and they left with them from Ur Kasdim to go to the Land of Canaan." Thus we see that the family set out for Canaan even before Hashem told Avraham to go there.

Based on these verses, Ibn Ezra (on *Bereishis* 11:26) maintains that Avraham was born in a place called Ur Kasdim, and that was where Haran died. According to him, Hashem's command to (*Bereishis* 12:1) "go to the land that I will show you" preceded the previous *parashah* where Avraham's departure from Ur Kasdim is related. Avraham's father set out with him but settled along the way, while Avraham continued on his own, following Hashem's order.

Ibn Ezra reflects on the *d'rush* of *Chazal* that Ur Kasdim was not the name of a place, but the location of the furnace into which Avraham had been thrown by Nimrod for believing in Hashem (*ur* is taken here as "fire"). If this *aggadah* is indeed the *p'shat*, asks Ibn Ezra, why is there no mention of it in the Torah? After all, this *mesiras nefesh* — devotion — of Avraham to Hashem was even greater than the *akeidah* of Yitzchak! He therefore says that the words Ur Kasdim have no such special meaning.

Ibn Ezra's opinion is met by strong resistance on the part of *Ramban*, because according to this, it means that Avraham was not born in the land of Shem but in the land of Cham (Ham), for that is where Kasdim is located. Yet the Torah always relates Avraham to Shem, referring to him as Avraham the *Ivri* and not the *Kasdi*. And there is also the verse, "Across the river (עֵבֶר הַנָּהָר — hence *Ivri*) your fathers lived perpetually, and I took Avraham from across the river." *Ramban* also asks: When Avraham sent Eliezer to bring Rivka, he said to him: "Go to my land and my birthplace;" we thus see that Aram Naharayim was his birthplace and not Kasdim! He also asks: If Avraham left Ur Kasdim by Hashem's command, and Terach his father only went to Charan and stopped there, why does the Torah say that Terach took Avraham, when in reality Terach *followed* Avraham?

Ramban therefore holds that Avraham was born in Charan, and not in Ur Kasdim. Terach first lived in Charan, and there two of his sons, Avraham and Nachor, were born. Afterwards the family moved to Ur Kasdim, where Haran was born. After Haran died, they returned to Charan. At first, when leaving Ur Kasdim, Terach thought of going to Canaan, but when he reached Charan he remained there. While they were in Charan, Hashem appeared to Avraham and told him to leave his land, his birthplace and his father's house, and to go to the Promised Land. Evidence of the fact that Charan was his birthplace is to be found in *Chazal* in *Bava Basra* 91 (and *Rambam* quotes this in *Moreh Nevuchim* 3:29, as being in the books of the other nations as well), that Avram was thrown into prison in the town of Kuta, where he remained for three years. Kuta is a large city across the river, and is far from Kasdim, the latter being in Babylon.

In regard to Ur Kasdim, *Ramban* follows in the footsteps of *Chazal* that there was a confrontation there between Avraham and the ruler over matters of faith, and that Avraham was saved in a miraculous way, either, according to *Chazal*, by an explicit miracle in which he survived the fiery furnace, or through a *nes nistar* — a "concealed miracle" — that Hashem "put into the heart of the king to expel him and not to kill him."

This is the significance of the verse (*Bereishis* 15:7), "I am Hashem אֲשֶׁר הוֹצֵאתִיךָ — Who removed you — from Ur Kasdim," which is similar to "Who removed you from the Land of Egypt," rather than אֲשֶׁר לְקַחְתִּיךָ — "Who took you." This shows that just as the removal of the Jews from Egypt was through a great miracle, the removal of Avraham from Ur Kasdim was also a great miracle. The reason that the Torah did not mention the furnace was that the other nations said that this was nothing but witchcraft, and the Torah did not want to mention what they said and how they mocked the miracle.

Abarbanel too rejects the opinion of Ibn Ezra and concurs with

Ramban. He says that Terach's leaving of Ur Kasdim was caused by Hashem in order to accomplish His designs. If Terach had not left Ur Kasdim, it might have been harder for Avraham to wander along the roads, to leave his dwelling place, and to leave for Canaan at Hashem's command. As he and his family had already left his birthplace and had stopped along the way in Charan, it was easier for him to go on from there to Canaan.

Abarbanel also quotes *Chazal* that Avraham left Ur Kasdim because of his fear of the king, after he had been sentenced to be burned to death for refusing to worship the sun. Avraham in his wisdom had realized that the sun is just the servant of Hashem. His departure was a *nes nistar*, and the means by which he was saved from a fiery death. This is not found in the Torah, because whatever Avraham did, he did on his own, not by Hashem's order but in his own wisdom and understanding.

According to *Chazal*, Avraham was forty-eight years old when he recognized his Creator. It is true that another source says that he was three, but that relies on the verse (*Vayikra* 19:23), "for three years it (i.e., the fruit of a new tree) shall be *arelim* (literally "uncircumcised," but here meaning "forbidden") to you." What *Chazal* mean is that Avraham was still uncircumcised when he realized that Hashem exists.

When he left Ur Kasdim, says Abarbanel, Avraham found that the land was full of idolatry. The entire region, including his own father's house, worshiped idols, and Hashem ordered him to move away from these people. Hashem deliberately did not tell him the land where he was to go, so that the others would not be able to follow him. The place, of course, was *Eretz Yisrael*, because of its special qualities, as the Wise Man told the king of the Khazars (in the *Kuzari*),

> for prophecy is a special quality of the Holy Land, and whoever prophesied only did so within it or on its behalf. Avraham was moved from his land when he became worthy of clinging to the concept of God, and that worthy heart needed to be in the place where it could be perfected. This is like a farmer who finds a tree which yields good fruit growing in the desert. He then transplants it into fertile soil, so that it will grow even better there.

The argument between Ibn Ezra and *Ramban* is thus about the Semitic origin of Avraham. *Ma'asei Hashem* offers an interesting compromise between the two. He says that Avraham never left Aram Naharayim (which is in the territory of Shem), but that the latter was then under the rule of Kasdim (of the territory of Ham). The beliefs of the Kasdim were predominant. Avraham began to rebel against that belief there, and was thrown into the furnace of Kasdim or was taken to

Kuta. Afterwards, when he had survived miraculously, he left the domain of Kasdim with his father, and they crossed the river to Charan, where idolatry was not as rampant as it was in other regions. Hashem, though, told him to leave the entire kingdom of Kasdim and to go to the land that He would show him. Thus Avraham never left the boundary of Shem. Instead, it was Nimrod, King of Cham, who governed Aram Naharayim at the time.

๛§ Avraham's Ascent

How Avraham ascended to the stage where Hashem appeared to him is not mentioned in the Torah. The Midrash is full of stories of how Avraham studied nature and finally realized on his own that Hashem exists. So too are we told in the Midrash how he argued with the people of his generation, who finally threw him into a fiery furnace, from which he emerged unscathed. It was by this *mesiras nefesh* that he publicized Hashem's existence to all. World literature is also full of such stories. *Rambam* in his *Moreh Nevuchim* (3:29) quotes from these books how Avraham debated with the other beliefs and how much he suffered for his faith, even before Hashem appeared to him. In his *Mishneh Torah* (Hil. Avodah Zarah), *Rambam* explains at length Avraham's spiritual progression until:

> He grasped the way of the truth and understood the just course by his true perception. And he knew that there is only one God, who rules the world, and He created all, and there is no other God except for Him. And he knew that the entire world erred and what caused them to err was that they worshiped the stars and other forms until they totally forgot the truth.

But none of this is mentioned in the Torah. It is only hinted at in *Yeshayahu* (29:22), "Hashem, who redeemed Avraham," which fits in with the story of how he was in great danger from those who opposed him in Ur Kasdim, and how he was saved from them. Beyond that, the Torah does not mention any special action which Avraham took before Hashem told him to leave his father's house and to go to Canaan.

Ramban discusses this in our *parashah* and asks: Why did Hashem tell Avraham to leave his land and birthplace, and to be His beloved and chosen one, without telling us first that Avraham served Hashem or was a righteous man? Nor does the Torah explain why he had to leave his land, the reason being so that he should be closer to Hashem in the Promised Land. In most cases, the Torah makes a precondition: "Walk with Me and listen to My voice, and I will be good to you," but with

Avraham there is no such prologue or reason given for Hashem to tell him to leave his home. The Torah though, says *Ramban*, relied on what was well known. It was known that the people of Ur Kasdim caused Avraham much grief because of his belief in Hashem, and he fled from them to go to the Land of Canaan, but was detained in Charan. Hashem therefore told him to do what he had planned at first: namely, to go to the Chosen Land, and to call upon the people there to serve Hashem. That was why Avraham was promised that in *Eretz Yisrael* his name would become famous and that nations would be blessed through him, unlike the way he had been treated in Ur Kasdim, where they insulted and humiliated him, and placed him in a pit or a furnace. Hashem promised him that He would bless those who blessed him and if any individual cursed him, that person would be cursed. That is the explanation of that *parashah*, but the Torah did not want to expound on the beliefs of the idolaters and to explain the argument that he had with the Kasdim on matters of faith, just as it dwelled very briefly on the topic of the generation of Enosh and their beliefs in the idolatry which they started.

Moreh Nevuchim (3:29) also refers our *parashah* to the events which preceded it in Kasdim, and says:

> When he argued with everyone there, they, who had strayed, would curse and humiliate him, and when he suffered all for Hashem, and the same for His glory, he was told, "I will bless those that bless you, and those that curse you I will curse," and the end of the matter was that we see that today most people in the world agree to exalt him (i.e., Avraham) and to be blessed through him, to the extent that even those that are not his seed refer to him. And there is none that disputes him and there is none that disputes his greatness, except for the remnants of the base nations which remain at the ends of the earth, as those who deny the Torah at the very north and the Indians at the very south.

Ma'asei Hashem explains the Midrash (*Midrash Rabbah Lech Lecha*) along these lines. The Midrash states:

> R' Yitzchak said: "This is analogous to a person who was going from one place to another and saw a certain building burning. He said, 'Can this building then be without someone who looks after it?' The owner of the building looked out at him and said, 'I am the owner of the building.'"

The *Midrash*, says *Ma'asei Hashem*, was bothered with the same question that preoccupied *Ramban*: Why does the Torah begin by telling Avraham to leave his land, without any prior prophecy or account of his life that would explain why he merited this? Therefore the Midrash tells us that Avraham had traveled from one place to another and investigated all the different beliefs, and while he was involved in his own investigation the "owner of the building" appeared to him and confirmed to him that he was to follow the path he himself had initiated.

Or HaChayim also asks why Hashem spoke to him before appearing to him in a prophecy. He gives two contradictory answers. (a) Hashem did not need to appear to him, because Avraham had already discovered Him by his own wisdom. Hashem could therefore turn to him without any need for an introduction. (b) Hashem did not want to appear to him until He had seen if Avraham would fulfill all of His commands without questioning them. Avraham appeared on the historical scene after ten generations had gone astray, and Hashem therefore wanted to test him and see if he was more worthy than the previous generations of having Hashem appear to him. In later generations, though, people already had faith in Hashem, and therefore Hashem could appear to His prophets and tell them His words directly.

Maharal has an entirely different approach in his *Netzach Yisrael*. According to him, the Torah does not first tell us why Avraham merited Hashem appearing to him, because that would imply that Hashem's choice of him was dependent on that fact, and if *chas veshalom* the Jews would not be worthy at some future time, He might annul His choice of them. The Torah thus did not reveal the merits of Avraham, so as to teach and inform us that the reason for Hashem's choice of the Jews is known only to Him, and that he will never annul or cancel it, and that Israel will always be a holy nation.

According to the Midrash, the *rishonim* and the *acharonim*, Avraham himself, by his investigation and study, ascended to the level of having Hashem appear to him. Therefore — says the Kotzker Rebbi — *Chazal* say that Avraham's question, "Can this building then be without someone who looks after it?" was the most profound one that contradicted all the beliefs of the ancient world, and was the basis for the faith which mankind has to this day.

✺§ Hashem Who Conceals Himself in His Hiding Place

Avraham's past is shrouded in mystery, as is the purpose for which he had to leave his home, just as Hashem concealed from him the name of the country to which he was to go. The reasons were only clear to Hashem, who extracted from this concealment the greatest clarity, and shaped the Jew out of it. Only one thing is stated clearly: that man must leave the surroundings in which he is and must forsake his land, his birthplace and his father's house. From the very outset he must be alone in the world, just as *Chazal* explained the word *Ivri* ("Hebrew") as meaning that the whole world was on one side (עֵבָר), while Avraham was on the other. "Lo, a nation that dwells alone, and is not reckoned among the nations." Avraham was commanded not only to separate himself physically, but also — and primarily — spiritually.

This physical separation, says *HaKesav VeHaKabalah*, is the exact opposite of the normal. At first, a person leaves his father's house; afterwards he leaves his area and his family; and in the end he leaves his country. Here, though, we are referring to leaving spiritually. In spiritual matters, the first thing a person will forget is his country, afterwards his family, and finally his father's house, where his roots are. Avraham was commanded to totally shatter the structure of his world and to break all ties that bound him to his parents, his family and his country. He was commanded to start over, like a newborn child, without any remnant of his past. He was not commanded to live any differently, because he had already changed his whole life style in accordance with his wisdom and understanding, but he was commanded to go to a new land, where his new and magnificent life could be realized in full.

The Tzaddik of Ostrovska holds that the first *mitzvah* that Avraham was commanded was that of living in *Eretz Yisrael*. *S'forno* says that when they left Kasdim, they planned to go to Canaan immediately, because it was famous at the time as the land where people were willing to contemplate and to serve Hashem, and had not been affected by the Flood. That was the reason why only Avraham continued on to it, leaving his father halfway there. Terach was not willing to assume the responsibilities involved in living in *Eretz Yisrael*.

Ramban, though, says that Avraham did not recognize the qualities of *Eretz Yisrael* until Hashem appeared to him and told him, "To your seed I will give this land." Before that, he had wandered from one country to another and from one nation to the next, until he reached his final destination, as it states,"Hashem caused me to wander from my father's house."

S'forno explains "to the land that I will show you" to mean "to the land where I will appear to you as God." He therefore passed throughout the land and did not pitch his tent until Hashem appeared to him, as it states, "And Avram passed through the land until the place of Shechem, and Hashem appeared to him and said, 'unto your seed I will give this land.'"

And out of this lack of clarity there emerged a great light. The blessing of "and all the families of the earth will be blessed through you," is, according to Abarbanel and other commentators, the purpose why Avraham left Ur Kasdim. Hashem explained to him, says Abarbanel, that the purpose of his going was to be a spiritual influence among all nations. "And you shall be a blessing" — not only will you be blessed, but you will bring a blessing to all, because when they call upon Hashem you will proclaim His kingdom over the world, and by this all of Creation will be perfected and will attain its purpose. "And all the families of the earth will be blessed through you" — through you the belief in Hashem will be spread, and that will radiate its light upon all of Creation.

II.
Because of Pure Belief

There is no specific commandment in the Torah pertaining to *emunah* — faith in Hashem. The commandments pertain only to actions. In the *parashah* of the *bris bein habesarim* — the "covenant between the pieces" (see *Bereishis* 15) — *emunah* appears as being the greatest quality, higher than knowledge or recognition of Hashem, and this is the key to all of Judaism. In that covenant, we are told, "And he believed in Hashem; and He considered it to him as *tzedakah* — righteousness." *Emunah* without the need to understand or study was what was considered to be *tzedakah*. It is this which is the basis for everything which stems from it. The choice of Avraham and his descendants as the Chosen People came because of this spiritual quality, which is greater than any other quality. Similarly, in *yetzias Mitzrayim* — when the Jews left Egypt — we are told (*Shemos* 14:31): "And Israel saw the Great Hand that Hashem put forth in Egypt, and the people feared Hashem and they believed." It was not what they saw — that only being a natural phenomenon — but their *emunah* that counted. Hashem recognized this wonderful trait in Avraham and his descendants, which is unrivaled in any other nation.

We know that Avraham came to the realization of the existence of Hashem through thought, study and investigation, according to *Chazal*. This is proven in various verses. But he was not chosen because of this, since the method he used cannot be used by all. Others might use the same methods and fail. Avraham did not ask Hashem for any signs to confirm His supernatural promise that old people would give birth to a child.

According to a number of great Chassidic rabbis, Avraham understood logically that it couldn't happen that (*Bereishis* 15:2) "I will remain childless." After all, without the promise of the continuation of the Chosen People, the most fundamental of all principles of "I am Hashem your God" would remain empty of content, with no one representing it, and without anyone willing to sacrifice himself to fulfill it. Avraham's life was not ruled by his intellect, but by his simple faith in Hashem, without any logical basis. Of course afterwards, once he had been told that the flame would continue, he could and was obligated to ask for the logical and rational answer to his question (*Bereishis* 15:8): בַּמָּה אֵדַע כִּי אִירָשֶׁנָּה — "How will I know that I will inherit it?" But Avraham's spiritual strength lay in that he had *emunah*; and even when there was no rational explanation that he could comprehend, he still believed. This was so even though man's five senses cannot comprehend *emunah*, which is above these senses and is in another sphere entirely. This is what the Torah teaches us in the introduction to the *bris bein habesarim*.

The commentators on the Torah, both *rishonim* and *acharonim*, attempt to understand the meaning within the verses. Each explains it in his own way. As we noted above, *Rashi* states that Avraham's merit lay in his *emunah*. On this *Ramban* asks:

> What is so *meritorious*? Why should he not believe in Hashem, especially as he himself was a prophet? And Hashem is not a man who might deceive. He who believed enough to slaughter his only beloved son, and the other trials — how would he not believe the good tidings?

Ramban concludes that "He considered it to him as *tzedakah*" does not mean that Hashem thought that Avraham's *emunah* was *tzedakah*, but that Avraham thought that Hashem's news to him was *tzedakah*. Avraham felt that he did not deserve such a reward, and it was only given to him because of Hashem's *tzedakah*. A number of *rishonim*, such as *Bechor Shor*, *Chizkuni*, and Rabbenu Bachya agree with *Ramban* in this.

Other commentators, such as *Rosh*, *Radak*, *S'forno*, and others, apply the *tzedakah* to Avraham. Hashem saw Avraham's *emunah* as being impossible according to the laws of nature, and as something which utterly surpassed the normal behavior of man.

It would seem that the other commentators were not concerned with the question posed by *Ramban* as to what *zechus* was involved in Avraham's *emunah* in the fact that he was willing to slaughter his only son. According to them, actions are not identical to *emunah*, for *emunah* means faith and belief that is beyond nature. Subjugating one's thoughts to Hashem is greater than subjugating one's deeds. *Emunah* does not apply to one's five senses. It is beyond the senses, and through it one does not only sacrifice a son to Hashem once, but builds a Chosen People. Therefore the Jew is willing to give his life even for something which he did not hear personally from Hashem Himself, but from His servants: the prophets and *Chazal*.

Rambam explains in *Moreh Nevuchim* (3:53) that the *tzedakah* here was Avraham's very *emunah*. He says,

> The word "*tzedakah*" comes from *tzedek* — righteousness... and because of this, every good virtue is referred to as *tzedakah*. (The verse) says, "And he believed in Hashem, and He considered it to him as *tzedakah*." This means that he had the virtue of *emunah*.

Acting according to the letter of the law, says *Rambam*, is referred to as *mishpat* (justice), while enhancing one's good qualities is known as *tzedek*.

Ikarim, also, in section 3 says: "And the signs and wonders are made for those with *emunah*, and not for those with knowledge from study. This teaches that *emunah* is higher than knowledge from study." And in section 1, chapter 23, *Ikarim* says: "And that is the reason why Avraham *Avinu*, peace be upon him, was praised for his *emunah*, as the verse says, 'And he believed in Hashem, and He considered it to him as *tzedakah*.'"

On *Ramban's* doubt as to what was so new in Avraham having *emunah*, after having been willing to sacrifice his son for that same *emunah*, *Chafetz Chaim* says that the *chiddush* was that by this stage, Avraham completely abandoned the way of investigation, and believed in simple faith. *Binah L'Itim* elaborates on this and uses this to explain the verses (*Devarim* 7:17-18), "If you say in your heart, 'These nations are more than I; how can I dispossess them?' — you shall not be afraid of them." When you reach the level of understanding that by natural means you have no way to dispossess the other nations, and when you realize that they cannot be dispossessed by man, only then will you attain *emunah*, through which He will do for you the impossible.

This is also the direction used by R' Shalom Mordechai Shwadron, in his *Techeiles Mordechai*. Hashem said to him: "From the same star that you see that you will not have a child, from there I will show you that

BEREISHIS — LECH LECHA / 57

you will have a child." From the same source which undermines your *emunah* will come the *emunah* which brings salvation.

I strongly recommend that the reader read the commentary and ideas of R' Samson Raphael Hirsch on this topic. He expands on and delves deeply into this concept, and discusses it at length.

One who studies the *rishonim* will find a certain line running through all the generations in understanding this *parashah* in this light. The most fundamental of all principles of Judaism, which stretches from our Patriarch Avraham, is that of *emunah* without investigation — supernatural *emunah*.

Chasam Sofer, in his commentary on the Torah, says that Hashem appeared to Moshe and Israel during *yetzias Mitzrayim* with His supernatural abilities. He did not appear to our *avos* — our Patriarchs — in that form (*Shemos* 14:3): "And my name Hashem I did not reveal to them." We know that "Hashem" is used to indicate God's supernatural powers. Hashem did not appear to the *avos* in this fashion. Here, though, Hashem took Avraham out of the realm of nature, and promised him that he would father a child at his age, that being a supernatural prophecy. Avraham believed in this great power of Hashem even before he met Him "face to face," as it were. And that was the *tzedakah* of his *emunah*. *Chasam Sofer* also explains "And he believed in Hashem" to mean that he implanted his *emunah* in the hearts of all the following generations, and Hashem bears in mind this *tzedakah* for him for all generations.

It appears to me that this is also the meaning of the Midrash at the beginning of the *parashah*:

> R' Yitzchak commenced with (*Tehillim* 45:11), " 'Listen, O daughter, and see, and incline your ear; also forget your own people, and your father's house.' This is analogous to a person who was going from one place to another and saw a certain building burning. He said, 'Can this building then be without someone who looks after it?' The owner of the building looked out at him and said, 'I am the owner of the building.' Similarly, our Father Avraham said, 'Can the world be without a guide?' Hashem looked out at him and said, 'I am the guide.'"

What this means is that at first Avraham began by investigating and studying, and this way he understood Hashem's existence. But Hashem saw that this understanding was insufficient. He appeared to Avraham and told him of the child he would father, and also commanded him regarding *emunah*. And this is the meaning of the verse brought in the Midrash, "Listen and see" — listening and *emunah* must precede seeing, even though seeing is better than investigating and studying. There are thus three levels: (a) investigation and study, with which Avraham began; (b) the supernatural vision that Israel saw at the Red Sea; (c) and the greatest of all levels, that of *emunah*, which Avraham attained after his investigation, and Israel after what it saw.

← The Proof — Inheriting the Land

After the simple faith of Avraham regarding fathering a child, a basic question must arise: If so, why was Avraham in doubt about inheriting the land, so that he asked: "How will I know that I will inherit it?" In fact *Chazal* tell us in *Nedarim* 32 that "He went too far in (questioning) Hashem's qualities in this matter," and because of that his children were enslaved in Egypt. In the Midrash, though, *Chazal* tell us that Avraham was not questioning Hashem, but was simply wondering: "What *zechus* do I have for such a great revelation?"

HaKesav VeHaKabalah quotes *Tzeidah LaDerech* that one cannot understand why, because of this question, *Bnei Yisrael* were destined to go into *galus*. He says: "Many great and learned men declared that all the reasons mentioned in *Maseches Nedarim* and in the Midrash on the exile in Egypt only come to explain why Hashem caused Avraham grief by telling him about the exile." In any event, as mentioned, there are also negative opinions among *Chazal* on the question raised by Avraham.

One of the *mussar* giants of the last generation, R' Eliyahu Dessler, quotes *Chazal* in *Sotah* 11, that Avraham's question was the "profound strategy of the *tzaddik* who is buried in Hebron," by which he acquired an explicit promise from Hashem concerning the inheritance of the land and the eternity of the Jewish people. The negative aspect, according to R' Dessler, results from what "appeared" to be doubt on the part of Avraham, and every such "appearance" is a flaw, not only in others, but also in Avraham.

Those *rishonim*, though, who primarily follow *p'shat*, explain Avraham's question not as a doubt, but as a request to clarify the promise, with each commentator following his own path.

Ramban says that Avraham was afraid lest inheriting the land would be dependent upon some condition. Even though Hashem had said, "to your seed I will give this land," He would not decree the gift to him, as He decreed seed to him (i.e., Avraham was afraid that there was no promise by Hashem concerning the land, it having been mentioned only incidentally, when Hashem said to him that He had taken him out of Ur Kasdim to give him the land), and that was why he said, "How will I know that I will inherit it?" This did not mean that he sought a sign. Neither did Hashem show him something extraordinary as He did with other signs. Rather, Avraham wanted to know how he could be certain that he would inherit it, and that his sins or those of his descendants would not deny them this heritage. Perhaps the Canaanites would do *t'shuvah*, and Hashem might fulfill with them the verse (*Yirmiyahu* 18:7-8), "At that instant I will speak about a nation, and about a kingdom, to pluck up, and to pull down, and to destroy it. But if that nation whom I have sentenced turns from its evil, I will repent of the evil that I thought to do to it." He therefore asked for a covenant from Hashem that he would inherit it.

Quite a few commentators also follow in the path of *Ramban*.

Ralbag, though, is astounded at this explanation. If Avraham's question was that he was afraid that the Jews' inheriting the land was conditional on their observing the Torah, what purpose would a covenant serve here? Would a covenant change the freewill of his descendants? After all, they might well sin and annul the covenant.

Bechor Shor says that Avraham's question dealt with the details of the inheritance. "What will I inherit? When will I inherit it? How much will I inherit?"

Chizkuni explains the matter simply. The Torah is not a chronological account of our history. Hashem's promise about the land was before His promise about having a child, even though in the Torah they appear in the reverse order. Avraham asked, "How shall I inherit it?" implying "Through whom?" I have no children, and how, then, can I inherit the land? Hashem then told him that he would have a child, and thus Avraham realized that the promise to inherit the land would indeed be fulfilled.

Tur quoting *yesh mefarshim* — "there are those that explain this" — has a beautiful interpretation. "How will I know that I will inherit it?" was not a display of a lack of faith in Hashem, but a request for clarification. How can You help me to fulfill this promise? I am living among gentiles, and will be forced to make a treaty with them in order not to be harmed by them, and the same will apply to the generations after me. On that, Hashem answered him:

> I will find a solution to your concerns. I will exile your children from this land to another land, and they will live there unto the fourth generation. When they return, they will have no ties with the inhabitants of the land, and will evict them without any qualms.

HaKesav VeHaKabalah has a simple explanation. According to him, the word אֵדַע (translated here as "I will know") in בַּמָּה אֵדַע כִּי אִירָשֶׁנָּה, means fondness, as in (Shemos 33:12) יְדַעְתִּיךָ "... I know you by name and you have found favor in my sight," or as in (Bereishis 18:19) כִּי יְדַעְתִּיו לְמַעַן אֲשֶׁר יְצַוֶּה אֶת בָּנָיו וְאֶת בֵּיתוֹ אַחֲרָיו — "For I have known him, so that he may command his children and his household after him..." Avraham asked Hashem, "What is the reason for this great love that You show me, to the extent of allowing me to inherit this land?"

R' David Zvi Hoffmann holds that Avraham only wanted to know what factors would cause him to inherit the land. How would he know when the time to inherit it had come? When would he know that the sins of the present inhabitants had reached the limit? What sign would he be able to give his children to know when this longed-for aim would be achieved?

One could perhaps say that the meaning may be yet deeper. The declaration that he would have a son was one that affected Avraham as an individual, while that of inheriting the land affected the entire nation. Avraham knew that Hashem's promise about a child would be fulfilled through him, but when would the promise to the nation be fulfilled? When would the nation be ready to inherit the land? When would Hashem's declaration become reality? To this, Hashem answered him, "And the fourth generation will return here," and Hashem made a covenant with him to validate that promise.

⊷§ The Covenant to Validate the Promise

The *bris bein habesarim*, says R' David Zvi Hoffmann, was the second covenant that Hashem made with mankind. The first was the covenant after the Flood, that humanity would never be wiped out. The second covenant, on the other hand, was to establish the Chosen People and the Kingdom of Heaven on earth through Avraham's descendants.

The promise (*Bereishis* 15:14), "And afterwards they will leave with great wealth," was, according to *HaKesav VeHaKabalah*, a promise of the spiritual wealth that they would acquire when they left Egypt on their way to *Eretz Yisrael*. For that, Israel had to be purified first by the crucible of affliction — the iron furnace of Egypt, where its dross would be removed. That is the reason why the Torah says בִּרְכֻשׁ גָּדוֹל — "great wealth" rather than בִּרְכֻשׁ רַב — "much wealth" — for the word "great" refers to quality, while "much" only refers to quantity, as we see from (*Shemos* 18:11), "that Hashem is great," and (*Shemos* 11:3), "the man Moshe was very great in the eyes of Egypt." Thus, here Hashem was telling Avraham not only that he would inherit the land, but also about the nature of that inheritance. The *parashah* begins with Avraham's great *emunah*, and ends with the reward that Hashem will give him for that *emunah*, both to him and his descendants: that He will give them the land, and will make them a kingdom of priests and a holy nation. This was what Hashem said to him when He told him (*Bereishis* 15:1), "Your reward will be very great."

III.
The Pronouncement of the Exile and the Redemption

In the *bris bein habesarim*, Hashem told Avraham the length of time that the Jews would be slaves, and when the slavery would come to an end. Why did Hashem decree that Avraham's descendants would go into exile? That the Torah does not explain. *Chazal* in *Nedarim* 32 tell us that Avraham was punished in having his descendants become slaves in Egypt, because "he questioned Hashem's attributes when he said, 'How shall I know?'" On this, there are *Midrashim* that disagree.

In *Bereishis Rabbah* 44, R' Chiya ben R' Chanina states that Avraham did not "complain to Hashem, but said to Him, 'With what *zechus* — merit?'" In addition, *Chazal* in *Berachos* 7b praise Avraham's words, and say: "From the time that Hashem created His world, there was no person who called him *Adon* (Master) except Avraham, as it states, '*Adon-ai Elokim*, how shall I know?' Indeed, as we will see below, the different commentators do not regard Avraham's question as being one of doubt, but as a request to know the time when the inheritance will take place, etc. That is the reason why the commentators attempt to understand the reason why Hashem decreed exile on Israel.

Ran holds that at the *bris bein habesarim*, Hashem told Avraham about what would occur in the future. After the twelve sons of Yaakov would die, Hashem would remove His *hashgachah* — His personal supervision — from them, whereupon the Egyptians would enslave them until they would cry to Hashem and He would redeem them.

Abarbanel, though, finds this surprising, and asks how it would be that the future of Avraham's descendants would be left to "chance." After all, in the Torah we see clearly that the actions leading to and after the sale of Yosef were part of a continuous chain of miracles; should those miracles then give way to nothing more than "coincidence" and the rule that "might makes right"?

In addition, we are told in the *bris bein habesarim* that (*Bereishis* 15:14): וְגַם אֶת הַגּוֹי אֲשֶׁר יַעֲבֹדוּ דָּן אָנֹכִי — "and the nation that they will serve, I will also judge." This appears to be a decree against the Egyptians in advance, with the exile in Egypt linked to the punishment of the Egyptians. If it was all to be a matter of coincidence, why should Hashem blame the Egyptians for enslaving a nation which did not have Hashem's *hashgachah* — Divine Providence — backing it?

Abarbanel deals with this question, and concludes that the exile in Egypt was a *gezeirah* by Hashem — a decree which man cannot fathom. The Egyptians were punished even though they were fulfilling a task imposed on them by Hashem, because they carried matters much further than they had been ordered.

Rabbenu Bachya and other commentators expand on this, and quote the words of *Zecharyah* (1:14-15), "I am jealous for Jerusalem and for Zion with a great jealousy. And I am very displeased with the heathens that remain at ease: for at first I was only a little displeased, and they helped increase the affliction." Thus we see that the punishment of the Egyptians was that they exaggerated in their treatment of Israel. Hashem only commanded that "they will enslave them and afflict them," but Pharaoh and his nation did everything possible to destroy the Jewish people by forcing them to work unusually hard and by drowning their sons. Thus, when the Torah states that Hashem would judge the Egyptians, it means that Hashem would examine whether they had indeed carried out what they were ordered to do, or whether they had exceeded their orders.

We also find in *Yeshayahu* 10, "O Assyria, the rod of My anger, and the staff in their hand is My indignation ... But his heart does not think so; but it is in his heart to destroy and cut off many nations ... therefore I will punish the fruit of the strong heart of the king Assyria."

There too, we see that Assyria is to be punished for exceeding the task imposed on it by Hashem. We see this in other places as well. Indeed, says Abarbanel, the plagues upon Egypt always came after it had been warned that it was doing more than it had been ordered, as it states (*Shemos* 9:17), "You yet exalt yourself over My people."

According to Abarbanel, the exile to Egypt was decreed because of the sin of the sale of Yosef (*Torah Sheleimah* quotes *Midrash Cheifetz* which explains why Yaakov's children went into exile, in a comment on *Bereishis* 15:13 — יָדֹעַ — *yado'a* — because you questioned My deeds; תֵּדַע — *teida* — because of the sin of your children in selling Yosef). What happened was *midah k'neged midah* — measure for measure.

Because Yosef was sold as a slave, all the tribes later became slaves. Yaakov's going down to Egypt began with the sale of Yosef. Yosef was a shepherd for his father, and the entire exile came about as a result of the fact that there was no place for their flocks to graze during the drought years. The brothers that sold Yosef deserved to go to exile, and their children suffered after them. As the punishments of Hashem go to "the third and fourth generations," the result will be that "the fourth generation will return here." When Israel left Egypt, they were ordered to slaughter a sheep for the *Pesach* sacrifice, so as to make them understand the reason why they had gone into exile — dating back to the sheep that Yosef tended. And at the *bris bein habesarim*, Hashem told Avraham what would happen to his children as a result of their deeds.

Abarbanel, though, gives another reason, which is brought in other works as well. The exile in Egypt was a necessary prologue for the Jews to understand the concepts which they were later taught at the giving of the Torah. Had they remained in their land at peace the entire time, they would not have been prepared to accept the yoke of the Torah and the *mitzvos*. Only after they had been beaten in Egypt were their souls refined and purified, did they become the Chosen People which received the Torah, and become a guide to the human race. According to this view, the exile in Egypt was a necessary stage in the people's spiritual development.

This idea already appears in *Ralbag* on the verse, "And the nation that they will serve, I will also judge," that this was a means to prepare Israel for receiving the Torah. Israel saw in the plagues brought on the Egyptians the hand of Hashem, and thus the *emunah* of their fathers became stronger within them, and it was through that *emunah* that they became worthy of receiving the Torah.

✎§ The Nature of Avraham's Question

Certain *rishonim* hold that Avraham's question, "How shall I know?" pertains to when the event would take place, and in which way. *Yosef Bechor Shor* finds a similar example with Achav (Ahab), who, when the prophet told him that he would be victorious over his enemies, asked, "With whom?" namely, through whom? In which way? Avraham too wanted to know what events would occur through which one would be able to tell that the conclusion of the promise was to come to pass.

One of the *acharonim*, the Dubno Magid, also explains it along these lines. Avraham's question was like the question a sick person asks his doctor, as to how and when he will be healed. Hashem's answer was that the redemption would come about the way things normally grow, with plowing followed by planting, where the seeds that are planted first have to decay in the ground before the plant can take root. The slavery and poverty would pave the way for redemption, as we see in *Chazal* (*Berachos* 5): "Three precious gifts were given, and all of them with suffering," and one of these is *Eretz Yisrael*. So too do we see in *Tehillim* (126:5): "They that sow in tears shall reap in joy."

R' David Zvi Hoffmann adds that Avraham asked Hashem for "a sign and token" with which he would know when the Emorites living in *Eretz Yisrael* had surpassed their limit of sins, which would mean that they were to be driven from the land. Hashem disclosed to him what sign would indicate that the time had arrived, by telling him that the oppression and the slavery in Egypt would be the signs that would foretell the Jews' redemption.

Meleches Machsheves states that at first Avraham had thought that he himself would inherit the land, and his question was when this would take place. Hashem then told him that he was mistaken, and that it was not he who would inherit the land, but his descendants of the fourth generation, and that only after enslavement of four hundred years. R' Samson Raphael Hirsch also follows a similar path. Avraham asked, "How will I know that the time has come for me to conquer the land?" Hashem answered him that it was not he who would inherit the land, but his descendants, and it would not be soon, but only after the Emorites had sinned to the extent that they deserved to be banished from the land.

Tur has an interesting interpretation: Avraham was afraid that the inhabitants of Canaan would force either him or his descendants to make a treaty with them, just as he had made one with Avimelech. Hashem then told him: Your children will be exiled from here, and they will not remain in Canaan until the time comes for them to inherit it. They will only come back after a certain amount of time, and only then will they inherit the land.

Kesav Sofer has an interesting interpretation: Avraham wished that the inheritance would take place at least in his days, so that he too would be able to spend some time living in peace and tranquility in the Promised Land, and he asked: "But I am a stranger here. How then will the inheritance be expressed?" Hashem then answered him:

> You at least are a stranger in your own land, but your children will be strangers in a land that is not theirs, and that is even worse. At least be happy with your situation, and await the day of redemption that will come, after the fourth generation returns here.

BEREISHIS — LECH LECHA / 65

◆§ From When Did the Calculation of the Exile Start?

At the *bris bein habesarim*, Hashem stated that the exile would be for "four hundred years." Rabbenu Bachya states that "the reason for this amount of time for the exile in Egypt is not known, and none of the commentators of the Torah tells us anything about it." R' Sa'adiah Gaon, in his *Emunos VeDeos* 8:4, says that the Torah contains three different time periods in regard to the exile in Egypt: (a) 430 years; (b) 400 years; (c) 210 years. He reconciles the differences as follows: The actual time the Jews stayed in Egypt was 210 years. It was 400 years from the time that Yitzchak was born, and the 430 years includes the thirty years that Avraham was a foreigner before Yitzchak was born.

Midrash Tanchuma on *Parashah Massei* 7 says that the verse (*Bamidbar* 23:19), "Hashem is not a man, that He should lie," refers only to His doing good and not doing bad. Thus, when Hashem states He will do something good, He will always do it, but if He states He will do something bad, He may later "change His mind," as it were. Here, then, Hashem took back what He had said, and reduced the years of exile.

Most of the commentators, though, follow *Rashi* based on *Mechilta* in *Parashas Bo*, that the exile began with the birth of Yitzchak, and then the time emerges as 400 years. Yitzchak was 60 years old when Yaakov was born. Yaakov was 130 years old when he stood before Pharaoh. Add to this the 210 years of slavery and oppression, and the figure is indeed 400 years. That is the reason why Avraham was not told (*Bereishis* 15:13) at the *bris bein habesarim* that his children would be strangers *in Egypt*, but that his seed would be a stranger "in a land which is not theirs." Our *avos* — Patriarchs — were also foreigners, even before the exile in Egypt began. Thus, with Yitzchak we are told, "And Yitzchak lived in Gerar," and with Yaakov it states that, "We have come to live in the land."

Rosh expands along these lines. In our *parashah* itself, the words "and your seed will be a stranger" refer to Yitzchak, who lived as a stranger in *Eretz Yisrael*. "In a land which is not theirs" is a reference to Yaakov and his sons, who lived as strangers in Aram Naharayim, where most of Yaakov's sons were born. "And they will enslave them and oppress them" alludes to to the children of Yaakov's sons, who already felt the slavery and oppression of Egypt.

Pa'aneach Raza finds an interesting principle regarding this number in the *trop* — the melody notations on the words. The Torah has an *esnachta*, which symbolizes a pause, dividing the verse between the words "and they will enslave them and oppress them" and the words "four hundred years," thus showing that the four hundred years includes both the period before the slavery and the slavery itself.

Chida, in his *Nachal Kedumim*, has an interesting interpretation. *Chazal* tell us in *Chullin* 60 that Yosef moved all the people of Egypt to live in different locations, "so that they would not refer to his brothers as being in exile." According to this, the Egyptians themselves lived in land which had not belonged to them originally. This is hinted at in the words, "in a land which is not theirs."

Sifsei Kohen finds in the expression "that is not theirs" a halachic rule. The land of Egypt can never belong to the Jews, as we see in the verse, "You shall not continue to see them (i.e., the Egyptians) again," on which *Chazal* tell us that one who lives in Egypt violates three prohibitions. As Hashem had stressed to Avraham that "I will give you this land from the great river, the Euphrates River," He now made it clear that Egypt was not included in this. Even if Israel would succeed in conquering that land, they would be forbidden to live in it. This interpretation, though, differs with the *halachah* as ruled by *Rambam* in *Hil. Melachim* 5:8: "And it appears to me that if a king of Israel conquered the land of Egypt, in accordance with (a ruling of) the *beis din*, it is permitted, and (the Torah) only warned against individuals returning to it, or to live there when it is in the hands of *akum* ("pagans")."

The Rogachover, in his commentary on *Rambam*, explains that *Rambam* means that only if Israel conquered Egypt would Jews be permitted to live in it, provided that the conquest was in accordance with a ruling of the *beis din*, but Jews are forever forbidden to annex the territory to *Eretz Yisrael*, as opposed to the other countries that they may conquer. The words "that is not theirs" thus have a halachic content, in regard to annexation.

R' Yisrael Salanter and a number of other commentators, such as *Mei Marom* and the Munkacher in his *Os Chaim VeShalom*, find a *hashkafah* lesson in this. The Jews in the diaspora will always be "in a land which is not theirs." They will not succeed in becoming citizens in the other lands and in forgetting their own land. The Munkacher expresses this well when he states, "He promised him that even when they are in exile they will feel that it is not their land, and their hearts will desire to return."

Unfortunately, we have learned this lesson from bitter experience. All the attempts of the Jewish people to assimilate have ended in tragedy. The Jews remained and still remain a foreign body among the other nations, and that is good news for their survivability and their eventual return to *Eretz Yisrael*. This was expressed well by *Chasam Sofer* in his *d'rashah* of 7 Av 5592 (1832), where he wrote: "The more we try to draw closer to the other nations, to forget Jerusalem, the more they place a yoke on us and the more hated we become in their eyes." That is what is meant by "a land that is not theirs."

◈§ Why Did Egypt Deserve to be Punished?

We have brought the words of the *rishonim* that the punishment brought on Egypt for enslaving Israel was that its people exceeded what they were assigned to do, because of their wickedness. *Rambam* (*Hil. T'shuvah* 6), though, gives another reason. According to him, the words of the Torah, "and they will enslave them and oppress them," were not a command by Hashem, but simply Hashem informing Avraham of what would take place. The fact that Hashem knows does not take away a person's free will. The Egyptians did not have to enslave Israel, and therefore they deserved a punishment when they did so.

Ramban in our *parashah* ponders the words of *Rambam*, and says, "I do not see his words as correct. When a king demands that any act take place, a person who does not carry out his orders and instead assigns the duty to another is worthy of the death penalty, while the one who does carry it out will find favor."

Perhaps, though, one can attempt to answer *Ramban's* question as follows. According to *Rambam*, after all, there was no decree, but an "announcement" to Avraham, and according to him that announcement in no way diminished from the Egyptians' free will. As is known, *Rambam* repeats this idea a number of times in his works. Hashem simply told Avraham that the other nations in their wickedness would seek to do evil to Israel and to enslave them. Thus, *Ramban's* statement, "One who fulfills the decree of Hashem is doing a *mitzvah*," can be answered. It is because of this question, though, that *Ramban* arrives at the same conclusion as other *rishonim*: that the Egyptians exceeded what they had been assigned to do. And the same applied to Nebuchadnezzar, who was sent by Hashem's orders, but was punished for being more cruel than he had been ordered to be.

Meshech Chochmah answers *Ramban's* question on *Rambam*. He too maintains that there was no *decree* by Hashem here, but merely an announcement of what was to happen. The Egyptians were punished because they showed such monumental ingratitude to the descendants of Yosef, the one who had saved them from starvation, and because they transgressed one of the seven *mitzvos* of Noach by killing the Jewish male infants.

Meshech Chochmah shows how Hashem's acknowledgment of events before they happen is not a decree, as indicated in the following comment by *Chazal*: The frogs that plagued the Egyptians were under no obligation to immolate themselves in order to sanctify Hashem's name, yet they voluntarily entered the ovens. From this incident we see that just because Hashem said, "They will enter into your ovens," does not mean that He decreed it so. And if this applies to creatures without free will, how much more so to humans.

Or HaChayim also explains the punishment in a similar fashion to *Ramban's* interpretation. When the Egyptians oppressed Israel, they did not do so to fulfill Hashem's commands, where Hashem had wanted this to purify Israel (as cited above in the name of *Ramban*). Instead, they wanted to force the Jews to abandon their beliefs, and there is no hatred as fierce as religious hatred. The Torah therefore states (*Bereishis* 15:14), וְאַחֲרֵי כֵן יֵצְאוּ בִּרְכֻשׁ גָּדוֹל — "And afterwards they will leave with great wealth," for as the Egyptians did things they were not commanded to do, it was only proper that they should pay Israel for the slavery which under the circumstances they had no right to impose.

HaKesav VeHaKabalah also explains the word "afterwards" (in *Bereishis* 15:14) as "the reason" — namely that the Jews would receive this wealth "after" the Egyptians had acted differently than they were supposed to. According to him, the words "and also" in the verse, "and also the Egyptians I will judge," means that the Egyptians "added" to what they were commanded. They were chastised for the *added* punishment they perpetrated on Israel. It was because of that addition that Israel deserved to receive great wealth in compensation. He adds though, as does Abarbanel, that this wealth was spiritual. Avraham would never have agreed to have his descendants serve as slaves for four hundred years so that the fourth generation would be paid money in compensation for all that labor. This "wealth" then was a spiritual one, where they prepared themselves to receive the Torah. For such wealth, the hard work was worthwhile.

The *Baal Shem Tov* has a beautiful explanation. The Egyptians already deserved to be destroyed because of other sins, and therefore Hashem used them as the tool to enslave the Jews, since bad things happen through those that are culpable. This is the meaning of the verse, "and also the nation that enslaves them, I shall judge." I, who knows what each nation's plans are and who knows which nation is guilty, will decide which nation is to be designated for destruction for having enslaved Israel. This interpretation is in keeping with that of *Rambam* in *Hil. T'shuvah*, who says that, "It is well known that the

Creator does not pay back a person except through someone who is more wicked than he, and then he pays back that person with one who is even more wicked than he."

◆§ The Fourth Generation Will Return

As we brought above from *Rashi* and the other commentators, the exile began with Yitzchak, but when the Torah refers to the "fourth generation" it means the fourth generation of those who entered into Egypt, namely the chain of Yehudah, Peretz, and Chetzron, with Calev the son of Chetzron already among those who came to *Eretz Yisrael*. But these words of *Rashi's* are surprising, for Calev was of the fifth generation that went down to Egypt, because Yaakov too went down to that land. R' Eliyahu Mizrachi suggests that Yaakov is excluded from the generations that went down to Egypt because of his advanced age. *Maharal*, in his *Gur Aryeh*, is not satisfied with Mizrachi's explanation. According to him, the count of the generations began with the children of the first people who went down to Egypt. But this interpretation is also surprising, for when the Torah states that the fourth generation of an Egyptian or an Edomite convert may intermarry freely, it begins the count from the person himself, and not from his children. *Maharal* answers that the reason why in the latter case the *halachah* counts from the person himself is that there the Torah uses an extra word לָהֶם, and the *gemara* in *Yevamos* deduces from this that the count begins with the person himself, and not with his children.

Ramban quotes a similar explanation, and says that it is not correct. According to him, the reference to "the fourth generation" has nothing to do with the Jews. Instead, it refers to the Canaanites, as we see that Hashem visits the sins of the fathers on the third and fourth generations. In the fourth generation of the Canaanites, Israel will return to the land.

Or HaChayim has his own interpretation. According to him, there are two different dates involved here: The end of living in a strange land and the oppression which would come to pass in exactly 400 years, and then Israel would leave Egypt, "on this very same day," as determined in advance. As to the fourth generation, that refers to the fourth generation of bondage. Yaakov's twelve sons were not enslaved. The Torah refers here to the generation which was under the age of twenty when it left Egypt, upon whom the decree of enslavement never applied. Thus the count of the generations begins with Peretz, the son of Yehudah. The sons of Calev were the fourth generation of the decree, and they were the first generation to enter *Eretz Yisrael*. It is true that Calev himself also entered the land, but he was an exception. The fourth generation was on the whole under the age of twenty when it left Egypt.

As we mentioned, according to *Rashi*, the fourth generation was in reality the fifth. This seems unusual, though, because it is possible to find those among the fourth generation itself who were redeemed. Moshe was the fourth generation of Levi, and he and Korach both left Egypt. This requires further study. (See Ibn Ezra whose explanation is along these lines.)

It is interesting that *Rashi's* explanation that the fourth generation is really the fifth is the source of a question in *She'elos u'T'shuvos Noda BiYehudah* (*Choshen Mishpat* 36), regarding a case where a person willed his possessions to the fourth generation. What did he mean by that? *Noda BiYehudah* deduces in accordance with *Rashi* that the fourth generation is the deceased's fifth generation, because even *Ramban*, who maintains that the verse applies to the Emorites, states that it pertains to the fifth generation, because the Torah refers to the four generations of descendants, and not to the sinner himself.

IV.

The Holy Sign of the Covenant

⋙ And I Have Made My Covenant Between Me and You

The covenant of circumcision (*bris milah*) is the seal of Hashem and a sign that the man who is so marked belongs to the community of believers. A Jew is not asked if he wants this sign. He is linked to it, and it is part of his flesh, without anyone asking his opinion or desires, from the age of eight days. The father is commanded to have his son circumcised, and if the father doesn't arrange for this, the court (*beis din*) must do so. *Bris milah* is a *mitzvah* which is forced on a person, and in that it is unique in the Torah. In the blessings of the circumcision, the father says לְהַכְנִיסוֹ — "to enter him" — implying that this is imposed. We are commanded to enter the Jew against his will into the yoke of the covenant, as his eternal link to the covenant of the Patriarchs.

The two blessings לְהַכְנִיסוֹ and עַל הַמִּילָה — "regarding the *milah*" — recited during the circumcision ceremony are a source of discussion among the halachic authorities. The first blessing, עַל הַמִּילָה, is recited just before the circumcision itself, as with all blessings that are recited in advance of the act, while the second, לְהַכְנִיסוֹ, is said between the *milah* itself and the *p'riyah* (splitting and pulling down the membrane).

Some *rishonim* hold that both blessings must be recited before the *bris milah*, but *Ran*, *Ritva*, and *Rashba* maintain that the second blessing does not relate to the circumcision as such, and is a blessing of thanks and praise to Hashem for our having arrived at this time.

Other authorities such as *Taz*, *Shach*, etc., consider the blessing before the *p'riyah* as a blessing recited in advance of the act, since circumcision without a *p'riyah* is not considered to be a *milah*.

R' Raphael Meizels uses this principle to explain why *Chazal* in *Shabbos* 137, on the *mishnah*, "The one who performs the *milah* says ... the father says ...," quote a *beraisa* to the effect that "one who did the *milah* without the *p'riyah* is as if he did not do the *milah*." What *Chazal* wanted to prove here by quoting the *beraisa* is that even though the second blessing, לְהַכְנִיסוֹ, is said between the *milah* and the *p'riyah*, it is still considered to have been said before the *mitzvah*, because a *milah* without the *p'riyah* is not considered to be a *milah*.

Chasam Sofer in his commentary on *Shabbos*, though, asks a profound question on *Taz* and *Shach*, whom we mentioned above. According to *Chazal*, Avraham was not instructed concerning the *p'riyah*. How then can we then make the blessing, "to enter him into the covenant of our Patriarch Avraham," just before and in regard to the *p'riyah*? (*Minchas Chinuch* leaves this question unanswered.)

It would therefore appear, as we began this section, that the blessing "to enter him" is a blessing in which we indicate that the *bris milah* is imposed without the person being given a choice, rather than a blessing on the actual act of *milah*.

P'rishah on *Yoreh De'ah* 265 also brings a similar answer in the name of *Abudraham*. According to him, the blessing was formulated because the father is commanded to circumcise his son, to teach him Torah, to redeem him if he is a firstborn, and to marry him off, and it is against this obligation that the blessing is said.

R' Yonah Emmanuel, in his work on R' Samson Raphael Hirsch, gives a beautiful description of R' Hirsch as a commentator who, when he was only twenty-eight years old, explained the blessing "to enter him" as a blessing relating to Jewish education, which from the *bris milah* on, the father is duty bound to give his son. He notes that this idea is already given in *T'shuvos R' Akiva Eiger* in the name of *Levush*. And indeed, in *T'shuvah* 42, R' Akiva Eiger dwells at length on the tie between the Torah and *milah*. Removing the *orlah* (foreskin) of flesh is a prelude to removing the *orlah* of the heart. Thus, the first blessing refers to the removing of the *orlah* of the flesh and the second to removing the *orlah* of the heart and entering into the gates of the Torah.

Indeed, one of the reasons of *milah* given by *Rambam* in his *Moreh Nevuchim* 3:49 is that through the *bris milah*, the child who is circumcised enters into the covenant of those who believe in the Oneness of Hashem, that being the *bris* of our Patriarch, Avraham, as it is written (*Bereishis* 17:7), "To be a God to you and to your seed after you." *Rambam* also stresses that this is a major reason for the *mitzvah*.

It is interesting that this reason is also to be found in *Midrash Sechel Tov*, "And it shall be a sign of a covenant that all the nations will recognize you, that you are the seed that Hashem has blessed." *Torah Sheleimah* also quotes *Midrash Cheifetz*, in which it states, "This teaches that the *milah* was only given as a sign to the holy seed of Avraham, which proclaims the unity of His name."

✺§ A Sign of the Holy Covenant

Rambam in *Moreh Nevuchim* 3:49 provides a number of reasons for *bris milah*. We have mentioned the reason that it is a sign that one is a member of the covenant of those who believe in the unity of Hashem. He also gives a pragmatic reason, in that it is a unifying mark of all those who belong to the same religion, who are bound to one another with bonds of love. All those who quote *Rambam*, though, only mention the other reason which he gives, which is to weaken one's sexual lust. *Rambam* states that "to me this is the strongest of the reasons of *milah*." *Ramban*, though, holds that *bris milah* is but a sign of the holy covenant, without any natural explanation. He too, though, mentions that one of the reasons for *bris milah* is to warn one to deal with the procreative organ properly, as the fundamental principle of *kedushah* — holiness.

In reality, there is a dispute if a person who did not have a *bris milah* is lacking something by that fact, or whether one who has had a *bris milah* has an added *kedushah*. According to *Rambam*, the absence of *bris milah* means that the person has greater sexual lust, whereas according to *Ramban*, *bris milah* increases one's *kedushah*.

HaMidrash VeHaMa'aseh says that the origin of these two views is in a *mishnah* in *Nedarim* 31. R' Elazar ben Azaryah says that the *orlah* (the foreskin, which is removed in the *bris milah*) is obnoxious, and the wicked are despicable with it. This implies that the body, without the rectification of the *bris milah*, is lacking. R' Yehoshua, on the other hand, says that *bris milah* is outstanding, because thirteen covenants were made about it; namely that by means of *bris milah*, *kedushah* is added to the body. He explains along these lines the words of *Chazal*:

> When the Holy One, Blessed be He, said to Avraham, "Walk before Me and be wholesome," he was overcome with fear. He said: "Is there then something within me that is despicable (as *Rambam* explains it)?" When he heard, "and I will give My covenant between Me and you," he was comforted.

Ibn Ezra does not seek an explanation for the *mitzvah*. He sees it as a *chok* (statute), a *mitzvah* whose meaning we cannot understand. He explains Hashem's statement to Avraham, "Walk before Me and be wholesome," in terms of "Do not ask me for the reasons why I commanded the *bris milah*."

Kuzari, too, in 3:7 says that "*Milah* is far from our comprehension," but in 1:115 he himself gives the reason for it as that given by *Ramban*, as a mark by Hashem specifically in the organ of procreation, and as a sign of overcoming one's bodily lusts. In that fashion man can come closer to accepting Hashem: "One who follows this path — he and his descendants will have a great portion in drawing closer to Hashem." Thus, according to *Kuzari*, holding one's lust in check is not a natural result of the *bris milah*, but comes about because by it the person understands the reasons for the covenant, which was made specifically in the procreative organ so as to guard the holiness of one's descendants.

Abarbanel, too, sees the *mitzvah* as a seal that was placed on the procreative power, so that one's sons and daughters will be born in *kedushah*, just as a person places a seal on his household that everyone who leaves it should act only in accordance with his orders.

Chinuch explains this more clearly. According to him, the purpose of *milah* is to separate the Jews from the Gentiles. Hashem wanted to differentiate between the two in their bodies, just as they are different in their souls. But the place of differentiation was made specifically in the procreative organ, because it is from it that the continuation of mankind originates.

Akeidah, too, after listing a number of reasons, in the way of *Rambam* in *Moreh Nevuchim*, adds the reason for the seal of *kedushah* being specifically in the place which the wicked use for evil purposes:

> There the Holy One, Blessed be He, sealed the holy covenant with the seed of those who loved Him forever, and as a sign that the fear of *Elokim* rules over all the world and there is none like Him. Just as that is the place from which the greatest

tum'ah can burst forth when one's lusts dominate, so too does the greatest *kedushah* come from that place.

The link of the covenant with Hashem to man, according to this, lies at the very place where man's ways split into good and evil. The purpose is to remind man of his spiritual obligations, and his links to the eternal.

Ikarim says that the sign of the *bris* is also evidence of *perseverance* and *eternity*, because it endures forever in the body of the nation. Therefore, "as long as we see this *bris* existing within the nation, we will know for sure that we still have the power to live, and through this tie the nation will return to its original state."

R' Samson Raphael Hirsch gives these very explanations in his *Horeb*. "The eternity of our nation," he says, "depends on the sign of the holy *bris* ... The maintenance of the *bris*, even when man is not good, will ensure a proper generation in the future." That is the meaning of the promise given to Avraham (*Bereishis* 17:7), "And I will establish My covenant between Me and you and between your descendants after you for their generations, as an eternal covenant ... And you observe My covenant, you and your descendants after you for their generations."

The procreative organ is what ensures the eternity of man, and it was there that the eternity of the Jew was implanted. Everything, says *Sefas Emes*, has an essential point, through which it is connected to its roots. *Eretz Yisrael* is the central point of the world, *Shabbos* is the central point of time, and the *milah* is the central point of man's bodily organs.

We also find that idea in *Akeidah*. Each organ has its own special attribute — the ear to listen, the eye to see — but all are linked to the procreative organ. That is why this organ was chosen to place an eternal seal on the Jew.

All these reasons combine into a single basic one of separation — between the holy and the profane, between Israel and the other nations. This holy sign serves to ensure this separation. Whenever it is within the Jewish body, the Jew remains separate from the other nations. This sign, says *Igra D'Kallah*, will always be part of the Jewish people, based on the verse, "And My covenant shall be in your flesh for an eternal covenant," to guarantee to Avraham's seed that the other nations will never abolish this *mitzvah* among Israel.

◆§ For You We Were Killed the Entire Day

Chazal, in *Yalkut Shimoni Va'Eschanan* 837 quoting *Sifri*, mention the verse (*Tehillim* 44:22), "For You we were killed the entire day." R' Shimon ben Mansia said, "Can a person then be killed the entire day?

Rather, this is a reference to *bris milah*." *Milah* here appears as a *korban* (sacrifice) and as a voluntary act of *Kiddush Hashem* by the Jew, who has shed his blood for Hashem.

We also find this same idea in regard to *milah* in other places. *Pirkei D'Rebbi Eliezer* 29 states that *milah* is as important as a *minchah* offering on the altar. In *Vayikra Rabbah* 27, the reason for *bris milah* on the eighth day is given as following the pattern that a newborn animal may be sacrificed only from the eighth day on.

Yalkut Shimoni on *Lech Lecha*, 81, says that, "Whoever presents his son for *milah* is as if the *kohen gadol* had sacrificed his *minchah* and his wine offering on the altar." *Zohar* states clearly that "When a person brings his son to the school or to *milah* it is a whole offering."

Olelos Efrayim 469 expands on the idea of the *milah* as being a test of *mesiras nefesh* for *Kiddush Hashem*. In this, he was preceded by Rabbenu Bachya who draws comparisons between *bris milah* and sacrifices. He adds that *milah* is greater than a sacrifice, and is considered as an *akeidah* on the altar, as we see in (*Tehillim* 50:5), "They have made a covenant with Me by sacrifice."

This idea is also used by *Sha'arei Simchah*, in explaining the verses (*Bereishis* 17:4-9), "As for Me, My covenant is with you, and you shall be a father of many nations ... You shall therefore keep My covenant, you, and your seed after you in their generations." Hashem said to Avraham, "You were willing to die for Me in Ur Kasdim, and you proved your readiness to have your blood spilled on the altar. 'My covenant is therefore with you' — it has already existed from ancient days, but I still want you to circumcise your own flesh, so as to instill this readiness to sacrifice their lives in your descendants."

And indeed it is well known that the *mitzvah* of *milah* is the source of the Jew's willingness to sacrifice his life. In addition to the blood of the *bris* at the time of the *milah*, our blood has also been offered on the altar of our holy Jewish history. "'Why are you being taken out to be killed?' 'Because I circumcised my son.'" This is a sign which is engraved in our flesh as a continuity of *Kiddush Hashem*. It is common knowledge that throughout the generations our enemies have used this sign to know who is a Jew, and who is to be offered up as a sacrifice on the altar of his faith. In the Holocaust too, *bris milah* was the sign the Nazis used to identify Jews who wanted to escape their fate. And yet, in spite of this, Jews circumcise themselves and their sons and accept their fate willingly in our Holy Land. In spite of the fact that there is no law requiring *milah*, almost no Jew frees himself voluntarily from this yoke. Even those who shout against "religious coercion" make sure that their children will receive a *bris milah*, and thereby accept the yoke of the sanctity of

Hashem. We thus see that this commandment is something engraved in our blood and our souls. This is one of the wonders which Hashem implanted in our holy nation.

Milah serves as an iron curtain between the Jew and the non-Jew. It is this which engraved the mark of *Kiddush Hashem* in our flesh. *Imrei Yosef* on the Torah sees in this the reason that Avraham did not perform a *bris milah* on himself until Hashem specifically ordered him to do so. All the commentators remark on this, for after all, Avraham obeyed all the *mitzvos* of Hashem even before he was commanded to do so. However, says *Imrei Yosef*, Avraham understood the *gevurah* — the strength — underlying this *mitzvah*. This quality is the opposite of Avraham's major quality, that of *chessed* — mercy and compassion. Avraham was therefore afraid to carry out this *mitzvah*, as we see in *Bereishis Rabbah* 47: "Avraham said, 'Before I was circumcised, passersby would come to me, yet now that I have had my *bris milah*, no one comes.'"

Avraham was hesitant as to whether it was permissible to put a barrier between Israel and the other nations, with such a total and radical separation. "Therefore," says the Sochachower, "Hashem was forced to encourage him and to tell him, 'Walk before Me and be trusting.' Do not be concerned with the change in your nature which took place by the *milah*. I know the nature of the Jew better than that of anyone else, and its nature is one of *Kiddush Hashem*, a nature of 'for You we were killed the entire day.'"

This feeling of a sacrifice and *Kiddush Hashem* in the *bris milah* is implanted deeply in our nation, and it is seen in the feelings of the father and the other participants in the *bris milah*. *Chazal* and the commentators give many other reasons, both rational and kabbalistic, for the *mitzvah* of *milah*. According to a number of statements by *Chazal*, it is a rectification of nature and a sign that man must complete Hashem's deeds. There are also numerous medical reasons given by various *rishonim*, including Abarbanel and *Akeidah*.

There are innumerable other reasons. For us, though, the major principle is that we find in the verse (*Yechezkel* 16:6), "And when I passed by you, and saw you soiled in your own blood, I said to you, 'With your blood, live; with your blood, live.'"

Vayeira – וירא

I.
Why Did Hashem Appear?

The *parashah* begins, וַיֵּרָא אֵלָיו ה׳ — "And Hashem appeared to him," but does not explain why He did so. It is followed by the story of the three angels. After Avraham had escorted the angels who came to destroy S'dom, Hashem appeared again to Avraham, and told him of the overturning of S'dom.

The *parashah* of S'dom begins with "And Hashem said," and ends with, "And Hashem went after he finished speaking to Avraham, and Avraham returned to his place." But Hashem's appearance at the beginning of our *parashah* does not include any communication as such, which makes it unlike any other revelation in the entire *Tanach*. According to *Rashi*, following in the footsteps of *Chazal*, this revelation was merely *bikkur cholim* — visiting the sick — on Hashem's part, as Avraham was recovering from his *bris milah*. Rabbenu Bachya confirms this by the fact that the Torah says, "And Hashem appeared to him (אֵלָיו)," and does not say, "Hashem appeared to Avraham." This indicates that our *parashah* is a continuation of the previous one, where we read that Avraham and his sons circumcised themselves. Thus this *parashah* tells us that as a result of the *bris milah*, Hashem came to visit him.

Rabbenu Chananel also holds that this appearance by Hashem was related to the *bris milah*, but according to him it was not only *bikkur cholim* but also a reward for observing the *mitzvah*.

R' Samson Raphael Hirsch goes into this idea in depth. There is, of course, no place where Hashem is not, but when a person offers himself completely to Hashem, as Avraham did, he is worthy of actually seeing the *Shechinah*.

According to *Malbim*, the Torah even explains the nature of this appearance, which came about because of Avraham's *mitzvah*. This occurred in Eilonei Mamre, far from the place that Avraham had made an altar to Hashem. It also occurred "at the entrance to the tent," among people. Avraham did not isolate himself from others before Hashem appeared to him, as is customary among prophets. This appearance by Hashem took place "at the heat of the day," when Avraham was not completely at ease. The Torah tells us how Avraham's soul was so elevated after his *bris milah* that he merited the revelation of the *Shechinah*, in spite of all those factors which would normally prevent such an appearance.

The Chassidic works all describe how great this appearance was, each in its own way. *Chiddushei HaRim* brings *Rashi's* view at the beginning of *Vayikra* that the word אֵלָיו ("to him"), as used at the beginning of our *parashah*, is much more personal than the word לוֹ ("to him").

Some commentators note that Bilaam said that he had (*Bamidbar* 24:4) "Fallen down, but with his eyes open." There, *Rashi* explains that Hashem appeared to Bilaam only at night, and that he fell on his face because he realized he was uncircumcised and therefore despicable. With Avraham, though, who had circumcised himself "on the very same day," Hashem appeared to him even when he was sitting and even "in the heat of the day."

HaKesav VeHaKabalah brings proof to *Rashi's* statement that "Hashem appeared" (וַיֵּרָא) means that He came to visit the sick, from the verse (*II Melachim* 8:29), "Achaziah the son of Yehoram, king of Judah, went down to see (לִרְאוֹת) Yoram the son of Achav in Jezreel, because he was sick." The same is true in *I Shmuel* 19:15, "to see David." And in both cases the Targum translates it as *l'mis'ad*, namely, "to assist." Here too this was the purpose of Hashem's appearance after the *bris milah*.

◈§ Hashem or an Angel?

Other commentators see this appearance as not just a visit or revelation, but as a prophetic vision. *Akeidah*, in one of his commentaries, says that Hashem appeared to Avraham to inspire and support him, so that he should not fear that in his weakened condition he might be attacked by strangers, just as happened later when his descendants attacked the inhabitants of Shechem after their *bris milah*.

R' Yosef Bechor Shor and other commentators maintain that Hashem

BEREISHIS — VAYEIRA / 79

appeared to Avraham after the angels had left, even though in the Torah it is written that this occurred before their arrival. *Chizkuni* explains this along similar lines. According to him, Hashem appeared to Avraham for the purpose of His later appearance, but the Torah interrupted this with the story of the angels. (In reality, that is the same explanation.) *Tzofnas Pane'ach* too says that these three sequences are a single long prophecy.

Rashbam goes even further, and says that whenever we read here of Hashem appearing, whether at the beginning of our *parashah* or to foretell the overturning of S'dom, it always refers to Hashem's angels, for in regard to the burning bush too we see an angel referred to as Hashem. In that case, it says (*Shemos* 3:2), "And an angel of Hashem appeared to him in a flame of fire," and afterwards it says, "And Hashem saw that he had turned to look."

According to *Rashbam*, all of the events mentioned in this *parashah* involve the three angels, each of whom came for a specific task. Avraham pleaded with the angel who told him that he had come to overturn S'dom not to fulfill his task if there were but ten righteous people in the city. And the answers that Avraham got were all from the angel.

Meleches Machsheves supports *Rashbam's* opinion from a number of sources in *Tanach*. Thus, for example, we read in *Yechezkel* (40:1-2): "The hand of Hashem was upon me ... in the visions of *Elokim* He brought me ..." And in reality, it was an angel that brought him and that spoke to him. In the Torah too there are places where angels are referred to as Hashem. Thus, with the *akeidah*, we are told (*Bereishis* 22:11-12), "And an angel of Hashem called to him," and nevertheless it says, "And you did not spare your son, your only one, from Me." So too does it say (*Shemos* 13:21), "And Hashem went before them in the day," and afterwards it says (14:19), "And the angel of *Elokim*, who went before the camp of Israel." And there are other such examples. He therefore concludes that every appearance of prophecy, even when it comes through an angel, is referred to as "the appearance of Hashem."

Rashbam's view is somewhat similar to that of *Rambam* in *Moreh Nevuchim*, which aroused a storm of controversy among the Sages. In *Moreh Nevuchim* 2:42, *Rambam* writes that all the events in this *parashah* before us were not physical manifestations, but only prophetic visions. The vision begins with the words, "And Hashem appeared." Afterwards we have the details of the words of the angels, and all the events which followed, including the overturning of S'dom and the saving of Lot, and all are part of the same vision. *Rambam's* view is somewhat similar to that of *Rashbam*, in that "And Hashem

80 / *Why Did Hashem Appear?*

appeared to him" was not an actual event, but there is a difference between the two commentators. According to *Rashbam*, the story with the angels actually took place, while according to *Rambam* even that was only a prophetic vision. *Rambam* strengthens his view quoting R' Chiya in *Chazal*, who holds that Avraham's plea, "*Adonai*, do not pass before your servant," was said to the greatest of the angels, and the word *Adonai* (either God or my master) in this instance is חול (secular) and not a reference to Hashem.

✥ An Actual Appearance or a Prophetic Vision

Rambam's view, which we quoted above, is met with strong opposition by *Ramban*. First, says *Ramban*, we never find in any other place that the words, "and Hashem appeared to him," are a prelude to a prophetic vision. In addition, *Ramban* has numerous questions on *Rambam's* view. Among these are: If Avraham's encounter with the angels was only a prophetic vision, why does the Torah tell us that Sarah kneaded cakes and Avraham prepared the cattle? What symbolism is there in these actions? Again, if *Rambam's* view is correct, we must assume that the angels did not actually appear to Lot either, and Lot did not actually bake matzos. But since Lot was not a prophet, how was he able to experience a prophetic vision? And if we conclude that Lot was a prophet, then who told the evil people of S'dom that some visitors had come to Lot? And again, if everything was but a prophetic vision, then the angels spurring Lot on to leave as soon as possible never actually occurred, and how then did Lot flee?

After continuing along this line with his strong disagreements with *Rambam's* view, *Ramban* concludes that *Rambam's* interpretation "contradicts the words of the Torah, and one is forbidden to hear or believe in them."

Abarbanel in his commentary on *Moreh Nevuchim* and *Akeidah* on our *parashah* attempts to justify's *Rambam's* words and to defend him from *Ramban's* attacks. Abarbanel refers to the words of R' Chiya who maintains that the word *Adonai* in "*Adonai*, do not pass before your servant" is a secular reference prompted by the presence of the angels. If that was the case, shouldn't Avraham have owed an apology to Hashem for interrupting His appearance by turning to the angels? Subsequently, Avraham resumes his encounter with Hashem and reverts to his prophecy. How can there be different appearances in a single prophecy, unless we explain that everything that happened was a prophetic vision, with different scenes within that same vision?

Ramban's questions on *Rambam* are answered by Abarbanel as follows: The form "and Hashem appeared to him" is also found in regard to prophetic visions. With the burning bush we are told (*Shemos* 3:2), "And an angel of Hashem appeared to him," and the Torah does not state for what purpose. All we are told is that Moshe turned aside to see the burning bush. Yaakov, too, who struggled with the angel, said (*Bereishis* 32:31), "For I saw *Elokim* face to face." There are different types of expressions regarding prophetic visions, and our *parashah* has one of these.

As to the descriptions of Sarah baking and Avraham going to get cattle, these were also part of the prophetic vision, for such visions often reflect reality. Avraham saw in his prophetic vision the way he and Sarah would normally treat their guests. Similar examples of this can be found throughout *Tanach*. In addition, these examples illustrate the generosity of Avraham and Sarah, because of which they were given a son. The vision also explained the reason why S'dom was going to be overturned, due to its terrible sins. But even if these descriptions were not to symbolism anything and were simply a description of the prophetic vision, that would not change the meaning.

Abarbanel says that for *Ramban*, reality is more significant than a prophetic vision, but he disagrees with that view. Even the story of Lot, according to *Rambam*, was only a prophetic vision that did not involve Lot in any way. It only comes to illustrate Lot's generosity, and to explain why he was saved when S'dom was overturned. The vision also included the behavior of the people of S'dom and the actions of the angels, just as in the descriptions of visions given by *Yechezkel*. The purpose of this *parashah* was to tell Avraham that he was to have a son, and to explain to him why S'dom was to be overturned and that his nephew would be saved, while Lot's wife would perish. Afterwards, this vision was reflected in reality, by the fact that Hashem put into Lot's heart the desire to flee.

After the destruction of S'dom, there are two verses in the Torah: "And he looked upon the face of S'dom and Amorah, and upon the face of the whole plain of the land, and he saw a pillar of smoke ascending, as the smoke of a furnace" (*Bereishis* 19:28). This verse is the end of the prophetic vision. Afterwards, the second verse states, "And it came to pass, when *Elokim* destroyed the cities of the plain, that *Elokim* remembered Abraham, and He sent Lot out from the overturning" (*Bereishis* 19:29). That verse already tells us how the prophecy was actually fulfilled.

Abarbanel goes into great length in justifying *Rambam*, but he himself doesn't agree with his view. He merely rejects *Ramban's* contention that *Rambam's* view contradicts basic Torah principles.

Instead, Abarbanel claims that "To state that seeing something in a prophetic vision is greater than actually seeing it is not something one is forbidden to hear."

Abarbanel's view, though, is different. He holds that the events actually took place. Even if the beginning of this *parashah* begins with a prophetic vision, the later events, including the overturning of S'dom and the saving of Lot, certainly took place, because the Torah concludes: "And Avraham returned to his place." Nor can we say that immediately after that, there was a new prophetic vision to Lot, because Lot was not a prophet, and that was certainly true for the people of S'dom.

According to *Akeidah*, one cannot, Heaven forbid, say that *Rambam's* words are such "that one is forbidden to hear them." The events which took place in the prophetic vision are symbolic of the reward to Avraham after his *bris milah* and a symbol of his generosity (*Bereishis* 18:7): "And Avraham ran to the flock." There is also veiled criticism of Avraham here, for laughing when he was told he would have a son. We see this in the words (verse 10), "And there will be a son to Sarah your wife." There is also a description of what happened to S'dom once the time came for it to pay for its sins. Avraham's prayer was certainly real, after he realized the meaning of his vision.

ᶧ§ Revelation as a Reward and as an Honor

Ramban follows in the path of the commentators we mentioned above, that Hashem's revelation was real, and every detail listed actually happened. The reason for this revelation was to glorify and exalt Avraham, and to honor him for his dedication. Hashem came to Avraham suddenly, without any previous preparation by Avraham. Something similar to this happened when the *Mishkan* was erected in the desert, where it states (*Vayikra* 9:23), "And they went out and blessed the nation, and the glory of Hashem appeared to them." The *Shechinah* did not come to issue any commands, but to honor them by its appearance, and as a sign that their deeds had found favor in Hashem's eyes. We find the same with Yaakov (*Bereishis* 32:2): "And the angels of Hashem met him," although the Torah doesn't say why. They only came to tell him that his deeds were proper and desirable.

According to *Ramban*, too, this *parashah* is a continuation of the previous one, in which we are told about the *bris milah*; now Hashem came to honor Avraham for it. This is stated specifically by *Chazal* in the Midrash: " 'You shall make Me an altar of earth.' If I will appear to one who makes Me an altar of earth and bless him, then with Avraham, who circumcised himself for My sake, all the more so." Thus we see here that the purpose of Hashem's appearance was to extol and exalt Avraham.

S'forno holds that the purpose of the revelation was in order to make a covenant. Avraham and his household had been circumcised, and now the *Shechinah* came to make a covenant with him. This is similar to (*Devarim* 29:9), "You are standing here today ... to pass through a covenant before Hashem ..." And the same is true with regard to Moshe, where we are told (*Shemos* 4:24), "And Hashem met him," but are not told of Hashem saying anything to him. There, too, the purpose was the making of a covenant, as it states, "between Me and you for your generations."

At first, Abarbanel says that the appearance of Hashem was only to appease and honor Avraham. At the end, though, he tends to the opinion of *Chazal*, that this was Hashem's attending to the sick, as he sees from the verses. Avraham was sitting at the entrance to his tent at the heat of the day because of his weakness. *Eilonei Mamre* was an isolated place, and he could sit there exposed, so that the sun's rays could heal the wound, for, as *Chazal* tell us, warmth is good for a wound. And indeed, after Hashem appeared to him to encourage him and offer him support, a healing sun shone forth, so that when the men appeared he was able to run to greet them. He stood by them to serve them, as all the other members of his household were still ailing from their *bris milah*, and therefore Avraham did not invite the visitors inside his tent. His home was full of sick people, and there was no place to receive visitors. Avraham, though, had been healed completely, so that he was able to serve them and even to escort them afterwards.

Abarbanel offers another explanation which he feels is better than the previous ones. The entire vision in this *parashah* was to tell Avraham of the wickedness of the people of S'dom and the destruction which was to be brought upon the city. Hashem wanted Avraham to come to their defense, as He is a merciful God who does not want the wicked to die. So, too, did Hashem want Avraham to warn his household to observe the Torah so that they should not become like the people of S'dom.

It is interesting that this explanation of Abarbanel is to be found in *Midrash HaGadol*, as quoted in *Torah Sheleimah*, and this is the statement: "He appeared to him in a prophetic vision, so as to tell him what would happen to S'dom, as it states, 'Hashem *Elokim* will not do a thing, without revealing His secret to His servants the prophets.' So too (did He come) to inform him about Yitzchak, as well as to heal him from his sickness."

What is especially interesting is that *Rambam* in *Moreh Nevuchim* bases his interpretation on R' Chiya that the word *Adonai* is secular (referring to the angels), while in *Hil. Yesodei HaTorah* 6:9 he himself rules that that reference is holy (i.e., to Hashem), and this requires further study.

II.
S'dom and the Pilegesh in Giv'ah

There is no specific statement in the Torah as to the sin of the people of S'dom. The Torah merely tells us that they were very wicked and sinned greatly, and that a cry had come up from S'dom to the Heavens, until Hashem, as it were, came down by Himself to see if indeed they had done "as its cry." But what this cry was, is not specified in the Torah. *Chazal* explain it as the cry of a certain young woman who had been sentenced by the city to either be exposed to bees or to be burned, because she had helped a poor man (*Midrash Rabbah, Vayera*). So, too, do *Chazal* tell us about the cruelty of the people of S'dom and Amorah to poor and unfortunate people. This cruelty is also mentioned in *Yechezkel* (16:49), "Behold, this was the sin of your sister S'dom: pride, an abundance of bread and an abundance of idleness in it and in its daughters; nor did it strengthen the hand of the poor and needy."

Akeidah is surprised that Yechezkel does not cite the specific sins of S'dom mentioned in the Torah, but attributes their punishment to the fact that the people were not charitable. He concludes from this that their abominable conduct toward their visitors was not typical of their behavior, but rather what was typical was their negative and hostile treatment of the poor and suffering. What they wanted to do to the people who came to Lot was meant simply to cause them not to return to S'dom any more, and was not meant to satisfy their own lust.

Chazal in *Sanhedrin* 109 find hints in the verses for various grave sins which the people of S'dom committed. The decree against them, however, was only because of their anti-social behavior.

Rabbenu Bachya says that there was never a nation whose people were completely uncharitable except for this one. And even though the Torah had not been given yet, their behavior was despicable. Their behavior was like that of a rich man who sees a poor man starving to death and does nothing to save his life. They acted this way even when the sufferer was a member of their own people.

Tiferes Shlomo holds that that is exactly what the Torah tells us. "The cry of S'dom and Amorah is great;" the cry which emerged came out from themselves. Each one was cruel to his fellow, and therefore, "their sin is very grave." Had there at least been peace among themselves, they would never have reached such a situation. But they were divided even among themselves, each out to get the other, and even at the very brink of the abyss they did not change. When Lot warned his sons-in-law what was liable to happen, "it was as laughter in the eyes of his sons-in-law."

Shem MiShmuel has a beautiful explanation here. "And the people at the door to the house they smote with blindness" — their minds were blinded, so that they did not understand. "And they were unable to find the door" — the door of repentance was not opened to them, and they continued in their evil ways until they were destroyed.

Ramban holds that their punishment came primarily because of the sanctity of *Eretz Yisrael*, a land which does not tolerate abominations. It vomited up these people, so that this would be a sign in the future for Jews who rebelled against Hashem, for, as the Torah warned (*Devarim* 29:22), "brimstone and salt, all its land burned, as the overturning of S'dom and Amorah, Admah and Tzevo'im, which Hashem overthrew in His anger and in His wrath."

◆§ The Differences Between S'dom and the Pilegesh in Giv'ah

Ramban analyzes the difference between the case of S'dom and that of the *pilegesh* (concubine) in Giv'ah (see *Shoftim* 19). At first glance, the two cases have an uncanny resemblance. In the case of S'dom, two men who have no acquaintances or friends come to the city, and Lot invites them into his house. The same is true with the *pilegesh* in Giv'ah. In S'dom, the local residents want to have the men come out, "so that we will know them," and at Giv'ah too the people say, "send out the man who came to your house and we will know him." In S'dom, Lot offered his daughters, while at Giv'ah, the man offered his concubine. In terms of the consequences, that of Giv'ah was worse, because there the people did unleash their lust, abusing the concubine until she died, while in S'dom they only tried to do so but were unsuccessful. Nevertheless, the punishment of the people of S'dom was far worse than that of Giv'ah. The people of S'dom and their entire families were killed when Hashem overturned the city, while in Giv'ah only those involved in the battle died. And not only that, in two of the battles they defeated all the other tribes and killed forty thousand people, and only in the third battle were they defeated, where twenty-five thousand one hundred men of the tribe of Binyamin were killed. Why, then, were the men of Giv'ah treated in a better way than the people of S'dom?

In explaining the difference, *Ramban* and the other commentators, whose views we will bring below, also clarify exactly what occurred in the case of Giv'ah. This was the first time that *Bnei Yisrael* asked Hashem, "Who will be the first among us to wage war against Binyamin?" and Hashem answered, "Yehudah will be first." Yet, even though they asked Hashem, twenty-two thousand of the attackers died. The next day, they again asked Hashem: "Shall I continue going out to war against Binyamin my brother?" Again Hashem told them to go, and again they were defeated, this time suffering eighteen thousand dead. The third time, they came to Beis-El, and fasted and cried before Hashem. Afterwards, they brought sacrifices. A third time they asked Hashem, this time through Pinchas ben Elazar the *kohen*, and Hashem answered them, "Go up, because tomorrow I will deliver him into your hands."

This whole sequence is astounding. If *Bnei Yisrael* were right in declaring war on Binyamin, then why were they beaten twice? And if they were not right, why did they win in the end? Below we will give the views of various commentators, who, following *Ramban's* lead, deal with this question.

The case of the *pilegesh* in Giv'ah, says *Ramban*, even though it resembles that of S'dom outwardly, is not the same in terms of the evil involved. The people of Giv'ah did not want to wipe out all the poor from their land, but were simply sexually licentious. When the man offered to bring out his virgin daughter and his concubine, they did not harm his daughter, but accepted the concubine. A concubine (*pilegesh*) does not have the status of a married woman. This particular *pilegesh* had also been unfaithful to her husband, as it states in *Shoftim*. In addition, whereas in S'dom every single man was there — "from the youth to the old man" — in Giv'ah, not everyone was present. Only some of them, who are referred to as *bnei b'lial* — "worthless ones" — came.

The rest of the people were too afraid to protest or to prevent them from doing what they did. By Torah law, they did not deserve the death penalty for abusing the *pilegesh*, but as their action was similar to that of the people of S'dom, *Bnei Yisrael* wanted to make a fence to the Torah, for, as we are told, the *beis din* (court) can inflict punishments that are not imposed by the Torah. Only the tribe of Binyamin were opposed to "making a fence." And it may be that the reason that *Bnei Yisrael* lost the first two battles was because it was the duty of Binyamin to do justice, and not that of the other tribes.

The members of the tribe of Binyamin, who did not deliver the *bnei b'lial* to those who sought them, were certainly not liable to the death penalty. They did not respond to the other tribes, who wished to make a fence. And it was their duty, not that of the other tribes, to punish wrongdoers within the tribe. *Bnei Yisrael* thus lost the first two battles, because the war that they had declared against Binyamin was not one in accordance with *halachah*.

In reality, both the other tribes and Binyamin deserved to be punished, the former for becoming involved in something which was not of their concern, and the latter because its members did not protest against the evildoers in their tribe. Nor did the other tribes ask advice from Hashem as to whether or not to go to battle, because they were so sure of their power. They only asked who should be first, to which Hashem responded that Yehudah should be first, as usual.

On the second day, having learned from their previous day's experience, they already asked if they should go out to war, but as they were still sure of their strength, they did not ask if they would emerge victorious. On the third day, they fasted and cried before Hashem, and then Binyamin was defeated. Thus in this entire episode, forty thousand people were killed of the other tribes, and twenty-five thousand of Binyamin. But it is possible that if we include women and children, the losses of Binyamin might have reached forty thousand so that both sides were punished equally. These are *Ramban's* words in brief.

Abarbanel, though, is strongly opposed to *Ramban's* interpretation. He asks a number of questions on this explanation. (a) Why didn't the *beis din* of the other tribes have the right to try the tribe of Binyamin? (b) If the only crime of *Bnei Yisrael* was that they declared war, why were they defeated twice? (c) If Binyamin did not sin, why were they defeated in the third battle? (d) If there is a sin in tribes meddling in other tribes' business, why was there no sin involved when Pinchas and the heads of the tribes sent a warning to the tribes of Reuven and Gad about the altar they had set up across the Jordan? Abarbanel notes the concluding words of *Ramban*, that the tribes were punished because of the idol of Michah. It appears from this, he says, that *Ramban* felt that his previous explanation was a weak one.

Regarding the men of the *pilegesh* in Giv'ah, Abarbanel says that they deserved the death penalty for a number of reasons: (a) homosexuality; (b) a *pilegesh* is considered a married woman, because she was betrothed (*kiddushin*) and is only lacking the *kesubah* (marriage contract); (c) they took the *pilegesh* by force; (d) they tortured her to death; (e) they disturbed public order so that no one would come there. Yet, in spite of all of their sins, there was a difference between them and the people of S'dom. The latter had sin deeply imbedded within themselves, and there was no way that they would ever return to the good, while the men of Giv'ah only sinned this one time. The sins of Binyamin were equal to those of the other tribes, and therefore Hashem did not listen to the other tribes until the latter had repented completely.

ও§ An Anti-Moral Regime

Akeidah, too, questions *Ramban's* differentiation between the deeds of the people of S'dom and those of Giv'ah, because the verses resemble one another, and even the wording is almost identical, as we showed above. Nor does he accept *Ramban's* view that the other tribes had no right to judge the people of Giv'ah. The *beis din hagadol* has the right to judge any tribe and render its verdict in accordance with the laws of the Torah.

According to *Akeidah*, the punishment of the people of S'dom was more severe than that of the people of Giv'ah because the entire regime of the former was based on so-called laws which were unjust by their nature. It is important to differentiate between a person who is "a sinner" and between institutionalized cruelty and wickedness. The people of Giv'ah were certainly sinners. In the case of a sinner, his lust gets the better of him, but his mind is sound. In the case of a wicked person, though, both his mind and his lusts are polluted. A wicked person will never repent, but a sinner, once his lust has passed, will return to his former ways. A wicked person carries out his deeds in secret, and that is the reason he is more dangerous, but a sinner does not act secretly. If a wall has been breached, one can repair it, but in the case of a wicked person there is simply no wall there to repair.

That was the sin of S'dom and Amorah. Not only did they not have a moral wall restraining them, but they had erected a wall of brambles — of "laws" which were unjust. They were not like the sinners in other places, where at least the laws were just, but the sinners had violated them. The people of S'dom acted wickedly in accordance with the law on the books, the law upon which their entire regime was based. The Torah constantly stresses the importance of those *mitzvos* between man and his fellow-man, but the people of S'dom transformed their justice into a mockery, and justified theft as being ethical. This is unlike the case of the *pilegesh* in Giv'ah, where the people lived under Torah law, and it is therefore not surprising that in that case Hashem did not bring fire and brimstone on them. Their society was a just one, and if there were criminal elements among them, those were the ones who needed to be punished. The people of Giv'ah saw what was happening and did not protest, and therefore they too were responsible. In S'dom, though, people were criminal with the blessings of the society.

The tribes were punished twice when they went out to battle against Binyamin, because they did not sanctify and prepare themselves properly before doing so. At first they asked, "Who will go up?" then they asked, "Shall I continue to wage war against Binyamin my brother?" This question proves that they did not realize why they had been punished the first time, and assumed that the punishment had come because they had gone out against their brother. Only before the third battle did they do *t'shuvah*, crying and fasting, and then they were able to punish the tribe of Binyamin which had sinned.

Ma'asei Hashem has an interesting explanation on this event. According to him, the first time, the people of Israel did not ask the *Urim* and *Tummim* as to what to do, but asked the idol of Michah. Regarding this idol, we are told (*Shoftim* 17:13), "Then Michah said, 'Now I know that Hashem will do me good, because I have a Levite as my priest.'" The answers that Hashem gave to the first two questions, where we are told, "And Hashem said," were really given by this Levite, as if in the name of Hashem. Alternately, Hashem had the Levite give these answers, so that they would blunder into the war, as a punishment. Only the third time are we told that they asked properly — from Pinchas ben Elazar the *kohen* — "and there was the Ark of God's covenant;" only then were they answered.

R' Samson Raphael Hirsch follows in the footsteps of *Akeidah*. Regarding S'dom, it states, "and the men of the city." These were the most important men in the city, those who ran it and represented the regime, and it was they who had come to protest the violation of the city law forbidding anyone from allowing a poor person into his house. In addition, everyone else came, "from the youth to the old," and they called out, "Send them out to us, so that we may know them." We will torment them, and then they will learn never to repeat their "offense" in our city. The reason that Hashem doomed them was because they had turned wickedness into the law of the land and cruelty into justice.

Sha'ar Bas Rabim quotes a certain commentator that explains the words "and we will know (וְנֵדְעָה) them" in accordance with this verb in *Shoftim* (8:16), "And he took the elders of the city, and thorns of the wilderness and briers, and with them he taught (וַיֹּדַע) the men of Sukkos." Here, too, the people of S'dom said, "Let us torment these people who came to our city."

R' Yosef Bechor Shor, though, says that had Lot not said, "I have two daughters ...," we would have thought that all that the people of S'dom wanted to do was to question the two men and to see whether they were spies or evil individuals. *Ramban* sees this proposal of Lot to give up his two daughters as part of the evil nature of his character. He was willing to have his daughters ravished to protect two strange men who had come to his house. Only someone whose character is such that debauchery is not foreign to him could do such a thing. *Chazal* therefore tell us that among most people, a person is willing to sacrifice himself to save his wife and daughters, whereas Lot was willing to give up his daughters to the people of S'dom.

☙ What Is Mine Is Mine and What Is Yours Is Yours

Chazal in *Avos* 5 tells us that there are four types of people. One of these is the person who says, "What is mine is mine and what is yours is yours," which *Chazal* take to be an average position, but some say that this is the way of the people of S'dom. All the commentators are astounded at these two diametrically opposed views. One sees this conduct as a neutral, average position for a person to take, and the other sees it as representative of conduct associated with the people of S'dom.

Countless explanations are given of this. *Akeidah* endeavors at length to reconcile the two views. He says that the "average" conduct referred to here is certainly not "the golden mean." Such conduct is without a doubt a bad quality, and is close to that of S'dom. It is only numerically "average" between the positions of, "What is mine is mine and what is yours is mine," and, "What is mine is yours and what is yours is yours." For example, if a person has ten loaves of bread, and if eating them all will make him sick while eating only one will leave him hungry, can we then say that eating five loaves is an average? It may be a numerical average, but it is not the golden mean, which is a combination of the two extremes. Here too, in *Avos*, the concept of "average" is a strictly numerical one, without discussing the values involved behind this position. On the other hand, those who say that it is the characteristic of the people of S'dom evaluate this position for itself rather than as relative to other positions, and therefore they say it is the characteristic of S'dom.

A beautiful interpretation, which is in keeping with *d'rush* and *mussar* values, is given by R' Moshe Avigdor Amiel. When is, "What is mine is mine and what is yours is yours," average? That is only if an individual acts that way, but if a community acts that way, it is the characteristic of S'dom. An individual can be egotistical and act only in accordance with the letter of the law, but a community must act with compassion, in contrast to the behavior of S'dom.

III.
The Fear of God Prevents Sin

In the verse (*Bereishis* 20:11), "Surely the fear of God is not in this place; they will kill me for my wife's sake," the Torah stresses that there are not, and there cannot be, human morals without faith in Hashem and fear of Heaven (*yiras shamayim*). A "synthetic" type of humanly devised moral code cannot prevent the committing of the worst possible sins when one's personal egotism demands it.

The regime of Avimelech, King of Gerar, was one of fine manners and human morals, and not a corrupt one such as that of Pharaoh. Avimelech's complaints to Hashem and to Avraham are convincing in their honesty. He is shocked about the accusations leveled against him. He justifies his actions and proves that he meant no evil. He appears to be justly indignant when asking Avraham, "What did you see?" Neither does Avraham claim that he saw any evil in the country's behavior or conduct. He only speaks about his own personal conviction. Avraham is convinced that in a place where there is no *yiras shamayim*, moral codes and upright behavior are valueless. He believes that in such places people can commit the worst crimes, including idolatry, sexual offenses, and bloodshed. Avraham stresses this in the words: "there is no fear of God" (idolatry); "they will kill me" (bloodshed); "for my wife's sake" (sexual offenses).

Chasam Sofer has a beautiful explanation of the word רַק (translated above as "surely" but which can also mean "only"). He explains this as meaning that "only" *yiras shamayim* was missing, but people certainly feared punishment for committing a crime. It was the very fact that the people feared being punished by mortals that caused Avraham to fear that they might kill him secretly, so that no one would complain when they took Sarah. Avraham was not concerned about this in Pharaoh's regime, because in Egypt they were not ashamed to sin or do evil. They felt no need to have to kill Avraham in order to take his wife. In Avimelech's Gerar, though, which was a "state based on law," they were afraid to take a woman from her husband as long as the husband was alive. They therefore would have no alternative but to either kill him secretly or to find a "legal" way to do so. Where there is no *yiras shamayim*, there is reason to worry about such a possibility.

Today we live in a time when culture and civilization have shown their true faces, as they did in World War II; we have also seen what "justice" is under the different communist regimes, and can thus appreciate how correct Avraham was in his statement. It is remarkable how one of the great commentators of the previous generation, *Malbim*, defined this:

> If we see a person (or a nation) who is a great philosopher, who is just in his ways, and has accustomed himself to act properly based on his intellect, we still cannot trust that person or nation, for at a time of passion he (or it) may act evilly ... rather than having his intellect dominate his passions, the fire of his passion may burn for a woman that he desires, or for the wealth of his fellow. In such circumstances, even his intellect will be led astray; to murder, to commit adultery, or any other evil act. There is only one force in man's soul which can guarantee that he will not sin, and that is the characteristic of *yirah* which is planted in his soul, which comes down to one thing — *yiras Elokim* (the fear of God).

Malbim's view is also that of the *mussar* giants of all generations. It can be found in both *rishonim* and *acharonim*. *Rambam*, too, in his *Moreh Nevuchim*, discusse at length the power of *yiras shamayim*, as preserving human morals within oneself, between man and wife, and at a time when there is none to see him.

Ikarim in 1:8 says that "The religion of ethics errs, and says that that which is ugly is beautiful." He brings proof from Plato, who proposed a regime in which the elite would share women. He lists many weaknesses in a religion based on human ethics, and especially the fact that it cannot prevent a person from committing a crime in private, when there is no one to see and he has no one to fear.

All the Chassidic and *mussar* literature discuss this. The basis for this indisputable truth is that in our *parashah*. At first glance, Avimelech's claim seems to be correct; after all, his statements are logical and ethical. He cries out against the suspicions leveled against him, as if he had wanted to steal his fellow's wife. Avraham, though, charges him with a much more serious crime: that with such a moral code he is liable to kill people when there are no observers, or under the cover of the law.

Hashem had already testified to Avimelech that Avraham was a prophet. Avraham was able to penetrate into the innermost thoughts of the people of this society who — only externally — appeared to be fine and upright. It is possible that Avimelech himself was a just person, but potentially he, too, belonged to the sinners. That is the nature of a regime which does not have *yiras shamayim*, for it always contains within itself the seeds of sin. Sometimes the sin only exists potentially, while at other times it is actually carried out in the open.

◆§ His Fear of Sin Precedes His Wisdom

Chazal in *Avos* expressed this view in a succinct form: "Whoever's fear of sin precedes his wisdom, his wisdom will continue to exist; if not, his wisdom will not continue to exist." In *Pirkei D'Rebbi Eliezer* 37, we are told, "Do not fear a person who is an officer or a ruler, but fear people that have no *yiras shamayim*." In the *Yerushalmi Berachos* 4, we are also told, "Act out of *yirah*, for if you wish to rebel, know that you fear, and one who fears does not rebel." We find this idea most clearly in the *Tosefta Shevuos* 3:

> Chanania ben Chachinai says (*Vayikra* 5:21), " 'וְכִחֵשׁ בַּעֲמִיתוֹ — And he denies his friend' — a person does not deny his friend unless he denies the *ikar*" (i.e., the very existence of Hashem). Once R' Reuven lodged in Tiberias and met a certain philosopher. He said to him, "Who is hated in the world?" He answered him, "One who denies He who created him." He said to him, "How?" He said to him, "Honor your father and your mother, do not kill, do not commit adultery, do not steal, do not bear false witness against your fellow, and do not covet. Thus a person does not deny anything unless he denies the *ikar*, and a person does not commit a sin unless he denies Him who commanded about it."

These words clarify the view of *Chazal* regarding the bond between religion and ethics. The strongest comments by *Chazal* on this subject are to be found in *Midrash HaGadol* on our *parashah*:

> Great is *yirah*, for whoever has *yiras shamayim* can be presumed to be free of sin, and whoever has no *yiras shamayim* is presumed not to refrain from committing any sin. So too does it say (*Shemos* 20:20), "So that His *yirah* shall be upon you that you do not sin."

As to the wicked, it states (*Tehillim* 14:1), "The fool says in his heart, 'There is no God.' They are corrupt, they have done abominable deeds, there is none that does good."

The words of this Midrash are piercing in their sharpness and clarity. A person who does not have *yiras shamayim* cannot be ethical in any way. Civilization without faith cannot survive.

Michtav Me'Eliyahu, vol. 1, p. 72, notes that Avimelech thought that he was a righteous person and was furious: "Will You then kill a righteous nation?" But Avraham did not believe in the culture of the Philistines. Everything was just external and an act. In secret, these people were quite capable of killing. Further, according to Rabbenu Bachya, Avimelech's fine words themselves contained an implied threat of killing Avraham. He explains the words, "Will You then kill a righteous nation?" in terms of *middah k'neged middah* — measure for measure. "If You kill me, my servants will kill Avraham." This is the typical ethical Philistine, who claims to rule an ethical people, but without *yiras shamayim*.

We can bring countless examples from various works of Jewish thought which deny the illusion that one can run a society without Hashem. We will content ourselves with the penetrating words of R' Kook in his *Igros Rayah*, p. 45. He says there, among others:

> There is no ideal which can survive without the life force of the fire of Godliness. The individual and social person remains as a *golem* without a soul, and there is nothing that moves in him except a small measure of mechanical life which the flow of blood gives technical power. As a result, there is nothing that is more frightening to the world than the wicked-foolish denial of the existence of God. This is the most senseless view, which finds its place in the hearts of the least worthy of the miserable masses, who are steeped in the wildest animal lusts of licentiousness, drink and murder...

This idea, as mentioned, is brought in our *parashah*, and primarily as a reaction to the *chutzpah* of Avimelech, who, having taken Sarah, then attempted to blame Avraham for his own misconduct. Not only did Avimelech steal his fellow's wife, while pretending that he had not known the facts, but he also had the audacity to reprimand Avraham for trying to avoid death by means of a ruse. That has always been the way of a secular regime. Not only is it not ethical at its very foundation, but it has the *chutzpah* to criticize the morals of others, and to blame them for its own ethical faults.

◆§ If a Person Thinks Something Is Permitted — Is He Guiltless or Guilty?

In *Makkos* 9 and *Bava Kama* 92, there is an argument between Abaye and Rava whether a person who sinned due to an error (e.g., if he erroneously thought a particular action is permitted or a particular food is kosher, and then performed that forbidden act or ate that forbidden food) is considered to be an *onus* — one who is guiltless, or a *meizid* — one who is considered to have committed the sin deliberately, and is thus guilty. He certainly is not *shogeig*, for a *shogeig* is one who acts without thinking, and here he knew exactly what he was doing. According to Rava, one who thinks something is permitted when it is in reality forbidden is considered to be close to *meizid*, because he should have studied and investigated more carefully. Abaye, though, holds he is *onus*. (*Rambam* and the other *poskim* rule like Rava, that he is *meizid*.)

Abaye wants to bring support to his assertion from our *parashah*, because Avimelech referred to himself as "righteous," based on the fact that he thought Sarah was permitted to him. Rava, though, answers that Hashem did not agree with Avimelech's view, and told him, "Return the woman regardless. As to what you said, 'Will You then kill a righteous nation?' know that he is a prophet, and you should learn from him." (According to *Rashi* and other commentators, the meaning of the *gemara* is that as he is a prophet, he knew that you had planned to kill him, and that was the reason that he lied to you.) If a stranger comes to town, one asks him about matters of food and drink. Does one then ask him about his wife? This shows clearly he was interested in taking Sarah. From the fact that Avimelech would have been killed if he had taken Sarah, the *gemara* concludes that a non-Jew is killed if he commits one of the sins for which there is a death penalty, even if he did not know what was involved, because it was his duty to study and find out about it.

According to the *gemara*, then, the case of Avimelech was like that of a person who commits a forbidden act, believing it is permitted. But this presents a problem: Avimelech's error was really one of faulty identification, which, according to the *gemara* in *Bava Kama* and the *poskim*, has a different law! Thus, if a person planned to kill another person and instead killed an animal, or if he thought a woman was unmarried and he found she was married, it is an error in identification and not an error of ignorance of the law. Avimelech believed that his error was one of identification.

On the other hand, the *gemara* in *Makkos* does not differentiate between these two types of errors, both according to Abaye and according to Rava.

Based on this *gemara*, R' Meir Arak finds a ruling of *Rambam* surprising, for in *Hilchos Melachim* 10, *Rambam* differentiates between a non-Jew who thought a woman was single and later found out she was married, and one who knew that she was married, but for some reason thought that she was nevertheless permitted to him. In the first case, he exempts the man, because a non-Jew is always exempt for *shogeig*, whereas in the latter case, *Rambam* rules that the person is guilty. The commentators on *Rambam* give as the source *Makkos* 9. R' Meir Arak, though, says that this *gemara* proves the exact opposite, because there, there is no difference between the two cases, and the law should thus be the same in both! This is indeed a forceful question.

R' Yechezkel Abramski goes further, and shows an apparent contradiction in *Rambam* himself. In *Hilchos Rotze'ach* 6:10, *Rambam* rules that an error in identification — e.g., where a person thought he was killing an animal and accidentally killed a person — is close to *meizid* and he cannot seek refuge in *arei miklat* — the cities of refuge — because he should have been more careful, whereas in *Hilchos Melachim* he rules that an error of identification is considered *onus*, and a *ben Noach* is not put to death for such an error.

R' Abramski gives a logical answer. In regard to going into exile in one of the *arei miklat*, the Torah insisted on complete *shogeig*. Thus, where a person did not investigate sufficiently, he is considered to be close to *meizid*, and he cannot take refuge. With the case of the *ben Noach*, though, he is only guilty if he did the act deliberately, and whenever he did not act deliberately he is exempt. This answer explains *Rambam's* view well, but we still need to understand why he rules that a person making an error of identification is exempt, whereas, according to *Chazal*, a *ben Noach* is guilty and incurs the death penalty for this.

Ritva asks another question. According to the conclusion of the *gemara*, "a *ben Noach* is put to death because he should have learned and did not learn." Now, according to *Rashi* and other commentators, *Chazal* were referring here to *hilchos derech eretz*. Can it be that a *ben Noach* will be killed for not learning the laws of *derech eretz*? *Ritva* therefore holds in *Makkos* 9 that the *gemara* is referring to a person who claimed something was permitted when it wasn't. Avimelech claimed that Avraham had deceived him, and that he had been acting in accordance with what Avraham the prophet had told him. Hashem answered that Avraham knew what Avimelech had been scheming, and that was why he lied to him. Thus Avraham was not deceiving him. The most that Avimelech could claim was that he thought he had been permitted to do what he did, but the law in such a case is that one who thinks something is permitted when it isn't is culpable, because he should have learned and he didn't learn. Thus, according to *Ritva*, both Avimelech and Hashem claimed that Avraham "is a prophet." The difference was that Avimelech used this to justify his conduct, while Hashem saw this as the reason why Avimelech should be guilty.

There are other commentators who ask questions on this passage in the *gemara*. I would like to propose an explanation of this *gemara*. It is possible that the meaning of the *gemara*, about the answer of Hashem that "he is a prophet," is that if Avimelech had his doubts, he could have asked Avraham, whom he acknowledged as a prophet. The text in *Makkos* is "because he is a prophet and he learned from you," but the text in *Bava Kama* 92 is, "he is a prophet and he has already taught: If a stranger comes to a town, does one ask him about matters of food and drink...?" This version is a rebuke to Avimelech, for having transgressed the words of the prophets. Avraham was a prophet, and he taught by his *gemilas chasadim* — his acts of compassion and lovingkindness — that a stranger who comes to a city is asked about food and drink. The conclusion of the *gemara* is that "a *ben Noach* is put to death because he should have learned and he didn't learn," namely that he should have learned this law from Avraham. He deserves the death penalty, in accordance with the view of *rishonim*, because a *ben Noach* is executed for those matters on which he heard rulings by his prophets. (See *Encyclopedia Talmudis*, "Ben-Noach.")

This may even be the meaning of the *gemara* in *Makkos* according to the version that we have: "He learned from you." This is a second point, and comes to justify Avraham's assertion: "She is my sister."

According to this interpretation, the conclusion of the *gemara* is that one is not killed for an error in identification, but for not knowing the law, where he should have known it. It is possible that it is based on this principle that *Rambam* rules that a *ben Noach* is only put to death if he thinks something is permitted which is not, and not if he makes a mistake in identification, and that would answer the question of R' Meir Arak.

Among the seventy facets of the Torah, this is one, and may Hashem show us wonders in His Torah.

IV.
The Influence of the Akeidah on Our People's Life

The test of the *akeidah* was the tenth and last one, according to *Chazal*, that Hashem tested Avraham. It was also the greatest test of all, and to this day we mention it daily in our prayers. Among the other tests that Avraham had undergone, he had been thrown into a furnace by Nimrod. It is evidently easier for a person to sacrifice himself than to sacrifice his son. In addition, in the test of the furnace, we have no idea how Avraham felt emotionally, whereas with the *akeidah* we see how Avraham planned in advance, set out eagerly, and did everything in a deliberate way. He was not overcome with emotion when his son asked him where the lamb was for sacrifice, and did not waver about performing the *mitzvah*, until he heard a voice from Heaven telling him to stop. After the test, Avraham was told, "Now I know that you fear God," and that was the end of the tests.

This "knowledge" by Hashem, which is given here as the reason for this great test, is, of course, a major point of discussion by the *rishonim* and *acharonim*. They ask: As Hashem knows the thoughts and feelings of every person, does He then need an actual test to prove His knowledge? What was the purpose of this test, and what is its meaning? All the commentators agree that this was not for the benefit of the One giving the test, but for the one being given the test, as it states (*Tehillim* 11:5), "Hashem will test the righteous."

According to Ibn Ezra, the purpose in such tests is to have the one tested receive a reward. *Ramban* delves into this deeply. The reward is ready for him for his spiritual righteousness even without the test, but Hashem is interested in having *tzaddikim* — the righteous — carry out their thoughts into action. Unless a person actually lives through such an experience, he has not really been tested about his *bechirah* — his free will. Hashem knows that His *tzaddikim* will do His will regardless, and he tests them with deeds, this way having them exercise the spiritual power that was only latent until then. The meaning of the verse "now I know" is that now Avraham's righteousness had been shown in action, whereas until then it had only been potential. Now Hashem had brought Avraham's soul to reveal itself.

Radak goes along the same path as *Ramban*, and was preceded in this by *Ran*. *S'forno*, too, explains the purpose of the test: "That he should in practice love and fear, just as he does in potential, and in this way he will more closely resemble the Creator, who is good to the world in practice; for the purpose of the existence of man is to resemble his Creator."

According to *S'forno*, carrying out a deed from potential to actual practice is a stage in man's elevation, that his image should be like that of Hashem, who transforms His good from potential to action.

Kuzari too gives this idea in a few words, and says (5:20), "The verse, 'And God tested,' means to (have Avraham) carry out the service of Hashem from potential to action, that this should be the reason for His goodness."

Ikarim (5:13) expands on this and says that as long as a person has not been tested in actual deed, he is not yet complete:

> Similarly, we read (*I Melachim* 20:11), "The one that puts on the harness should not boast as the one who takes it off" — one who has not actually shown his strength should not be proud. One who is ready and dressed for battle is not the same as one who has already acted in a heroic manner. Many times, Hashem brings suffering on a *tzaddik* to have him coordinate his good deeds with his good thoughts.

∾§ To Publicize His Righteousness among the Other Nations

Rambam in *Moreh Nevuchim* (3:24) also sees the *akeidah* as being for the one who was tested, but instead of viewing this as being directed at giving Avraham a reward, he stresses that this was meant to publicize his name among all the nations, so that all might become aware of his righteousness. The word יָדַעְתִּי — "I know" — is explained by him as if written הוֹדַעְתִּי — "I have informed." In other words, Hashem now informed all and publicized what type of person Avraham was, and the extent of his *emunah*. According to *Moreh Nevuchim*, the *akeidah* was the peak of spiritual greatness in the love of Hashem and in *yiras shomayim*:

> It comes to inform us the extent and the limit of the love of Hashem, may He be blessed, and how far the *yirah* for Him extends. Avraham is commanded to do a certain act, which cannot be equaled by any surrender of property or by any sacrifice of life,

for it goes beyond anything else that can be done, and belongs to a class of actions which are believed to be contrary to human feelings. He had been without a child and had been longing for a child; he had great riches, and was expecting that a nation would come forth from his seed. After he had given up all hope, a son was born to him. How delighted he must have been with that child! How intensely he must have loved him! And yet, because he feared Hashem and loved to do what Hashem commanded, he thought little of that beloved child, and set aside all his hopes concerning him, and consented to kill him after a journey of three days ... The fact that he performed it three days after he received the commandment proves that this followed thought, proper consideration, and careful examination of what is due to the Divine command, and what is in accordance with the love and fear of Hashem.

In this short passage, *Rambam* encompasses a number of reasons and explanations for the *akeidah*, which fill countless pages in the different commentaries and *d'rush* volumes. Avraham knew that when his son was sacrificed, Hashem's promise of setting up the Jewish people would be nullified. And it involved the very son whose birth had come only after much prayer and supplication. Nor was Hashem promising him anything in return for this great sacrifice. And in spite of this, Avraham did not hesitate, and planned to carry out the action in three days, without his conscience bothering him. Rabbenu Bachya too says that "the test of the *akeidah* was to publicize among the nations how great is the duty to fear and love Hashem."

According to these commentators, who were already preceded by R' Sa'adiah Gaon, the test of the *akeidah* was primarily educational. By it, the knowledge of Hashem and how much one must love Him penetrated into the heart of humanity. The one who is tested serves as a tool by Hashem to prove that mortals can reach this lofty height.

Avnei Shoham increases the impact of the test in that Hashem did not include Sarah in the action. Had He included her, it would have been easier for Avraham emotionally. She would have encouraged him, and Hashem had already told him (*Bereishis* 21:12), "Whatever Sarah tells you, listen to her voice." Now he himself had to make the decision, while hiding it from his wife, who had given birth to their son in her old age.

Abarbanel explains the word נִסָּה (which we have translated above as "tested") as derived from נֵס — "a sign" — because the great action which Avraham did in regard to Hashem was a sign to all the nations, like a mighty banner, which the nations all look up to. As opposed to *Moreh Nevuchim*, though, who sees the *akeidah* as an educational act for the other nations, Abarbanel sees it as being meant to implant into the deepest recesses of the Jewish soul the most exalted of all values. In the act of the *akeidah*, there was a mighty vision of love and fear, one which cannot be described in words. Not only was Yitzchak bound on the altar, but also the entire Jewish people, which at that time was contained completely in Yitzchak, "so that from that time on they would declare the Oneness of God, and would not follow the arbitrariness of their hearts." Thus the *akeidah* was an educational act for Israel, through which a nation was established which became a sign and banner to the other nations.

This answers the question of Ibn Ezra directed at those commentators who hold that the *akeidah* was done to publicize Avraham. He asks, if no one else was present at the *akeidah*, not even Avraham's two youths, how was this then to be publicized? According to Abarbanel, though, this is simple. The world receives its inspiration in this regard from Israel, and Israel reads this *parashah* in the Torah, and by this reading, it is as if the test had been done before all of Israel, past, present and future, without a single person who did not see this great test with true prophetic vision, and its validity and the depth of its faith, through which this faith was implanted in the entire world.

Israel, the children of Yitzchak, saw this vision, and they carry it as a sign to the entire world, so that they should understand the reason why Israel was chosen, and should recognize their mission in the world.

HaKesav VeHaKabalah also follows these lines. He brings countless examples that the word נִסָּה means an example or sign. The extraordinary love that Avraham showed for Hashem is a sign for all future generations as to how much man is capable of in elevating himself to the level of loving Hashem.

A very interesting and unusual interpretation is brought by *Rashbam*. He says that the word נִסָּה means "to anger" or "provoke" someone. Hashem provoked and tormented Avraham for having made a covenant with Avimelech, "to him, his grandson and his great-grandson," and for having given him seven lambs as a gift: "You were boastful about the son I had given you, to make a covenant between him and your children, and now go and offer him as a burnt offering, and we will see what will become of your covenant."

In this vein, *Rashbam* notes that the *parashah* of the *akeidah* is introduced with the words (*Bereishis* 15:1), "After these things," referring back to the covenant between Avraham and Avimelech.

And indeed, *Chazal* in the *gemara* and the Midrash discuss why the *parashah* of Avimelech comes directly before the *akeidah*, and according to *Rashbam* there is a direct link between the two.

~§ The Akeidah as a Sign for Future Generations

The *akeidah* has become a symbol for future generations, because it contains not only the *parashah* of the *akeidah* of Yitzchak, but also the millions of *akeidos* throughout the generations of Jews who died for *Kiddush Hashem*. As *Pesikta* puts it, Yitzchak was "the first of the *ne'ekadim*." *Chazal* in *Gittin* 57 tell us, regarding the story of Channah and her seven sons, that she exclaimed: "You made an *akeidah* of one sacrifice, and I made an *akeidah* of seven sacrifices." There is no doubt that the *parashah* of the *akeidah* was sanctified by our nation not only because of the one-time act of Avraham's *akeidah*, but because of the continuous *mesiras nefesh* and sacrifice of people being willing to die for *Kiddush Hashem* in all generations. Mentioning the *akeidah* brings to mind all the millions of *akeidos* that the Jewish people have sacrificed since Avraham to our very day for *Kiddush Hashem*.

This is a reminder, but it is also a prayer that we should have happen to us that which happened to Avraham, whereby a ram appeared to take Yitzchak's place, and Avraham was told, "Do not stretch forth your hand to the lad." Unfortunately, we have had too many occurrences of the first part of the *parashah*, and much fewer of the second, and we remind Hashem of that fact.

In any event, the chain of *Kiddush Hashem* on the altar of Judaism has continued from Avraham. It was he who implanted this great spiritual power in us. The Chassidic works explain the verse, "And your seed will inherit," that in the future the Jewish people will inherit this great and holy characteristic, by which they will implant the knowledge of Hashem in the world. There is no doubt that that is the reason that the *akeidah* was raised to the highest symbolic level on the Jewish scale. This was especially stressed by *Chasam Sofer*, when he stated:

> In my humble opinion, Hashem did not test Avraham and Yitzchak to see if they would maintain their righteousness, but He tested the holy nation that would in the future come out of them. At first Hashem tested our fathers as they wandered from one nation to the other, so that they would be the source for their children to be able to withstand suffering. And later he tested them, to see if they would withstand the murders and conversion campaigns for *Kiddush Hashem*. After Hashem had given

(Avraham) an only son and he had raised him for thirty-seven years honorably and to greatness, he gave him over to be slaughtered. And this would be the source for their children after them that suffer this. After they had been supreme among the nations of the world, they were, Heaven forbid, given over to captivity, plunder, murder and destruction, and all suffer. And when Hashem saw that "and the two of them went together" — He perceived that from such a holy source a holy people would emerge.

Continuing these remarkable words of *Chasam Sofer*, I heard from R' K. Reinetz, who gave over in the name of his grandfather, R' Zusman Fishel Sofer, his interpretation of the verse, "It will be seen; as it is said to this day, in the mountain of Hashem it will be seen." Then, at the *akeidah*, only Hashem saw that great act, because even the youths weren't with Avraham, but today the whole world sees the *akeidos* of Israel. All saw how fathers and mothers sacrificed their children: "As it is said" — that which we were told about Avraham — is "to this day" to be seen.

That is the historic significance of the *akeidah* for future generations. How true this is for our generation of the Holocaust, where we were subject to the most terrible tests, "and yet we did not forget Your name."

Tosefes B'rachah has a beautiful explanation, which belongs to the category of *d'rush*. The Midrash tells us that Avraham said to Hashem: "You know that when You told me, 'Take your son and offer him up as a burnt offering,' I could have answered You: 'Yesterday you told me, "For by Yitzchak will your seed be known" and now You tell me, "Offer him up as a burnt offering;" ' but I nevertheless suppressed my desires to perform Your desires with a perfect heart." This statement of Avraham seems surprising. How can any man argue with Hashem? Who can understand His meaning?

Rambam, though, in his explanation to the *mishnah* (*Sanhedrin* 10) discusses when one must listen to prophecy and when not, based on what *Chazal* tell us (*Shabbos* 55), that Hashem never made a positive promise which He later changed to a negative one. It follows that if Hashem promised Avraham something good — that his seed would continue through Yitzchak — he did not need to pay attention to Hashem if He, as it were, reversed himself. Only when Hashem changes from bad to good do we need to listen to Him. And that was what Avraham claimed: "I did not see the *akeidah* as a change to the bad, which would imply that You changed a promise from the good to the bad, and consequently I did not disobey Your order. To me, I saw the *akeidah* as being perfectly good, and I was therefore willing to forgo the prophecy of my seed, which too was perfectly good." And that was the test for which Avraham was praised, because even emotionally he felt that the *akeidah* was good.

Sha'arei Simchah explains the *akeidah* in an interesting manner: Avraham chased away Yishmael because Sarah saw him involved in idolatry. But in order for people not to say that Avraham was influenced by Sarah to chase Yishmael away for egotistical reasons, Hashem tested Avraham and ordered him to slaughter his own son to whom Sarah had given birth, and then afterwards everyone agreed that the case of Yishmael was also based on Hashem's command and on prophecy, and that is the meaning of the verse, "After these things."

There is a more simple explanation of the nature of the test in the *rishonim* and *acharonim*. Avraham, whose entire mission in life was to spread the idea of Hashem and to smash the idols, was suddenly ordered to offer a human sacrifice, and to take an action that he had been fighting against the whole time, and yet he did not question Hashem's actions but did as he was told.

I would like to bring here a remarkable interpretation of *Malbim*, who says that the phrase (*Bereishis* 22:2), אֲשֶׁר אֹמַר אֵלֶיךָ — "that I will tell you," does not refer to the place, because Hashem had already told him its name in advance: "Go to the land of Moriah." Rather, "that I will tell you" refers to what I will tell you to sacrifice. The fact that the Torah says "and offer him up" did not have to imply that Yitzchak was to be the sacrifice, because the phrase could equally be translated "and offer it up" and applied to the ram that Avraham later sacrificed. Hashem gave Avraham a hint that another sacrifice was to be ready there, but Avraham did not investigate or examine the words, and ran to do as Hashem had commanded him.

Afterwards, when Avraham took Yitzchak down, He said to him, "Now I know that you fear God, and you did not spare your son, your only one, from Me," the stress being on the words "from Me." I testify that you only took him down because of a direct command "from Me," just as you brought him up there because of your love for Me, without questioning Me.

It is interesting what *Peninim Yekarim* says about "from Me." This was said by the angel that had been created through this *mitzvah* that Avraham had performed. It was this angel who said to Avraham: "Look at me, and you will understand with what *shleimus* — completeness — you performed your *mitzvah*, without any outside considerations, for I was created from that *mitzvah*."

✑ Against the Idolatrous Beliefs of Christianity

Chazal in *Ta'anis* 4 comment on the verse (*Yirmiyahu* 7:31), "That I did not command, and did not say, and did not come into My heart," as follows: "I did not command" — refers to the son of Misha, king of Moab; "And did not say" — refers to Yiftach, who sacrificed his daughter; "And did not come into My mind" — refers to Yitzchak, son of Avraham. The commentators discuss this *Chazal* at length. After all, what do these three have in common? This quotation, with some changes, is brought in *Midrash Rabbah* on our *parashah* and in *Yalkut Shimoni* on Michah, with the following text (*Michah* 6:6), "With what shall I come before Hashem and bow before the high God?" Even though this refers to Misha, the king of Moab, who performed that action and offered his son as a burnt offering, it really refers to Yitzchak, as it states, "With what shall I come before Hashem and bow before the high God?" ... With Yitzchak, even though the action was not carried out, it was accepted as if it had been carried out, and with Misha it was not accepted by Him.

Of course the glaring question is why *Chazal* saw fit to equate the *akeidah* to the human sacrifice of the king of Moab, so much so that they felt it necessary to answer that in one case the action was taken and in the other it wasn't. It is true that there are scholars who see the *akeidah* as not only coming to let us know the spiritual greatness of Avraham, but as bearing an educational message, whose aim was to fight against the idolatry that prevailed in the world at the time, which included human sacrifices. The cry, "Do not stretch forth your hand to the lad," and the sacrifice of the ram instead of Yitzchak teach us that Hashem does not want human sacrifices, and He rejects utterly any attempt to worship Him in this way. But it is still difficult to understand why *Chazal* found it so necessary to reject a practice that already in their days no longer existed among the other nations as well, and felt it necessary to differentiate between the actions of Misha and of Avraham.

Perhaps one could venture to say that *Chazal* were really debating here with Christianity. It is known that the church fathers included the *akeidah* in their glorification of the "sacrifice" of Christianity's founder. R' Yair ben Shabasi, in *Cherev Pifi'os*, debated with the Christians and proved to them that the *akeidah* was not a "sacrifice" but a "test." It appears that the Christians had inherited from their forefathers, who were all idolaters, perverted ideas about the need to bring human sacrifices, and then fitted these concepts into their new religion. *Chazal* wanted to stress the foreign nature and the idolatry in this idea, and attributed it back to Misha, king of Moab, while in reality meaning the idolatry in Christianity. Misha brought a human sacrifice, and his offering was not accepted, as the prophet says (*Michah* 6:7), "Shall I give my firstborn for my transgression?" *Lehavdil*, Yitzchak, was not sacrificed, because that was not what Hashem wanted; yet Hashem considered it, because of Avraham's thoughts and devotion, as if Avraham had actually brought the sacrifice.

It is possible that the reason it is called the trial of *Avraham* and not that of *Yitzchak* is to stress that the Torah was interested in showing the qualities of the one bringing the sacrifice, and not the one who was meant to be a sacrifice. Avraham was ready to sacrifice to Hashem his most precious possession. That is the content and the essence of the *parashah* of the *akeidah*.

Chayei Sarah – חיי שרה

I.

Avraham Buys the Cave of Machpelah

The importance which the Torah attaches to Avraham's purchase of a burial plot arouses our attention. An entire *parashah*, of unusual length, is devoted to this sale. In *Parashas Vayechi*, Yaakov reiterates the details of the sale in his will to his sons. When the Torah tells us about the execution of the will, it again gives all the details of the sale. If that is not enough, *Chazal* also tell us that "ten times it states 'the children of Cheis,' paralleling the Ten Commandments, to teach you that whoever clarifies the transaction of that *tzaddik* (i.e., Avraham) is as if he observed all the Ten Commandments" (*Bava Basra* 69). This special importance that the Torah imparts to the acquisition of a piece of land for a burial plot demands an explanation. There is obviously a deep meaning in this, and we must search for and find it.

Ibn Ezra holds that what the Torah meant was "to tell us the virtues of *Eretz Yisrael* for the living and for the dead," and also to fulfill Hashem's promise to give Avraham a *nachalah* — "an inheritance" — in the land. *Ramban* disagrees with this. He asks: "What is the virtue of this land, that he would not take her (i.e., Sarah) to be buried in another land?" The second explanation of Ibn Ezra, that Hashem gave Avraham an inheritance here, is also not approved of by *Ramban*, for the whole land was promised to him, and that promise was only fulfilled with Avraham's descendants. Therefore, says *Ramban*, what the Torah wanted to tell us is the mercy Hashem had for Avraham, that He fulfilled His blessing to him, as stated in the words, "And I will exalt your name." Avraham came to a foreign land, and in spite of that they honored him, and referred to him as *"nasi Elokim"* — a prince of God.

Ramban has another explanation. The purpose of this *parashah* is to tell us where our forefathers are buried, because everyone is required to honor their burial place. *Ramban* also cites the view of *Chazal* that this *parashah* was one of Avraham's tests. He was forced to buy a burial plot in the land which was promised to him as an inheritance, and yet he didn't question Hashem's ways. It is true that *Chazal* in *Sanhedrin* 111 did not refer to this as a test, but they nevertheless praised him for having accepted everything lovingly. R' Yosef Bechor Shor, though, quotes Rabbenu Yonah, the teacher of *Ramban*, that it was indeed a test.

Chasam Sofer, in his commentary on the Torah, explains that the nature of the test lies in the distress caused to Avraham, in that his first acquisition in *Eretz Yisrael* had to be for a burial plot, and not for any other purpose. This comment of *Chasam Sofer* is in keeping with his explanation of the *tefillah*, וְתוֹלִיכֵנוּ קוֹמְמִיּוּת לְאַרְצֵנוּ — "and gather us upright to our land." *Chasam Sofer* explains this to mean that we wish to come to *Eretz Yisrael* while we are still alive ("upright"), and not through the tunnels underground, which, we are told, those buried outside *Eretz Yisrael* will have to roll through to get to *Eretz Yisrael* at the time of *techiyas hameisim* — "resurrection of the dead" (*Teshuvos Chasam Sofer*, *Yoreh De'ah* 332).

There are, however, commentators who see this *parashah* as having *halachic* implications, regarding buying a burial plot for money. Avraham did not want to receive the grave as a gift, says *Chafetz Chaim*, because one must buy a grave with money. We find hints of this obligation in *Chazal* as well. In *Bava Basra* 112, *Chazal* tell us that "we find a *tzaddik* buried in a grave not belonging to him." *Yerushalmi* too, quoted by *Tosafos* on *Mo'ed Katan* 13, states, "It is good for a person to rest in his own." Based on this, *Chasam Sofer* concludes, in his *Teshuvos* on *Yoreh De'ah* 331, that it is a *mitzvah* to take some payment for a piece of land for a grave even from a poor person. On the other hand, he is furious (in 329) at those *chevra kadishas* — "burial societies" — that charge fantastic prices for grave sites, and demand that these practices should be fought against. He nevertheless finds an *asmachta* — a "hint," as it were — though, for paying a high price to be buried near the grave of a *tzaddik*. *Chazal* refer to Efron (עפרן — by rearranging the letters of his name and changing the letter פ, which has a *gematria* of eighty, to עי which have a combined *gematria* of eighty) as רַע עַיִן — "one with a bad eye" — for asking for an exorbitant amount for the grave plot of Sarah, but they do not say anything against Esav, who sold his share in the cave to Yaakov for "piles of gold." The reason

BEREISHIS — CHAYEI SARAH / 109

for the difference is simple: Efron had no idea who would be buried in this cave, so he had no right to charge so high a price. Esav, though, already knew that his forefathers were buried there, and therefore he had the right to demand a high price.

Rabbenu Bachya also sees special significance in this *parashah* in that it stresses that the cave was bought בְּכֶסֶף מָלֵא — for the full price, and not by conquest. He names three exceptional places which were bought for money, and these are: the Cave of Machpelah; Mount Gerizim and Mount Eival, where the covenant about keeping the Torah was made; and Mount Moriah, where the *Batei Mikdash* stood. The words of Rabbenu Bachya need clarification, as they differ from *Midrash Rabbah* 79. There, the Midrash does not include Mount Gerizim and Mount Eival among the three. R' Chavel, however, points out that Rabbenu Bachya's source is R' Sa'adiah Gaon.

✥ Give Me a Burial Plot

After studying the verses, it would seem that the Torah meant to stress the conquest of the land by Avraham, specifically by acquiring this burial plot. It would appear that according to the laws of the nations at the time, burial, just as birth today, was the sign and symbol of being attached to a specific area, and it was from this that one would acquire citizenship rights. *S'forno* points out a verse in *Yeshayahu* (22:16), "What have you here, and whom have you here, that you have carved out for yourself a grave here?" This verse shows that the place a person was buried was considered proof of his citizenship in that place, and a foreigner would not be permitted to be buried in that place. Avraham, too, was not considered to be a citizen of the land until he bought this burial plot. That was the first step in his ownership of the land. From that time on, the children of Avraham have merely returned to their father's possession, as a result of that first acquisition. It appears that was the law in those days.

A burial place was evidently the first condition necessary in those days for ownership of land. We find a hidden hint of this in *Yalkut Shimoni* on the verse (*Tehillim* 20:2), "May Hashem hear you in the day of trouble." Once — the Midrash tells us — a father and son were walking along the road. The son became tired and said to his father, "Father, where is our destination?" He answered him, "I will give you a sign to look for. If you see a graveyard, you will know our destination is near." This Midrash is often quoted by others who interpret it symbolically as referring to the sacrifices that come before the establishment of a state and that foretell its emergence.

But there is a deeper meaning here. A grave, in the perception of the ancients, was the link which bound the fathers to the sons and symbolized their ownership of the land. That is the reason we refer to a grave as *kever avos* — "grave of the fathers." It was not for nothing that Jews struggled for our right to the Cave of Machpelah long before there was a Jewish state. Even though people may not recognize the import of what they do, their inner souls recognize it. We succeeded in understanding the significance of this ancient burial plot, that testifies to our eternal roots in this land.

◈§ And I Will Bury My Dead Before Me

Even the most superficial study of this *parashah* teaches us the value of *kever Yisrael* — to be buried in a Jewish cemetery — in our perceptions. Avraham searches for a place to bury Sarah. *Ramban* explains the verse, "If you are willing to bury my dead," as a threat by Avraham, where Avraham told the children of Cheis that if they did not consent to allow Sarah to be buried in the ground, he would leave her body in a coffin above the ground.

Kli Yakar and others are surprised at *Ramban*, because he himself, in his *Toras Ha'Adam*, says that a person who leaves a body in a coffin without burial in the ground violates a positive *mitzvah* of the Torah which states, "You shall surely bury him," which implies in the ground. It appears to me, though, that *Ramban* does not disagree here with his ruling, but on the contrary, reinforces it, stressing that even the children of Cheis realized that burial must be in the ground. The threat of not burying the coffin frightened them, and forced them to accept Avraham's demands.

Akeidas Yitzchak in *Parashas Ki Seitsei* expands on the importance of burial in the ground, and quotes *Koheles* (12:7), "The dust shall return to the earth as it was: and the spirit shall return unto Hashem who gave it," as proof that there is a link between the return of the body to the ground and the soul to Hashem.

Chazal in *Sanhedrin* 46 prove that the requirement of burial is a Torah law, and the commentators establish that burial in the ground is specifically required. There is no doubt that our *parashah* is the source for that ruling.

In the *rishonim* and *acharonim* we find numerous reasons why burial must be in the ground. The Sochachower holds that this is in the category of "and he shall return the theft," for the Torah states, "and you shall return unto the earth." Based on this, he explains the words of *Chazal* in *Chullin* 92, that the fact that *bnei Noach* do not sell human flesh in their butcher stores is considered to be the performance of a *mitzvah*. Where is the source for this? The answer is that *bnei Noach* are forbidden to steal, and as a result they must bury their dead and not sell their flesh.

One who delves into *Tanach* and *Chazal* will soon see that the concept of *kever Yisrael* is a major concept in Jewish belief. There are hundreds of verses about this in *Tanach*. Let us discuss but a few of them. Regarding Adam, the Torah states, "Until you return to the earth, for from it you were taken." Avraham went to great effort to buy a burial plot for Sarah. Yaakov ordered his sons to bury him in that grave, and to bring his body up from Egypt. He also placed a grave marker on the grave of Rachel. We are told in regard to Moshe that Hashem "buried him in the valley." A person put to death by the *beis din* must be buried. Yehoshua was buried at the border of his land. The old prophet from Beis-El was punished in that "his carcass was not brought to *kever Yisrael*." David took the bones of Shaul and buried them in the graves of his fathers. One of the curses of the *tochechah* is that the body will not be buried. That same curse was said about Yerovam ben Nevat. Yoav went to Edom to bury the people who had been killed by Edom. These cases are but a few of the many in *Tanach*, and there are a far greater number in *Chazal*. When those who had been killed in Betar were finally buried, a special blessing was added in the *bircas hamazon* in gratitude to Hashem.

This idea is discussed by both the *rishonim* and *acharonim*, who explain that this emphasis is to stress to our nation the belief in the continued existence of the soul after death. The body deserves to be treated respectfully, as it served as the vessel for the soul, and it exemplified the image of God (*tzelem Elokim*) in creation. Thus it was not for nothing that *Chazal* compared the purchase of the Cave of Machpelah to the Ten Commandments. According to the commentators, by his actions Avraham established a strong basis for the continued existence of the soul, "for in the image of God He created man." Therefore Avraham's deed is associated with the Ten Commandments.

We can thus understand the insistence of religious Jews that autopsies and disrespect for the bodies of the dead undermine the very foundations of Jewish belief, in addition to the fact that such actions are grave violations of *halachah* regarding disrespect for the dead and the prohibition against deriving benefit from a dead body. All this applies equally even if the entire body is brought to burial after the autopsy. If organs are removed from the body, there is a further violation of the Torah prohibition of "you shall surely bury him," which, according to the commentators, is a positive and a negative *mitzvah*. *Yerushalmi* states clearly (*Nazir* 7:1), "You are to bury him completely, and do not bury part of him." From this it follows that if any part was left unburied, (the person doing the burying) has done nothing.

That is the reason why all the *acharonim*, without exception, refuse to countenance autopsies. R' Yitzchak Elchanan in his *Teshuvos Beis Yitzchak* (*Yoreh De'ah* 33) rules that where there is fear that there might be an autopsy, one is permitted to hide a body in a stone coffin and not bury it in the ground, until conditions have changed.

There is not a single *posek* who permits autopsies unless there is at hand an immediate occasion where the purpose is to save other lives (*pikuach nefesh*), although R' Yaakov Ettlinger even forbids this. In his *teshuvos* (74), R' Meir Shapira has a detailed discussion on this question. According to him, even if our actions in forbidding autopsies will result in the scoffers and heretics denying the whole Torah, that is irrelevant. One must only be concerned about scoffers in order to reprimand them, but cannot permit something which is prohibited because of such considerations.

◆§ You Are a Prince of Hashem in Our Midst

Avraham was aware of his status in a land ruled by others. He knew that he was a "stranger" to them, even when they referred to him as "a prince of God." Avraham was very wealthy, but he didn't own even a sliver of the land, and he was able to evaluate this situation accurately. But the children of Cheis wanted to create the impression that not only was he equal to them, but that he was superior to them, because of his great wealth.

"And Avraham came to mourn for Sarah and to weep for her." *Chizkuni* says that he came to weep because he did not even have a burial plot in the land. It appears that that is the reason Avraham referred to himself as "a stranger and sojourner." To the casual observer, he appeared to be a resident of the land, because he was wealthy and famous among the people, who referred to him as "the prince of God," but in reality he had nothing. The children of Cheis referred to him constantly as *adon* — "master" — but he was not impressed. It is true that he felt in his heart that he was indeed the master; not, however, because of their flattery, but rather as a result of Hashem's promise. He could not rest until he had bought this piece of ground, and from it his ownership of the entire country would expand and grow: "The field, and the cave in it, and all the trees in the field, which is within its border around it."

II.

The Beauty of the Speech of our Forefathers' Servants

Abarbanel points out a number of differences between what Avraham told Eliezer to say, and what Eliezer actually said. The other commentators also point out tens of differences. Abarbanel explains that these changes were intended to gain the confidence of Lavan and Besuel, and to persuade them how essential it was for them to bind themselves to Avraham through the marriage of Rivkah to Yitzchak. In accordance with this, he explains a statement of *Chazal* in *Midrash Rabbah* 11: "The speech of the servants is more beautiful than the Torah of children." *Chazal* stress the wisdom of Eliezer, Avraham's servant, who understood the mentality of such people as Lavan and Besuel, and was able to influence them.

According to Abarbanel, these were the changes that Eliezer made, and the reasons why he made them:

(a) Avraham told Eliezer, "But go to my land and my birthplace." When Eliezer related this, he changed it and said that Avraham had commanded him to go "to the house of my father and to my family." By this, he wanted to stress to them how strongly Avraham felt about them, and that he had chosen only them and not the other residents of this area.

(b) Avraham said, "Hashem, the God of the Heavens, who took me from my father's house," while Eliezer said, "And Hashem, before whom I walked, said to me." Eliezer made this change so as not to arouse their hostility, for Avraham was boasting, as it were, that Hashem had taken him out of their midst to give him a special land. He also did not want to reveal to them Hashem's promise to Avraham of the land.

(c) Avraham said to him: "Beware lest you bring my son back there," in the event that he would not find the bride he was looking for, while Eliezer changed it and said, "In that case you will be absolved of my oath." The reason for this change is an obvious one. Eliezer did not want to reveal to them how little Avraham thought of them, and that under no circumstances was he willing to have his son remain with them.

(d) Eliezer asked for a sign for himself and said, "It shall be that the young maiden ... It is she that You have chosen for Your servant, for

Yitzchak, and thus I will know that You were merciful to my master." When he told of this, though, he said, "That is the woman that Hashem chose for the son of my master." He did not mention the idea of this being *chessed* — "kindness" — by Hashem, so as not to equate their worth with that of Avraham, as if they are doing Avraham a *favor* by agreeing to the marriage.

(e) Rivkah said, "I will also draw for your camels," whereas when Eliezer told the story, he changed it and said, "I will also give your camels to drink." There is perhaps no special significance in this, as Rivkah could not have known at the time whether she would be successful in giving the camels to drink. Hence, she only spoke about drawing the water. By the time he told it, though, Eliezer already knew what had happened.

(f) Rivkah said, "I am the daughter of Besuel, the son of Milkah, who bore to Nachor," while Eliezer stated shortly, "the daughter of Besuel, the son of Nachor," and did not mention the mother.

(g) First Eliezer gave her the jewelry and only afterwards did he ask her who she was, while when he told the story, he reversed the order, so that they should not be astonished that he gave her gifts before he even knew who she was.

(h) Eliezer did not mention his prayer after the test, "Blessed is Hashem, the God of my master Avraham, who did not forsake His mercy and truth ...," and that, too, out of respect for Avraham.

(i) At first, Eliezer said, "In the way, Hashem led me to the house of my master's brother," but when he told it, he said, "who led me in the true way, to take the daughter of my master's brother for his son." His first words implied that he had no other choice, whereas according to the way he told it, if they refused him he would go someplace else.

In addition to these changes that Abarbanel pointed out, there are other substantial and stylistic differences regarding almost every single detail. For example, the Torah states regarding Avraham, "And Hashem blessed Avraham בַּכֹּל — in all," while Eliezer went far beyond this and told them, "And he grew prosperous, and He gave him flocks and cattle and gold and silver ..." With Avraham we are told, "And I will make you swear by Hashem the God of the Heavens and the God of the earth," whereas Eliezer said, "And my master made me swear, saying." Avraham said, "And you will take a wife for my son, for Yitzchak," and Eliezer said only, "and you will take a wife for my son." Avraham said later, "And you will take a wife for my son from there," and Eliezer said, "And you will take a wife for my son from my family and from my father's house." Avraham said, "from the daughters of Canaan in whose midst I dwell," and Eliezer said, "in whose land I dwell." There

BEREISHIS — CHAYEI SARAH / 115

are many other differences similar to these. The *rishonim*, such as *Rashbam*, *Akeidah* and others, discuss these differences at length. All have one element in common: that the story shows us Eliezer's wisdom and psychological insights, in his attempt to prove to them that this marriage came from Hashem.

R' Samson Raphael Hirsch also follows the *rishonim* and says that the entire purpose of this story was to make the matter acceptable to Avraham's relatives. Eliezer understood how they thought. He made a point of not arousing suspicion, and skipped whatever he felt might seem to be too great a concern for the success of his mission. The compassionate elements of the previous story were deliberately left out, because these are people to whom it is dangerous to appear to be emotional. Eliezer limited himself to stressing the fact that Hashem's hand was directly involved, so that Lavan would be afraid to oppose the move.

Radak is the only commentator who states that there is no significance in the differences. He says: "We cannot give a reason for the deletions or additions, because there are so many." Eliezer told them everything so as to show them that Hashem loved Avraham and did what Avraham wished. Thus they could not keep the maiden from Yitzchak, because this had come from Hashem.

In the repetition of these matters there are differences in the words, but the gist is the same, because that is the way the Torah works when it repeats matters, where it gives the same gist, but not the same words.

As opposed to this, *Akeidah* holds that this *parashah* is educational, so as to teach us how to accomplish such tasks properly and efficiently. This *parashah* contains a wealth of ideas and philosophical concepts, and the reason why the Torah repeated the *parashah* was "to add, to make us understand better, to teach us from its wisdom how to accomplish matters."

✡ The Speech of the Servants of Our Avos

Chazal were amazed at how the Torah dwells at such great length on the story of Eliezer, to the extent that they exclaimed: "R' Acha said, 'The everyday speech of the servants of the *avos* is more beautiful than the Torah of the children.' " The *parashah* of Eliezer occupies a number of pages. It says what it has to say, and then repeats itself. Why is this so?

R' Moshe Avigdor Amiel in his *Hegionos el Ami* says that *Chazal* wanted to stress the importance of the historical events at the time of the *avos*, which became part of the very fabric of the Torah.

Rambam in *Moreh Nevuchim* says that Hashem's *hashgachah* (Divine Providence) on individuals is directly related to their understanding. The reason the Torah deals with every little detail over here is to teach us how great was Divine Providence in the everyday life of the *avos*. Already in the very first verse in *Bereishis*, *Rashi* quotes R' Yitzchak, who says Hashem should have commenced the Torah with "This month is for you . . .," which is the first *mitzvah* all of *Klal Yisrael* received, but He began the Torah with *Bereishis* to stress at the very beginning our right to *Eretz Yisrael*, which we would inherit from the *avos*. By the same token, the speech of the *avos* is permeated with *hashkafah* and *halachah*, which makes these *parashiyos* extremely important. Thus we can learn from Eliezer's action in looking for a wife for Yitzchak the way one should look for a spouse, in accordance with the words of *Mishle* (31:30), שֶׁקֶר הַחֵן וְהֶבֶל הַיֹּפִי — "Grace is deceptive, and beauty is vain." Eliezer did not check anything about Rivkah except her generosity and the way she would treat a stranger. That was enough for him to recognize that she was suitable to be Yitzchak's wife.

Chazal point out that in using this method of finding a wife for Yitzchak, Eliezer was making an improper request of Hashem, but in this case Hashem nevertheless answered him properly. He asked improperly, because all he checked was Rivkah's spiritual state, but he never checked to see if she was physically well. When *Chazal* tell us that Eliezer asked improperly, we can see that other factors should also be checked out, and "a person is forbidden to marry a woman until he has seen her."

In any event, the Torah stresses here only the spiritual quality as the basis for the choice of a marriage partner. Eliezer didn't look any further once he found that quality. He relied on Avraham's power, and knew that Hashem would lead him along the right path.

Besides this, the *parashah* also contains other important *halachos*, such as that of having humans drink before animals do. We learn this from the fact that Rivkah said, "Drink and I will also draw for your camels." With food, though, one must feed animals first before one eats himself. R' Yosef Zvi Dushinski also mentions the *halachah* of a "double condition" in *Kiddushin* 61 as seen in this *parashah*, as well as many other *halachos*.

The speech of the *avos* is also Torah, and not only in terms of proper manners and *middos*. This *parashah* is valuable for the different *halachos*, values, and customs that we find in it. Thus *Degel Machanei Efrayim* said that the speech of the *avos* is beautiful because it itself became Torah for their descendants.

The Chassidic works examine the story of Eliezer and find in it an abundance of ideas. We can learn from it how much a person must dedicate himself to achieve something worthwhile. Avraham said to Eliezer that if his — Avraham's — family did not wish to give their daughter, "you will be absolved of this oath," but Eliezer nevertheless did everything possible to change their minds and to have them accept his proposal. And he did this even though, as *Chazal* tell us, he had a personal interest in the case, because he too had a daughter, whom he would have liked Yitzchak to marry. Eliezer nevertheless did what he was sent to do and refused to budge from there until he achieved the parents' consent to bring Rivkah back with him as a wife for Yitzchak.

Nachal Kedumim, by *Chida*, explains why *Chazal* referred their statement, "The everyday speech of the servants of the *avos* is more beautiful than the Torah of the children," to the verse, "And I came today to the well." *Chazal* learned from this verse that Eliezer had a miraculous speeding up of his journey (*kefitzas haderech*), to the extent that he arrived in Padan Aram on the same day he had left Avraham. "Today I left and today I arrived." Had he traveled for a number of days, says *Chida*, the Torah would no doubt have told us what happened on those days, because "The everyday speech of the servants of the *avos* is more beautiful than the Torah of the children." As the Torah only tells us about a single day, that is a clear indication of the miraculous speeding up of his journey.

⇜§ In Whose Midst — In Whose Land — I Dwell

The commentators tell us what Eliezer had in mind when he changed what Avraham had said, "in whose midst I dwell," to "in whose land I dwell." Avraham had intended by this to exclude anyone in whose midst he was living — and that included Eliezer's daughter as well. By ignoring Avraham's choice of words, Eliezer discredited only the Canaanites, as if he himself and his family would not be excluded.

Tosafos HaRosh has a beautiful explanation of this change in the language. Avraham said "in whose midst" and not "in whose land," because by then Hashem had already promised the land to him. Eliezer, though, did not want to tell Avraham's relatives that Avraham was to inherit the land, and he therefore changed the words. He also used "to my family" rather than the words "to my birthplace" that Avraham had used, so as not to draw their attention to Avraham's ties to his "birthplace."

HaKesav VeHaKabalah, though, says that Avraham did not use the phrase "to my family," because the word מִשְׁפָּחָה — "family" — is close to the root ספח — meaning "joining" or "annexing." Avraham did not want to use a word which expresses a spiritual link and tie with his family. Eliezer, though, wanted to influence them, and that was why he used a term which indicated spiritual closeness.

◆§ Perhaps She Will Not Consent

Rashi quotes *Chazal* who point out that the word "perhaps" is not written אוּלַי here, as it normally is, but rather אֵלַי, which (since the Torah scroll is not vowelized) may be pronounced אֵלַי — "to me." In other words, Eliezer was looking for a way for Yitzchak to marry his own daughter. A common question asked on *Rashi* is why he makes this comment over here, where Eliezer is repeating his story, because earlier too the Torah uses "perhaps," and there too *Rashi* could explain that Eliezer hoped that the woman would not wish to go, in which case Avraham would have to come back to him. The Kotzker answers that in the earlier case, when the events were actually happening, his personal interest so blinded Eliezer's eyes that he did not even realize that the question, "Perhaps the woman will not wish to go," stemmed from his egotism. Now, after Eliezer already knew that the sister of Lavan and daughter of Besuel was certainly going to marry Yitzchak, he finally realized that he had raised as a doubt, "perhaps (written אֵלַי) the woman will not go," because his egotism had made him think and ask that way.

Sefas Emes has a beautiful interpretation. At the time, Eliezer carried out his mission properly and never even thought about himself at all, as we see in how he did everything possible to persuade the family to permit Rivkah to go. Only afterwards, when he was retelling the story, did he reveal to them that he too had a daughter who was suitable for Yitzchak, yet he had not even thought of suggesting her, and had let Avraham's interests take precedence over his own. By the same token, they now had to place Avraham's interests before their own.

Oznayim LaTorah has a similar explanation. In order to make the match acceptable to Lavan and Besuel, Eliezer told them that he personally had wanted his daughter to marry Yitzchak, but Avraham had not wanted it and had refused him.

Maharshal uses a similar line of reasoning with minor changes. He uses this hint of אֵלַי as a threat to Lavan and Besuel, that if they did not give Rivkah to Yitzchak as a wife, Avraham's son would marry Eliezer's daughter.

R' Avraham Mordechai of Gur gives an interesting interpretation. When Eliezer was with Avraham, he never thought of so disloyal a thought, that he would become Yitzchak's father-in-law. Now though, when he was in the home of Lavan and saw who Yitzchak's in-laws would be, he thought to himself: "Am I not as worthy as they?"

(As to the question asked earlier on *Rashi*, the answer is quite simple. In the first reference the Torah writes it as אֻלַי, and only in the second is it written אֵלַי. Thus it is the latter reference that induced *Rashi's* question and comment.)

Afikei Yehudah — and some give this in the name of *Gra* — explains the words of *Rashi* as follows: There is a difference in the words פֶּן and אוּלַי. אוּלַי is positive, and is used in a case of doubt, where the person wants the event to happen, while פֶּן is negative, and is used where a person has a doubt which he hopes will not take place. And this is what bothered *Rashi*. The Torah should have used פֶּן to tell us "perhaps the woman will not consent," rather than using אוּלַי. Since the Torah used אוּלַי, *Rashi* explained that in his heart Eliezer wanted the woman not to want to follow after him, because he had a daughter.

R' Yosef Chaim Nathanson, in his *Divrei Shaul*, disagrees with the latter explanation, because we sometimes see the word אוּלַי used even when a person does not want something to happen, such as with Avraham and S'dom, where he pleaded, "אוּלַי there will be five missing," or with Yaakov when he was told to visit Yitzchak and pretend that he was Esav, he exclaimed, "אוּלַי my father will touch me." He therefore explains that the word אוּלַי is used when the person thinks that that is the more likely possibility, and פֶּן is used where it is a less likely possibility.

There is, however, another interesting answer in a number of commentators. They explain the word אֵלַי as if the punctuation were אֵ-לִי — "My God" — and this was a prayer by Eliezer to Hashem that the woman should not want to go with him.

III.

The Torah of Kindness on Her Tongue

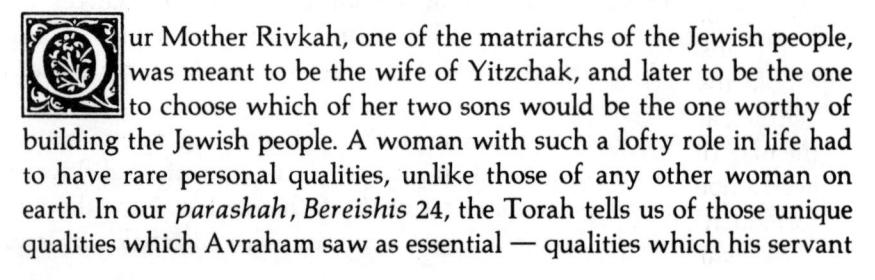

Our Mother Rivkah, one of the matriarchs of the Jewish people, was meant to be the wife of Yitzchak, and later to be the one to choose which of her two sons would be the one worthy of building the Jewish people. A woman with such a lofty role in life had to have rare personal qualities, unlike those of any other woman on earth. In our *parashah*, *Bereishis* 24, the Torah tells us of those unique qualities which Avraham saw as essential — qualities which his servant

Eliezer had in turn learned to appreciate from Avraham — in the choice of a wife for Yitzchak, one of the fathers of our nation.

The conditions that Avraham set were: (a) "You shall not take a wife for my son from the daughters of the Canaanites in whose midst I dwell"; (b) "but you are to go to my land and my birthplace." The oath that Avraham made Eliezer swear was to fulfill those two conditions. After Eliezer asked him what to do if the woman refused to come: "Shall I bring your son back to the land from which you departed?" Avraham answered him that if the woman refused to come, Eliezer would be absolved of the vow. But Avraham stressed, "Guard yourself lest you return my son there." And he made a condition that "You will be absolved from this vow of mine; only do not return my son there."

Each commentator explains the significance of this oath in his own way: which conditions apply if the woman does consent to come and which if she refuses to consent. The commentators also discuss what is meant by, "to my land and to my birthplace." Let us first examine the clear warning not to take a wife from the Canaanite daughters. Why were they worse than the women of any country? Who was included and who excluded in "the daughters of the Canaanites"?

◆§ The Purity of the Jewish Family

There is no doubt that Avraham's intention in his oath was to set up a firm foundation for the purity of the Jewish family, and to protect it from any foreign mixture. After studying the text, though, it would seem that this warning is mixed into and interwoven with the love of *Eretz Yisrael* and our ownership of it. Avraham forbids Yitzchak to leave the country, even if the woman meant for him refuses to come to him. Yitzchak, who was offered as a sacrifice, is not permitted to leave the country and to settle elsewhere, because the unique qualities of the land are one of the basic components of the Jewish people, which is to be forged by Yitzchak. Those who live in the country with Yitzchak are flawed and their friendship and closeness are not desired. The land of Canaan, though, is one that was sanctified, and one may not leave it. In the case of Yitzchak that even applies to leaving it to find a wife.

This instruction by Avraham parallels what *Chazal* tell us: "A person should always live in *Eretz Yisrael*, even in a city where the majority are gentiles, and should not live outside *Eretz Yisrael*, even in a city where the majority are Jews." Yitzchak was commanded to remain in Canaan, even among the most despicable of nations, but at the same time he was forbidden under any circumstances to take a wife from there.

Ramban understood clearly this stress, when he explained why this is the first time that the Torah uses the phrase (*Bereishis* 24:3) "The God of the Heavens and the earth," whereas until now the Torah has always referred to Hashem as "the God of the Heavens." He says:

> God is referred to as the God of *Eretz Yisrael*, as it states (*II Melachim* 17:26), "They do not know the manner of the God of the land." In the verse, "Who took me out of the house of my father," though, it does not say, "the God of the land," because he was in Charan or Ur Kasdim. So, too, did (*Chazal*) say, "One who lives outside *Eretz Yisrael* resembles one who does not have a God."

Ramban's words are clear. When Avraham commanded Yitzchak not to leave the land even to marry, he used the phrase, "the God of the Heavens and the earth," so as to stress the principle that was stated later by David (*I Shmuel* 26:19), "They have driven me out this day from dwelling in the inheritance of Hashem, saying, 'Go, serve other gods.'" From this *Chazal* learned that whoever lives outside *Eretz Yisrael* is as if he is without a God (*Kesubos* 110). (The commentators note that according to *halachah* a person is permitted to leave *Eretz Yisrael* to marry, but explain that as Yitzchak had been prepared as an *olah* — a "burnt offering" — he was not allowed to leave the country. One could explain this better yet. One is allowed to leave *Eretz Yisrael* to marry, but if Yitzchak would have left, he would not have returned to *Eretz Yisrael*, because the only reason he would have left would have been if "the woman does not consent to go after me.")

In any event, this remarkable *parashah* illustrates clearly the unique nature of the Jewish people. On the one hand, it is essential to maintain family purity for the continued existence of this holy people, but, on the other hand, living in *Eretz Yisrael* is of a similarly high spiritual value. Both conditions are necessary for the building of the Jewish people. Avraham commanded Yitzchak not to leave the country, and not to intermarry and assimilate with the people of the land. This is the basis for the words of *Chazal*, as we see in (*Bereishis* 17:8), " 'And I will give to you and to your seed after you ... the land of Canaan' — that you may not marry a Canaanite woman, so that your seed will not go after her" (*Yevamos* 100b). Here we find that Avraham commanded Yitzchak about both matters at the same time, because they are bound together.

As we mentioned, the commentators struggle to understand the difference between the daughters of Canaan and those of Aram Naharayim. After all, all of the people were immersed in the idolatry of the time. *Ran*, and after him various *rishonim* and *acharonim*, hold that the Canaanites were also morally degenerate, steeped in sexual offenses and disgusting acts, as we see in the verse (*Vayikra* 18:3), "And after the doings of the land of Canaan, where I am bringing you, you shall not do." Avraham's family, on the other hand, was on a high moral level, even though they were still idolaters. Thus we see from this that idolatry does not leave its mark on a person's soul as strongly as certain other sins do.

R' Avraham of Sochachow explains this: In regard to virtues and personal characteristics, children follow their parents. Questions of faith, though, depend on one's intellect and understanding, and these change in accordance with the condition of the generation. In any event, they are not passed on genetically.

It would also be possible to say that even though the people in both places were idolaters, idolatry itself is not identical in every place. There are places where idolatry involves abominable practices, such as those of Baal Peor. In other places, idolatry consists of no more than erroneous beliefs. Avraham recognized the type of idolatry they had in Canaan, and that of Aram Naharayim. He chose the idolatry that did not include abominable acts.

Kli Yakar, though, does not see any substantial difference between the two. What Avraham wanted to do was uproot Yitzchak's future wife from her surroundings and heritage, so as to save her from the influence of the area where she had been raised. By bringing her to Canaan, to a place where she was not part of the society, Yitzchak would be more easily able to influence her. Eliezer, though, changed Avraham's words and stressed that Avraham had told him to "go to my father's house and to my family," as if Avraham's concern was only his family ties to Lavan, and not his desire to remove Yitzchak's future wife from her surroundings, and to bring her to Canaan. If he had told Rivkah's relatives the truth, they would not have agreed and would have felt humiliated. Eliezer therefore changed Avraham's words, so as to persuade the family members to continue with their family affection.

◆§ In Whose Midst I Dwell

The statement made by Avraham not to take a daughter of the Canaanites "in whose midst I dwell" requires an explanation. Is this a reason for the prohibition or is there some other special meaning involved? R' Samson Raphael Hirsch says that this is a statement regarding a prohibition and the explanation for the prohibition. I am living in their midst, and therefore the family members of Yitzchak's wife will always be living in the vicinity. This would not be the case if he takes a wife from Aram Naharayim (as *Kli Yakar* above).

Or HaChayim explains the word אֲשֶׁר as "even though," so that the words mean "even though I am living in their midst." The meaning is thus that even though I am living among them, I still don't want my son to intermarry with them.

Maharal in *Gur Aryeh* says that Avraham deliberately used words that had an ambiguous meaning. He was referring to the Canaanites in general, but also to Aner, Eshkol and Mamre, in whose midst he was actually living. He deliberately excluded the last three from the general category of the Canaanites to tell us that the law which applied to the Canaanites did not apply to them, for if the woman from Aram Naharayim refused to come back to Yitzchak, the oath against intermarriage would no longer apply to Aner, Eshkol and Mamre, and would then apply only to the other Canaanites.

This is the source for the words of *Rashi* on "you will be absolved from my oath." There *Rashi* says, "Take for him a wife of the daughters of Aner, Eshkol or Mamre." At first glance, it would appear that *Rashi's* source for this is unclear. However, from the Torah's statement "in whose midst I dwell" *Rashi* learned that this prohibition was only to apply at the outset, but if there was no choice Eliezer would be absolved from his oath. Yitzchak would then be permitted to marry a woman from one of these three groups, because they were still closer to the concepts of Avraham than were the other nations.

Ramban is strongly opposed to *Rashi's* interpretation, and says, "Heaven forbid for him" to take as a wife one of the daughters of Aner, Eshkol and Mamre, who were Canaanites just as the others. This is especially true considering the fact that *Bereishis Rabbah* says that the primary decree was against them. In fact, as *Tur* explains it, Avraham specially had to warn Eliezer about these three, because they had made a covenant with him. Therefore, says *Ramban*, if the woman refused to follow him, Eliezer would be totally absolved from his oath, having done what he could and having not succeeded. And from that point, "Hashem would do what was right in His eyes." Avraham knew that in such a case Yitzchak would realize that he was forbidden to marry one of the Canaanite women, and would go to Yishmael, Lot, or the other nations.

At the end, though, *Ramban* adds that it is possible that the words "this oath" hint at the fact that Eliezer would be free from the oath of taking a wife from Aram Naharayim, but not from the oath of not taking a Canaanite woman for Yitzchak. In such a case, Eliezer was ordered to search for a wife for Yitzchak from another place, as Eliezer himself said: "And I will turn to the right or to the left." He did not, though, say that he would "return" to Canaan, because regardless of what happened, he was forbidden to take a wife for Yitzchak from there.

Ramban's view is in line with R' Yitzchak (brought in *Tosafos Kiddushin* 61b), that Avraham made Eliezer take two oaths: (a) not to take a Canaanite woman; and (b) to take a woman from his family. If the woman refused to follow after him, he would be exempt from the second oath, but would still have to keep the first one.

Regarding the condition of taking as a wife only a member of his family, Avraham used words which are open to different interpretations, "to my country and to my birthplace." Only when Eliezer repeated Avraham's words did he explain them as if Avraham had told him to, "Go to the house of my father and to my family." Did Avraham mean something else? And why did he not specify what he meant?

Rashbam explains Avraham's words in the sense that Eliezer understood them, to go "to my land," as opposed to those that are not near. Go to my birthplace in my land. The word "my birthplace" is thus explained as "my family," as it is in many places in *Tanach*. *Rashi* though, below in verse 7, explains "from my father's house and from the land of birth" to refer to Charan and Ur Kasdim.

According to *Rashi*, "the land in which I was born" is Ur Kasdim. This explanation is greeted by *Ramban* with astonishment. If "my birthplace" refers to Ur Kasdim, how could Avraham have commanded his servant to bring a wife to Yitzchak from the daughters of Cham? *Ramban* attempts to resolve this problem in various ways, but in each case rejects them. He finally concludes, as he did before, that Avraham's birthplace was not Ur Kasdim, but Aram Naharayim. Terach arrived in Ur Kasdim with his family at a later time, after Avraham was born. According to this, when Avraham said "to my land and to my birthplace," he was referring to Aram Naharayim, where his family had come from originally. Thus Eliezer's words reflect those of Avraham.

It appears that according to *Rashi* there is a difference between "my birthplace," which refers to the family, and "the land of my birthplace," which is Ur Kasdim. *Rashi* here follows his own interpretation above, at the beginning of *Parashas Lech Lecha*, where he asks what "from your land" means, as Avraham and his father had already left his land and come to Charan. Therefore, when the Torah tells us here in verse 7, "who took me from the house of my father and from the land of my birth," it refers to two departures, one with his father from Ur Kasdim and one from the house of his father. However above, in verse 4, where it states, "to my land and to my birthplace," Avraham refers to his family.

Ramban's question on *Rashi* that in verse 7 it says, "And you will

BEREISHIS — CHAYEI SARAH / 125

take a wife for my son from there," can be answered. Who says that the word "from there" refers to "the land of my birth"? Maybe it refers to what we had above: "to my land and to my birthplace" — "from there" — from the place I told you.

The *tzaddik* of Spinka in his *Chakal Yitzchak* says that when Eliezer said "my family" rather than "my birthplace," as Avraham used, he did not mean to diminish the concept, but to expand it. The family also included Lot and Yishmael. If Eliezer had told Lavan and Besuel Avraham's words exactly, they would have realized that he meant only them, and they would thus have thought that they had the power to prevent the Jewish people from being established. Eliezer threatened that Avraham had a large family, and if they did not give their daughter he would go to the other parts of the family, and Hashem's wishes would still be fulfilled.

❧ Kindness as a Basic Quality

Just as the servant understood that when Avraham said "to my land and to my birthplace" it meant to his family, he also understood that when Avraham said "and you shall take a wife for my son, for Yitzchak," he meant a woman who was worthy for Yitzchak based on her personal qualities — to be a wife "for my son" and "for Yitzchak." From this, the servant took upon himself the right to test the woman, to see if her devotion to *chessed* was of a degree that would enable her to fit into Yitzchak's household, for he knew that that was the cornerstone of Avraham's house — a house which was always open to everyone. When he set up the test, he said, "It is she whom You chose for your servant, for Yitzchak," namely that this was the woman whom Avraham meant when he said "for my son, for Yitzchak." Indeed, Eliezer ended his words with, "for You have done *chessed* (kindness) with my master." And when he repeated his words to Lavan and Besuel, he said, "That is the woman that Hashem has chosen for the son of my master." It was not a guess on Eliezer's part, but a deep-rooted understanding of the virtues required of Avraham's daughter-in-law, the wife of Yitzchak. The virtue of *chessed* is the foundation of Avraham's nation. "A bride whose eyes are beautiful — her whole body need not be examined" (*Taanis* 24). The *darshanim* explain this to mean that if a bride is "of good eye," namely that she is generous, then she has everything. There is no doubt that Eliezer fulfilled Avraham's mission completely, in his task to find a wife that would continue his deeds in the field of *chessed*.

IV.
Hashem Determines One's Wife

The *parashah* of how Yitzchak found his mate is a very long one in the Torah. There is much in the story about how a person should behave, and if that had not been the case, the Torah would not have dwelled on this episode at such great length. It is thus not surprising that every commentator attempts to analyze the messages contained in this *parashah* in his own fashion.

Chazal learned from here many basic *halachos* and lofty concepts, as we see in *Shas* and in the Midrash. The most comprehensive analysis of this is what *Chazal* tell us in *Bereishis Rabbah*: that Hashem determines the wife each man will have, and this fact is learned from the Torah, *Nevi'im* and *Kesuvim*. The source for this statement is the words of Lavan and Besuel, "This matter comes from Hashem."

R' Amiel discusses the meaning of the expression, "From Hashem a woman (is matched) to a man." Why is the woman matched to the man and not the man to the woman? So too are we told, "Forty days before the child is created, it is proclaimed in Heaven, 'The daughter of so-and-so to so-and-so,'" and there too it is the woman who is matched to the man.

He answers this according to the question asked by *Rambam* in the last of the *Shemoneh P'rakim*, *Rambam's* introduction to *Pirkei Avos*. There, *Rambam* asks: If one's free will in keeping the *mitzvos* is a major principle of Judaism, as we see from the statement of *Chazal* that "Everything is in the hands of Heaven except for *yiras shomayim*," how is it that a man's spouse is predetermined, when the first *mitzvah* in the Torah is to "be fruitful and multiply," and that — just like all other *mitzvos* — is in man's power to keep or not to keep. Thus, just as they do not proclaim in Heaven whether a person will be a *tzaddik* or a *rasha*, leaving this decision to him, the same should be true about choosing a wife.

That is the reason, says R' Amiel, that *Chazal* tell us the proclamation refers to the woman and not the man, because women were not commanded to "be fruitful and multiply" (*Yevamos* 65). A woman is not required to be married but has the option to do so, and it is therefore possible to guide her choice. That is why it says "From Hashem a woman (is matched) to a man" (*Moed Katan* 9). The absence of free will in matching a mate applies only to the woman, for she has no *mitzvah* to marry. So too did Lavan and Besuel say, "This matter comes from Hashem."

Indeed one who studies the verses here cannot deny that, as far as Rivkah's desire was concerned, Heaven preordained her marriage to Yitzchak. The entire *parashah* is a series of wonders, and a great deal of *d'rush* has been said about it. Its conclusion shows that Divine Providence (*hashgachah*) was involved. Underneath the surface of the *parashah*, we see the struggle between the good and the bad and between the profane and the holy; in the end the holy conquers the profane, and the desires of Hashem's *hashgachah* are filled.

Countless obstacles lie in the path of Eliezer as he comes to fulfill Avraham's mission — to find a wife for Yitzchak, through whom the future nation of Israel will be built. All the powers of *tumah* — of impurity — encompass Rivkah's family in an attempt to prevent the fulfillment of Hashem's mission, which, as all know, has been assigned to Avraham's seed. Already in *Parashas Vayeira* we found that Avimelech came to Avraham and asked him for a covenant, and according to the commentators that shows that he knew of Avraham's mission, and wanted to prevent any disaster from befalling his own family, at least to the third generation. Earlier in *Bereishis*, R' Samson Raphael Hirsch states, "This whole episode cannot be understood without the assumption that Avimelech had heard about the promise that had been told to Avraham." Similarly, regarding the blessing with which Lavan and his mother blessed Rivkah (*Bereishis* 24:60), "Our sister, be the mother of thousands of ten-thousands, and let your seed possess the gate of those who hate them," R' Hirsch, following in the path of the *rishonim*, says: "Such words, in the mouths of such simple people as Lavan and his mother, are only understandable if we assume that they had heard of the mission of Rivkah to become the mother of a nation."

According to the commentators, Lavan appears in this *parashah* as the symbol of wickedness, as one who runs after gifts, and as a hypocrite. The Torah tells us this only through hints. But the Torah does say: "And when he saw the earring and bracelets, and when he heard the words of Rivkah his sister (who had been given so much for a little water) ... he came to the man." So too does the Torah say, "we cannot speak to you good or evil" — implying that if they were able to speak, they would have done so, and certainly not positively. It is not a far leap from here to the conclusion of *Chazal* that their father, Besuel, refused to accept this marriage until the very last minute, and was finally struck down and died.

We also see the family using delaying tactics until the very end. Even after they had given their consent, they attempted to detain Rivkah for some time before she was to leave. When Eliezer opposed this delay, they suddenly remembered that (*Bereishis Rabbah* 60) "a woman may not be married without her consent," and ask Rivkah in sweet innocence: "Will you go with this man?" Rivkah answers categorically: "אֵלֵךְ — I will go!" *Chazal* add that she informed them, "I will go even against your will." That decision is the final victory of good over evil.

All the commentators attempt to find what the source was for *Chazal's* explanation of Rivkah's answer. *HaKesav VeHaKabalah* has a very logical explanation. He says that there is a difference between the word אֵלְכָה, which implies "I am willing to go," and אֵלֵךְ — which means an adamant decision to go. This word was decisive, and brought an end to the great amount of effort that Avraham had expended, through his servant Eliezer, to find a suitable wife for Yitzchak — one who would be a mother of the Jewish people.

Oznayim LaTorah explains beautifully that Rivkah's conduct and actions, from the very beginning to the end, show her righteousness and integrity, and how much this rose suffered among the thorns. After all, she knew less about Avraham's home than did the older members of her family, but when she saw how Eliezer conducted himself, with his prayers and thanks to Hashem, something moved within her, and she decided to leave her father's home, to believe this foreign man, and to travel on an unknown road to her ultimate destiny.

✇§ The Importance of the Mother in the Education of Her Children

Chasam Sofer in his *Toras Moshe* stresses the moral that we are to deduce from this episode, regarding the importance of the mother's own education, and the role which she plays in molding the family's life. He says:

> Avraham our Patriarch was a prince of the land, and like a king to them, and all the greatest people came to him, Avimelech, Shem and Ever. He was extremely wealthy, "and Hashem blessed Avraham in all." He had an only son from his wife Sarah, to whom he gave all his possessions. As for Yitzchak — who could compare to him? How many times did they bow and prostrate themselves in awe, and how many prayers did Avraham offer for a proper spouse for his only son, for the proper service of Hashem, as well as all worldly matters, depend on the wife, as is obvious to

anyone who is intelligent and understanding. Later, after all had agreed to give Rivkah to Yitzchak to build a home in Israel, Lavan and his mother raised obstacles. It was for this reason that Eliezer hastened matters so that the proper and good match would not unravel, so as to confound the plans of the *yetzer hara*, and he concluded it properly, speedily, and as soon as possible.

That is the essence of this *parashah* and its true meaning. As this is true for every Jewish marriage, it was all the more true for a woman who would not become the mother of a single family, but of all Israel.

Thus, the Brisker Rav comments on the *Targum* of the verse, "And Yitzchak brought her to the tent of Sarah his mother," which the *Targum* translates, "And he saw that her actions were as the actions of his mother Sarah." In the previous verse we read: "And the servant told Yitzchak all the things which he had done," which *Rashi* explains to mean that he told him of all the miracles that had occurred to him, as, for example, that he arrived in a single day. But Yitzchak felt this was not sufficient proof for him. He only took her as a wife after he saw that her actions were as those of his mother. This is only hinted at in the verse: "And Yitzchak brought her to the tent of Sarah his mother." The commentators explain that she took the place of Sarah. Then, and only then, was Yitzchak consoled over the loss of his mother.

Chazal in *Bereishis Rabbah* on our *parashah* expand on this, and explain what "place" Rivkah filled. The Midrash says that this consisted of five elements (the number five is evidently deduced from the numerical value of the letter ה at the end of the word הָאֹהֱלָה — "to the tent"): (a) a cloud had constantly stood guard at the entrance to his mother's tent; when she died, the cloud disappeared, now it reappeared; (b) the doors were now once again wide open, as they had been during Sarah's lifetime; (c) there was a special blessing in the dough, as it had been before; (d) a candle burned from one *erev Shabbos* to the next; and (e) Rivkah would separate her *challah* in *taharah* — in purity — just as his mother Sarah had done.

There are numerous explanations of the significance of these five virtues, but the main point is that when Rivkah came, she restored the tent as in the days of Sarah, and only because of that was Yitzchak consoled.

R' Samson Raphael Hirsch, following in the footsteps of *Ramban*, *Tur*, Rabbenu Bachya, *Radak* and other *rishonim*, states that the four Hebrew words וַיִּנָּחֵם יִצְחָק אַחֲרֵי אִמּוֹ — "and Yitzchak was consoled after his mother" — are among the most lofty in all the history of mankind. "A forty-year-old man cannot be consoled for the death of his very old mother, and behold he is consoled through his wife. That is the status of the woman in Israel!"

Ma'asei Hashem explains the righteousness of Yitzchak in building his new home, based on *Chazal* that Yitzchak went to bring Hagar to Avraham before he himself married Rivkah. He explains "And Yitzchak brought *her* to the tent of Sarah his mother" as referring to Hagar and not to Rivkah. He first took care of his father. Only afterwards did he marry Rivkah. This is seen from the above verse, which should have otherwise been written, "And Yitzchak brought his wife to the tent of Sarah his mother."

Ma'asei Hashem also explains the fact that Yitzchak was consoled in that he had brought a wife for his father. There is remarkable generosity here on both sides: On Rivkah's part, we see this in the fact that she consented to go after the man, and on Yitzchak's part, that he was concerned first about his father. It was the union of these exceptional traits which led to the birth of the father of the Jewish people. It is here that the glory of the mother in Israel appears in all its beauty, as *Chazal* tell us in *Bereishis Rabbah* on *Parashas Noach:* "Before the sun of Moshe had set, that of Yehoshua had risen ... Before the sun of Sarah had set, that of Rivkah had risen." That sun shines forth in all its splendor in our *parashah*, and all the elements of the story come to enhance that light. But let us return to the last stages of the *parashah* that we have been dealing with.

∽§ Let Us Call for the Maiden and Ask for Her Reply

As we have mentioned, all the commentators are puzzled by the statement, "Let us call for the maiden and ask for her reply," after Lavan and his mother had already given their consent. Why did they suddenly decide that they had to go back to Rivkah and ask if she was ready to go?

According to numerous *d'rush* works, this was all one long attempt to refuse to submit to Divine Providence. Other commentators, though, see this as an innocent and straightforward question. Abarbanel says that they simply asked her if she would go by herself, or if she preferred to be escorted. To this she replied that she was not afraid to go alone with Eliezer.

Rivash holds that Besuel kept his word and was not interested in presenting any obstacles, but her mother and brother had changed their minds, and wished to prevent Rivkah from leaving. This explanation, of course, is not in keeping with that of *Chazal* that Besuel was killed by an angel because he was the primary opponent.

Sha'arei Simchah holds that the addition of the words "afterwards she will go" is evidence that their motive was pragmatic, and that they had no intention of going back on their word. It is the Torah that points out that they were willing to have Rivkah go. Had they not agreed, they too would have died like Besuel, because one cannot defeat Hashem's plans.

Other commentators, though, hold that these last few words show that the family did not want her to go at all. *Alshech* suggests that the reason they resisted was because Eliezer had not given them anything. They saw that Eliezer carried a great deal of money, and they thought it was meant for them. After they saw that they were not the recipients of any of the money, they changed their minds.

R' Yosef Shaul Nathanson explains their refusal in a *d'rush* manner. *Chazal* tell us in *Kesubos*, "One who betroths a minor girl — both she and her father can refuse; she, because she is afraid and does not want the husband, and her father, because she may rebel and return to him." *Mordechai* in *Kiddushin* quotes *Rach*, that if the father died, her brothers cannot refuse, because as far as they are concerned the reason of "she might rebel" does not apply, as she does not return to her brothers in any event. That is the ruling in *Shulchan Aruch Even HaEzer* 56. According to *Baalei Tosafos*, Rivkah was a minor and hence Besuel had the right to refuse. Therefore, once the angel killed him, all that were left were the brothers, and they had no legal way to refuse to let the marriage go through. They therefore decided to outwit Eliezer by calling Rivkah herself, because she had the right to refuse as well. But she expressed her desire to go.

Meshech Chochmah also explains this according to *d'rush*. On the verse, "Let us call for the maiden and ask for her reply," *Rashi* quotes *Chazal* that a woman cannot be married against her will. The *Midrash* brings this differently: "One may not marry an orphan against her will." Therefore, says *Meshech Chochmah*, as long as her father was alive, they told Eliezer, "Here is Rivkah before you; take her and go." But after Besuel died and she became an orphan, they said, "Let us call for the maiden and ask for her reply," as an orphan can only be married of her own free will.

This entire *parashah* is full of hints, and there is much *d'rush* concerning it. Even *S'forno*, who normally deals with *p'shat*, resorts here to *d'rush*. After Rivkah agreed, it states, "And the servant took Rivkah and went." Why is Eliezer suddenly referred to here as "the servant"? *S'forno* answers that here the words "and he took" refers to the fact that Eliezer was acting as Avraham's agent, which means that from that time on Rivkah was already married. As a result, Yitzchak's servant now became Rivkah's servant as well.

If that is the way *S'forno* explains it, it is not surprising that *Imrei Shefer* goes even further in explaining the *d'rush* here. *Chazal* in *Kesubos* 48 said: "She is always in the father's care, until she enters the *chupah*. If the agents of the father went with the agents of the husband, she is still in the father's care. If the agents for the father delivered her to the agents of the husband, she is in the care of the husband." *Imrei Shefer* provides an innovative interpretation here, which is basically what *S'forno* says. As long as Rivkah was under her father's care, even if she was traveling along the way with the maidens that escorted her, who were her father's agents, Eliezer was not yet considered her servant. It therefore says, "And they went after the man." But after they gave her to the husband's agent, as it says, "And the servant took Rivkah," she went into her husband's care, and Eliezer became her servant.

☙ All's Well that Ends Well

The meeting of Yitzchak and Rivkah was at the crossroads, when Yitzchak went out לָשׂוּחַ (normally translated "to meditate") in the field. Each commentator explains the word differently. According to Abarbanel, he went for a walk in the fields. According to *Rashbam*, he went to plant trees. *Pa'aneach Raza* also explains this along these lines, but he says that Yitzchak was symbolically about to plant a tree in Israel, for the Torah states (*Devarim* 20:19), "Man is the tree of the field."

Chazal say that לָשׂוּחַ means that he went "to pray." Abarbanel too, in spite of his interpretation, tends to follow *Chazal's* interpretation. He says that the major struggle against idolatry at that time was against those who worshiped the sun. Thus, the reason that Yitzchak instituted the *Minchah* ritual was to stress that the sun is not a deity, but that it too was created by Hashem.

Kli Yakar says that because of Yitzchak's prayer as the sun was setting, *Chazal* tell us that "a person should always be careful about praying *Minchah*, because Eliyahu was only answered at *Minchah*." Yitzchak, too, was answered then. He went out "to meditate in the fields," and immediately, "he raised his eyes and behold, camels were approaching." He prayed and was answered immediately.

The *parashah* ends on a happy note. Righteousness and the good triumph over evil. Yitzchak found the one he had been looking for, the mother of the people of Israel. The *parashah* ends with, "And she became his wife and he loved her." *Meleches Machsheves*, following R' Samson Raphael Hirsch in this regard, comments that here the Torah wants to teach us the proper way of marital love in Israel. And this is the way R' Samson Raphael Hirsch explains it:

> This is a characteristic which, thank God, was never abandoned by the seed of Avraham and Sarah, Yitzchak and Rivkah. The longer she was his wife, the more he loved her. This example of the marriage of the first Jewish son is the basis for all marriages. Most marriages in Israel are based not on lust, but on careful intelligent consideration. Parents and relatives discuss among themselves if the young ones are suitable for one another. Most marriages in the non-Jewish world are based on what they call "love," and one has but to look at all the descriptions in novels, taken from life, to see immediately how different is the love before a marriage to that after it. The love afterwards is insignificant and tasteless. How different it is from how it is imagined to be. That "love" is blind, and every step in the future will be a disappointment. That, however, is not the case with marriages in Israel, where we are told, "And she became his wife and he loved her." There the marriage was not the peak of love, but the source of love.
>
> It was from that source of love, generosity, and righteousness that our Patriarch Yaakov — the father of the Jewish people — developed.

Toldos – תולדות

I.
An Eternal Struggle Between Yaakov and Esav

According to the commentators, the struggle in the womb between the two unborn sons of Rivkah was an indication of the future relations between Yaakov and Esav and an allusion to their eternal struggle. From the very beginning, this struggle has encompassed all the confrontations between good and evil, between the spiritual and the material, and between light and darkness, that are personified by the two brothers. The forces of evil in all their different variations are associated with the evil Esav, who is the *yetzer hara*, while the forces of good are associated with Yaakov.

Abarbanel clarifies the response given to Rivkah when she went to seek an answer from Hashem. The two sons will be two nations, who will be different from one another even *racially*, as if one had been an Indian and the other a German. They will also be the sources of other nations which will branch off from them. There will be perpetual war between the two, and unceasing strife throughout history. As Esav represents materialism, Yaakov represents spiritualism, and the fate of the struggle has already been decided: "The older will serve the younger."

Abarbanel gives historical details of the actual warfare between Yaakov and Esav. There were kings in Edom even before the Jews became a nation, but David subjugated Edom and placed his own officers over it. Similarly, in the time of the second *Beis HaMikdash*, Hyrcanos defeated Edom and forced its people to convert.

These examples by Abarbanel are by no means a complete list of the eternal war between Jerusalem and Edom. *Chazal* refer to the exile by Rome as "the exile of Edom," because it is after this exile that *Mashiach* will come, as it states, "and his hand was clutching the heel of Esav." It is possible that the Romans began to be referred to as Edomites as a result of the reign of Herod. Herod was an Edomite slave who subjugated Judea, and it was he who brought about the catastrophe on his people, by enslaving it to Rome, and by making his sons — who kowtowed to Rome — kings over Judea. Later, when war came, Herod's sons joined the Romans and fought against their own nation and country.

Another hypothesis is that the Edomites, who had converted and had become Jews by compulsion, later became the standard-bearers of Christianity in the Roman world, and that is the reason that Christianity is identified with Edom.

Edom symbolizes the wicked kingdom, which comprises all the forces of evil from time immemorial, which has always clashed with the spiritual world of Israel in different ways and forms. The ancient nucleus of this confrontation appears in the struggle between the two sons even before they are born. The commentators demonstrate the growth from this nucleus throughout all stages of Jewish history. *Sefer Chassidim* 833 says that Hashem deliberately implanted hatred between the two even while they were still in the womb. Hashem wanted this hostility to serve as an iron curtain between Yaakov and Esav.

The Chassidic works yield pearls of wisdom about this struggle inside the womb. At first Esav pushed to leave the womb, but later changed his mind so that Yaakov would not emerge either. That is the character of the wicked Esav in all generations. He is willing to relinquish everything, if by that means he can ensure that Yaakov does not study Torah.

Chazal make a point of stressing that the struggle inside the womb occurred whenever Rivkah stood before synagogues or passed by idolatrous places. The commentators also see this *parashah* as being an introduction to a later *parashah*, where Rivkah demonstrates her love for Yaakov. The granting of the *bechorah* — the rights of the firstborn — to Yaakov had already been decided in the womb, when Rivkah was told that "the older will serve the younger." Only she knew that, but not Yitzchak, and that was why she helped Yaakov receive his father's blessings that were meant for the firstborn.

Different commentaries and *d'rush sefarim* discuss at length everything said to Rivkah, for this contains a host of ideas and visions. Jewish history is encapsulated here in just a few sentences. It is the purpose of Israel, says *Malbim*, to have the spiritual dimension control the material one. Yaakov was the son that represented the spiritual dimension, and that was why he was to dominate the materialism of Esav. Chronologically, matter always comes into being before its purpose is achieved, but in planning and concept, the purpose is envisioned first. So, too, Esav was born first even though Yaakov represents the purpose of creation. In the beginning of human history, before Avraham, materialism dominated in the world; afterwards Avraham and his offspring made their appearance in the historical arena. All of this is contained in the verse, "and his hand was clutching the heel of Esav." Hashem wanted to prepare a nation in the world that would be inspired from the spirit above, and would be a receptacle for prophecy and *kedushah*. This preparation was finally revealed in the personality of Yaakov, the father of the twelve tribes, who already in his mother's womb struggled with evil. Good opposed evil from the very first moment they appeared. Esav and Yaakov are symbols of the mighty forces which have been clashing in the world from its creation to the present. The conclusion of this struggle is also contained in the *parashah*, and has been engraved in fiery lettering, through the prophets and Sages of Israel, from the beginning.

◆§ If So, Why Do I Exist?

Or HaChayim wonders at Rivkah, for according to *Rashi* she regretted becoming pregnant. Could it be that just because of physical distress she would be willing to do without children? As a result, *Or HaChayim* interprets this episode differently. Rivkah was afraid that she might not give birth to a live child because of the struggle she felt in her womb. That was why she went to ask from Hashem that her pregnancy should result in a live birth. *Sha'ar Bas Rabim* quotes the interpretation of *Yerushalmi* that what Rivkah said was, "If I have such great pain, I must ask Hashem what the end will be with this struggle."

Kli Yakar, though, says that Rivkah's concerns were spiritual. She saw this struggle at the entrances to the synagogues and, *lehavdil*, to the idolatrous temples, and became afraid that there might *chas veshalom* be two deities in the world. She therefore went to seek the cause of this struggle. When she was told that there were two children in her womb, her fears subsided, and she realized that there is only one God in the world, who controls both good and evil.

The Chassidic works deal with the idea in almost the same way. Rivkah was not afraid of there being two deities in the world, but that her child might shift back and forth between good and evil, torn between the synagogue and the temples of idolatry. Such a child could very well be a hypocrite without a conscience. She was told that this was not the case. There were two children in her womb, one all good and the other all evil, and that was the cause of the struggle. This allayed her fears, and she lovingly accepted the misery caused by the struggle, in the knowledge that one son would be devoted entirely to Hashem.

What is very interesting is the interpretation of *Tur*. The struggle was entirely natural. Esav was hairy and Yaakov was smooth skinned. Esav's hair bothered Yaakov, and he tried to get away from it. This interpretation is different from that of Ibn Ezra, who says that the two children were in separate sacs, and only when they were born were both sacs opened at the same time. If there were two sacs, Yaakov couldn't be bothered by Esav's hair. *Yeshu'os Malko* says that the two boys were miraculously in a single sac, and it was essential for the two to struggle, so that they should not develop as Siamese twins.

The Brisker Rav gives a reason along *d'rush* lines for the struggle. *Chazal* in *Berachos* 3 say on the verse (*Yeshayahu* 38:1), "In those days Chizkiyahu was sick, and Yeshayahu the prophet, the son of Amotz, came unto him," that when Yeshayahu visited the king, a bitter argument broke out between the two, as to whether Chizkiyahu was required to have children after he found out that the wicked Menasheh would be one of his descendants. Yeshayahu rebuked Chizkiyahu for not fulfilling the *mitzvah* of *piryah v'rivyah* — "to be fruitful and multiply." Chizkiyahu replied that he had decided on this step when it had been prophetically revealed to him that one of his descendants would be wicked. Chizkiyahu also knew that his descendants would include generations of *tzaddikim* (righteous people), such as Yoshiyahu and Tzidkiyahu, but even so did not want to father his son Menasheh and the wicked Amon. Yeshayahu conceded that Chizkiyahu's fears were justified, but told him that one has no choice but to fulfill Hashem's commandment. If one has been commanded to do something, there is no way that one can avoid the commandment.

And She Went to Inquire of Hashem

Rashi explains that she went to the *beis midrash* of Shem and Ever to ask what the end would be. Some Chassidic sources say that what *Rashi* meant was that she thought this was one child with a double soul, who sometimes chose the *beis midrash* and at other times chose idolatry. She therefore went to ask which of the two forces would win in the end. She was then told that she was not carrying one son with a double soul, but two sons.

Ramban disagrees with *Rashi* that Rivkah went to see what the end would be. He says that wherever the Torah uses the concept of דְּרִישָׁה

(which we translated above as "to inquire") it also refers to prayer. She went to pray, as we see in the verse (*Tehillim* 34:5), דָּרַשְׁתִּי אֶת ה' — "I sought Hashem." *Ran*, though, in his *d'rashos*, disagrees with *Ramban*, because there is a verse which states (*II Melachim* 8:8), "And the king said to Hazael, 'Take a present in your hand, and go, meet the man of Hashem, and inquire (וְדָרַשְׁתָּ) of Hashem by him, saying: Shall I recover of this disease?'" Thus we see that the root דרש can certainly mean an inquiry.

Abarbanel too disagrees with *Rashi*. According to him, Rivkah went to ask Avraham, and not, as *Rashi* states, that she went to the *beis midrash* of Shem and Ever. Abarbanel also explains the verse, לָמָּה זֶה אָנֹכִי (which we translated above as "why do I exist") in an original fashion. Rivkah said as follows: "Both of us (Sarah and I) were barren and were unable to have children. Hashem then heard our prayers and gave us sons. Why should I suffer more than you (Sarah) with the pains of pregnancy? Why just I (אָנֹכִי)?"

She was answered that her pregnancy was a normal one in the case of twins. Carrying two children is twice as painful as carrying one. According to *Rashbam*, that was the answer to allay her worries about the struggle in her womb. All the rest was an additional prophecy. The prophet who told her that she would have twins also told her the future of her children and their fate.

Ramban, too, explains the verse in this way. He says that once she understood what was causing the struggle, she was no longer worried and was at ease.

Or HaChayim also sees these verses as dealing with one issue — to clarify the reason for the struggle. There would be two distinct nations, each fighting for its own survival, separate from their birth, and in the end, "the older will serve the younger." It was not that she was suffering from any disease, but what was happening in her womb was a reflection of things to come.

"You have a nation which is similar in build and characteristics to another nation," says R' Samson Raphael Hirsch, "just as the European nations resemble one another. But this is not a struggle of two nations, but of two *goyim* — two separate ideologies, which will leave their imprint on history." "And the older will serve the younger" — it is like a balance scale: sometimes the pen is on top, and other times the sword. In the end it will become clear that (*Zecharyah* 4:6), " 'Not by might, nor by power, but by My spirit,' says Hashem." Brute force will vanish from the world and on that day "Hashem will be one and His name will be one."

Sefas Emes gives a Chassidic explanation of "the older will serve the younger." *Chazal* said that "if he is worthy, he will serve," means that if *Yaakov* is worthy, then Esav will serve him. *Sefas Emes*, though, interprets the verse to refer to Esav. If he is worthy and is willing to be subservient to Yaakov and accept his authority, then there is hope for him to survive, and if not, then the verdict is sealed for him to perish from the earth.

↜§ The Fetus in Halachah

Our *parashah* is a source for clarifications in *halachah* as to whether a fetus is considered one's child or not. The Torah here refers to the two fetuses as Rivkah's children, when it states, "and the children (הַבָּנִים) struggled within her." *Maharshal* in *Yam shel Shlomo* in the third chapter of *Yevamos* deduces from here that *halachically* a fetus is considered to be a child. Other commentators say that the Torah used this language because that is what the fetus will eventually become, as where the Torah writes, "when the dead one dies," or "when the fallen one falls," where the language is used even though the event has not yet taken place.

HaDrush VeHaIyun brings proof to *Yam shel Shlomo* from *Bava Basra* 142, regarding somebody who makes a *kinyan* — "an act of acquisition" — on behalf of a fetus. The *halachah* in such a case is that the fetus does not acquire the object unless that fetus is the child of the one who makes the *kinyan*. Thus we see that the fetus is referred to in the Torah as בֵּן — "a son."

But *HaDrush VeHaIyun* asks a major question on this *halachah*. *Chazal* in *Bava Basra* 63 tell us:

> A Levite who sold a field to an Israelite, and said to him, "Provided the *ma'aser rishon* — the first tithe — is given to me," it (the *ma'aser rishon*) is his. And if he said, "To me and my sons," and he died, the tithe is to be given to his sons ... And why should this be so, when a person cannot transfer possession to another of something which does not yet exist?

On this, *Ri* in *Tosafos* says that the *gemara* refers here to a case where the man's sons are already living. The implication, then, is that the condition made by the Levite would not apply to his as yet unborn sons. Thus we see that before it is born, a fetus is not considered to be a child.

Revid HaZahav also argues with *Maharshal*. In *Yevamos* (35), the *gemara* tells us that R' Yochanan holds, regarding a woman whose husband died without any children (where the *halachah* is that his brother must either marry her through *yibum* or give her *chalitzah*, thus freeing her to marry others), that if a man died and his wife was pregnant, it is considered as if he died childless, because the Torah says "and he has no son," implying one that was born, and not a fetus. Even Reish Lakish, who argues with R' Yochanan, does not dispute that a fetus is not yet considered one's child, but holds that we must wait to see if the woman will give birth to a child that will live. Similarly, we are told in *Bava Basra* 142 that "and he has no child" refers to an actual child, and not a fetus.

Torah Sheleimah also brings the view of *Itur* (*Sha'ar* 2, *Hil. Shechitah*), that the Torah prohibition against slaughtering a mother and its young on the same day only applies to its young that was alive at the time the mother was slaughtered. If the mother was slaughtered and the young found inside her was then slaughtered on the same day, there is no prohibition in this, because a child is not called such until it emerges into the world. This we see in the verse, "Behold you will conceive, and will give birth to a son."

Vayosef Avraham, though, by R' Avraham Lefkowitz, brings the opinion of *rishonim* in a number of places that a fetus is also considered one's child. The source of this is in his commentary to our *parashah*.

⋄§ Train the Youth in Accordance with His Way

The two sons in this *parashah* play a decisive role in *hashkafah*. The different commentaries and *d'rush* works are filled with this. I would like to bring here a very surprising and striking view on this by R' Samson Raphael Hirsch. In discussing the development of Yaakov and Esav, he quotes *Bereishis Rabbah* 63:14, that until the age of thirteen the boys attended the same school, and afterwards they separated. R' Hirsch uses this to voice strong criticism against the fact that all boys receive the same education, without anyone paying attention to their individual characteristics and abilities. Among other things, he says (on *Bereishis* 25:27) that *Chazal* did not refrain from revealing deficiencies in the acts of our great forefathers; and it was just through that, that they enhanced and exalted the message for future generations. Here too, by saying that Yaakov and Eisav both received an identical upbringing, the Sages suggest to us that the differences between them (verse 24) were not taken into account. By pointing this out, the Sages wish to point out to us that we should be careful to heed the great principle of education (*Mishle* 22:6), "Train the youth in accordance with his way."

> Education must be directed in accordance with the child's special path in the future, which is in keeping with his characteristics and

the latent tendencies in the depths of his soul, and must educate him toward the holy goal of a pure human and Jewish life. In its essence, the Jewish role is a single and unique one, but the ways it is realized are many and varied, in accordance with the varied nature of man, and the different ways of life which result from this.

When the sons of Yaakov gathered to hear the blessing of their father, and he saw them as the future tribes of Israel, he did not only see priests and religious leaders — here was the tribe of Levi, the tribe of the monarchy, the tribe of merchants, the tribe of farmers and the tribe of warriors; the entire nation stood there before his eyes, with all its multi-faceted qualities, in all the ways it would develop; and he blessed them all, "each one according to his blessing, he blessed them" (*Bereishis* 49:28), each one according to his own unique qualities, because the covenant of Hashem that had been sealed with Avraham required a healthy, whole and fresh nation; its aim was to build the full life of a nation, with all its variegated forms, in order to direct them all to the one great task: to preserve the way of Hashem, to act justly and fairly. Strength and bravery, no less than thought and emotion, will find heroes who worship Hashem, and with their different occupations, they will all be performing the great task of the community.

It is just because of this — "train the youth in accordance with his way" — that each must be educated for the great goal based on his own personal way, in accordance with the future which can be foreseen for him based on his qualities. One who places Yaakov and Esav on the same study bench, and teaches them both together the same way toward a life of study and thought, is guaranteed to ruin one of them. Yaakov will draw from the well of wisdom with increasing desire, while Esav will only wait for the day where he can toss all the old books behind him, and together with them the whole great purpose in life, which he only recognized from one point of view — one which by his nature he detested.

Had Yitzchak and Rivkah penetrated more keenly into the soul of Esav, had they asked themselves how the latent energy, strength and flexibility in Esav's soul could be harnessed toward the ways of Hashem, then the future גִּבּוֹר — "mighty man" — might not merely be a גִּבּוֹר צַיִד — "an excellent hunter" — but he could be a "mighty man before Hashem." Yaakov and Esav, with all their differences, could have remained brothers who complemented one another in their spirits and in their ways of life; at the very outset, Esav's sword would then have made a covenant with

Yaakov's spirit; and who knows what difference that would make in history. But that was not the way it happened. "And the boys grew up." Only after the boys grew into men were all astonished to see that even though both came from the same mother's womb, were educated and trained together, they were so totally different from one another in their actions.

This analysis comes from the distinguished R' Samson Raphael Hirsch, who perceives all human development as dependent upon coordination between the person's innate qualities and the way he is educated.

II.
The Sale of the Birthright

The *parashah* of *Toldos* serves as an introduction to the selection of Yaakov's offspring to receive the Torah and inherit the land, and an explanation of why the younger brother, Yaakov, was chosen over Esav, to continue the traditions of Avraham and Yitzchak. The most striking point in the events leading to this is the sale of the rights of the firstborn and its transfer from Esav to Yaakov. This birthright (*bechorah*) symbolizes spiritual and moral superiority, as we will see. But even if the sale appears to be no more than a deception and a ruse by Yaakov, and the exploitation of Esav's predicament at a critical juncture, the fact is that the chain of events before the transfer of the birthright and after it show us that this action was required by circumstances. Esav was simply not fit to carry out the mission that had been imposed on Avraham and Yitzchak, and a kingdom of priests and holy nation could not have been built from him. In the end, everyone, including Yitzchak who had been in doubt about it, agreed that the task was to be placed on Yaakov's shoulders.

The *parashah* begins with the prophecy told to Rivkah even before her children were born, that "the older will serve the younger." And already in their youth, the differences between the two become apparent. Yaakov continued with the traditions of his fathers, as an אִישׁ תָּם יֹשֵׁב אֹהָלִים — "guileless man, dwelling in tents," while Esav followed in the footsteps of Nimrod and those like him, and became a hunter. Yitzchak loved Esav, but that was a love which was dependent on an outside factor, because "he gave him venison to eat." Rivkah, though, loved Yaakov, only because of his behavior and because of the prophecy which she had been told, and not because of any external reason.

Esav's rejection of all spiritual possessions is seen in his readiness to sell his birthright for a little bit of food, and in his taking of wives from the daughters of Cheis, who were "a source of grief to Yitzchak and Rivkah." On the other hand, from the very first moment Yaakov listens to his father not to marry a woman from that land, and he, like his father before him, will only marry a woman who is of his family. Only afterwards does Esav copy Yaakov and take a daughter of Yishmael, to "add to his wives." But that deed does not change his environment and his view of the world. Because of this, and especially as Yaakov is the firstborn in regard to his spiritual qualities, he deserves his father's blessing which is meant for Yitzchak's "older son."

Yitzchak, though, does not know about the sale of the birthright, and, according to *Chazal*, is not aware of Esav's spiritual deterioration, because Esav keeps asking him all types of *halachic* questions, such as how to take *ma'aser* from straw. Yitzchak thus calls Esav and orders him to take the action — to hunt and bring him a dish of food — which will result in his receiving the blessing.

But it is Hashem's will that Rivkah should hear this. Rivkah knows full well the true nature of Esav, and she remembers the prophecy. She arranges matters, with the will of Hashem, to have the blessing which Yitzchak meant for Esav to be given to Yaakov. In the end, Yitzchak too agrees to this unexpected development, and says, "Let him be blessed."

This is the meaning of the verses and their intent, from the beginning of this *parashah* until the end. Thus, as mentioned, we must regard this *parashah* as an introduction to the later development of the choosing of the seed of Yaakov as a kingdom of priests and a holy nation.

~§ The Rights of the Firstborn in Those Days

Ramban says that it is possible that the law stating the firstborn receives a double portion in the inheritance did not yet apply in those days. The main aspect of the birthright was "to inherit the father's prestige and his authority, that [the firstborn son] should be more respected and have greater distinction than the younger one." That is why Esav said, "I am your son, your firstborn," meaning that he should be the one to receive the blessing.

Ramban reaches this conclusion because of Ibn Ezra's view, that the reason that Esav sold his birthright and was not concerned about its effects on his inheritance was that by that time his father Yitzchak was poor, having used up all the money left him by Avraham. Ibn Ezra says that proof of this is that Yitzchak needed Esav to hunt for him for food. Yaakov, too, had nothing in his father's house, and did not have fine clothes. When he left his father's house, he left with nothing, as we see when he asked Hashem, "and if He gives me bread to eat and clothes to wear." Had his father's house been a wealthy one, his mother would have given him money for his journey.

Ramban does not agree with this assumption, and says about Ibn Ezra: "His reasoning was blinded here." According to him, Yitzchak was wealthy all his life, as the Torah itself tells us that he returned and became wealthy in the land of the Philistines, to the extent that they became jealous of him. Hashem had promised him, "I will be with you and I will bless you," and a blessing implies wealth and happiness. How then could he have lost all of this to the extent that at the end of his days he had no food to eat?

Ramban therefore maintains that Yitzchak told Esav to bring him venison, because by means of that gift their souls would be linked together, and he would be able to bless him. Alternately, he knew in his heart that eating would make him joyful, and would cause Hashem's spirit to rest on him. The reason Yaakov's parents did not give him money for the journey was so that Esav should not try to ambush him and kill him. At the time the firstborn evidently did not get a double portion of the inheritance, and therefore Esav was quite willing to forgo the birthright, which he only saw as a spiritual burden which he was not interested in.

Abarbanel, too, maintains that Yaakov did not want the birthright for material pleasure, and it is even possible that in the agreement between the brothers they decided that Esav would still receive the double portion. Yaakov's concern was only about the spiritual promise that Hashem had made to Avraham and Yitzchak. In his heart, he was doubtful whether Esav could be the heir and the one who would carry on the rich spiritual inheritance. He expressed his concern and thoughts when Esav demanded that Yaakov prepare him some food. Yaakov then told Esav, "If you are the firstborn, then you must fulfill your obligations to your family, and don't expect me to support you." Esav answered that Yaakov was right, and that indeed as far as he, Esav, was concerned, he had no interest in the birthright.

This path is followed by *Ran*, too, in his explanation. He adds that Esav came from the field when all were in mourning for Avraham. Esav was not disturbed by this terrible loss, and in fact showed only his interest in gorging himself. Yaakov saw that the birthright was not suitable for such a person, and did everything to save the family's honor.

Ralbag maintains that Yaakov wanted the birthright only so as to receive his father's blessing, and not for any other purpose. The custom at the time was that the firstborn received an additional blessing, above the blessing received by his other brothers, as we see in the blessing of Yaakov to Yosef's sons. Yaakov bought the right to this blessing from Esav, because he realized its value. Esav, on the other hand, ridiculed it.

Rashi, too, maintains that Yaakov wanted to rescue the spiritual service of Hashem from Esav's hands, that being the position filled by the firstborn at the time. He suggested to Esav, "sell today," namely in a clear and decisive sale, as clear as the day. Esav declared that he had no interest in the birthright, because the *mitzvos* involved in the service of Hashem could result in the person's death if he did not carry them out properly. He thus agreed to sell the birthright.

For what? The Torah says clearly, "For a lentil stew." But *Rashbam* gives his own novel interpretation — that the lentil stew was just the way the sale was ratified, as was evidently the custom in those days. Yaakov paid Esav as much money as he asked for, and bought the birthright for its full price. Esav thought little of the birthright because he was a hunter, and he could at any time be torn apart by a wild animal and die. He therefore thought nothing of the inheritance it might bring him if his father died. Thus, when he received a good price, and, in addition, was given the lentil stew which he loved, to ratify the sale, he was quite satisfied.

S'forno also holds that the lentils served only as the way to seal the agreement. He describes the sequence in the following fashion: Esav arrived from the hunt so tired and confused that he did not even recognize the food that he loved, and simply referred to it as הָאָדֹם, הָאָדֹם הַזֶּה — "this red, red one." When everyone else saw that Esav no longer referred to things by their names but by their colors, they called him *Edom*, because of the way he became red all over when he devoured the food. Yaakov agreed to give Esav to eat and said, "If you are so preoccupied with your material work to the extent that you become so tired, you certainly will not be able to devote yourself to the work of the firstborn, which requires close attention and concentration." Esav agreed that that was true. "I am going to die of tiredness, and I cannot carry out the work of the firstborn." He thus voluntarily gave up the birthright. Yaakov then asked him to swear about this, so that he would not have any complaints later.

✥ Heresy and Relinquishment of the Legacy to the Land

There are commentators who view Esav's attitude towards the birthright as demonstrating his disbelief in Hashem, and also his renouncement of his legacy to the land. *Ma'asei Hashem* says that the sanctity of the birthright in those days was linked to acknowledging that Hashem is the master of the entire universe, and that He created everything. It was based on this recognition that it was ordained that the first of everything belongs to Hashem, such as *challah* (the *Kohen's* share of the dough), the first fruits, the first shearing, etc. All of these things express the idea that there was a start to creation and that it was created by Hashem. The birthright also symbolizes the recognition of Hashem and the beginning of the world. According to *Chazal*, Esav denied all this, and that was why he despised the birthright and offered to sell it for a lentil stew — as a way of displaying his heresy. It was thus essential that Yaakov, the great believer in the Lordship of Hashem — who continued in the traditions of his fathers — should acquire this possession for himself, and should thus announce to all that there is a Master in the world, and a beginning and a start to creation. This act of acquiring the birthright was thus a demonstrative gesture, showing all that Hashem is the Creator of the world and the One who guides it.

Chizkuni says — and the idea is already found in *Midrash Lekach Tov* — that Yaakov wanted the birthright so that he would be the one in whom the promise of the inheritance of the land would be fulfilled. Esav, who knew Yaakov's intentions, agreed voluntarily to this, and said to him:

> I am giving you this promise voluntarily and as an absolute acquisition. In any event, Hashem said that "the fourth generation will return here," and I myself would stand to gain nothing from this promise. "Behold, I will die" as a stranger in a foreign land, and what do I have to worry about the fourth generation, after my death?

All the commentators attempt to interpret the matter of the selling of the birthright differently from the way it appears superficially. It is surely not that Yaakov cheated Esav and exploited a momentary weakness in order to acquire the birthright, as we see when Esav cried later, "He has held me back these two times." This is the direction used by most commentators, from the time the Torah was given to this day.

HaKesav VeHaKabalah says that Yaakov was not the one who

BEREISHIS — TOLDOS / 147

proposed the trade, but it was Esav who spoke derisively of the birthright and laughed at its value. Yaakov then said to him:

> You talk as if the birthright is already sold (*mechurah* — rather than *michrah* — "sell"), because according to you it has no value. That being the case, I claim it as ownerless (*hefker*). And Esav continued to mock the birthright even after he had eaten his fill, showing that his desire to be rid of it was not because he had momentarily preferred the food, but that he wished to be free of something he truly scorned. "And Esav despised the birthright," even after he had eaten, thereby indicating that he had indeed sold the birthright to Yaakov as a full and final sale, the way one says: "Take this thing that I do not want at all."

The Nullifying of Idolatry

It would seem that the *parashah* of the birthright underscores the fact that not only had Yaakov acquired the birthright, but that this event marked the termination of the birthright as a value in itself, whereby the firstborn played an important part in the idolatrous practices of those days. Yaakov showed by his action, for all future generations, that a person's value does not depend on his birth, but on his own spiritual qualities and superiority. Above, we brought the view of *Ma'asei Hashem* that the concept of the birthright expresses faith in the creation of the world and that it was created by a Creator. But in the idolatrous world before the Torah was given, this concept was corrupted and perverted. It was detached from its original purpose and intention, and became a part of the idolatrous practices that were meant to ensure fertility in man.

We find evidence of this perversion in later generations, when the king of Moab sacrificed his own firstborn son (*II Melachim* 26). *Chazal* in *Mechilta* on *Shemos* 13 tell us that in Egypt they even made their firstborn into gods; Hashem therefore killed all the firstborn in Egypt. The Torah canceled the service of the firstborn, and left them with only one right, to inherit a double portion. The rest of the *mitzvos* that apply to the firstborn today are only remembrances of the exodus from Egypt.

All this comes to teach us that a person is not to be evaluated by his birth, but by his spiritual characteristics. Only after Hashem had smitten all the firstborn in Egypt was there a short time that the firstborn played a role, and only in commemoration of the exodus from Egypt. Afterwards, when the Jews sinned with the Golden Calf, the firstborn were replaced by the Levites, and the firstborn no longer appear as a spiritual factor. (*Ramban* uses this concept later to explain the reason for the argument by Korach.)

This opposition to the worship of the firstborn is to be found a number of times in the Torah. Avraham ousted Yishmael his firstborn. Yitzchak recognized the *bechorah* of Yaakov. Yaakov transferred the *bechorah* to Yosef. Yaakov crossed his hands and placed his right hand on Ephraim. By the orders of Hashem, Shmuel chose David, who was the youngest of his brothers. David, by order of the prophet, chose Shlomo, who was younger than his brothers. All these events are not mere coincidence, but they are meant to teach us that the superiority of a person depends on *his conduct*. If the son follows in his father's ways, he has a double virtue, because then there is the combination of the continuity of generations and the son's own personal attributes.

This idea is expressed clearly in our *parashah*. Yaakov was afraid "that this wicked man will be the one to stand and offer sacrifices." He saw Esav coming from the field tired and excited after having killed, with his eyes only on gluttony, without any spiritual values. Yaakov therefore came to teach all future generations that the firstborn only has a *financial* right, but the special *attributes* of *bechorah* depend on the person's personality. The stressing of this principle continues afterwards in the greatest men of the following generations. It is possible that what Yaakov meant when he said, "today" ("sell to me today"), was that he was abolishing the whole concept of the birthright, as it was understood at the time, as a spiritual value, but he was not coming to abrogate the legal definition of the birthright regarding financial rights.

I have found something along these lines in *Akeidah*, who explains this whole incident at length. *Akeidah* says that one has the right to fight for spiritual possessions and to take them away from those that are not worthy of them. He states (*Akeidas Yitzchak* 23):

> One is obligated to try diligently to return the virtue of perfection to the good and just, as is fitting. And from him and on, this *bechorah* was weakened and its force was nullified, and it was no longer able to prevent a good person from achieving the attainments of which he is worthy, neither in terms of justice nor in terms of the law.

Later he says:

> Yaakov understood with his intelligence, as had occurred with the blessings and with this matter itself, that because of the previous conditions the right was being transferred to one who was unworthy of it, and Hashem was not pleased with him (i.e., Esav).

[Yaakov] was zealous for Hashem and said: "How can this wicked one get up and sacrifice? That cannot be, because a flatterer cannot come before Him. If I do not hurry to shift Hashem's good to me, then neither I nor he will have it." He therefore sacrificed himself for the *bechorah* and abolished it, and returned Hashem's abundance to the place where His name and praise will be recognized.

According to *Chazal*, this *parashah* does not come to extol the virtue of the birthright in the fact that it was transferred to Yaakov, but rather to stress that it was nullified as something which granted the person spiritual rights. These rights are dependent only on man's good deeds, and on nothing else. That is why the Torah said, "My son, My firstborn, Israel."

III.
Forerunners for the Hatred of Israel

The major factor in the argument between Yitzchak and Avimelech about the wells was simply *sinas Yisrael* — anti-Semitism — which has been characteristic of all arguments and disputes between Israel and other nations, from those times to the present.

The Torah gives as the reason why Yitzchak's wells were sealed up as the jealousy of the Philistines for Yitzchak. Avimelech, who once made a covenant with Avraham not to lie to him or to his children or grandchildren, converts his nation's jealousy into *action*, and orders Yitzchak to be evicted, telling him (*Bereishis* 26:16), "Go from us, because you are much wealthier than we are." Yitzchak moves to another place, but the hatred still pursues him. There, too, they argue with him over the wells which he has dug. Then, when Avimelech comes to him and asks that they sign a new treaty between themselves, Yitzchak rebukes him and says, "You hate me, so why do you come to me?"

Avimelech's answer is a paradigm of the approach of the non-Jews to the Jews, already at that time. Avimelech prides himself in the fact that, "We have done you nothing but good, and we sent you away in peace." He wants Yitzchak to appreciate the fact that he was not sent to a concentration camp, but was allowed to leave the country after his wells and his land had been confiscated.

Bereishis Rabbah 64 gives a marvelous parable to explain this strange view of Avimelech. There was once a lion which had a bone stuck in its throat. It called out and offered a reward to anyone that would remove the bone. Finally a bird with a long beak came, stuck its beak into the lion's throat, and removed the bone. The bird then asked for the promised reward. The lion answered him: "Isn't it enough for you that you put your beak in my mouth and survived, without my swallowing you? Now you want a reward?" That, the Midrash tells us, was what Avimelech said to Yitzchak. "You were in my land and I sent you out penniless, but intact. For that you must be grateful to me."

Both the *p'shat* and *d'rush* works discuss the hatred/jealousy involved in the *parashah* of the wells. *Alshech* holds that Avimelech was the one who encouraged this hatred among his people. He wanted to get rid of Yitzchak, and that was why he sent his servants to seal Yitzchak's wells. This way, Yitzchak would be prompted to leave the country.

S'forno, though, holds that Avimilech's servants sealed the wells without his knowledge. On the contrary, Avimelech's servants were afraid to do anything openly against Yitzchak, because they were afraid of their master. They only sealed up his wells, so as to harass him.

According to *HaAmek Davar*, the ones who were most *jealous* were the Philistines who lived in the capital city, who were the elite of the kingdom. The ones who sealed up the wells, though, were those who lived in the countryside. The king ignored what they had done, because he too was happy about this harassment. The words of the Midrash indicate Avimelech's satisfaction and his agreement with the general hatred. He and his nation made a claim which we have known well in our exile: "All the wealth which you acquired, was that not from us? Once you had only a single flock, and now you have many flocks." The fact that Yitzchak had tended and guarded the flocks was irrelevant. "Go from us, because you are much wealthier than we."

According to *Chafetz Chaim*, that is the typical complaint of the anti-Semite. Pharaoh said, "Behold the people of the Children of Israel are greater and mightier than we." The anti-Semites hate the Jews, says *HaD'rush VeHalyun*, regardless of whether they are lazy and are not involved in constructive work, or whether they are constructive and productive members of society. Judea was exiled both (*Eichah* 1:3) "because of its poverty" and "because it was too productive." In this, Yitzchak serves as a model, as it were, for his descendants. When he came to Gerar with nothing, an order was issued, "He who touches this man or his wife will be put to death," indicating that the people wanted to harm Yitzchak for having nothing. Afterwards, when he worked hard and accumulated wealth, the cry went forth, "Go from us, because you have become much wealthier than us."

Oznayim LaTorah adds another detail to the plots of the anti-Semites against the Jew. They always come with their complaints after the Jew has become successful, and not before. After Yitzchak has increased his flocks and dug his wells, they come and say: "The water is ours." In reality, they are claiming that the land on which Yitzchak dug his well is theirs. Why then did they let him dig the well? The reason is that they want the Jew to do all the work, and afterwards they will come and take what he has acquired with all his sweat and effort.

Otzar Chayim also adds a *hashkafah* element in the words of the Torah as a solution to the problem of anti-Semitism. The Torah does not only tell us the plots of Avimelech and his servants, but also the way to deal with these plots: "And he moved away from there." One must leave their midst and move to *Eretz Yisrael*. Yitzchak moved all the way to Beersheva.

According to *Ramban*, Hashem's promise, "Do not fear, for I am with you," was stated specifically because of this hatred which Yitzchak experienced. He saw that Avimelech in his hatred had chased him away, and that the shepherds of Gerar had also argued with him, and he was afraid that all of them would assemble against him and attack his family. Hashem therefore promised him that there was no need to fear them. It was then that Hashem placed the idea in the mind of Avimelech to come to Yitzchak and to treat him with the utmost respect, even more than his respect for Avraham. And not only did he not harm him, but he asked him for a treaty.

⇦§ The Reason for the Treaty

The fact that Avimelech came to Yitzchak after all he had done to him, and his request that they make a treaty, is somewhat surprising. Did he do this because he was just? According to *Ramban*, his conscience bothered him because he had violated the treaty he had made with Avraham, and he was afraid that Yitzchak's descendants might expel his descendants at some future time. That was the reason he came to make a new treaty, claiming that until then he had only done good to Yitzchak.

Chizkuni, too, says that he came to propose a new treaty, after he had violated the first. But why did he do it?

Ramban raises the possibility that Avimelech was afraid of

Yitzchak's power. Avraham had had more than three hundred mighty warriors as well as many allies, and he had pursued the four kings. Now Avimelech was afraid when he saw how successful Yitzchak was; he was fearful that Yitzchak would take revenge and conquer his kingdom.

Kol David finds an example similar to the words of Yitzchak in the words of Yiftach to the elders of Gilead. There, Yiftach used the same words as Yitzchak, "You hate me, so why do you come to me?" Just as the elders of Gilead approached Yiftach in a time of distress, here, too, Avimelech was in distress, and was afraid that Yitzchak would join his enemies.

The words of Avimelech and his men show no sign of *regret* for what they did. On the contrary, they justify themselves, claiming they had only made a mistake. This is the way a number of commentators explain this. Thus Avimelech's men say: "We have seen that Hashem is with you." *Be'er Mayim Chayim* explains that at first they had claimed, "'Because you are wealthier than we are'. (The phrase מִמֶּנּוּ 'than we' may also be translated 'from us' or 'because of us.' Thus) you became rich 'through us.' You exploited us and that was how you became rich." Now that they saw that Yitzchak was successful in a different location, they had to admit that they were mistaken, and that Yitzchak's success was because, "Hashem is with you."

Chasam Sofer too explains this in a similar way. That was a year of famine in *Eretz Yisrael*. The land of the Philistines was not as good as *Eretz Yisrael*, but it did not suffer from the famine. The Philistines saw this stranger who came to them from *Eretz Yisrael* and were jealous of him, as they felt he had become rich from them. They believed that had he continued to live in his famine-stricken land he would not have become rich. But when Yitzchak left their land and returned to *Eretz Yisrael* and was extremely successful there, they were finally convinced that his success was because of Hashem. They finally admitted, "'We have seen that Hashem is with you.' In retrospect, we now realize that whatever you acquired was not from us, but because *Hashem* helped you."

This idea is also brought by *Riva*, one of the *Ba'alei HaTosafos*. He says that before that, Avimelech and his men had thought that the land where Yitzchak had sowed his grain was fertile land, and that was why his crop increased a hundred-fold. However, after he left the place and he had the same success with his crops elsewhere, they realized that it was because of Hashem's blessing.

Ralbag is amazed at Yitzchak's bold approach and courage, when Avimelech came to him to make a treaty. He was a stranger in the land,

and Avimelech was the ruler. Yet Yitzchak did not demean himself before Avimelech. He told him straight to his face, "You hate me, so why do you come to me?" Yitzchak was so much a man of truth that he had to tell them his feelings, even if he endangered his life by doing so.

✥ The Quarrel about the Wells

Twice in a row the Torah tells us how Yitzchak's wells were sealed up by the Philistines. The first time, we are told, "And all the wells that they dug in the days of Avraham his father, the Philistines sealed up, and they filled them with earth." The second time, it states, "And Yitzchak again dug the wells of water that they had dug in the days of Avraham his father, and the Philistines had sealed them after the death of Avraham."

According to *Rashi*, there was only one act of sealing up the wells. The Philistines sealed them, because they "were afraid of marauding troops." The second time, the Torah only tells us that Yitzchak dug again the wells that the Philistines had sealed up in the past. The question then arises: If the reason the wells were sealed up was because the Philistines were afraid that they might help marauding troops fight them, how did Yitzchak dare to reopen them? On this question by *Ramban*, both *Mizrachi* and *Maharal* offer answers. By the time that Yitzchak reopened them, there was no longer a fear of invasion in the land.

According to *Rashbam*, too, there was only one act of sealing up the wells. *Or HaChayim* adds that when Avraham died, they only sealed up the wells, but after they became jealous of Yitzchak, they also filled them with earth.

Ramban has a different view. He holds that there were two acts of sealing up the wells. In Gerar, the leaders of the land sealed up the wells dug by Avraham, because they were jealous of Yitzchak. Avimelech told Yitzchak to go to another place. He then moved to Nachal Gerar. Here, there were the wells which Avraham had dug and which had been sealed up when he died, not because of jealousy, but because the Philistines believed that no one would settle there after Avraham died. It was those wells which Yitzchak dug up again. And here he had another confrontation with the shepherds of Gerar. They claimed that the water in the well came from the river (*nachal*) of Gerar, and that he was stealing their water. Yitzchak, though, claimed that these were waters from the underground water basin.

Tzofnas Pa'aneach quotes a number of statements of *Chazal*, from which he deduces the *halachah* that if the well was dug in private property, all would have agreed that the well belonged to Yitzchak. And if the water gushed forth into public property, Yitzchak's shepherds would not have claimed, "The water is ours." Here, though, was a well in addition to a natural spring. That was what the argument was about. In any event the reason for the argument was the first well, where each side had a case. With the second well, though, there was no case for the shepherds of Gerar. That was why Yitzchak called the second well *Sitnah*, namely unwarranted hatred. Only when he dug his third well did they remain silent.

What happened to the first two wells? *Ma'asei Hashem* concludes from *Ramban* that the Philistines took them away from Yitzchak. But he disagrees with *Ramban*. If they had stolen the wells from him, why would he give them the names that his father had given them? *Ma'asei Hashem* therefore holds that the Philistines did indeed argue about the wells, but Hashem did not allow them to be taken away from Yitzchak. *HaKesav VeHaKabalah* also says that a person does not give a name to something which he doesn't own. The wells remained in Yitzchak's hands. That is *Rosh's* opinion as well.

Abarbanel goes further in this direction, and says that the wells remained in Yitzchak's hands, and, in fact, he maintains that that is the whole purpose of this *parashah*.

Ramban wonders why this *parashah* is related in the Torah. It is possible that what the Torah wanted to stress was that Hashem kept his promise to Avraham, "To you and to your seed I will give this land," by having Yitzchak take possession of these wells. If we look in the story, we will see that this promise was kept. Even though the Philistines in their wickedness had sealed up the wells which Avraham had dug, and Avimelech had told Yitzchak, "Go from us, because you are much wealthier than we are," Yitzchak did not fear them and settled near Gerar (unlike *Rashi* and other commentators, who hold that Nachal Gerar was far from Gerar). Yitzchak opened the sealed-up wells and again called them by the names his father had used, and by this, in spite of the wickedness of the Philistines, he returned matters to the way they had been before. He also found a well of fresh water, over which the shepherds of Gerar argued with him, claiming it was their water, but their complaint was in vain. They also argued about the second well, and that, too, remained in his possession. Finally, when it came to the third well, they no longer argued. Yitzchak displayed clear dominance and was able to ensure that his deeds remained intact. In the end, his opponents gave up and admitted that Hashem was with him. And that, according to Abarbanel, is the purpose of this episode.

Taking a diametrically opposite approach to this, in an original interpretation of this story, is R' Samson Raphael Hirsch. According to him, here the Torah does not stress Yitzchak's dominance, but rather the beginning of the exile in his days. The Philistines' jealousy of Yitzchak initiated a chain of events, which indicated the commencement of a new phase. Avraham, with his great wealth, walked as a prince of Hashem among the inhabitants of the land, and only once was there enmity between him and Avimelech, and this was denied by Avimelech. That was not true for Yitzchak. The period of exile began with him, and the prophecy of "your seed will be a stranger" was fulfilled in him. He already felt what it was like to be a stranger. After him, Yaakov was drawn into the total bondage which marks the beginning of the exile in Egypt.

∽§ The Purpose of this Parashah

Ramban says that this episode served no purpose for Yitzchak and did not bring him glory, and he therefore explains the *parashah* in a symbolic fashion. The three wells symbolize the three *Batei Mikdash* that the Jewish people were to have in their history. The well of fresh water refers to the House of Hashem, whose light we follow. The first *Beis HaMikdash* was called *Eisek* (quarrel), because the other nations would quarrel with us and wage war against us until the *Beis HaMikdash* was destroyed. The second *Beis HaMikdash* was named *Sitnah* (enmity), which is a worse term than the first, because we are told, "In the days of Achashverosh at the beginning of his reign, they wrote *sitnah* ("words of enmity") against the dwellers of Zion and Jerusalem." Throughout the entire second *Beis HaMikdash*, we suffered from enmity, and we were exiled into our present bitter exile. The third *Beis HaMikdash*, which will be built at the time of the *Mashiach*, will be called *Rechovos* ("wide expanses"), because "now Hashem has made room for us, and we will be fruitful in the land."

Kli Yakar takes this idea and expands on it. In the first well there was a quarrel between the shepherds of Gerar and those of Yitzchak, as a sign of the quarrel that would exist between the kings of Judah and the kings of Israel. The second well was called *Sitnah*, because there was enmity among the Jews themselves, for, as *Chazal* tell us, "The second *Beis HaMikdash* was destroyed because of senseless hatred."

According to *Or HaChayim*, the whole incident of the wells was a test. Hashem wanted to test Yitzchak, to see if even after He had promised him that the land would be his, he would angered by these incidents, which were all contrary to Hashem's promise.

Rabbenu Bachya sees this *parashah* as a moral lesson, that a person should not diverge from his fathers' path the slightest fraction. Yitzchak even gave the wells the same names his father had given them.

Chafetz Chaim holds that this *parashah* is meant to teach us that one should not give up when confronted by obstacles, but should trust in Hashem for deliverance and continue with whatever action he began. Yitzchak was confronted by so many obstacles. He dug to find water, and when he finally found it, the local residents argued with him about to whom it belonged. And in spite of this, he did not give up, but continued until he was finally able to live in peace.

Rabbenu Bachya, though, in a different interpretation, provides a new *hashkafah* idea, which is then expanded on beautifully by *HaKesav VeHaKabalah*. There are commentators, says Rabbenu Bachya, who hold that the wells were the converts whom Avraham drew close to Judaism and to Hashem. After Avraham died, the Philistine converts went back to their old ways. Yitzchak finally succeeded in bringing them back to the right path, and gave them the same names his father had given them.

HaKesav VeHaKabalah says that Avraham gave the wells names based on Hashem's mercies and His wonders, such as, "and Avraham named the place, 'Hashem will see,'" or "And he named that place, 'Beis El.'" Avraham gave a name related to holiness to each well, so as to indicate that the world was not run by fate, as some believed. The names of these wells created concepts. Those who went to drink from these wells referred to them by the name of Hashem, as these were names given by Avraham. When Avraham died, the idolaters sealed up the wells, and Hashem's name was no longer heard. Yitzchak did not accept that, and dug the wells a second time, again giving them the names his father had given them. The struggle over the wells was a spiritual one, and that is the purpose of the story.

One can add to this the words of the *Yehudi HaKadosh*, who explained in a Chassidic way that Avraham ordered his men to dig wells of water, and water always refers to Torah. These wells were used for giving the flocks to drink, and that refers to Israel, the "holy flock." The Philistines came "and sealed them up," namely giving them a simple, superficial explanation, devoid of any content, until Yitzchak came and restored the conditions to the way they had been.

IV.
This Is from Hashem

The *parashah* of how Yaakov received the blessing from his father is a remarkable one, full of dramatic events. All the Torah commentators delve into this *parashah*, not only to clarify those parts which are unclear, but also to rebuff the attacks of both non-Jewish and Jewish critics. Yet this *parashah* needs to be clarified. There are so many questions in it: Why did Hashem transfer the blessing to Yaakov in this fashion? What was Yitzchak's role in this whole sequence? If Yitzchak was against blessing Yaakov, why did he conclude with, "He shall be blessed"? What type of blessing was it, that Yitzchak could have given it to either son? How did Rivkah and Yaakov permit themselves to foil Yitzchak's plans with deceit? There are numerous such questions, which have produced a wealth of ideas and explanations in the various commentaries through the ages.

◆§ The Nature of the Blessing

Ralbag is perplexed and asks by what power Yitzchak could bless. Was he a prophet? What did his sons want from him if he was unable to transfer a blessing from a person for whom it was meant? And as he was a perfect *tzaddik*, and whoever he blessed was indeed blessed, then Esav was right when he asked: "Do you then have but one blessing?"

Ralbag answers as follows: A *tzaddik* does not give his own blessing. He gives each person the blessing that is meant for him, as it says (*Bereishis* 49:28), "Each one according to his blessing he blessed them." The *tzaddik's* blessing only serves to increase the good that the person is to receive. The person who is about to be blessed by the *tzaddik* gives him a gift. As a result, the *tzaddik* turns his thoughts to him and concentrates on him to give him his blessing, and to know what has been decreed for him from Above.

Abarbanel rejects this explanation. According to him, and *S'forno* concurs in this view, one cannot expect that a material gift will draw the *tzaddik* to concentrate on the person's needs. Rather, the Torah is referring here to the blessing that Hashem gave Avraham to inherit the land, and to instill in humanity the Oneness of Hashem. Yitzchak sought an heir to this blessing before his death. It was natural for him to choose his older son. But as Esav's behavior did not find favor in his eyes, he wanted to prepare him for the blessing by giving him the opportunity to fulfill the *mitzvah* of *kibud av* — "honoring one's father." That was the reason he sent Esav to hunt for him.

Abarbanel also brings the view of *Ran*, that the purpose of the hunt was to please Yitzchak, and thereby to increase the abundance of the blessing through that. Rabbenu Bachya and other commentators also see the purpose of the hunt to make Yitzchak rejoice thereby enabling him to prophesize, as in the verse, "And when the musician played, the hand of Hashem rested on him." (*Beis Yosef* in *Orach Chayim* 128 uses this as the basis for a *halachah* in the name of the *rishonim*, that a *kohen* who is not in a joyous state should not bless the people.)

Rabbenu Bachya asks: If that is so, why didn't Yitzchak ask for a harp rather than venison? He answers that Yitzchak wanted to see the thing to which the blessing would apply, as *Chazal* tell us: "(Hashem said,) 'Pour water before Me on the *Chag* (*Sukkos*),' so that rain will be plentiful that year."

Akeidah also follows in the footsteps of Abarbanel. Yitzchak wanted to give the blessing to Esav by virtue of the *mitzvah* of *kibud av*. Thus the reason that Rivkah told Yaakov, "Listen to my voice that I command you," was so that he too would be ready for a blessing because of the merit of that *mitzvah*.

Ramban maintains that the blessing mentioned here refers to the inheriting of the land. But this is hard to understand, because the blessing makes no mention of that inheritance. The blessing of the land is emphasized only when Yitzchak blesses Yaakov before he goes to Padan Aram.

Sefas Emes has an interesting explanation. The blessing that is mentioned in this *parashah* refers only to this world, and even this Yaakov did not want to leave directly in Esav's hands, but rather wanted Esav to receive it through him. Yitzchak never planned to transmit the blessing of Avraham to Esav.

There are many other interpretations of the meaning of the blessing. Some are symbolic (R' Samson Raphael Hirsch), or take the venison as referring to a sacrifice (*Meshech Chochmah*), and other interpretations. The Chassidic works find much support here for their view. *Chassidim* understand this as the first time a real *tzaddik*, in the form of Yitzchak, appears, and he brings blessings down from Heaven.

◆§ I, Wisdom, Live with Cunning (Mishle 8:12)

There is no doubt that Yaakov used *cunning* in order to achieve what he wanted. According to many commentators, this action is a continuation of the one when he bought the birthright from Esav. The blessing is linked to the birthright, because Yitzchak called here for his older son. According to *Akeidah*, as Yaakov was convinced that it was forbidden for a wicked person like Esav to be the one to serve Hashem (in those days, the firstborn would bring the sacrifices), he had to do whatever he could to defeat this plan. Esav helped him in achieving his aim. He didn't even ask for a fair price for the birthright, thus showing how little it meant to him. "And Esav scorned the birthright" — R' Simcha Zisl of Kelm says that the very fact that Esav sold the birthright for a lentil stew shows how he detested it. *Melo HaOmer* says that even the claim that Esav did what he did because of his hunger is also irrelevant, because the Torah says clearly that he scorned the birthright after he had finished eating and was full.

Yitzchak was missing two details to be able to evaluate the situation properly. He did not know how Esav had scorned the birthright and had even sold it to Yaakov, and did not know how corrupt Esav was and what a hypocrite he was. Rivkah recognized this in Esav, because she had grown up in a home of swindlers and corrupt people, while Yitzchak was unfamiliar with such matters in the world. When Rivkah decided not to allow Esav the right to the blessing, she taught us a lesson for subsequent generations: not to come to terms with injustice, and not to bow to a negative situation. Rivkah did not want to anger Yitzchak by telling him the painful truth, and that was why she used cunning. "Cunning," not "lies."

Ibn Ezra (on v. 13) proves from *Nevi'im* that one may use this method in such circumstances. That is the reason why all the commentators seek to find in the verses themselves the ambiguous meaning in the words of Yaakov, when he spoke to Yitzchak while impersonating Esav. They find meanings in each word, indicating that Yaakov was indeed telling the truth, and all this in order to have justice triumph.

Yaakov's words, "I am Esav your firstborn," are explained in the Midrash and the *rishonim* as two separate statements: "I am as I am, and Esav is your firstborn." There are also commentators who explain the verse by rearranging the words. It is not, "And Yaakov said to his father 'I am Esav your firstborn,'" but "And he said to his father, 'I am Yaakov; Esav is your firstborn.'" This explanation is difficult, because if so, Yaakov is admitting that Esav is the firstborn. There are therefore many commentators who explain the verse as a "substitution" — "I by my presence represent the firstborn to whom you wish to give the blessing, because I bought the birthright." The rest of Yaakov's words are also explained as cunning, whose meaning is true. Thus *Ari* explains the words, "I have done 'as' you spoke to me," in the sense of "I have done 'as if' you spoke to me." And indeed we see this from the fact that the Torah does not use the word אֲשֶׁר for "as," but instead uses כַּאֲשֶׁר.

HaKesav VeHaKabalah finds a number of stylistic changes in the words of Yaakov, whose purpose is to achieve the overall aim, and as much as possible by truthful means. Yaakov used the אָנֹכִי for "I," rather than אֲנִי. He said עֵשָׂו בְּכֹרֶךָ — "Esav your firstborn" — rather than בְּכֹרְךָ עֵשָׂו — "your firstborn Esav." Esav, on the other hand, said, אֲנִי בִּנְךָ בְּכֹרְךָ עֵשָׂו — "I am your son your firstborn, Esav." Yaakov did not use the word "your son" in connection with "your firstborn," because that would imply that he was firstborn by birth, and he didn't want to lie. Similarly, Yaakov used the word דִּבַּרְתָּ for "you said" rather than אָמַרְתָּ. The first is more general, and means "as you were wont to speak," whereas the second refers to what was said only on this occasion. *Megaleh Amukos* explains "I am Esav your firstborn" in the spiritual sense. Right now, I am clothed in Esav's manner of deceit. That is also the way the Sochachower explains the verse, "rise and eat from my hunt," i.e., from my pursuit of deceit.

The Torah states clearly that Yitzchak's love of Esav was dependent on a thing — says *Sefas Emes*. We are told, "And Yitzchak loved Esav because he (brought him) venison in his mouth." Once that thing disappeared, the love disappeared with it, and that was why Yitzchak finally concluded, regarding Yaakov, "He shall be blessed."

Or Rashaz notes that a person who uses cunning to save the truth deserves to be blessed. A hypocrite who acts like a *tzaddik* is a liar, but if a doctor uses deceptive talk to reassure his patient, he is a man of truth.

But in spite of these different explanations which seek to justify Yaakov's actions, there is a position adopted by *Chazal*, which does not accept cunning for the sake of truth. It sees the tears and cry of Esav at the time as the reason for the troubles which befell the Jews in Shushan and throughout our exile (see the *Midrashim*).

⋖§ This Was from Hashem

Yitzchak's actions are slow and deliberate, but in the end they are all blended into a general picture. At first he turns directly to Esav, and the explanation for this is to be found in the *rishonim*. Yitzchak in his innocence does not understand who Esav really is, and therefore seeks to draw Esav to his ways. Afterwards, he is a partner to the unraveling of the Divine plot. As much as Yaakov has disguised himself, there is still doubt in Yitzchak's heart about the blessing. When Yaakov says, "My father," he asks, "Who are you, my son?" When Yaakov claims he is Esav, Yitzchak asks: "How did you hurry to find, my son?" Afterwards he asks Yaakov to come closer so that he can feel him. Once that has also been carried out successfully, Yitzchak again remarks, "The voice is the voice of Yaakov, but the hands are the hands of Esav." And finally he asks him again, "Are you my son Esav?" These doubts, which are expressed aloud, show that Yitzchak was divinely guided to be actively involved in the action, by means of knowledge in his heart.

Tzofnas Pa'aneach proves from many places in *Shas* that the fact that Yitzchak carried out the action in spite of his clear uncertainty shows that what he did was halachically binding. The fact that in the end Yitzchak confirmed the blessing shows that he was inwardly aware of what he was doing, and that this *potential* was now realized in action.

The Chassidic works devote themselves to analyzing why Yitzchak was outwardly unaware of what he was doing. They quote *Zohar* that from Heaven they wanted the blessing to have the concurrence of the *Shechinah*, and not the concurrence of Yitzchak.

When I studied this *parashah*, I was amazed at the clear message to us in the verses themselves that this came from Hashem. Yitzchak's eyes were weak, the Torah tells us in introducing the *parashah*, and this was not purely coincidental. This was Heavenly decreed, as a prologue to the chain of events that would take place. And indeed *Chazal* in the *Midrash* and the commentators stress the link between the fact that Yitzchak's eyes were weak and what happened as a result.

Again the Torah stresses that when Yitzchak told Esav to go and hunt so that he could bless him, "Rivkah overheard." This fact is also not coincidental, and reminds us of a similar, but different, incident where Mordechai happened to overhear Bigsan and Teresh plotting. We should also pay attention to the verses directly before and at the conclusion of the *parashah*. In both places we are told how Yitzchak and Rivkah were upset with Esav's choice of wives of the daughters of the land. The presence of these verses in the *parashah* is not coincidental, and comes to explain the events and analyze their reason. After Esav had taken a "daughter of Cheis" as a wife, he was no longer worthy of the blessing, and could not receive the spiritual inheritance. There is no doubt that the purpose of this *parashah* is to teach us to be on our guard, because Hashem helps man in his efforts — and where one frees himself of the Yoke of Heaven, Hashem, as it were, frees Himself of the person. Thus we are encouraged to fight against injustice and evil.

Likutei Basar Likutei cites an interesting idea in the name of *Chiddushei HaRim*. At first, Yitzchak wanted to give the blessing of this world to Esav, seeing that he was capable of dealing with worldly matters. But after Yitzchak saw that Yaakov was not as naive as he had thought and was capable of achieving what he wanted by cunning, there was no reason why he should not receive the blessing of this world as well. That was why Yitzchak later exclaimed, " He shall be blessed."

The *Chozeh* of Lublin also has a penetrating explanation here. "Yaakov was a guileless man" — he was the one who controlled his guile and used it as he needed to. He was not always guileless as people thought. If there was the need, then "Your brother came with cunning." To him to be guileless was only because that was what he wanted, and it was his nature as such. When he needed to, though, he was able in his cunning to achieve what he could not in any other way.

And why did all this happen the way it did? The Chassidic works give a remarkable reason for it all. Hashem wanted there to be enmity between Yaakov and Esav, so as to separate between the two, and by this act He accomplished that goal. The Gaon of Brizhan explains with this concept the words of *Chazal* on the verse, "Your brother came with cunning" — with the wisdom of the Torah. The purpose of the cunning was to separate Yaakov to Torah and to keep him apart from Esav.

R' Samson Raphael Hirsch says that the purpose of this cunning was to make Yitzchak confront reality, and to show him that there is cunning in the world. If Yaakov was able to use Esav's clothes to deceive Yitzchak, why should he not believe that Esav was always wearing a disguise, when he acted as an innocent with *yiras Shomayim*? This plot was meant to make Yitzchak see things with open eyes. When he did this, he realized that *Yaakov*, and not Esav, was worthy of the blessing, and he said, "He shall be blessed."

Vayeitzei – ויצא

I.
Who Is Rich?
He Who Is Satisfied with His Lot

Yaakov's vow is discussed by the commentators. Are the words, "And Hashem will be a God (*Elokim*) unto me," part of Yaakov's request, or are they a promise by him? If this is a request, what does it mean? And if it is a promise, is there any reason why he should make his promise conditional on the fulfillment of his request from Hashem?

Most commentators say that this phrase is part of Yaakov's prayer. According to *Rashi*, he was asking Hashem to fulfill the promise made to Avraham, "And I will be God to you and your descendants" (*Bereishis* 17:7). Yaakov prayed that that blessing would be fulfilled for him, and that his children should not have any blemish. *Rashi's* source is *Sifri*. Thus, he explains Yaakov's prayer as being "that no unworthy ones would emerge out of him, from the beginning to the end."

Rashbam, too, says that this is a prayer, that Hashem should aid him in all his deeds. Alternately, this is a condition, as *Rashi* mentions, if Hashem helps him in all his actions.

Ramban has a very interesting explanation. According to him, this is a continuation of the words, "And I will return to my father's house in peace."

> When I return to my father's house and settle in *Eretz Yisrael*, then Hashem will be my God, in accordance with the words of *Chazal*, "Whoever lives in *Eretz Yisrael* is as if he has a God, and whoever lives outside *Eretz Yisrael* is as if he does not have a God." In *Eretz Yisrael* I will be able to accept upon myself His Godhood and feel His existence.

Ramban states this same idea in various places. The rest of Yaakov's words are a continuation of this theme: If Hashem does indeed appear to him in *Eretz Yisrael*, he will build Him a "house of God" there, because that is His place.

HaAmek Davar also explains it along these lines. According to him, this was a promise by Yaakov that even in *Eretz Yisrael* he would not rely on his physical powers, but would trust to Hashem and wait for His salvation. Outside *Eretz Yisrael* he certainly needed Hashem's aid every moment, but Yaakov promised that even when he would no longer be faced with all the dangers involved in being outside *Eretz Yisrael*, there too his faith in Hashem would not decrease.

Ibn Ezra in *Parashas Shemos* explains the verse as an exchange offered by Yaakov. If Hashem protected him and gave him bread to eat and clothes to wear, he would devote himself entirely to serving Hashem, and he would "separate himself his whole life to cling to Him."

S'forno also explains the verse as a promise made by Yaakov. Yaakov was so sure of his attachment to God that he had no fear in saying that Hashem would become his "Judge" (*Elokim*), who would punish him if he transgressed any of the *mitzvos*. He did not mind if Hashem used His attribute of *din* — "strict justice" — if he did not keep his promise.

R' Samson Raphael Hirsch follows a similar line, and says that Yaakov promised that the service of Hashem would be for him a requirement, and not merely something which is optional. He would be obligated to Hashem for all of His mercies.

These commentators are all preceded by *Zohar*, who says that outside *Eretz Yisrael* Yaakov needed Hashem's mercies, but in *Eretz Yisrael* he did not want any mercy (*chessed*), and promised that he would earn everything strictly according to *din* (see *Michtav Me'Eliyahu* volume 3).

According to various commentators, Yaakov's promise was not a condition but a prayer. The way *HaKesav VeHaKabalah* interprets the word אִם (which we translated above as "if") at the beginning of the prayer is most appropriate in this regard. He sees the word as derived from the word אָמֵן — amen — namely that Yaakov announced, "I hope that this will all take place," but it was not that he made this a condition. As proof to this meaning, *HaKesav VeHaKabalah* brings the verses (*Mishle* 3:34), "Surely (אִם) He scorns the scorners," and (*Bamidbar* 24:22), "Nevertheless (אִם) the Kenite shall be wasted," where in both cases אִם is taken as an affirmation. Indeed, the word אִם often means, "hopefully, this will occur." Thus the meaning of the verse is, "I hope that Hashem will be my God and that my God will protect me wherever I go, and will give me bread to eat and clothing to wear."

BEREISHIS — VAYEITZEI / 165

৺§ Bread to Eat and Clothing to Wear

Chazal in *Bereishis Rabbah* tell us:

> Aquila the convert came to R' Elazar and said to him, "Does the entire benefit for the convert lie in what we are told (*Devarim* 10:18), 'He loves the convert, giving him food and clothing'?" He answered him, "Is that then such a minor thing in your eyes? Our ancestor prayed for just that, 'If He will give me bread to eat and clothing to wear,' and yet here [the convert] comes and [Hashem] offers it to him on a reed" (i.e., without effort). He went to R' Yehoshua. He began to comfort him, saying, " 'Bread' refers to Torah ... And not only that, but his daughters may marry *kohanim*, and their children can be *kohanim gedolim*." Had R' Yehoshua not spoken to him at length, he would have returned to his previous ways.

This Midrash illuminates how man's mind works. He is constantly in search of luxuries and is not willing to settle for only bread and clothing, which were for Yaakov the maximum to ask for. Aquila the convert, who, *Chazal* tell us in numerous times, was selflessly dedicated to Judaism, almost abandoned it because "bread and clothing" seemed so minor to him. It was only when these words were reinterpreted that he was willing to be reconciled. Many interpretations have been given about Yaakov's request, in order to make this request more palatable to those who, like Aquila, are not satisfied with it in its simple form.

Rishonim such as *Ralbag*, though, are not afraid to explain the verse as it stands. "It is not fitting for a person to be eager for wealth. Rather, he should be content with what is essential, just as we see that Yaakov only asked Hashem for what was essential, 'bread to eat and clothing to wear.' "

So, too, are we told in *Mishle* (30:8), "Give me neither poverty nor riches; feed me with food convenient for me." And that was exactly the prayer of our Patriarch Yaakov. He asked Hashem to enable him to live a natural and modest life in the land of his fathers, and then Hashem would be his God — Hashem, and not a god of gold or silver.

Rabbenu Bachya has a very interesting view of this, which should serve to be our guide, and these are his words:

> This is what *tzaddikim* ask Hashem. They do not ask for luxuries, but only for what is essential, that without which a person cannot live. As is known, a person who seeks luxuries is subject to all types of confusions. Therefore a person who fears Hashem should be happy with what he has and be content with less, and should not lust for luxuries. Instead, he should be happy in his awe of Hashem ...

And know that had it not been for the fact that man's inclination is evil from his youth, so that he desires all the wealth and honor in this world, he would not have wanted any of the luxuries, and would have been content with the necessities, because what is necessary is given by Hashem each day.

This is as we see with the manna: "They gathered it for themselves each day," because they were not able to set aside manna for any length of time, and not even from one day to the next. As they trusted Hashem, he provided it to them each day ...

We see with our own eyes how the world is conducted, with great and marvelous wisdom. Hashem takes care of His creatures and gives them what is essential. Whatever is needed more is more plentiful, and whatever is needed less, such as pearls and precious stones, is not so common in the world. But food, which is necessary, is common, for you will find wheat in the markets and streets. And so with water, which is more necessary than food. As to air, which is more necessary than water, you will not find a place without air. Thus we see that the more needed a thing is, the more it is available in the world. And that is why Yaakov asked for bread to eat and clothes to wear — they are the essentials. He asked for the minimum, which is the way of the *tzaddikim*. He did not ask for luxuries, because the Torah detests them, to the extent that even a king should refrain from them, as it states, "Only let him not have too many horses, and not too many wives, and he should not have an exceedingly great amount of silver and gold."

Kli Yakar too explains the verses in the same manner. According to him, Yaakov not only wanted to ask that which Hashem should give him, but also that which Hashem should not give him. When he said, "Bread to eat and clothing to wear," this meant not to give him more food than he needed to eat, nor more clothing than he needed to wear. Yaakov prayed to Hashem not to give him gold and fine jewels, but only to give him what was absolutely essential for his needs.

Ma'asei Hashem also explains the following verse in the *parashah* along the same lines, where Yaakov said, "And whatever You give me, I will surely tithe to You." The word וְכֹל (translated above as "whatever") implies being satisfied with what he had. Hashem blessed Avraham בַּכֹּל — "with all" — namely to be content with whatever he had. Esav the wicked did not use the word כֹּל. He said, "I have a lot (רַב), my brother." But Yaakov stressed כֹּל — "all that You give me," implying that all he wanted was bread and clothing.

BEREISHIS — VAYEITZEI / 167

This view regarding contenting oneself with little and not seeking luxuries is also to be found in Abarbanel, when he explains the fate of the Generation of the Dispersion (the Tower of Babel). He says that the sin of Adam and of Cain was that they forsook the simple life and strove for great things, above and beyond what they needed. The same was true of the Generation of the Dispersion, which had unrestrained lust to obtain what couldn't be received by normal means — to conquer all the expanses of the world — in opposition to what Hashem wanted in nature. Abarbanel quotes *Rambam's Moreh Nevuchim*, which also is opposed to man's accumulation of vast sums and his abandonment of the simple and just life.

Chazal, too, see the willingness to content oneself with what he has as being part of one's faith in Hashem, and they tell us in *Sotah* 48:

> R' Eliezer the great would say, "Whoever has bread in his basket and says, 'What will I eat tomorrow?' is of little faith."
>
> So, too, did R' Eliezer say (in explanation of the verse *Zecharyah* 4:10), " 'For who has despised the day of petty things' — What causes the *tzaddikim* to waste (the portion of) their tables in the World to Come? the petty things within them."

It is true that *Chazal* are dealing here with faith (*emunah*) and trust (*bitachon*), but the question of contenting oneself with what he has is a question of *bitachon*. Man's desires stem from his worries about the future for himself and for his family. *Chazal* say, "Whoever has bread in his basket," and not, "Whoever has nothing," because here they are referring to a person who has what to eat, but wants to save for tomorrow. He has what he needs, but wants more. Such a person is of little faith.

Using this saying of *Chazal*, the Kotzker explained another saying of *Chazal* in *Mechilta*: "The Torah was only given to those who ate the manna." Torah and *emunah* are only truly appreciated by those with the special qualities of those who ate the manna. They had food for that day and did not worry about the next day, and that was why their hearts were open to Torah and *emunah*. The Torah could only be given to people who did not worry about tomorrow.

In this spirit, one can explain the words of Yaakov, "And he will give me bread to eat and clothing to wear," to mean that, and no more. That was an introduction to "and Hashem will be my *Elokim*." Yaakov would be worthy, as a result of the above, to כל that Hashem would give him, namely that he would feel that he had כל — "everything" — that he needed. By the same token, "And whatever You give me, I will surely tithe to You," means, "whatever tithe I give will be for You alone, and not for me." *Chazal* say, "עַשֵּׂר בִּשְׁבִיל שֶׁתִּתְעַשֵּׁר — tithe in order that you may become rich (deduced from the root עשר in both cases)." Yaakov, though, did not want wealth. He only wanted bread to eat and clothing to wear, and then he would have כֹּל.

ೞ§ Who Is Rich? One Who Is Satisfied with His Lot

The *mussar* works extol the value of the person who is satisfied with his lot, and consider him to be the perfect person. *Maharal* of Prague, in his commentary on *Avos* 4, says that the person who is satisfied with his lot is a perfect person, unlike all the rich people who strive for more. The rich person is never satisfied, and he therefore always feels that he is not rich enough. But one who is satisfied with his lot is not missing anything and therefore is richer than anyone else.

Nesivos Olam explains this idea. He quotes the words of David in *Tehillim* (128:2), "Happy shall you be, and it shall be well with you," which *Chazal* explain to mean, "You shall be happy in this world, and it shall be well with you in the World to Come." According to *Nesivos Olam*, the essence of the World to Come is that no one there receives anything from anyone else. Only someone who is material can receive something, but a spiritual being is complete in itself, and does not receive anything from anyone. Thus a person who is satisfied with his lot is like one who is already in the World to Come.

From the preceding discussion, we can also see why Yaakov is always referred to as שְׁלִימָתָא — "the perfect one." The Torah says (*Bereishis* 33:18) וַיָּבֹא יַעֲקֹב שָׁלֵם — "and Yaakov came *Shalem*." The word *shalem* means "in peace," but it also means, "complete, whole, perfect." The word "perfect" applies to Yaakov more than to anyone else, because he showed he was perfect when he asked only for "bread to eat and clothing to wear," and for nothing else.

Yaa'aros D'vash also is opposed to the search for luxuries. He sees this as "the mother of all sin." He concludes by saying,

> I can call the Heavens and earth to testify about myself, that my heart aches when in the middle of the week I put on a woolen garment and on *Shabbos* a silk one. And even if on *Shabbos* (this can be justified as) it is in honor of *Shabbos*, my heart nevertheless hurts in the middle of the week.

Yaakov's prayer, "And you will give me bread to eat and clothing to wear," is a basic principle of the Torah, which is all too often ignored because of our evil inclination. Whatever has been said or written against luxury is already included in these words of Yaakov. This is a directive and an admonition for future generations, and happy are those who follow in the ways of the *avos* and discern from their words not only what is proper and good for them, but that which is proper and good in the eyes of Hashem.

II.

The Modesty of the Mothers

Yaakov's choice of Rachel on the basis of her outward appearance is, according to R' Samson Raphael Hirsch, the reason why half the tribes were descended from Leah's children. According to R' Hirsch, we can learn from the names which Leah gave her sons how she allowed herself to be humiliated without humiliating others in return, and how she loved her husband and trusted that Hashem would bring peace to her house, for the happiness of the family. She loved her husband without reservation, and hoped that each son would be yet another tier in her flawless love and the shaping of her home. The end was that Leah obtained what she had not achieved when she was first married: pure love for herself and her children, and total trust in Divine Providence.

We can learn from the names that she gave her sons how each additional one she bore endeared her more to Yaakov. At first, with Reuven, it was, "Hashem saw my affliction." Until that time, it was clear to all that Yaakov preferred Rachel to Leah. That was rectified when Reuven was born. But she still had not won her husband's heart completely, and when her second son was born she named him Shimon, "For Hashem heard that I was hated and He gave me this one as well." The third son was Levi, "Now my husband will accompany me." Now the difference between the two wives was totally blurred, and she expressed her faith that from then on she and her husband would have a pure and honest marriage relationship. "That was why he called him Levi" — he, Yaakov, named his third son, and not she. These were glad tidings. When the fourth son was born, she no longer saw any need for seeking the love of her husband, because she already had acquired it. Now she was totally happy with the birth of her son, and as a content mother she said about herself, "This time I will thank Hashem" merely for His gift, "she therefore named him Yehudah."

◆§ Was It Indeed on the Basis of External Observation?

R' Samson Raphael Hirsch's explanation is in keeping with the content of the verses, but his statement that Yaakov chose Rachel on the basis of her outward appearance, even though this may be in accordance with the verses, is nevertheless not the view of all the *rishonim*.

S'forno explains the verse, "And he loved Rachel," as meaning that Yaakov loved her personality because she was Rachel, and not for any other reason. Even though the Torah (*Bereishis* 29:17) tells us that Rachel was "shapely and beautiful," many of the *rishonim* see in the words, "and the eyes of Leah were soft," that her sister's eyes were beautiful as well. That is the way Onkelos, *Rashbam* and others perceive it. According to this explanation, both sisters were outstanding in their appearance, therefore it was not appearance that was the decisive factor in Yaakov's choice.

Da'as Zekeinim MiBa'alei HaTosafos also points out the beauty of Leah's eyes. According to him, though, her eyes were painful because of her weeping, as she was afraid that she would have to marry the wicked Esav. In this interpretation, he differs with *Rashi*, who, based on *Chazal* in *Bava Basra* 123, says that Leah's eyes were homely because of this weeping.

Ibn Ezra quotes Ben Efra'im that the word רַכּוֹת, which the Torah uses to describe Leah's eyes, is missing the letter א, as if it should have been ארכות — "long." Ibn Ezra derides this interpretation.

Rivash too holds that the phrase, "and the eyes of Leah were רַכּוֹת" is not meant to be negative. The Torah only explains why Rachel went out with the sheep and not Leah, because Leah's eyes were sensitive to the wind. That was the reason why Lavan sent his younger daughter with the flock, and she was the first one to meet Yaakov.

Chizkuni gives another reason why Yaakov chose the younger sister. A rumor had circulated that the older daughter was meant for the older brother, Esav. Yaakov was thus afraid to ask for the older daughter, because this might anger Esav even further after the sale of the birthright. Esav might then say, "Not only did he take my birthright, he also took my wife."

According to *Rashi* in the name of *Chazal*, Leah's eyes were painful from weeping because she was intended for Esav. *Likutei Basar Likutei* brings a beautiful statement based on *d'rush*. *Chazal* said in the Midrash that when Yaakov complained vigorously to Lavan, "Why have you cheated me?" Leah responded, "But you too cheated your father when you said, 'I am Esav your firstborn.'" It seems very strange that Leah should appear here as defending Esav, but, says *Likutei Basar Likutei*, she was not defending Esav, but herself. She told him, "I was meant for the firstborn, but after you bought the birthright, you also acquired me through that action."

It is interesting that this beautiful idea is already found in different words in *Ma'asei Hashem*. He says that when Lavan said, "It is not done so in our place, to give the younger one before the older one," he was really trying to provoke Yaakov about the birthright. He did not mention the words גְּדֹלָה and קְטַנָּה — "older" and "younger" — but rather צְעִירָה and בְּכִירָה — here implying the "later-born" and the "firstborn." Yaakov was the צָעִיר and Esav was the בְּכוֹר. Thus, what Lavan was telling him was that maybe in your place one can sell the birthright to a younger brother, but in our place the customs are different. (This is also to be found in *Chasam Sofer* on the Torah and in *Beis HaLevi*.)

This idea is basically *d'rush*, but it might even be the simple meaning of the verse. The words, "It is not done so in our place," contain much more than the simple text itself. Lavan bases his trickery on the basis of "logic and justice." He places the blame for his dishonest behavior on others. On the contrary, he is the righteous one. He claims that he is acting according to the custom of the land, and that Yaakov is the cheater.

⊷§ The Trickery of Lavan

The trickery of Lavan already appears in his first answer to Yaakov. He understands very well that Yaakov wants his younger daughter. According to *Ramban's* first explanation, Yaakov agreed to tend Lavan's flocks in place of Rachel, even before Lavan suggested it. Based on this, Lavan said to Yaakov, "Are you then my brother that you should work for me for nothing?" But as to Yaakov's demand that he give him his daughter Rachel as a wife in exchange for his work, Lavan did not answer him directly. He only said, "It is better for me to give her to you than to give her to another man." According to *S'forno*, Yaakov's demand was indeed in keeping with the custom of the land, because he did not ask to marry Rachel immediately, but after seven years of work, and by that time Leah could well be married.

Abarbanel, however, maintains that Lavan meant that he was willing to give Rachel to Yaakov, but in accordance with the customs of the land.

The *d'rush* and *kabbalah* commentaries see Lavan's answer as having a devious aim. The word תִּתִּי ("to give") has a *gematria* by *mispar katan* (where all the zeroes are removed in the calculation, so that ת is 4 rather than 400) of 9, which is the same as לֵאָה, while מִתִּתִּי ("than to give") has a *gematria* of 13, which is the same as רָחֵל. Thus, it was as if he said, "I will give Leah to you, and Rachel to someone else."

Lavan also made a big feast for Rachel (who was in reality Leah), which he did not do later when Rachel was actually married. According to Abarbanel, the feast was meant to publicize the wedding, so that Yaakov would be ashamed later to divorce Leah.

Tosafos HaRosh, though, holds that Lavan also cheated the local people. He did not make a wedding feast, but a feast in general. He invited all the local people to a celebration without any reason, whereas Yaakov thought it was a wedding celebration.

Torah Temimah says that the celebration was done to confuse Yaakov by means of the feast and the large number of guests. The second time, when Yaakov married Rachel, there was no need to confuse him, so Lavan did not make any feast.

Sifsei Kohen holds that the purpose of the feast was to involve everyone in the deceit and to make all accomplices to the deed. *Oznayim LaTorah* explains that Lavan invited all the people of the place in order to be able to claim later on that it was they who had not allowed him to diverge from the local custom. Many commentators see as part of Lavan's plot the fact that he gave Zilpah, the younger maidservant, to Leah, so that Yaakov would believe that he was given the younger maidservant together with the younger daughter. (See *Rashi* below on 30:10 that Zilpah was the younger maidservant.)

I found a beautiful comment in *Avnei Shoham*. Regarding Rachel, we are told below, "And Lavan gave to Rachel his daughter Bilhah his maidservant to her as a maidservant," while with Leah it says, "And Lavan gave her Zilpah his maidservant, to her as a maidservant." Here it does not say "to Leah his daughter." The reason appears to be that Lavan hid from Zilpah that he was giving her to Leah. He just made a general statement. Zilpah did not know to whom she was being given, because he cheated her as well.

In any event, once his trickery was exposed, the *rishonim* tell us, Lavan refused to take any responsibility for his actions, and blamed it on the local people. He told Yaakov, "Complete this week, and we will give this one as well." This stress on and "we" will give in the plural tells us, says *S'forno*, that now the local people would consent to the marriage. Before that time, it was they who had refused to allow the wedding to be held, because "it is not done so in our place."

Ramban, too, says that it appears to him that Lavan's words were uttered as a mere subterfuge. He claimed that the local people thought it detestable that the younger daughter would be married off before the older, but now that Leah was married, the way was open for Yaakov to marry Rachel. Now the local people would agree.

Chizkuni goes further. Yaakov no longer believed Lavan's promises. He wanted the local people to guarantee that Lavan would keep his word, and they attested to it.

Malbim and R' Samson Raphael Hirsch explain Lavan's "justification" of his deed in the following way:

> "Don't think," said Lavan, "that I wanted to go back on what I told you to give you Rachel, or that I wanted to marry Leah to you against her will. Whatever I did was only in order to keep my promise. I promised you Rachel, but the custom of the place prevented this. I therefore observed the custom and gave you Leah first, so that I could keep my promise to you and Rachel. You do not have to work another seven years before you can take her. Not at all. Just 'complete this week,' and I will give you Rachel on credit. Then you can work the seven years afterwards. I gave you Leah first only so that I could give you Rachel. You don't know the customs of the place. By us, one who asks to marry the younger sister implies that he wants the older as well. Thus everything is in order, in accordance with my promise and the customs of the place."

Lavan the swindler is also a man of "justice." He is not willing to admit that he duped Yaakov. On the contrary, whatever he did to deceive Yaakov was only so as to fulfill his promise.

◆§ To Give the Younger Before the Older

It is interesting that what Lavan said to deceive Yaakov: "It is not done so in our place, to give the younger before the older," is used by a number of *rishonim* and *acharonim* as the basis for *halachah*. *Revid HaZahav* notes an argument among *Ba'alei HaTosafos* regarding this in *Kiddushin* 52. There *Ba'alei HaTosafos* bring a case which came before Rabbenu Tam, regarding the son of R' Oshiya HaLevi who was betrothed to a daughter of a certain wealthy man, without specifying which daughter it was. Rabbenu Tam says that the oldest daughter was the one he betrothed, because, "It is not done so in our place, to give the younger before the older." R' Menachem, though, argues with him on this.

Rashbam in *Bava Basra* 120a also writes that when *Chazal* tell us that the daughters of Tzelofchad are listed by age in the verse stating that they married their cousins, that is because, "It is not done so in our place, to give the younger before the older." This position supports that of R' Ami, who says, "In seating (in the *beis medrash*) one goes according to wisdom, but at a festive gathering, such as one convened for a *mitzvah* or at a wedding, one goes by age."

HaD'rush VeHaIyun brings in this regard the view of *Ramban* in his comments on *Rambam's Sefer HaMitzvos*, that the law requiring one to respect his older brother is derived from the law of respecting one's parents, because it is the wish of parents to have the younger children respect the older ones. According to this, the rule of not having the younger daughter marry before the older is also derived from the law of respecting one's parents, because that is their desire.

Bach in *Yoreh De'ah* 244:13 says that when *Tur* wrote, "At a festive gathering or wedding one goes by age in seating," he meant to tell us that even though a person might be greater than another in wisdom, one should not let him take precedence over someone who is older, in accordance with *Rashbam* which we brought above. This view is supported by many *poskim*.

Techeiles Mordechai asks how it can be that this *halachah* is derived from Lavan's behavior rather than from that of Yaakov, who was willing to take the younger before the older. And indeed *Maharsham* 3:136 rules that the prohibition is only a matter of *derech eretz* and proper manners.

But there are a number of laws that *Chazal* deduced from Lavan. For example, the rule that אֵין מְעָרְבִין שִׂמְחָה בְּשִׂמְחָה — "one does not mix one festivity with another" — is derived in *Yerushalmi Mo'ed Katan* 27 from Lavan's offer to Yaakov: "Complete this week, and we will give this one as well." And the law that the period of betrothal for a maiden is twelve months is determined in tractate *Kesuvos* from Lavan's suggestion to Eliezer (*Bereishis* 24:55), "Let the damsel abide with us a few days, at least ten," which *Chazal* render as "a full year or ten months." Also, the blessings of the *chuppah* are derived from "and they blessed Rivkah."

✥ And Hashem Saw that Leah Was Hated

All the commentators state that Yaakov's dislike of Leah was only relative, compared to his love of Rachel. One cannot explain the words simply as hatred, because the Torah said earlier, "And he also loved Rachel more than Leah." Thus we see that he loved Leah, but loved Rachel more. (*Chazal* in *Bava Basra* 123 tell us about the virtue of Leah: "Hashem saw that the deeds of Esav were detested by her, and he therefore opened her womb.")

It is man's nature, says *Ramban*, to love more the woman he first knew (as in "Adam knew Chavah"). Thus, when Yaakov loved Rachel more than Leah, it was not normal. He was angry at Leah for having collaborated with her father in having tricked him, without offering even the slightest hint that she was Leah. But she did this, *Chazal* tell us, because she did not want to fall into Esav's hands.

Rabbenu Bachya also sees in these verses a reflection of the fact that Yaakov did indeed love Leah, but loved Rachel more. R' Samson Raphael Hirsch and other commentators also explain the verses along these lines: "That Leah was disliked" — in comparison to Rachel.

S'forno says that Yaakov saw in Leah signs of barrenness, for we see that it was necessary for Hashem to "open her womb," and he thought that was the reason that Lavan wanted to deceive him. Thus Leah said about her first son, "because Hashem saw my affliction" — that Yaakov had suspected her in vain. With the second son, it was "because I was hated" — because of Yaakov's suspicion. With the third son, though, "Now my husband will accompany me" — because now he knows I am not barren, for having three children is a *chazakah* — an established claim. "Now," Leah was saying, "he can see that there was no deception in our marriage, for I am not barren."

HaKesav VeHaKabalah notes that the word יֶאֱהָבַנִי ("he will love me") has a *patach* under the *beis* (*ye'ehavani*) and not a *tzeireh* (*ye'ehaveini*). This teaches that the verb is a composite of both the past and the future tenses, and this means, "from now on, I will be beloved by him retroactively as well." This in keeping with *Chazal* in *Bereishis Rabbah* 71: "When our father Yaakov saw how Leah had tricked her sister, he thought of divorcing her. When Hashem gave her children, he said, 'Shall I divorce the mother of these?' In the end he relented." That is what the Midrash indicates regarding the verse (*Bereishis* 47:31), " 'And Yisrael bowed himself upon the head of the bed.' Who was the 'head' of Yaakov's bed?" the Midrash asks, and responds, "Was this not Leah?" Thus we see that the Midrash says that Leah enjoyed his love retroactively, as a result of the action which took place in the present.

III.
The Sources of Work Ethics

The chosen one of the *avos*, Yaakov, appears in our *parashah* as an example of what proper work ethics should be. *Halachah* includes a comprehensive set of social laws to protect the worker and his rights, but also imposes on him obligations in his relations with his employer. A worker who fulfills his duties is called a פּוֹעֵל צֶדֶק — "a just worker," a name that *Chazal* called Abba Chilkiyah (see *Ta'anis* 23; *Makkos* 24). *Rambam* (*Hil. Sechirus* 13:7) sums up these duties in the following words:

> He may not be idle from the employer's work, here a little and there a little, spending the whole day deceitfully, but must be careful with himself regarding the time, because *Chazal* were careful about the fourth blessing (i.e., *Chazal* say a worker is exempt from reciting the fourth blessing of the *bircas hamazon* — "grace after meals" — so as not to take any of his employer's time).

Rambam also rules that one has a moral obligation, as he states: "He must work with all his might, for Yaakov said, 'with all my might I worked for your father.' " This law, in regard to Yaakov, has no source in *Chazal*. *Rambam* took it directly from the Torah verse, and it is from there that it went to the authorities, such as *Tur, Shulchan Aruch*, etc.

Many similar laws are derived from the above verse. *Rambam* brings these as well, their source being *Chazal* and the *rishonim*. *Tosefta, Bava Metzia*, ch. 8, mentions the *halachah* that employees are not allowed to stay up late at night, or to afflict their bodies. In *Yerushalmi Demai* (7:3) we are told: "If that is forbidden in regard to the work of flesh and blood, how much more it is true for the work of Heaven." Yaakov was the first in Jewish history to embody this principle. He was the first worker of our people who made demands on his employer, based on the responsibility that he himself had undertaken.

Beis Yosef (*Tur Hil. Po'alim* 337) brings a view that the right granted to a worker to partake of food with which he is working is in the best interests of the employer, because then the employee will become stronger, and thus work better. That is why, he explains, this right cannot be transferred to the employee's family. But *Beis Yosef* himself disagrees with this view. First, the right to partake of the employer's food applies equally to the satiated employee who had already eaten his full. In addition, we are taught that the employee may not eat bread with the grapes he is picking, because that will lead to his consuming more of his employer's crops. Now, if the reason the employee is permitted to eat is for the employer's advantage, by all means he should eat more and thus increase his capacity for work. The latter question, though, can be answered. The fact that the employer may benefit does not necessarily mean that the employee has to be fed by him. If the employer and employee did not set any conditions about it, the employee must eat at home and not afflict his body, so that he will have strength to work to capacity. He is, however, permitted to partake of whatever food he works with, but only that, in order to strengthen his body, either for the benefit of his work or in order not to be distracted from his work by the temptation that the food induces. This therefore limits the eating rights of the employee to the food which he is processing. It is possible that *Beis Yosef's* statement, that the purpose of the allowance made to the employee is to prevent his discomfort, is also for the benefit of the employer. A worker who is suffering is incapable of working properly.

✶§ In the Day the Drought Consumed Me, and the Frost by Night

The duties of shepherds, who are paid watchmen — שׁוֹמְרֵי שָׂכָר — are also derived from the words of Yaakov (*Bereishis* 31:40): "In the day the drought consumed me, and the frost by night, and my sleep departed from my eyes." These laws are stated by *Chazal* in *Bava Metzia* 93 as stemming from Yaakov. It is interesting that *Rambam* does not mention these laws, not even in the name of Yaakov.

It appears that *Rambam* didn't want to learn these laws from Yaakov, because we do not deduce laws from events before the giving of the Torah. The duty to work with all one's might is a moral one which is left to one's own conscience. Yaakov can serve as a model for the Jewish worker, but the responsibility depicted by the verse, "in the day the drought consumed me, and the frost by night," refers primarily to the financial responsibility for an employer's property when it is in the workman's possession. The Torah requires the worker to pay for any loss to that property — according to *Rashba* even if the loss was due to an *oneis* (an accident which was no fault of the worker, i.e., if the animal died, etc.), or, according to the other commentators, only for theft or loss. This is not a moral obligation, but a clear halachic one which obligates the worker, and it cannot be deduced from events that took place before the Torah was given to the Jewish people.

✶§ Great Is Work

There are thousands of statements throughout *Chazal* on the virtue of work and physical labor. The work ethic of the chosen one of the *avos*, Yaakov, enhances the value of work to the greatest heights. *Chazal* in *Tanchuma Vayeitzei* even go as far as to say:

The virtue of work is greater than the *zechus* — virtue — of the

> *avos* ... From this we learn that a person should not say, "I will eat and drink and be well without exerting myself, and Heaven will have mercy" (on me and supply my needs). ... Rather, a person must exert himself and work with his two hands, and *Hashem* will send his blessing.

One who is not familiar with the social views of *Chazal* will stand amazed at the clarity of this definition (see in the Midrash: R' Yirmiyahu said, "More precious is work than the *zechus* of the *avos*, because the *zechus* of the *avos* rescued money, as it states, 'Had it not been for the God of my fathers ...', whereas work rescued lives, as it states, '*Hashem* saw my poverty and the work of my hands.' "). This is a basic Jewish view, which extends from the time of Yaakov to the modern day.

Ralbag, though, draws different conclusions from the Torah regarding how we should act, and summarizes the *parashah* in the following words:

> It is proper for a person ... to try to do any type of work, and even if it is below his level, so that he should not need the assistance of others. Thus we see that Yaakov, the perfect, was willing to work for Lavan in this type of work so that he would not need Lavan's favors. That is what *Chazal* meant: One should take work which is foreign to oneself rather than come to others for help.

Of course there were differences over this issue throughout the generations, just as there are in our days. We find a view which disagrees with *Ralbag*, especially as regards Yaakov, among the Chassidic sources. Thus *Tiferes Shlomo* states that a specific aim of Lavan was to uproot Yaakov from the Torah, by keeping him constantly busy and harassed with endless work. He explains the verse (*Bereishis* 31:24), "Take heed that you do not speak to Yaakov either good or bad," that one must beware not to adopt Lavan's ideas as to what is "good" or "bad." Lavan wants us to believe that combining Torah with work is good, but in reality, his intention was "bad" — to uproot those who study the Torah from the tents of Yaakov. *Tiferes Shlomo* then turns to the young men with a call: "Go out and learn" — Go to the *yeshivos* and learn *lishmah* — "for its own sake" — without any foreign intervention, because the exact opposite of this is what "Lavan the Aramean wanted," and it is not for your benefit.

Certainly everyone agrees that Lavan was not interested in helping Yaakov in any way. He definitely had Yaakov engage in exhausting work, by the use of trickery. Yet the value of work as a virtue is based on the words of Yaakov, and not on Lavan's plans, although both the *rishonim* and the *acharonim* differ here on this.

What is interesting is how the commentators point out the deceptive plans of Lavan. Before he got Yaakov to work for him, and even before Yaakov had even mentioned the idea of work, Lavan already told him, "Are you then my brother that you should work for me for nothing?" which *Rambam* explains beautifully as, "You have already been here a month without doing anything. I realize that you are an ethical person and would not like to continue to live that way. I am sure you would like to work, but I don't want you to work for nothing." Thus, with this thinly veiled hint, he obliged Yaakov to engage in the exhausting labor of tending Lavan's flocks.

Other commentators see this hint in the previous verse, where Lavan says, "You are my flesh and bone." You came here without a thing, like a slave, of whom we are told (*Shemos* 21:3), "If he comes in by himself." You brought nothing with you to keep you alive. That being the case, it is only natural that we must presume that you will begin to work for me.

But after Yaakov had already worked for fourteen years and asked to be paid for his work, Lavan suddenly puts on the cloak of *"yiras Shamayim,"* and told him, "Your work brought me no income. While it is true that I have been blessed since you arrived, that is because I kept the *mitzvah* of *tzedakah* by supporting you, who are nothing but a loafer. And it was not because of your ability."

Commentators with different approaches, such as *Kli Yakar*, the Dubno Magid, R' Samson Raphael Hirsch and others, all explain the dispute between Lavan and Yaakov on that basis. Lavan claimed that, "Hashem blessed me because of you" — the blessing was from Hashem because he had been supporting Yaakov, while Yaakov claimed that Hashem's blessing was due to his work and toil, "You know how I worked for you." That is why I want you to stop being sanctimonious when you are asked to pay me for my work. Don't use Hashem's name to justify your scheming, when you try to steal the poor man's lamb.

S'forno is the only one among the commentators who holds that Yaakov was already wealthy when he came to Lavan, because he wouldn't have married if he had nothing. What Yaakov meant when he exclaimed, "With my staff I crossed the Jordan," was that he had come without any flock or any skill. Yaakov worked for his wives, not because he was poor, but because that was the customary way of paying the bride price. The daughters of Lavan said (*Bereishis* 31:15), "For he has sold us," because the bride price that Lavan took was inflated. To

Yaakov, though, the years of work were "as few as days," and he thought that the bride price was cheap. This view of *S'forno*, which is different from that of the other commentators, is based on his view that Yaakov wanted to teach future generations not to take a wife in marriage unless one has the means to support her.

◆§ Return to the Land of Your Fathers

Both *rishonim* and *acharonim* attempt to explain Yaakov's actions in placing the rods before the cattle. It appears that this, too, was meant to be an object lesson for future generations, not to give in to injustice and evil, and not to be afraid to work to recover something stolen from the thief who stole it. This idea is central to a number of other *parashiyos* in the Torah, in regard to the *avos*. Indeed this is the way a number of commentators explain this incident.

The *acharonim* explain the words of Lavan's sons, "Yaakov took all that is to our father" in terms of the fact that Yaakov adopted Lavan's methods in order to foil his plots. Yaakov managed to get what rightfully belonged to him by "trickery," which Lavan's sons had thought was only something their father was familiar with.

Some commentators see in this clash not only social dispute between Yaakov the employee and Lavan the exploiter, but a general clash between Israel and the other nations. It has always been the way of the other nations, says *Chasam Sofer*, that even though they are supported by the work of the Jews, not to allow the Jews themselves to earn a living except through trickery. Afterwards they come and complain, as did the sons of Lavan, that "It is from that of our father that he acquired all this wealth."

The *tzaddik*, R' Shlomo Leib of Lenchna, uses this to explain one of the verses that we say in the *Hoshanos*, "Save us because of the rods that were used in the water troughs." It seems strange to call upon Hashem for the *zechus* — the merit — of the rods used by Yaakov. But, says the *tzaddik*, these words are used to oppose the claim against us by the prosecuting angel, as to how Israel earns its money among the nations. What should we do, when we have no other choice? Even Yaakov the *tzaddik* was forced to use cunning in order to claim what rightfully belonged to him from Lavan.

From this, the logical and practical conclusion follows that it was time for Yaakov to "return to the land of your fathers," as explained by *Chazal* in *Bereishis Rabbah* 74: "Your possessions outside *Eretz Yisrael* have no blessing, but once you return to the land of your fathers, I will be with you."

What *Chafetz Chaim* has to say on this in our *parashah* is remarkable:

> When the other nations criticize the Jewish people, they make all types of accusations against us, in terms of, "And he heard the words of the sons of Lavan." We, though, remain silent, absorb our shame, and do not react. We go our way and they theirs. But when we see that their faces are not the way they used to be toward us, when the heads of states exhibit their anger to us, then we must leave for a place of refuge, and the most safe refuge is the land of our fathers — "Return to the land of your fathers."

IV.
A "Double" Theft from Lavan's House

In the *parashah* of how Yaakov and his family fled from Lavan's house, Lavan accuses Yaakov of two types of "theft." He accuses him of stealing "his *terafim*" — a form of idol used for divining the future — and again, of stealing "his heart." The first was an actual theft, which was done by Rachel without Yaakov's knowledge. The Torah does not explain why she did this. Nor are we told if Yaakov ever found out about the theft.

As the theft of Lavan's *terafim* is juxtaposed with what follows, "And Yaakov stole the heart of Lavan the Aramean, because he did not tell him that he was fleeing," it appears that the commentary of *Rashbam* and other commentators is appropriate, when they state that the theft of the *terafim* was meant to ensure that Lavan would not find out that Yaakov had fled.

Rashbam brings proof of the ability of the *terafim* to tell the future from what we are told in *Zecharyah* (10:2), "The *terafim* have spoken vanity." But if that is so, and if, as *Rashi* states, Rachel intended to wrest her father away from idol worship, it is surprising she didn't tell Yaakov about the theft. The fact that she did not tell Yaakov led him to tell Lavan, "By whoever your gods are found, shall not live," and, according to *Chazal*, that is the reason why Rachel died on the way.

In the Torah, we are only told of the theft of the *terafim* as a fact and no more, without the Torah adopting either a positive or negative position on the matter. Lavan's complaint, "Why have you stolen my gods?" seems somewhat ludicrous, coming from a boor who believed in a god that could be stolen.

There are commentators who hold that the reason why Rachel stole them was similar to the argument that Yoash offered to the people of his city (*Shoftim* 6:31): "If he is a god, let him plead for himself, because someone has thrown down his altar." It would also appear that by placing the *terafim* in the saddle of the camel, Rachel was showing contempt for them, and demonstrated that she did not, Heaven forbid, believe in them. Thus the explanation of *Chazal*, as brought by *Rashi*, appears logical — that Rachel took the *terafim* so as to remove her father from idolatry.

Ibn Ezra, though, disagrees with this interpretation. If that was the case, he says, why didn't she simply throw them away, or bury them someplace? Why was she carrying them with her? *Ibn Ezra* thus explains that the idols were like zodiacal charms. Rachel was afraid if she left the idols, her father could use them to find out in which direction Yaakov had fled, and that was why she stole them. She did not dispose of them on the way, because they were not actually idols that were worshiped. *Ramban*, along the same lines, says that they were an instrument used for telling time.

The word used for idols here, *terafim*, is found often in *Tanach*, and in connection with magic or various idolatrous practices. Thus we are told in *Hoshea* (3:4), "... without a prince, and without a sacrifice, and without an image, and without an *efod*, and without *terafim*." The *efod* was a holy utensil, and yet we see the word *terafim* linked to it. And we see similar usages in *I Shmuel* 15 and in *Yechezkel* 21. All of these show that *terafim* were used for magical purposes. On the other hand, we are told that Michal, David's wife, placed *terafim* and a pillow of goat's hair in her bed, so that those looking for David would think that he was still in his bed (*I Shmuel* 19:13). If it was meant for magic, why was it to be found in David's house?

Ramban therefore holds that *terafim* were used for telling time, but magicians used them for their magic, and would employ them to tell the future. They were called תְּרָפִים from the root רפה, meaning "weak," because their prophecy was weak and unreliable. It is possible that Lavan worshiped them, as it says, "Why did you steal my gods?" In general, though, they were not worshiped, but were used for telling the future. Thus we see (*Shoftim* 17) that Michah made for himself a copy of the *efod* used in the *Beis HaMikdash* as well as *terafim*, and that way became known as one who could tell the future. Aram, the home of Lavan, was a place filled with witchcraft. Bilaam also came from Aram, and it appears that Lavan was also a magician, as he said (*Bereishis*

30:27), "I divined." [See *Targum Yehonasan* to *Bamidbar* 22:5 where Lavan and Bilaam are identified as one and the same person.]

Rachel took from Lavan the tools he used to do his magic, but for what purpose? Was it because she was afraid of the *terafim*, or was it to have her father stop worshiping idols? *Ramban* does not answer that question. According to him, the *terafim* in themselves were not bad. They were only a tool for telling the hours, and thus it is not surprising that they were found in David's house.

But *Zohar*, *Targum Yehonasan*, *Pirkei D'Rebbi Eliezer* and others hold that the *terafim* were actual *avodah zarah* — idolatry. They say that this idol was a firstborn son that had been killed and embalmed. A certain potion was placed under the tongue, and then the idol would tell the future. *Ma'asei Hashem* adopts the view of *Zohar* here, and says that the word תְּרָפִים is a word indicating condemnation, such as מְקוֹם תּוֹרְפָה. The *terafim* in David's house, on the other hand, were simply objects in the form of a human body, upon which clothes were placed to be cleaned. Because of their similarity to the shape of a human body, Michal placed the *terafim* in bed with goat's hair at the top, so as to fool those looking for David.

Shaloh holds that Rachel's words, "it is the way of women upon me," were the truth, and by this she was hinting at the presence of the idols. *Chazal* in *Shabbos* 82 tell us that touching *avodah zarah* makes one *tameh* as does a menstruating woman (*niddah*), and thus Rachel was indeed a *niddah*.

Ramban, *Rabbenu Bachya* and others, though, hold that Rachel was trying to frighten her father away through the impurity (*tum'ah*) of *niddah*. A *niddah* was regarded as impure and harmful to anyone who came into contact with her, where even her breath and the ground she walked on were *tameh* and harmful, as *Rabbenu Bachya* explains in *Parashas Tazria*. When Rachel told her father that she was a *niddah*, he avoided entering her tent.

In any event, the theft of the *terafim* by Rachel is an unclear episode in the Torah, of whose reason we are not sure. According to *Chazal*, who say she wanted to remove her father from idol worship, Yaakov's words, as explained by *Chasam Sofer*, become quite clear. Yaakov said, "By whoever your gods are found, shall not live." By this he meant, "Even if your gods are found in the hands of one of us, you will see that what you found is only a lifeless corpse." Therefore, "Recognize for yourself what is with me," i.e., learn my faith in Hashem, "and take for yourself" faith in Hashem when you go back home. That, of course, is *d'rush*, but fits in with the above idea of *Chazal*.

◆§ Stealing Lavan's "Heart"

Lavan claimed that his heart had been stolen (i.e., that he had been deceived). The Torah also tells us, "Yaakov stole the heart of Lavan the Aramean, because he did not tell him that he was fleeing." The Torah commentators are astonished. Should Yaakov then have told Lavan that he was fleeing? And if he didn't tell him, was that "stealing his heart"? *S'forno* says that Yaakov knew how to deal with Lavan cunningly. He acted as if he didn't realize how Lavan had turned against him, and as if he hadn't heard the words of the sons of Lavan, "It is from that of our father that he acquired all this wealth." He pretended that he hadn't sensed the hostility in the air, and didn't show by his actions that he, Yaakov, planned to leave. It was not that he was unethical or ungrateful, but because he realized that "he was fleeing." Yaakov was afraid that Lavan, assisted by the town's people, would steal everything he owned if they suspected that he wanted to leave. By his cunning, says *Akeidah*, Yaakov was able to prevent Lavan from suspecting anything, even though people sometimes have a feeling of what will happen, especially those like Lavan who are involved in magic.

Or HaChayim adds another detail about this "theft of the heart." Yaakov had asked Lavan earlier to send him home, and from this Lavan understood that Yaakov would not go unless he gave him his permission. Afterwards, when Lavan realized that Yaakov had fled, he understood that Yaakov's asking for permission had been a ruse, so as to lessen Lavan's alertness.

Alshech, and following him other commentators, explains the meaning of the verse in the exact opposite manner. Yaakov would threaten Lavan over every small matter, claiming that he would go back to his father's house. Thus Lavan did not believe that Yaakov would ever carry out his threat (*Bereishis* 31:20): "And Yaakov stole Lavan's heart" — he stole it — "by telling not" — by turning every nothing into a threat "that he was fleeing." This way, Lavan did not realize when Yaakov actually made plans to leave.

Abarbanel has an interesting interpretation. Yaakov's "theft of the heart" consisted of the fact that he never told Lavan "that he was fleeing" from Esav. Had he told Lavan about his troubles with Esav and that he had been forced to flee from him, Lavan would have known that this "naive" person was indeed cunning, and that Yaakov might flee from him as well.

To'ali'os LeRalbag explains the objective of this flight. Yaakov was sure that Hashem would deliver him, but at the same time he did

BEREISHIS — VAYEITZEI / 185

whatever he could to save himself from Lavan by natural means. He waited until Lavan had gone to shear his sheep, and then he departed before anyone would notice. Even when Hashem offers assurance, He wants the person to help himself by natural means. Similarly, Hashem wanted Yaakov to use the rods with the sheep, even though He had promised him that even without these the sheep would be spotted and speckled.

That is not the view of *Chasam Sofer*. He expresses his amazement that Yaakov fled. And these are his words in our *parashah*:

> It is surprising that our old father fled, for after Hashem had told him, "Go, leave this land," he should have trusted in Hashem and should have left openly, and not as one who flees after committing a theft or trickery. And it may have been because of this that Dinah his daughter was stolen from him in the same fashion.

~§ Lavan Wished to Uproot All

Lavan expressed his true feelings when he exclaimed (*Bereishis* 31:29), "I have the power in my hand to do you evil." He wanted to do evil not only to Yaakov, but also "to you" — to all of you. Lavan wanted to uproot all. He wanted to kill his own daughters and his grandchildren together with Yaakov. The *rishonim* are surprised at this comment of Lavan, that he had the power to do evil to Yaakov and his family, when immediately afterwards he explained that Hashem had appeared to him in a dream and told him, "Watch out for yourself not to speak to Yaakov good or bad." Abarbanel and *S'forno* both explain that what Lavan was saying was that he had the right legally and morally to punish Yaakov severely for fleeing. But Hashem had intervened, and had told him to treat Yaakov *lifnim mishuras hadin* — "beyond that the law stipulates" — i.e., to be merciful to him.

Rabbenu Bachya has a different explanation. Lavan claimed that he had had the opportunity to treat Yaakov evilly for the past twenty years, because only the previous night had Hashem told him not to do so. If he had not acted evilly to Yaakov until that time, that was proof that his intentions to Yaakov were honorable.

Pardes Yosef, in the name of *Cheshek Shlomo*, brings a beautiful explanation of the words of Lavan in our *parashah*. Lavan claimed: "Hashem only told me not to do anything bad to you, but did not deny me the freedom of choice to do whatever I want regardless. Had that not been the case, he would have told you not to be afraid, rather than telling me not to do anything bad to you. Hashem said to me whatever

He did, but I can do whatever I want. It is true that I will be punished for it, but not because I did something bad to you, but because I didn't listen to Hashem."

R' Mendl of Riminov, in his *Mevaser Tov*, finds in the words of Lavan, "I have the power in my hand to do you evil," an attempt to deceive Yaakov as to what Hashem actually said. Hashem had told him, "from good to bad." This Lavan explained to mean that he was forbidden anything in the range of "from good to bad," but there was nothing forbidding him from doing something which was completely bad.

Meleches Machsheves explains that Lavan acted as a "sweet" innocent, and said, "Hashem forbade me to talk to you from good to bad, but I am permitted to do to you whatever bad I want."

⋄§ Why Should He Do "Good" to Him?

Hashem forbade Lavan even to do good to Yaakov, just as he forbade him to do bad. *Rashi*, quoting the Midrash, says: "All the good of the wicked ones is bad for the righteous ones." *S'forno* explains the "good and bad" in terms of Yaakov's remaining with Lavan. Lavan claimed that if Yaakov remained with him, it would be good for him. That was why Hashem forbade Lavan even to seek to do good to Yaakov. Not everything which seemed bad in Lavan's eyes seemed bad to Yaakov, and vice versa. The ideas of good and bad appear different to a wicked person; in fact they are the exact opposite of how they appear to a righteous person.

Kesav Sofer has a nice *d'rush* on this. In the *Haggadah*, we are told, "And if the Holy One, Blessed be He, had not taken our fathers out of Egypt, we and our children and our children's children would have been slaves to Pharaoh in Egypt." The *d'rush sefarim* explain that had Hashem Himself not taken us out of Egypt, but instead allowed Pharaoh to send us out voluntarily, all our lives we would have owed Pharaoh thanks, and we would have been enslaved to him in our bodies and souls. Here too, Hashem did not want Lavan to do any "good" to Yaakov, so that Yaakov should not have to be grateful and indebted to him for having done that good to him.

Kedushas Levi says: Lavan was surprised to hear words in defense of Yaakov from Hashem, as well as the directive that forbade him to do any bad. Until then, Lavan had thought that Yaakov was a man of his own kind. He did not recognize Yaakov's *kedushah* — "sanctity" — because Yaakov knew how to conceal his behavior from Lavan. Lavan was full of lies, and thought Yaakov was the same. Now, when he heard the greatness of Yaakov from Hashem, he came with a complaint to Yaakov, "Why did you conceal yourself to flee?" Why did you hide your actions, so that I didn't know your true nature? Why didn't you reveal to me what you are, and then, "I would have sent you out joyfully and with song, with drum and harp."

R' Moshe Leib of Sasov adds: Had I known you are a *tzaddik*, I would have sent you from me long ago, because I don't want to have such people near me, who can "ruin" whatever I "fixed."

◆§ Between Yaakov and Lavan the Aramean

It is said, in the name of R' Eliyahu Chaim Meisel, that Yaakov was terrified by the kind and sweet words of Lavan. He knew that Lavan by his nature was his opponent, and here suddenly Lavan was telling him, "Why did you conceal yourself to flee, and did not tell me? And I would have sent you out joyfully and with song, with drum and harp." In response to these friendly words, we are told, "Yaakov was angry and he quarreled with Lavan. And he said, 'What is my sin and what is my transgression that you pursued me?' " Yaakov was angry at Lavan's good spirits, and the love which he was showing.

This idea is expanded upon in the Chassidic works. As long as Yaakov lived with Lavan and Lavan was not happy with him, Yaakov knew that he himself was following the proper path. A person like Lavan by his very nature and essence had to hate Yaakov, because *tum'ah* and *kedushah* cannot dwell side by side. Now, though, that he saw that Lavan had suddenly begun to love him, claiming, "Why did you not permit me to kiss my daughters?" and had told him, "I would have sent you out joyfully and with song, with drum and harp," Yaakov became terrified at this love, and said, "What is my sin and what is my transgression?" I must have sinned, because "you pursued me." If you are so eager to come to me and you love me, it must mean that I have sinned, to the extent that even you have begun to like me and to long for me.

The commentators discuss the complaints between Yaakov and Lavan. *Akeidah* gives *six* strong complaints of Yaakov against his father-in-law: (a) You have checked all of my things and didn't find anything belonging to you; how could you have accused me of such a thing? (b) I worked for you for twenty years, and I did not make you lose a penny, "Your ewes and your she-goats never lost their young;" (c) I never took anything of yours nor derived benefit from it, "and the rams of your flock I never ate;" (d) I was never negligent in my work, "I never brought you a *treifah*" — an animal torn by a predator; I paid for every loss, whether it occurred during the day or night; (e) my work was very difficult, "In the day the drought consumed me, and the frost by night;" (f) I owe you nothing, because "I served you fourteen years for your two daughters, and six years for your sheep."

Regarding all these correct complaints, Lavan gave a single cynical answer, as stated by *HaKesav VeHaKabalah*. "The women are my daughters." When you claim that you were afraid that I would steal them from you, that is irrelevant, because they are mine anyway. Similarly, "the cattle are my cattle," and don't tell me that it was because of you that I did so well. All of the cattle are mine, and you got them by fraud. "Whatever you see is mine." I did not search your things but was searching mine, because everything is mine, and you own nothing.

Chafetz Chaim says that Lavan's complaints have been at the base of the anti-Semitic ideology throughout the ages:

> That is the way of the nations in the land of our *galus*. We work with the sweat of our brow and acquire every penny by דָּמִים (*damim*), in both senses of the term (i.e., "blood" and "money"), and not only that, but the nations become wealthy by the fruit of our labor. We are careful not to touch what belongs to them in the slightest, "from a string to a shoelace," and yet they complain, "Whatever you see is mine." All is theirs. Both we ourselves and all our work. In their eyes, they are the masters and we are their slaves, and whatever a slave acquires belongs to his master.

It is not for nothing that this *parashah* comes after Hashem tells Yaakov, "Return to the land of your fathers." Hashem wanted to prove to Yaakov how essential that commandment was, and how we do not belong in a hostile land. If Yaakov had not realized earlier how essential this was, he was now convinced of it following the cynical remarks of Lavan.

Vayishlach – וישלח

I.
Lesson of the Meeting Between Yaakov and Esav

The meeting between Yaakov and Esav, when Yaakov returned from Lavan's house was, according to *Ramban*, a lesson for all future generations. It teaches us that Hashem saved His servant and redeemed him from one who was stronger than he by sending an angel to save him. Further, it teaches us that Yaakov did not trust his own righteousness, but did whatever he could on his own. There is, however, also an intimation for all future generations, that whatever happened to Yaakov will happen to us in regard to the children of Esav, and we too should prepare ourselves in the three ways that Yaakov prepared himself: by prayer, by gifts, and for war.

R' Samson Raphael Hirsch also explains this *parashah*, following in the footsteps of the *rishonim*, as a lesson for future generations, but he transfers the emphasis to the substantive spiritual differences between the Jewish people and the other nations throughout history. Yaakov is absorbed in his concern for the wholeness and welfare of his family. He builds himself up gradually, and finally attains internal happiness and a tranquil family life, but the political strength is always in the hands of others. Yaakov must always depend on the favors of others. While Yaakov is preparing to settle down, Esav is already established as both ruler and warlord of his people. For thousands of years, says Hirsch, this struggle has continued between Yaakov and Esav. The former has the most glorious family life, while the latter has all the strength and power. Is it enough to be a person and to forgo political power, or has man been created only to serve the interests of political power? That is the question to which the Torah with all its *mitzvos* and commands gives us a clear answer. The final victory will belong to the moral side, and not to the one with power.

As opposed to other commentators who see this as a hypocritical gesture, Hirsch sees the kiss which Esav kissed Yaakov as a hint to what will happen in the end of days. Esav's kisses and tears show that deep within him there beats a spark of humanity, as an inheritance from Avraham. Esav will eventually put aside the sword from his hand and will lend a hand to progressive humanity, to the light of Godly ethical values. His position regarding Yaakov proves to what extent humanity beats in his heart. When the strong supports the strong, there is nothing remarkable about that, but when the strong, like Esav, falls on the neck of Yaakov, that is a victory for justice. That will be the final stage in the extended struggle between Yaakov and Esav.

Rabbenu Bachya sees the details of the *parashah* as illustrating the abyss that lies between Yaakov and Esav. Yaakov speaks at length, but Esav is curt, which signifies his conceit. But there is something else that is interesting. Esav does not mention Hashem in his words, and Yaakov mentions Him many times. Yaakov says, "The children that God favored to your servant;" "as seeing the face of God;" "for God favored me." These hints in the Torah are all filled with significance and are characteristic of the difference between the two.

The Dubno Magid quotes a Midrash and then explains it. The Midrash on our *parashah* states: "Yaakov lifted his eyes and saw Esav coming from afar, and then lifted his eyes to Heaven." The term "from afar" tells us that Esav's deeds would apply not only to that time, but to the future generations, namely not only to the Esav of that time, but to all future Esavs. It tells us how we are to act to him in order to be saved from his clutches. What, then, is the lesson the *rishonim* and *acharonim* learn from our *parashah*, that was meant to be a lesson for future generations?

❧ Gifts, Prayer, Battle

Yaakov used three means in his preparation to meet Esav: gifts, prayer, and battle. *Rashi* explains on the verse, "and the remaining camp will be a refuge," that Yaakov would, against his will, if necessary, engage in battle, thus allowing the other camp to escape. *HaKesav VeHaKabalah* sees this interpretation in the verses themselves. If the first camp comes "and he will smite him" — will smite Esav — then the second camp will come to the aid of the first. This view of the battle with Esav is that of the Midrash and those commentators that follow in its path.

But many commentators reject, or do not mention at all, this means as one of the possible ways for Yaakov to save himself. This was meant as a lesson for future generations, says Rabbenu Bachya, and we must follow in the paths of our forefathers and prepare ourselves to meet our enemies with gifts, with a soft tongue, and with prayers to Hashem; but we cannot meet them in battle, because Hashem made us swear not to get involved in battles with our enemies.

Ramban, too, does not mention battle as a possible means for Yaakov to be saved. According to him, the meaning of *against his will* refers to the will of the other nations, who will not be able to destroy us, because that is the wish of Hashem. The Children of Esav cannot wipe us all out at the same time. If one king enacts evil decrees against us and orders us exiled from his land, another king arises to save and redeem us, and opens his doors to the refugees.

Akeidas Yitzchak has an interesting opinion of the meaning of the Torah here. I will summarize his view below, but it needs thorough study in the original, because it deals, in terms of *hashkafah*, with all the plots of man. According to *Akeidah*, what the Torah meant to teach us is that one must combine *emunah* with whatever one is able to do under natural conditions, and cannot under any circumstances rely on a miracle, without doing something to try to prevent the danger. When we are told (*Tehillim* 33:18), "Behold, the eye of Hashem is upon those that fear Him ... to deliver their soul from death," that is only where the person does whatever he himself is capable of doing, but not when he sits with folded hands and waits for Hashem to save him. Not trying to help oneself is a sin. *Akeidah* quotes *Midrash Shochar Tov* on *Tehillim* 23, which brings the verse (*Devarim* 2:7): " 'For Hashem your God has blessed you in all the works of your hand.' One might imagine that (this applies) even if one sits by idly; it therefore states, 'in all the work of your hands.' If one worked, one is blessed, and if not, one is not blessed."

Man, continues *Akeidah*, is forbidden to trust in miracles, just as he is forbidden to give up hope but must do whatever he can, and must hope that Hashem will save him. Shmuel was afraid to go and anoint David by Hashem's orders, because he feared that Shaul might kill him. Hashem then advised him how to save himself in a natural manner: "Take a heifer in your hand, and say, 'I have come to sacrifice to Hashem'" (*I Shmuel* 16:2). Who is greater than David, whom Hashem promised to save from all his enemies? And yet he did not rely on miracles when he went to Achish, king of Gas. David did what he could by acting as if he were insane, allowing his saliva to drip on his beard and so on, and thoroughly humiliating himself, and all this so as to save himself in a natural manner. After he had done whatever he could, he turned to Hashem to save him and said (*Tehillim* 142:4-5), "I looked on my right hand and saw, but there was no one that would know me —

escape failed me; no one cared for my soul. I cried unto you, Hashem." And indeed, after man has tried all the natural avenues and thinks that he may be forced to accept the evil decree, that is when Hashem's deliverance comes. Thus, when Achish went out to war against Israel and called upon David to go out with him in battle against Shaul, their joint enemy, David was in serious trouble, as he had never been before. He was invited by an ally, as it were, to fight against the Jewish people. What could he do? How could he emerge from his distress? But Hashem looks after *tzaddikim*, and He had the servants of Achish persuade him to send David back from the battle, because he might act treacherously, or, as they put it (*I Shmuel* 29:5), "How can he reconcile himself unto his master? Will it not be with the heads of these men?" Hashem's plan, as arranged through Achish's men, saved David from his predicament.

These examples from *Akeidah* are penetrating and decisive, and, in his opinion, they justify the plans that Yaakov made in trying to save himself from Esav, even though he had a promise from Hashem that He would preserve him wherever he went.

◆§ Yaakov's Fear

Ramban explains that Yaakov was afraid because he was forced to pass through the area where Esav lived. Edom is in the south of *Eretz Yisrael*, and Yitzchak lived in "the land of the south." Yaakov thus had to pass through Edom, or near it. That was why he was afraid, and sent messengers before him. *Chazal* are especially taken aback by this action of Yaakov, and quote the verse (*Mishle* 26:17), "He that passes by, and meddles with strife that does not belong to him, is like one that takes a dog by the ears." Hashem said to him, "Esav was going along the way and had nothing against you," yet you drew attention to yourself by sending messengers.

According to *Ramban*, this is a hint that it was the same type of flattery of Edom later on that brought about the destruction of the Second *Beis HaMikdash*. The Chashmona'im made a treaty with Rome where there was no necessity for this (this refers to the first Chashmona'im), and that eventually brought about the intervention of the Romans and the destruction.

Oznayim LaTorah points out a second possibility that Yaakov had available to him, which he only used at the end. After he had met Esav, he changed his mind and did not pass through Seir, but instead crossed the Jordan and went by way of Shechem. He had this same opportunity from the very beginning, and had no need to send messengers to Esav. And that is why *Chazal* were upset about Yaakov as "meddling with strife that did not belong to him."

Both *rishonim* and *acharonim* attempt to understand Yaakov's fear. After all, Hashem had promised him, "I will preserve you wherever you go, and I will return you to this land." *Chazal's* words (*Berachos* 4), that Yaakov was afraid that he might have sinned and thus lost Hashem's protection, are well known, but most of the *rishonim* do not content themselves with that explanation alone, and explain the fear and its cause, each in his own way.

According to Ibn Ezra, the promise was not enough to dissolve Yaakov's fears for the fate of his children and household, because Esav might kill them all, and Hashem's promise might have applied only to Yaakov himself.

Ramban does not hold that the promise did not include his children and household. If his children would have been killed, Hashem's promise would not have been fulfilled. *Ramban* bases himself on *Chazal*, in explaining that the reason for this fear was that the messengers came back and told him that they saw that Esav still hated him. To bolster this view, *Ramban* says that it is logical to assume that Esav did not greet the messengers respectfully, and may not even have allowed them to talk to him. Had this not been the case, the Torah would have told us what Esav answered the messengers. That is why the messengers said, "We came to your brother, to Esav," but they did not receive any reply from him. Instead of answering, he was coming to meet him with four hundred men, and that was enough of a reason for Yaakov to be afraid.

Rashbam holds the opposite, that the messengers told him that Esav was coming out of respect for him, and was bringing four hundred men with him as a sign of this respect. Yaakov, though, did not believe that Esav meant him well. He crossed the river, seeking to avoid a confrontation, just as we see when David fled before Avshalom and disobeyed the counsel of his advisors.

Chizkuni explains that when the Torah says that Yaakov was "afraid and distressed," it refers to doubts that build up in one's heart. Esav did not answer the messengers, but only said that he was going to meet Yaakov. Yaakov did not know if this trip was for good or for evil. Had he known that Esav's intentions were bad, says R' Yosef Bechor Shor, he would have fled before him to the fortified cities. But if Esav was coming only as a sign of respect, then Yaakov's fleeing would make Esav angry at him, as in the folk-expression, "If someone is running away, it means that someone is chasing him." A doubt in one's heart is the worst possible situation in which to find oneself. Yaakov did not know what to do.

In Yaakov's condition, explains *Or HaChayim*, if he did not take up arms, Esav was liable to kill him, so that meant that he should take up arms. But then again, Esav might be coming in peace. In the end, he decided "to divide" his household into two camps, one of which would be ready for peace and the other for war.

Beis Halevi, too, explains this along similar lines, and he uses this interpretation to explain Yaakov's prayer: "Save me please from my brother, from Esav." Both of these possibilities were negative. If he appeared as a brother who wanted peace, Yaakov would be harmed spiritually by becoming too friendly with him, and if he appeared as Esav the Wicked, there would be bloodshed. Either scenario was a bad one, and Yaakov prayed to be saved from both.

Malbim says — and this is found in many Chassidic works — that Yaakov's fear was the reason why he was distressed. A person who really trusts Hashem will not fear mortals. This is as we see in *Yeshayahu* (51:12-13), "Who are you, that you should be afraid of a man that shall die... And forget Hashem your maker." This certainly applied to Yaakov, who had received a promise from Hashem that He would guard him. Yaakov realized that in spite of that promise he was still afraid, and therefore "he was distressed." He was afraid that Hashem might not perform a miracle for him, because he did not have perfect *bitachon*, and therefore he wanted to see if he could save himself by natural means.

The Chassidic works add that in his weakness, man often runs away from a situation which Hashem had wanted for his benefit. The person evaluates his situation logically, and does not realize what Hashem's true meaning is in this. The reason that Esav was to meet Yaakov was so as to have Esav come to terms with the events of the past, and to recognize the right of Yaakov, but Yaakov, because of his realistic approach, was afraid of this meeting.

Baal Shem Tov explains a verse in keeping with this. We are told (*Tehillim* 23:6), "Surely goodness and mercy will pursue me." David prayed and asked Hashem that if, through ignorance, he ran away from goodness and mercy, that they should nevertheless run after him and catch him, and that was what happened with Yaakov.

Abarbanel has an original interpretation of Yaakov's fear. It was not because his *emunah* was weak or that he was unsure of his ultimate mission, but, on the contrary, this is the fear of the truly mighty man. When he goes to war, he is afraid of death, and yet in spite of this he goes out to fight. If a mighty person is fearless and does not fear death, that is nothing new, just as there is nothing new about a rich person who wastes money, because he doesn't realize the value of money. Had Yaakov not been afraid, it would have been a sign that he trusted his brother, but now that he was afraid and still went to meet Esav, it was a clear sign that he had *bitachon* in Hashem.

∽§ One May Flatter the Wicked

Together with preparing for war, Yaakov humbled himself before Esav and referred to him eight times as "my master." *Chazal* in *Sotah* 41 learn from this *parashah* that one is permitted to flatter wicked people in this world. We are also told in *Bereishis Rabbah* that Rebbi referred to Antoninus with all types of exaggerated titles, and based himself on Yaakov, who flattered Esav. Rav Afas has a different opinion about this. The Midrash there also states that at the time that Yaakov referred to Esav as "my master," Hashem said to him, "You humiliated yourself and referred to Esav as 'my master' eight times. By your life that I will anoint eight of his sons kings before your sons." These two views are expressed by *Chazal* in countless places. R' Samson Raphael Hirsch gives an interesting interpretation of this: We cannot learn an object lesson from the way Yaakov related to Esav, because when it came to Lavan he treated him entirely differently, in a much more forceful and lordly manner. Only before Esav did he humble himself in such a way, as he felt himself obligated to Esav because of the birthright and the blessing, and therefore wanted to appease him.

Abarbanel and *Ramban* also say that Yaakov wanted to have Esav forget about the birthright, and to act as if he recognized him as his older brother.

Chazal in *Sotah* 41 are astonished at the expression, "For I have seen your face as the face of *Elokim*." They say that this expression was said because Yaakov was afraid for his life. Various commentators, such as *Ramban* and *S'forno*, explain that Yaakov asked Esav to accept his gift and be appeased with it, just as Hashem is appeased when a person brings a sacrifice, or just as high officials are appeased in this way. High officials, too, are sometimes referred to as *elohim*.

Yaakov was interested, says *Tosefes Brachah*, to have Esav take from him the gift and be bribed by it. But Esav refused it and said, "I have much, my brother." Yaakov therefore said to him, "I am not giving you this as a gift of generosity, but as the courtesy one shows to high officials," and then Esav accepted the gift.

The commentators are also astounded by something which appears to be a lie. Yaakov told Esav when he met with him, "Until I come to my master to Se'ir," but he never did arrive there. *Chazal* in *Avodah Zarah* 25 learn from this a *halachah*, that if a Jew meets a non-Jew on the way, and the non-Jew asks him where he is going, he should always mention a destination beyond where he is going, just as Yaakov did with Esav (for he went to Sukkos, which is before Se'ir).

Ramban says that Yaakov did not say clearly that he was going to Se'ir, but, "If I pass in that direction, I will visit you." *Ramban* also brings the view of *Chazal* that when the *Mashiach* comes, Yaakov will indeed go to Se'ir, as in the verse (*Ovadya* 1:21), "And saviors will come up on Mount Zion to judge the Mount of Esav."

Abarbanel takes the verse and rearranges its parts as follows: "Let my master go before his servant to Se'ir, and I will proceed at a slow pace." But *Ma'asei Hashem* tells us a *chiddush*, that Yaakov did keep his word. *Se'ir* is the name of a district. Yaakov passed through that district on his way to Sukkos. He never said he would visit Esav, but would reach the region where Esav ruled, and from there he would continue on his way.

II.
A Nation Which Dwells Alone

The *parashah* of the struggle between Yaakov and the mystery "man" until the dawn broke is quite extraordinary. It is clear that this was an angel in the form of a man, whose arrival was for a specific mission, since it is evident that he conferred a new name, Yisrael, upon Yaakov, because "you have contended (שָׂרִיתָ) with Hashem and prevailed," yet he did not reveal his name and who he was.

Why did the angel suddenly appear to Yaakov here, in the middle of his journey to Esav? This is not answered by the Torah itself, but is discussed by various commentators, each in his own way. What is clear from the verses is that the angel strived to vanquish Yaakov and to subdue him for a purpose known to the angel, but in the end was beaten, and blessed Yaakov instead of harming him. Still, during the encounter Yaakov suffered an injured thigh and this led to the prohibition of *gid hanasheh*, the sinew of the femoral vein.

The ending makes this *parashah* even more astounding. If Yaakov vanquished the angel, why was he hurt in the thigh? There is no doubt that there are matters here that need considerable explaining. It is thus not surprising that the commentators explained this *parashah* in widely differing ways, some of them symbolically in a way which is far from the simple meaning of the text. If there is so much that is hidden, each person may explain the *parashah* as he sees fit, from his own vantage point. The Torah itself offers a challenge to commentators to attempt to explain those matters that are not explained, and if these explanations are logical, even if they are far from *p'shat*, they have fulfilled their duty faithfully. This event, in the middle of these *parashiyos*, must be hinting to us of symbols of some kind, and the different commentators find themselves somewhat at a loss.

According to the simple *p'shat*, it appears that there was a hint here to Yaakov that no power in the world would be able to withstand him when he built the House of Israel, which was his mission from Hashem. There is also a hidden confirmation of Yitzchak's blessings. Who confirmed them? *Chazal* say they were confirmed by the angel (שַׂר) of Esav. *Rashi* even explains that Yaakov did not let Esav's angel go until he had admitted openly to the blessing that Yaakov had received from his father. While the Torah only relates that Yaakov asked the angel for a blessing, *Zohar* in *Parashas Tazria* notes that as the Torah says בֵּרַכְתָּנִי, it means the past tense, and not the future tense, proving that this was referring to the blessing of the past, namely a reference back to the blessing that his father had given him. But if that is the case, why was Yaakov injured in the thigh?

⋄§ Prophetic Vision and Actual Appearance

The *rishonim*, as we mentioned, are confronted here by a *parashah* which seems to be "sealed," and they attempt to explain it in a philosophical way. *Rambam* in *Moreh Nevuchim* (2:42) tells us that wherever the Torah mentions a meeting between an angel and a human, this refers to a prophetic vision and not to an actual appearance. As an example of this view, he cites the instance of our *parashah*, "and a man struggled with him." Since the Torah does not tell us here that it was an angel, the commentators explain that *Rambam* views this *parashah* as merely a continuation and explanation of what precedes it: "And the angels of *Elokim* met him."

This basic principle of *Rambam* leads *Ramban* to pose seven questions, based on different verses in the Torah, where, in each case, the Torah uses the word "angel," and which cannot be explained in any other way than an actual encounter between man and an angel.

R' Chisdai Crescas also expresses his astonishment at *Rambam*. How can *Rambam* say that the story here with Yaakov and his struggle with an angel was a prophetic vision, when it states clearly, "And he smote the thigh of Yaakov," and on that basis we were forbidden to eat the *gid hanasheh*?

Ralbag and Abarbanel attempt to answer this question. *Ralbag* holds that the vision was indeed a prophetic one, but the result of it was a physical affliction, and was caused by Yaakov's being impressionable. According to him, the body is often afflicted by mental feelings.

Abarbanel, though, holds that, according to *Rambam*, there were two actions in regard to the prophetic vision. The first was mental and abstract, while the second was tangible and physical. The struggle was a prophetic vision, whereas the other actions in the *parashah* were real. It is true, of course, that this answer is a difficult one.

Abarbanel, who seeks to preserve the honor of *Rambam*, attempts to answer all those who argue with him. Abarbanel, himself, though, does not agree with *Rambam* on the question of meetings between men and angels, and states many times that miracles should not be taken out of the plain meaning — the *p'shat*.

The significance of the struggle, in any event, requires symbolic explanations, and no one argues about that. All the commentators see this event as a prophecy for all future generations, and they only differ about the content and nature of this prophecy.

The only exception is *Rashbam*, who says that the angel came to prevent Yaakov from fleeing before Esav, and to trust in Hashem. Yaakov was afraid and got up in the middle of the night to flee, but the angel detained him for not having trusted in Hashem that Esav would not harm him. When the angel saw that his intervention was not helping and Yaakov still insisted upon fleeing, the angel damaged Yaakov's thigh and forced him to remain behind. When it began to become light and the angel told him, "Send me," Yaakov realized that it was an angel, not a man, that he had struggled with. Yaakov then asked the angel to bless him, so that he should not be harmed from the struggle, but the angel refused to listen to him. Yaakov was hurt and crippled for not having enough *bitachon* in Hashem, and that is what happens to everyone who does not follow in Hashem's ways, or who goes in a way which is against Hashem's will. Such people are punished.

◆§ An Eternal Struggle Between Yaakov and Esav

Chazal said that when Yaakov and the angel struggled, "They raised dust from their legs to the Throne of Glory." *Rashba* explains in his *chiddushim* that "dust of the legs" is an allusion to one's descendants. *Chazal* said that this angel was the angel of Esav. There was a hint to Yaakov in this struggle that his children would struggle with the children of Esav, until Hashem's name and throne are whole, as in the verse (*Ovadya* 1:21), "And saviors will come up on Mount Zion to judge the Mount of Esav."

Chazal in the Midrash follow this view, as in *Bereishis Rabbah*, where it is said that when the angel injured Yaakov, he also "touched all the *tzadikkim* who are his descendants, that being a reference to the generation of persecution."

Ramban explains that Hashem hinted to Yaakov that there would be very difficult times of persecution in future generations, in which Esav would succeed in undermining and harming Yaakov's righteous and pure descendants, to the extent that they might almost not be able to arise, Heaven forbid:

> But we have suffered all and endured it, as it states, "and Yaakov came whole." "And he saw that he was unable to vanquish him," because that is Hashem's desire. When Yaakov asked the angel his name, he answered him, "Why do you ask my name?" I am not a person that acts on his own initiative, that should have an independent nature. I am only a messenger who is fulfilling his mission. I was sent to bless you right now and to inform you what awaits you in the future.

Abarbanel, too, follows in this direction. The angel was sent to reassure Yaakov that in his days he would be at peace with Esav, and Esav would not be able to do him any harm. In the future, though, there would be difficult and bitter struggles "until the dawn." Yaakov's descendants would suffer much from the blows of Esav — "And he touched his thigh." In the end, Yaakov will emerge victorious, and Esav will even beg him to "send me" free. At that time, even Esav will agree about the blessings, and will bow his head before the spiritual superiority of Yaakov. The blow to the thigh is a symbol of the time the Jews will spend in *galus*, after which the sun will again shine, as the prophet said (*Michah* 4:6-7):

> "On that day," says Hashem, "I will gather the one that limps, and I will gather the one that was driven out, and the one that I afflicted. And I will make the one that limped a remnant, and the one that was cast far off into a strong nation." And Hashem will reign over them in Mount Zion from then on, forever.

In keeping with this symbolic way of interpreting the verses, *Chasam Sofer* explains the comment of *Chazal* on the word וַיֵּאָבֵק — "and he struggled" — which *Chazal* interpret in two ways: "that they raised dust" (אָבָק), or that "he hugged him (חִיבְּקוֹ) in his arms." These are the two ways that Esav has tried to destroy Israel throughout history. Sometimes Esav struggles with Yaakov, makes all types of accusations against him, and threatens to destroy him. At other times, he hugs him in his arms, and wants to assimilate him and to kill him with kindness.

The Chassidic works use this idea to explain another saying of *Chazal*: "He (the angel of Esav) appeared to him (Yaakov) as an armed robber," or, "He appeared to him as a *talmid chacham.*" This is a hint at the two ways Esav can fight us: either by means of decrees and forced conversions, or by trying to be persuasive.

Chasam Sofer sees a plan here by Esav's angel to undermine the agreement about the birthright. He says that the angel argued: "If you are the 'firstborn' then give me the 'עֵקֶב' — the 'heel' (from which the name יַעֲקֹב is derived), that being the symbol that the younger brother will seize the kingdom in the end of days." According to the Midrash, Esav's angel said to Yaakov, "Move your flock across first," namely you be the firstborn right now, and institute your monarchy before Esav has his, but give me the privilege of the kingdom in the end of days. But Yaakov vanquished him in this as well. "The coming of the dawn" was and remained his. Of course this is all *d'rush*, but the symbolic meaning of these verses is such that it is almost impossible to separate *d'rush* and *p'shat* here.

R' Samson Raphael Hirsch uses this *parashah* to discuss the current events of his time. The struggle with Esav will only continue as long as there is night and darkness on the earth, and people's understanding is overcast. During that struggle at night, Yaakov's opponent will try to wrest the ground from underneath Yaakov's feet and to hinder his means to survive. And indeed they have succeeded in weakening Yaakov's material power and have prevented him from using his natural gifts and powers to prosper. All that is true as long as the night exists in the world. When the day breaks, though, it will mark the end of the battle with Yaakov, and all the nations of the world will realize that Yaakov deserves to be blessed and not cursed. Instead of attempting to devour Yaakov, they will now acknowledge the truth of his beliefs, for which he fought throughout the ages.

➥ And Yaakov Remained Alone

If the entire *parashah* has a symbolic meaning, then this is all the more true for the words, "and Yaakov remained alone," which signifies the way Yaakov appears alone in history. Yaakov always was and has remained alone, ever since we became a nation, to this very day. It is the only nation throughout all of history which has remained separate from all the others in terms of its fate, staying as "a nation that dwells alone" in all generations and all eras.

The Chassidic works explain the verse in their typical fashion: Yaakov bequeathed to his sons the hope and dream of "remaining alone." They would always strive and hope for the period when (*Yeshayahu*, 2:11), "Hashem alone will be exalted on that day"

(*Bereishis Rabbah* on *Parashas Vayishlach*). It is not merely coincidental that in a *parashah* which hints so much at future events, the events begin and end with Yaakov remaining לְבַדּוֹ — "alone."

The prohibition against *gid hanasheh* is also deliberately interwoven into the general pattern of the story. The people of Israel was and remains alone, and has been that way throughout all generations. Until the dawn, Esav will struggle with Yaakov, and all of Yaakov's attempts to rid himself of Esav will be unsuccessful. This struggle will harm those who come out of the loins of Yaakov — his descendants — and that is where the *gid hanasheh* is located. Thus, the Jewish people may not eat the *gid hanasheh*, so as to remind us perpetually of the meaning contained in "and Yaakov remained alone," namely that we should not try to be assimilated with the descendants of Esav.

After studying the *parashah*, we see a resemblance between this *parashah* and that of Bilaam, with both involving the same aim. Bilaam came to curse Israel, and finally blessed them, and the same thing happened with the angel that struggled with Yaakov. The fact that "Yaakov remained alone" parallels the words of Bilaam: "Behold, a nation that dwells alone." The explanation about "and a man struggled with him," which, according to *Chazal* refers to the fact that "they raised dust to the Heavens," is indirectly hinted at in the words of Bilaam (*Bamidbar* 23:10), "Who can count the dust of Jacob?" Thus, it is not in vain that *Chazal* attribute the virtue of aloneness to Yaakov. *Rashi*, too, explains: "Behold a nation that dwells alone" is in accordance with our forefathers, who had the merit of dwelling alone. Yaakov was the first to symbolize for the future generations that "Yaakov remained alone," because our nation has no ties or links to any other people or tongue, but is single and unique in the world.

III.

Not by Might Nor by Power

There are innumerable reasons given by the commentators for the prohibition of *gid hanasheh* (the sinew of the femoral vein). At first glance, it appears that this is one of the *mitzvos* whose reason is specified in the Torah: "Therefore the Children of Israel shall not eat the *gid hanasheh* ... because he smote the thigh of Yaakov." Yet the commentators discuss the meaning of "therefore" in the verse. What is the connection between the subject and the object? What action is commemorated by the prohibition of the *gid hanasheh*? Is it the fact that Yaakov was injured, or the fact that he was saved, and a miracle occurred to him?

Chazal in *Chullin* 101 say that this *mitzvah* belongs with the others which were given at Sinai, "but it was written in its place, so as to know for what reason it was prohibited to them." It appears from the words of *Chazal* that the reason for the prohibition was clear to them. The commentators, though, examine not only the reason for the prohibition, but primarily its purpose. What did it teach the succeeding generations, as a result of what happened to Yaakov?

Three of the *rishonim, Ba'alei HaTosafos, Tur* and *Chizkuni*, explain the purpose of the prohibition in different ways: (a) as a remembrance; (b) to separate oneself from danger; (c) as a penalty.

(a) It is a "remembrance" of the great event where Yaakov fought with an angel and vanquished him, and yet came out unharmed except for his injured thigh.

(b) "To separate oneself from danger" refers to the fact that Yaakov's descendants separated themselves from the thing connected to the injury of their father. This is like the case of a person who has a headache or pain in another part of his body, and as a result resolves to abstain from eating that part of any animal. This acceptance was recognized by Hashem as a *mitzvah*, as one of the 613 *mitzvos*.

(c) "As a penalty," it reminds us of the sin of Yaakov's sons, who left their father alone without an escort. This last reason is discussed by various *acharonim*. They wonder what type of penalty was involved in the fact that we cannot eat the *gid hanasheh*. After all, sinews have no meat taste anyway. Maybe, they conclude, *Chazal* were not referring to the prohibition of eating the *gid hanasheh* as being the penalty, but to the great amount of work involved in removing it, or, failing that, the fact that Jews have to forget about eating the hindquarters.

Rashbam and *Rivash*, too, hold that the reason for the prohibition was in order to commemorate the miraculous event to future generations. Yaakov vanquished the angel; that was a source of encouragement to his children, that whoever attempts to vanquish them will not succeed.

Abarbanel explains this along similar lines. Yaakov and the angel were engaged in a mighty battle. When the angel saw that Yaakov was stronger than he, he stretched out his leg to trip Yaakov, and succeeded. But the damage was minor. Yaakov's thigh was dislocated, and nothing else. On the other hand, the spectacle was an exalted one. The angel struggling with Yaakov is the symbol of the eternal struggle between Yaakov and Esav, between the spiritual and the material. It is true that the angel managed to injure Yaakov's thigh, which is the symbol of his descendants, who would be subject to Esav, but the final victory would be Yaakov's. In the end (*Ovadya* 1:21), "Saviors will come up on Mount Zion to judge the Mount of Esav," and Esav's angel will yet beg and plead from Yaakov, "Send me because the dawn has come," a reference to our full redemption. In order to commemorate that great event, Israel were commanded at Sinai not to eat the *gid hanasheh*.

Ma'asei Hashem has an interesting interpretation of the struggle and its purpose. According to *Chazal*, the angel that struggled with Yaakov was the angel of Esav. The reason for the struggle was that the angel wanted to take back from Yaakov the bill of sale of the birthright. In those days, people used to guard their deeds by strapping them to their thighs, as we see from *Chazal* in *Bava Basra*: "If a person died, and a deed was found strapped to his thigh ..." The angel touched Yaakov's thigh in order to steal the deed, but did not achieve his objective. Yaakov, however, was injured from the touch of the angel and from then on he never fathered any more children. That is the reason why Jews do not eat the *gid hanasheh*.

A deep Chassidic significance is to be found in the blow to Yaakov's thigh, as brought by *Noam Elimelech*. The *poskim* say that one does not recite a blessing on the act of procreation, because one cannot perform the *mitzvah* without the involvement of physical lust. Esav's angel wanted in his struggle with Yaakov to inject his poison into Yaakov's nature, but he was only able to affect "his thigh." He was able to inject just a little of his venom into the *mitzvah* that is related to that organ, so that it is impossible to observe the *mitzvah* without physical sensation.

S'forno is the only one among the commentators who explains why the prohibition is specifically with the *gid hanasheh* and not anything else. By this prohibition, we want to publicize that the damage which the angel did to Yaakov was insignificant. What he apparently means is in keeping with the fact that *Chazal* tell us that the *gid hanasheh* has no taste. Forbidding the *gid hanasheh* to us thus does not limit what is permitted us, just as the damage to Yaakov was insignificant.

✥ A Place for the "Others" to Take Hold

Zohar sees the *gid hanasheh* as a place for the forces of *tum'ah* to take hold, and that was why Esav's angel succeeded in injuring Yaakov just there. The kabbalistic works follow the same lines as *Zohar*. Rabbenu Bachya maintains that the *gid hanasheh* in itself is symbolic of sin, as this sinew is as strong as a rope, and we are told in *Yeshayahu* (5:18),

"Woe to them that draw sin with cords of vanity, and transgression as it were with a cart rope." Following a certain philosopher, he explains the verse, "Therefore the Children of Israel shall not eat the *gid hanasheh*," as a moral lesson for Israel: that man must follow his mind, and not only his bodily lusts.

Akeidah gives this idea a broad meaning. The angel found no other easy place to harm Yaakov except in his thigh, that being a sign that this is a vulnerable place, as brought by *Zohar* above. The Torah wishes to teach us by this prohibition that we must destroy our hard-heartedness, as we see in the verse (*Yeshayahu* 48:4), "Because I knew that you are obstinate, and your neck is an iron sinew, and your brow is brass." We must keep away from all the hard things which the *gid hanasheh* symbolizes, so that we should not have happen to us what happened to Yaakov. At the same time, according to *Akeidah*, the *parashah* means to encourage the person who sinned, so that he should realize that there is a cure for his wound, as we see in *Michah* (4:6-7):

> "On that day," says Hashem, "I will gather the one that limps, and I will gather the one that was driven out, and the one that I afflicted. And I will make the one that limped a remnant, and the one that was cast far off into a strong nation." And Hashem will reign over them in Mount Zion from then on, forever.

Akeidah adds that he heard there was a saying in the *Zohar* as follows: "'Therefore the Children of Israel shall not eat the *gid hanasheh*' — to include *Tishah B'av*." He explains the *Zohar* according to *d'rush*. In the verse before us, there is a hint of the different fast days. The ג in גִּיד has a *gematria* of three and refers to the third of *Tishrei*, or *Tzom Gedalyah*. The י refers to the tenth of *Teves* — *Asarah B'Teves*. The word גִּיד in *gematria* adds up to seventeen and alludes to the seventeenth of *Tammuz*. Finally, the word אֶת which precedes the words *gid hanasheh* in the verse, when its letters are reversed, forms the acronym of תִּשְׁעָה (בְּ)אָב — *Tishah (B')Av*. In other words, all the fasts which symbolize our troubles stem from the blow to the *gid hanasheh*.

Sifsei Kohen, too, who was a disciple of *Ari*, explains the words of the *Zohar* in a similar fashion, and adds that he found it written that, of the 365 sinews in man, each controls another day of the year. The *gid hanasheh* controls *Tishah B'Av*, and that is the reason that both *Batei Mikdash* were destroyed on that day, one representing the right *gid hanasheh* and the other representing the left *gid hanasheh*. Whoever eats on *Tishah B'Av* is as if he ate the *gid hanasheh*, because both of these have the same source, that of evil.

The Chassidic works expand on this idea. *Be'er Mayim Chayim* says that the image of Yaakov is engraved on Hashem's "Chariot," and there was no place for evil to attach itself to even the smallest fraction of this image. But as we see that the angel of Esav was nevertheless able to hurt Yaakov in the *gid hanasheh*, that is a sign that here, in this place, Yaakov is vulnerable.

Kli Yakar regards the *gid hanasheh* as symbolizing something which is hard and difficult to digest. According to him, this refers to various philosophical books, and one who deals with them too much can easily become a heretic. When the Torah warns us not to eat the *gid hanasheh*, that is a symbol for future generations to watch out and not to fall into the trap, because if what happened to Yaakov could happen to him, how much more are we lowly mortals in danger.

These interpretations give an actual significance for the prohibition of *gid hanasheh* throughout all generations. They make it a symbol of the power of the forces of evil, and warn us to keep away from them.

ৼ§ A Symbol of Hope and Trust

Chinuch, as Abarbanel that we brought above, sees the prohibition of *gid hanasheh* as a sign of hope and *emunah*, just as Yaakov fought the angel and vanquished him, and even the small amount of injury that he suffered was healed when the sun came up. By the same token, the sun of redemption will shine for Yaakov's descendants, and will heal all their wounds.

Shem MiShmuel discusses this encouraging interpretation at length. He says that the entire event came to hint to us that a time will come when the descendants of Yaakov will be at the lowest point, as symbolized by "and he smote the thigh of Yaakov." But even at that point Israel will recover, just as Yaakov was healed from his wound. We should not despair regardless of how bad the situation is. We are the descendants of Yaakov, and whatever happened to him is a sign for what will happen to us. We must hope for Hashem's salvation, and for the day that the sun of redemption will shine for us.

This is also the approach used by R' Samson Raphael Hirsch in his *Horeb*. He says that on that dreadful night, Yaakov realized the place that Israel would have among the other nations, as it would carry the message of Hashem on the earth as a nation of vision and of the spirit. Many times Yaakov is injured in the thigh, but he nevertheless emerges victorious, and his name alone testifies to that fact. At first glance, his name appears to be "Yaakov," whose hands holds onto the *akev* — the "heel," but in reality he is "Yisrael," the "master and lord," who by his nature is decisive over all. In order to explain this better, and so that the

Jews, too, should not think that our physical strength will be what defends us, we are told, "Therefore the Children of Israel shall not eat the *gid hanasheh*," as a sign and symbol, that " 'not by power nor by might, but by My spirit,' says Hashem." The prohibition against the *gid hanasheh* is not merely a matter of remembering, but is a *symbol* for future generations.

Chazal in *Chullin* 91 tell us: " 'Hashem sent a word' (*Yeshayahu* 9:8-13) — that refers to the *gid hanasheh*." Let us quote the whole section:

> Hashem sent a word to Yaakov, and it fell upon Israel. And all the people shall know, even Ephraim and the inhabitants of Samaria, who say in their pride and strongness of heart: "The bricks have fallen down, but we will build with hewn stones: the sycamores have been cut down, but we will change them into cedars." Therefore Hashem will set up the enemies of Rezin against him, and join his enemies together; the Syrians at the front, and the Philistines behind; and they will devour Israel with open mouth. For all this, His anger is not turned away, but His hand is still stretched out. For the people do not turn to him that smites them, neither do they seek the Lord of hosts.

This *parashah* shows the meaning of *Chazal* when they said, " 'Hashem sent a word' (*Yeshayahu* 9:8-13) — that refers to the *gid hanasheh*." Their idea is reflected in the above idea of R' Samson Raphael Hirsch. "Hashem sent a word" — namely, Hashem gave us a mission to bear witness to Him and to serve to educate the world not to place its reliance on strength or physical might. The Jewish people must not eat the *gid hanasheh*, namely they should not see themselves as relying and dependent on physical strength. If their spiritual house is in order, the nation will be rehabilitated and strengthened. That is the word that Hashem sent to Yaakov when he struggled with the angel. Even though the angel weakened Yaakov physically somewhat, Yaakov still emerged victorious, until the angel had to plead to him, "Send me."

◆§ The Prohibition of Gid HaNasheh and When It Applies

The Mishnah in *Chullin* 89 says: "The (prohibition of) *gid hanasheh* applies in *Eretz Yisrael* and outside it, whether the *Beis HaMikdash* exists or does not exist, in both regular meat and sacrifices." The *gemara* there asks: "It is obvious that it applies to sacrifices (so why did the

Mishnah have to mention it)? Just because a person sanctified it, should that mean that the prohibition of *gid hanasheh* should no longer apply?" *Chazal* discuss the matter at length, but the commentators on the *gemara* ask: How do we know that the Mishnah was referring to eating of a sacrifice? Maybe the Mishnah is referring to the fact that one cannot sacrifice an animal without first removing the *gid hanasheh*? We see that the *Chachamim* and Rebbi argue over this later, and maybe the Mishnah is telling us that the *halachah* is like the *Chachamim*, just as there are many *mishnayos* that Rebbi listed as *stam* — "without argument" — even though they are opposed by him personally. I saw that *HaD'rush VeHaIyun* brings a beautiful answer in the name of *She'elos U'Teshuvos Beis Yitzchak*, 85. *Rashi* in *Zevachim* 35 says that wherever the *gemara* uses the term מְקוּדָּשִׁין (the word which is used in *Chullin* 89 to describe the sacrifices as opposed to regular meat), it refers to female animals. Thus the Mishnah in *Chullin* must be referring to females. As the only animals that are burned on the altar for an *olah* are males, it follows that the prohibition of *gid hanasheh* in regard to animals cannot apply to removing the *gid hanasheh* before burning the sacrifice. We are thus forced to say that the prohibition in regard to sacrifices refers to eating, and therefore the *gemara's* question, "Just because a person sanctified it, should that mean that the prohibition of *gid hanasheh* should no longer apply to it?" is a valid one.

And let us go from this topic to a related one. As we are discussing males and females in reference to *gid hanasheh*, I would like to mention an extraordinary matter concerning this. R' Yehonasan Eibeschutz in his *Kreisi U'Pleisi* says that in his times there was a certain מְנַקֵּר (a specialist in removing the *gid hanasheh*) who concluded that the sinew being removed by other *menakrim* was the wrong one, and he claimed that the *gid hanasheh* was a different sinew. He wanted to establish for all that everyone had erred until that time by removing the wrong sinew. He traveled throughout Germany preaching of his conclusions, until he reached Prague. "And I," says R' Yehonasan, "checked and studied and examined the matter, and I found that the particular sinew (mentioned by the man) only exists in males and not in females, and then I showed him the *Semag*, that states, '*gid hanasheh* applies to both males and females,' and he ceased his talk."

When *Kreisi U'Pleisi* appeared, this statement amazed all the Torah scholars. After all, the meaning of the words "applies to both males and females" is in terms of who is forbidden to eat the *gid hanasheh*, namely that the prohibition applies to both men and women, but does not refer to the animals involved.

This question has been dealt with by the *acharonim*. *Chasam Sofer* in

Yoreh De'ah 69 attempts to answer the question by *pilpul*. I do not have a *Kreisi U'Pleisi* right now at hand to study the question, but it is possible that the author, R' Yehonasan Eibeschutz, was only trying to expose the ignorance of the man, and that was why he showed him up by quoting the words of *Semag*.

I also saw that *Pardes Yosef* wrote that all those that discuss this matter did not look into *Semag* itself, because had they done so, they would have found there that there is no such statement as "it applies to both males and females." Therefore the whole question needs to be studied further. (R' Meir Gellis of Jerusalem pointed out to me that the reference here should have been to *Sefer HaNikur* and not *Semag*, and indeed, he told me, the first edition of *Kreisi U'Pleisi* carried the abbreviation סה"נ, rather than סמ"ג.)

IV.
Punishment According to Justice and Halachah

The severe punishment that Shimon and Levi dealt the people of Shechem is a major topic of this *parashah*. Is it proper that when one person sins the entire city should be punished? In addition, the form of punishment by trickery is difficult to understand. Indeed, Yaakov was not angry at the deed itself, but was only concerned about the reactions of the inhabitants of the land. The Torah itself, though, evidently indirectly justifies the sons of Yaakov, as we will see later.

Ramban holds that Yaakov agreed to the trickery of the circumcision. He became angry only after his sons' actions, because he did not know that they were planning to kill the inhabitants of Shechem. He thought that the people of Shechem would not agree to the circumcision, and that would be a perfect excuse to demand that they return Dinah. Even if they agreed to be circumcised, he and his sons would take Dinah by force when the men of Shechem were weak. Shimon and Levi, though, exploited the opportunity to take revenge on behalf of their sister, and killed those that were guilty. They did this without their father's consent. There were also other disagreements between Yaakov and his sons, as *Ramban* explains.

Other commentators hold that Yaakov thought that his sons would only kill the people who committed the outrage, and only if the people of Shechem defended the criminals would his sons have the right to take revenge on all.

Yaakov was against the "trickery" and the fact that the people were killed not in accordance with the law, says *Ma'asei Hashem*. He was embarrassed by his sons' breach of faith. He mentions the fact of the "honor" that was violated by the actions of Shimon and Levi, as we see in his blessings of his sons later, where he said of the two, "Let my assembly not be united with their honor." His sons responded that when one deals with swindlers, one must sometimes overlook "honor" and use cunning. The people of Shechem had slandered Dinah, claiming that she had wanted to be with Shechem and had acted as a "harlot." In such circumstances, all means were proper to save their sister.

As opposed to this, there are those who say that the people of Shechem regretted the fact that they had been circumcised, and it was they who rejected their treaty. *Ba'alei HaTosafos* and others, both *rishonim* and *acharonim*, explain the words, "while they were in pain," as meaning that they regretted their actions. This interpretation is in keeping with what we are told in *Sefer HaYashar*, that the people of Shechem regretted their action and gathered to attack the sons of Yaakov, so that whatever the sons of Yaakov did was carried out in self-defense.

HaKesav VeHaKabalah follows this same path in his interpretation of the verses. One of the *rishonim* confirms this from a verse in *Tehillim* 69:30 where the word כּוֹאֵב (translated above as "in pain") is explained as regretting one's actions. On the other hand, various commentators find other hints in the Torah that the idea of agreeing to be circumcised was just a ruse by the people of Shechem to deceive the hearts of Yaakov and his sons, and afterwards to kill them and take all their goods. When they suggested that all the men in their town be circumcised, Shechem and Chamor told their people, "Their flocks and their possessions and all their cattle will all be ours." (*Midrash Lekach Tov* says that the purpose of their circumcision was not spiritual, and all they were interested in was the property of Yaakov and his sons.) In these words of theirs, they showed their true intentions — that they planned to kill everyone and plunder all their possessions. This is also mentioned by *S'forno* and others.

Malbim gives three reasons why the sons of Yaakov were justified according to the *halachah* in killing the people of Shechem: (a) They had abducted a woman, and the people of the city had not meted out the judgment due the wrongdoers and had not killed them; (b) the people of the city had even defended the kidnappers when the sons of Yaakov demanded that Dinah be returned, and there was no alternative available to her brothers except for "one who comes to kill you, take the initiative and kill him first"; (c) they coveted the wealth of Yaakov and his sons, and were willing to kill them to receive this wealth.

Akeidah's interpretation is both extremely interesting and remarkable. He finds full justification in the verses themselves for all the steps taken by Yaakov's sons. At first glance, it appears that Yaakov's sons show certain negative character traits: (a) In general, a person who is ethically superior will not show his anger and distress outwardly, yet with Yaakov's sons, "when they heard, they were distressed"; (b) a physically strong person will confront his enemy face to face, and will not deceive him, whereas Yaakov's sons used trickery to achieve their aim; (c) a person who is spiritually strong will not be hasty in endangering his life, whereas Yaakov's sons were so angry that they completely ignored the masses of people who lived in the area; (d) a refined person is one who is generous and does not covet other people's money and possessions, yet Yaakov's sons looted Shechem after killing its inhabitants. But what is remarkable is that for each of the above, the Torah supplies a positive reason for the action. When we are told, "they were distressed," the Torah adds, "because an abomination had been done in Israel." In regard to the trickery, the Torah adds, "because he had defiled their sister." And the Torah notes the same thing in regard to their looting. As to Yaakov's complaints that they were too hasty, the Torah ends with their reply to Yaakov, "Shall our sister then be made as a harlot?" These statements all come to stress that where there is *chilul Hashem*, one does not take into account one's subjective manners. The reaction of Yaakov's sons came because of objective justice, and in such cases one does not use ordinary logic to prevent the doing of absolute justice.

∽§ Punishment According to the Halachah and the Torah

Whereas those who interpret the Torah in terms of *p'shat* and *mussar* seek the reason for the punishment in accordance with the rules of ethics and justice, we find that *Rambam* gives a *halachic* reason for the punishment of the people of Shechem, in accordance with the laws governing *B'nei Noach* (i.e., non-Jews). A *Ben Noach*, rules *Rambam* (*Hil. Melachim* 9:14), is killed for violating any one of the seven commandments which non-Jews must observe. Chamor son of Shechem was liable for the death penalty for having kidnapped a woman, while the rest of the people of Shechem were liable to the death penalty for not having established courts to judge such offenses, and setting up courts is one of the seven commandments of *B'nei Noach*.

Ramban disagrees with this. According to him, the law regarding courts means that *B'nei Noach* must have courts to decide monetary disputes, questions of swindling, theft, non-payment of wages, watchmen, borrowing and lending, etc. But *B'nei Noach* are not liable to the death penalty if they do not set up such courts, because they can only be punished for violating a *lo sa'aseh* — a "prohibition," and not for failure to implement an *asei* — a "positive commandment." *Ramban* adds, though, that there is no reason to have to justify the killing of the people of Shechem. They were liable to the death penalty because they worshiped idolatry and did every type of abomination (as we are told that Yaakov said to his sons, "remove all the foreign gods from among you"). And indeed, Yaakov never complained about *the deed itself*, but about the fact that by doing it the brothers endangered everyone's lives.

Chasam Sofer in his *Teshuvos* (6:14) attempts to justify *Rambam's* words. It is true that failing to implement an *asei* is not grounds for inflicting the death penalty on a *Ben Noach*, but in any event "he deserves to die," as we see, for example that *Chazal* tell us, "A non-Jew who keeps *Shabbos* is חַיָּב מִיתָה — worthy of death," even though he will not be sentenced to die for it. What *Rambam* meant, says *Chasam Sofer*, is that since in any event they deserved to die, Yaakov's sons were not guilty for killing them.

Chemdas Yisrael, on the 613 *mitzvos*, disproves *Chasam Sofer*, because *Rambam* says clearly that the people of Shechem were liable "to be killed" and not "to die." And indeed, one who studies *Rambam* there, will see that he referred to the people of Shechem as being executed by law. He defines the *mitzvah* for *B'nei Noach* of establishing courts of law as follows: "They must establish judges and magistrates," and he continues, "and for that reason the people of Shechem were liable to be executed."

Lechem Mishneh wants to explain *Rambam's* view, claiming that the establishing of judges includes a *lo sa'aseh*, as we are told, "You shall not do iniquity." But the *acharonim* are surprised at this reason, because that *lo sa'aseh* refers to the judges, and not to the people of Shechem themselves.

It appears to me that when *Ramban* lists the establishing of judges as a *mitzvah* that *B'nei Noach* are also liable for, he does not leave out liability for the laws themselves, for the *gemara* in *Sanhedrin* 56 includes both in the *mitzvah*. The setting up of judges is a precondition for the laws themselves, because one cannot have a social order without some type of enforcement mechanism. If there is no such mechanism, then everyone will do whatever he feels like. Where there are no judges to enforce the laws, the laws themselves are not kept. Such a society deserves to be put to death, because it has violated the seven commandments of *B'nei Noach*, for failure to have any one enforce them. *Rambam* only stresses the point of "establishing judges" to tell us that the seven commandments apply to the community as a whole, and not only to the individual, and that is expressed in a regime which has enforcement provisions. The people of Shechem did not appoint judges, and it followed that they did not follow any of the other laws either. They were therefore liable to the death penalty, even though in theory the seven laws had been adopted by them.

◆§ And Thus Shall Not Be Done

This phrase does not seem to add anything to the part of the verse before it, "because an abomination has been done in Israel." *Rashi* explains that the Torah wished to convict those who had done the abomination for having violated a law that everyone had accepted after the Flood, namely not to engage in sexual offenses.

Ramban is surprised at *Rashi*, because we know that the Canaanites were steeped in sexual offenses, and such actions were everyday occurrences by them. After all, wasn't Avraham afraid that they would kill him for his wife? Moreover, the Torah informs us that they did "all those abominations."

R' Eliyahu Mizrachi, though, justifies *Rashi*. Avraham was afraid that they would kill him so as take his wife "legally," since they were careful not to commit sexual offenses, such as taking another person's wife. When the Torah refers to the Canaanites, it refers to a later time, when they had changed and had begun violating these laws as well, and that was indeed the reason why their fate was decreed. The meaning of "and thus shall not be done" is thus that an abomination had been done in Israel, and that was against the practices of the people of the time. It was a revolting sin.

S'forno does not consider that the people of Shechem were that "ethical," but he explains that "thus shall not be done" means that even among such people, who were guilty of immorality, it was unheard of for someone to defile the daughter of someone as prominent as Yaakov.

On the other hand, *Hadar Zekeinim* of the *Ba'alei Tosafos* (and *Or HaChayim*) explain it in the exact opposite way. Such a disgusting act does not even take place even among the lowest of people.

Kanfei Nesharim explains that what the Torah wanted to say was that as it was impossible to punish them "measure for measure," there was no alternative but to kill them by the sword.

Shach has an interesting explanation of the fact that Yaakov's sons used cunning by telling them all to be circumcised. They wanted to punish them measure for measure, in the same organ with which the sin had been committed.

HaKesav VeHaKabalah has a very original interpretation. The word וְכֵן (translated above as "and thus") is linked to כֵּנוּת — "integrity and truth." Thus he explains the phrase as "and justice shall not be (i.e., was not) done." There was no one in all of Shechem that was just. These people carried out a despicable crime, and no one felt the need to bring them to justice. (*Chazal* in *Bereishis Rabbah* tell us that "and thus shall not be done" means that such things are not done among the nations of the world.)

It appears to me that the purpose of the Torah is plainly and simply to justify the punishment, and not to come to terms with a sin that had already been committed. The situation could not remain the way it had been. This type of crime could not be tolerated under any circumstances. Justice had to be done for the sake of society, so that such offenses would not be repeated, as well as to ensure the existence of the world on the basis of justice and righteousness.

◆§ Shall Our Sister then Be Made as a Harlot?

Shimon and Levi carried out justice, even at the risk of their own lives. As we mentioned, Yaakov was angry at their hasty decision. Yaakov was not opposed in principle to their actions to fight evil, and their battle to defend the moral code that had been violated. He was only opposed to having their action glorified as being of so great a value that it even exceeded the value of life itself.

R' Samson Raphael Hirsch explains the complaint of Yaakov's sons in a realistic manner. Had we not been Jews, the inhabitants of the land would never have permitted themselves to act this way. Only in respect to the Jew do they feel that everything is permissible, and that they can do whatever they want without fear of punishment. It is therefore necessary to take an action which will prove that the Jew's blood is not valueless, and that anyone that attempts to harm us will be punished. R' Hirsch continues: It is true that the hands are the hands of Esav, and we refrain from shedding blood, but that is not a sign of weakness. Sometimes we too lift our swords against our oppressors. The last days of the Second *Beis HaMikdash* showed our bravery and might. Yaakov split up Shimon and Levi among the other tribes rather than giving them their own territories, because we do not want to do justice by the sword. Our strength is spiritual, but that is a product of education and our own wish, and is not a natural, inborn characteristic.

Abarbanel, who perceived the affliction of his people and tasted the sword of Esav on his own body in the exile from Spain, has a marvelous explanation. According to him, Hashem agreed with the words of Yaakov's sons, as we see in the verse (*Bereishis* 35:5), "And the terror of God was on the cities that were around about them, and they did not pursue the sons of Yaakov." Yaakov's sons claimed, "In the case of such a disgrace, one must be willing to risk one's life, because death in honor is better than life in humiliation." The purpose of this *parashah* is to teach us that "they must take their lives in their hands, they and their wives and their children and all that they own, in order to take revenge on their enemies."

Or HaChayim too makes the words of Yaakov's sons relevant to us today. On Yaakov's words that their actions were endangering their lives, they answered:

> On the contrary, we will be in greater danger among the nations if they see that a single despicable person ruled over the daughter of Yaakov, and did as he wished and desired. And [the Jews] will not be able to maintain themselves among the other nations. On the contrary, [by our actions] the nations are afraid and will fear us.

Here there is a dispute about whether one should respond or should practice restraint. And indeed the Midrash stresses that even Yaakov, who at first was opposed to the fact that they had placed themselves in danger by their confrontation with the other nations, came to his sons' defense after the event had already taken place, and he too drew his sword among the fighters. And these are the words of the Midrash:

> Yaakov did not want his sons to carry out that deed. But once they did it, he said, "Shall I then let my sons fall into the hands of the other nations?" What did he do? He took his sword and bow and stood at the entrance to Shechem ... This we see in (*Bereishis* 48:22), "Which I took out of the hand of the Emori with my sword and with my bow."

Yaakov did not reject self-defense as a matter of principle. But he made a cold-blooded calculation as to if and when he should use these weapons against the other nations. From that point of view, history justified Yaakov. The hastiness of Shimon and Levi happened to come to a successful conclusion in Shechem, and in those conditions, and with the help of Heaven. But for the time that we were in exile (*Bereishis* 49:7), "Cursed be their anger, for it was fierce; and their wrath, for it was cruel."

Vayeishev – וישב

I.

Brotherly Hatred as a Factor in the Exile to Egypt

Israel's exile in Egypt was already ordained in the decree at the *bris bein habesarim*. Its purpose is not stated clearly, and the different commentators have offered their own views. The sequence of events in the Torah would imply that the exile in Egypt was meant as a prelude to the giving of the Torah. It was not a punishment, but a way to refine the people's hearts in anticipation of receiving the Torah. We will yet discuss this on various occasions.

The *parashah* begins with the story of how the decree of the *bris bein habesarim* begins to unfold, leading eventually to the exile in Egypt. Throughout history, entire nations were forced into exile, but at this time the Children of Israel were not yet a nation. Yaakov and his sons were the nucleus from whom the nation was formed, and that was the beginning of the exile to Egypt.

Tzofnas Pane'ach points out beautifully that the *parashah* here mentions that Yisrael loved Yosef more than his other sons. The word "Yisrael" normally implies the entire nation, and the choice of the word here was to hint to us that this was the beginning of the exile of the Israelite nation, in accordance with what Hashem told Avraham at the *bris bein habesarim*. This was also when the Jewish nation began to take form. The persons involved in this sequence appeared to be acting of their own free will, but were in reality directed by Hashem from Above. This we see when, at the end of these events, Yosef tells his brothers, "*Elokim* thought it for the good" — whatever they thought was irrelevant.

But we cannot ignore the educational purpose in the Torah when it relates the sequence of events leading to the exile. It is true that the decree of exile was ordained at the *bris bein habesarim*, but it evolved through שִׂנְאַת חִנָּם — "senseless hatred," to teach us that senseless hatred was a major factor in these events, even if it was not the major cause. This is what *Chazal* mean when they said (*Shabbos* 10):

> R' Chama bar Giora said in the name of Rav: "A person should never favor one son among his sons, for because of the value of two *sela'im* of a striped garment that Yaakov gave to Yosef above his other sons, his brothers were jealous of him, and the matter was brought about that our forefathers went down to Egypt."

Tosafos there asks: Wasn't the slavery already decreed at the time of Avraham, in the *bris bein habesarim*? It seems to me, however, that *Chazal* did not say that the exile in Egypt was caused by the jealousy and hatred of the brothers. They only said that the events were "brought about," namely that these events caused things to happen according to a certain sequence, in accordance with the rule of *Chazal* that Hashem causes "good events to be brought about by the worthy and bad deeds by the unworthy." The events themselves, whether good or bad, are not dependent on the person who will cause them to be brought about; but the person who causes them to be brought about is either worthy or unworthy, depending on the events which he sets in motion. Thus, when the Torah tells us that the jealousy and hatred of the brothers set in motion the sequence that eventually led to the exile in Egypt, this teaches us that we cannot indulge in either of these traits.

Indeed, one who studies this *parashah* will see that the true reason for the exile to Egypt was something entirely different. "Hashem's plan will be fulfilled." This is stressed especially in the way *Ramban* explains the story. A "man" happened to find Yosef and showed him how to find his brothers. This story, then, teaches us that, under natural conditions, whatever happened should not have happened. Yosef would have been lost and would not have found his brothers, but Hashem pointed out to Yosef how to find his brothers. Thus we see that the true "reason" had already been dictated by Hashem, and it would have taken place one way or another. By teaching us that baseless hatred was the tool that propelled the chain of events, the Torah shows all future generations the negative results of senseless hatred.

רֶמֶז — "hint" — is one of the ways of explaining the Torah, and it is worth noting the hint that *Tosafos* finds for the exile in the words וְהִנֵּה תֹעֶה בַּשָּׂדֶה — "and behold he was wandering in the field." The numerical value of the letter ת, four hundred, hints at the four hundred years of exile in Egypt; ע, seventy, at the seventy years of the exile in Babylon; and ה, five, alludes to the exile of Edom, which will end some time after five thousand years after the Creation.

BEREISHIS — VAYEISHEV / 217

☙ The Dislike Between the Different Brothers

The Torah includes all the brothers in their dislike of Yosef, but differentiates between them at the beginning of the event, when we are told (*Bereishis* 37:2), "And he tended the sheep with his brothers." Here, the Torah does not specify who "his brothers" were, but immediately afterwards it adds, "and the boy (נַעַר) was with the sons of Bilhah and the sons of Zilpah." In other words, there was some type of difference between Leah's sons and the sons of the handmaidens in regard to their treatment of Yosef. What difference was there? What is meant by נַעַר? We are not offered an explanation. Later on, we are told that Yosef "brought his father an evil report," but the Torah does not say about whom. What was this evil report? The only thing we are told clearly is that Yaakov "loved Yosef more than all his children," and that clearly implies more than the sons of Leah and those of the handmaidens.

According to *Rashi*, the Torah tells us here Yosef's weakness, which resulted in all the troubles. He was occupied by נַעֲרוּת — "juvenile things" — combing his hair and attending to his eyes. He would be friendly with the sons of the handmaidens, whom the sons of Leah kept away from. This was, of course, another reason for the brothers' dislike. Yosef would then bring evil reports to his father about Leah's sons.

This explanation naturally is a cause for astonishment by *Ramban*. If what *Rashi* says is correct, then only Leah's sons should have disliked him, and why didn't the handmaidens' sons rescue him? After all, it was he who could not stand the way they were being humiliated and it was he who had come to their defense! Even if there were only four sons of the handmaidens, they and Yosef, as well as Reuven (who tried to save Yosef), were six people. In addition, from the verses it appears that all his brothers were involved in the plan against Yosef, and all agreed to sell him.

As a result, *Ramban* explains that Yaakov placed Yosef at the disposal of the sons of the handmaidens, who were the shepherds. As Yosef was a נַעַר and they were ordered to watch over him, he never left their sides and saw everything they did. Yosef then reported back to his father about what the sons of the handmaidens had done, and that was why they disliked him. As to Leah's sons, they disliked him out of jealousy, because their father made him a coat of many colors and loved him more than any of the other sons.

The Torah refers to him as a נַעַר, even though he was already seventeen. The meaning of the word נַעַר is a young boy who is still not independent. That was why his father had him tend the sheep under the supervision of his brothers who were the sons of the handmaidens.

Rashbam explains the dislike of the brothers in a different way. Yosef tended the flock with Leah's children, but spent time with the children of the handmaidens, with whom he played in his childish way. This led to the malice that Leah's children had toward him. Moreover, Yosef was in the habit of divulging his brothers' faults to his father, who also loved him more than the other brothers. This accumulation of dislike on the part of the brothers led them to act as they did.

Rashbam adds that the other commentators did not discuss the nature of Yosef's disclosures to his father, except where we find what *Chazal* tell us, as we will explain below. (Incidentally, at the beginning of this *parashah*, *Rashbam* explains the difference between his interpretation and that of others, in that while the others all use *d'rush* and *remez*, he uses only *p'shat*, without straying from it. He notes that his grandfather, *Rashi*, wrote a commentary on the Torah, and "I, Shmuel ben Meir, debated with him and before him, and he told me that if he had had the time he would have written other commentaries, in accordance with the *p'shat* which is revealed each day.")

Ibn Ezra holds that the essence of Yosef's disclosures to his father is stated clearly in the Torah. As he was young, Yosef was sent by the sons of the handmaidens to do their errands. If the sons of Leah had done that to him, he would not have minded. He then reported to his father that the sons of the handmaidens were using him, a son of Rachel, as their errand boy.

S'forno has a different approach to these verses. Yosef was the one who told his brothers what they had to do in regard to the flock. The coat of many colors was the outward sign that he had been chosen to lead his brothers both at home and in the field. As he was young and not mature, he brought bad reports back to his father, claiming that his brothers were not tending the sheep properly. His brothers, who had been ordered by their father to obey Yosef, were unable, because of their jealousy, to speak to him civilly. In his interpretation, *S'forno* does not mention the role of the sons of the handmaidens in this sequence of events, even though the Torah specifically mentions them.

Chasam Sofer explains that Yaakov had given Yosef over to Leah's sons, to tend the sheep with them. They transferred him to the sons of the handmaidens without Yaakov's permission. That was the negative behavior which Yosef reported to his father about Leah's sons. When he was with the sons of the handmaidens, he heard that the latter were complaining about Yaakov for keeping silent even though Leah's sons were humiliating them. Yosef then brought Yaakov the evil report that they were talking about "their father."

There are countless other commentaries on this, among both *rishonim* and *acharonim*. R' Samson Raphael Hirsch explains that their "evil report" referred to the gossip about his brothers that Yosef picked up from people in the streets, and which he repeated to his father.

One could also say that the Torah wishes to accentuate here the differences between the sons of Yaakov's wives and the sons of the handmaidens, this too having been part of the cause of the animosity and the sequence of events which followed. Yosef was the only brother to have dealings with both groups. He tended sheep with Leah's sons, and was friendly with the sons of the handmaidens. He then told his father those bad things each group had said of the other. Thus all the brothers disliked him and teamed up to get rid of him, in spite of the differences between the two groups. These differences were also responsible for what happened, because Yosef used these differences to bring back evil reports to his father, and it was this that led them to unite in an attempt to kill him, and eventually to sell him as a slave.

~§ The Nature of the Evil Reports

As we mentioned, Ibn Ezra discusses the nature of these evil reports in terms of *p'shat*. In *Midrash Rabbah*, there is a dispute between R' Meir, R' Yehudah and R' Shimon about the nature of these evil reports. *Rashi* in his commentary includes all three together. He told his father that: (a) His brothers ate אֵבֶר מִן הַחַי — meat taken from an animal before the animal has been slaughtered; (b) the sons of Leah mocked the sons of the handmaidens, calling them slaves; and (c) they behaved licentiously. *Rashi* says that the punishment for Yosef's sin of bringing an evil report was "measure for measure." As he told his father about אֵבֶר מִן הַחַי, he was punished in that the brothers "slaughtered a goat kid." The brothers killed the animal when they sold Yosef, and did not eat the meat of an unslaughtered animal. As to the report that Leah's sons were calling the other sons slaves, Yosef was punished by being sold as a slave. In regard to the evil report about sexual conduct, he was punished through the accusation made by Potiphar's wife.

It appears that *Chazal* deduced from the punishments which Yosef endured what sort of wicked reports he brought back to his father. Many commentators, though, seek to find, within the words of the Torah, a source for the views brought in *Midrash Rabbah*. R' Eliyahu Mizrachi holds that *Chazal* deduced the nature of the wicked reports from a *gezeirah shavah*, i.e., from the similarity of words or phrases occurring in two passages, whereby it is inferred that what is expressed in one applies to the other. The word רָעָה ("wicked"), that is used in reference to Yosef's reports, is also used in reference to all three of the prohibitions mentioned. Thus, in regard to Potiphar's wife, Yosef said to her (*Bereishis* 39:9), "How can I do this terrible wicked (רָעָה) deed?" In regard to slavery (*Shemos* 21:8), the Torah says, "If she is bad (רָעָה) in the eyes of her master ..." Finally, regarding non-kosher species of animals which are not fit for *shechitah*, the Torah says (*Bereishis* 37:33), "a bad (רָעָה) animal ate him."

Maharal in *Gur Aryeh* rejects this explanation. Firstly, there is a general principle that a person cannot deduce a *gezeirah shavah* by himself, and the only *gezeirah shavah* we can use is one handed down by tradition from Sinai. Secondly, the word רָעָה is used in reference to many other things as well. Thus, for example, we are told about *tzedakah*, "If your eye is bad (רָעָה) concerning your poor brother." Does that then mean that the sin of the brothers was that they didn't give *tzedakah*?

Maharal attempts to find a basis in the verses for the *d'rash* used by *Chazal*, but in the end he explains the verses in a symbolic and *hashkafah* manner, and maybe the *p'shat* of the words of *Chazal* remains unclarified.

Other commentators also attempt to find the source for *Chazal*. *Kli Yakar* finds the word רוֹעֶה ("one who tends") four times in *Tanach*: (a) a רוֹעֶה of flocks; (b) a רוֹעֶה of harlots; (c) a רוֹעֶה of Israel; and (d) a person who is רוֹעֶה himself (in the sense of feeding oneself). From this *Chazal* learned that the sons of Leah lorded it over their brothers (in the first sense above: the רוֹעֶה of Israel); that they sought the women of the land (the רוֹעֶה of harlots); and the word רוֹעֶה in the sense of eating. But this interpretation is *d'rush*, and in any event is somewhat difficult to comprehend, because who says that the "eating" refers to anything forbidden?

Or HaChayim says that *Chazal* deduced their interpretations from the meaning of the verses themselves. Yosef saw his brothers "with the flock," and that hints at an evil report about the flock (i.e., that they ate meat of animals that had not yet been slaughtered); while "the wives of his father" hints at the fact that they took liberties with the concubines, not regarding them as "legal" wives. This explanation is difficult to understand, because the Midrash says that they looked at "the daughters of Canaan," and what does that have to do with their father's wives?

One may venture to say that the three items mentioned in *Bereishis Rabbah* are deduced from words which seem unnecessary in the verses themselves. We are told that Yosef tended with his brothers "in the sheep." The word "in the sheep" is unnecessary in the context. So too are the words "his father's wives" and the word "evil" ("evil report"). Each of the *Tannaim* in the Midrash learns what he does from the extra word, as he understands it. The first says that the evil report was "about the flock." The second says it concerned the way Leah's sons treated the children of "his father's wives." Finally, the one who finds the word "evil" to be superfluous sees this as a reference to the daughters of Canaan, as we are told, "for the daughters of Canaan were evil." This may well be the intent of *Chazal*.

✺§ Hashem's Plan Will be Fulfilled

As mentioned, from this *parashah* and the one following it, we deduce that Hashem's plan will prevail. Various people act and different events take place in this tragedy. Yaakov favors Yosef over his other sons, and thus causes jealousy among them. Yosef brings an evil report about his brothers to his father, and draws their dislike. His brothers, Hashem's tribes, are driven by dislike to do the undoable. All of these events are instrumental in the family's descent to Egypt, in order to bring about the fulfillment of the Divine plan revealed at the *bris bein habesarim*.

Abarbanel says that in spite of what the Torah says about the events, no person was to blame, for they were all fulfilling roles which were dictated by the events. All were directed by Hashem, who moves the wheel of history according to His desires and plans. The Torah does not want to disparage Yosef, but rather extols and praises him for being diligent and wise. It applauds him for his righteousness in bringing evil reports about his brothers to his father, so as to keep them from sinning. The brothers are not to blame either. They thought that Yosef and Yaakov wanted to reject them, just as Avraham did with Yishmael and Yitzchak with Esav.

Akeidah expands on this idea. Until the era of the brothers, only one son was chosen as the successor to his father. Here, the other sons were afraid that Yaakov was choosing Yosef for this role, and would give him his blessings. In their opinion, they were permitted to foil this plan, just as Rivkah did in regard to Yaakov. But they did not know that their deeds were directed from on High, so as to bring about the exile to Egypt.

Michtav Me'Eliyahu brings two seemingly diametrically opposed views, as brought in *Chazal* and in *rishonim*, as to Yosef's nature and his being a "נַעַר." He explains that both are true. Yosef was a great *tzaddik*, and tried very carefully not to stumble in his deeds, but Hashem removed His watch over him, so that matters would progress as they did. That is why some of the kabbalists interpret that the words "he was a נַעַר" mean that he was as great as the cherubs on Hashem's throne of glory. The *p'shat*, though, is that the fact that he was a נַעַר brought about all the troubles and suffering. Both are true. The one refers to how Yosef was really, spiritually, while the other was the way he was forced to act, based on Hashem's desires, and Hashem's plan will always be fulfilled.

II.
"Come and See the Works of Elokim"

Chazal in *Midrash Tanchuma* tell us:

"Come and see the works of *Elokim*; He is awesome in His plans toward the children of men." R' Yudan said, "Hashem wanted to fulfill the decree of 'You shall surely know that your seed will be a stranger ...' and He instituted a design for all these matters, so that Yaakov would love Yosef, and his brothers would hate him, and would sell him to Ishmaelites, who would bring him down to Egypt.

Indeed we see that the first cause of all the events which occurred later was when Yisrael said to Yosef, "Your brothers are tending their flocks in Shechem. Go and I will send you to them." From then on, the events follow one another by themselves, as it were, until finally, "He went down to Egypt, against his will, by [Hashem's] word." The "word" referred to here is the word of Hashem at the *bris bein habesarim*, but it was fulfilled through Yaakov speaking to Yosef.

Chazal look at this in *hashkafah* terms and see the unity of the events, when they say: "And he sent him from the valley of Chevron" — with the guidance of the *tzaddik* buried in Chevron, to fulfill what had been said to Avraham *bein habesarim*, "For your seed will be a stranger."

Yaakov was forced to do what he did. That did not take away his free will, says Abarbanel, because the events did not have to unfold in the sequence in which they unfolded. The exile would have occurred in one way or another. And even if the details would have developed in a different fashion, the decree would still have been fulfilled. The way things actually happened, with the free will of all concerned, helped in the realization of the decree, through the events described in the Torah.

This hatred by the brothers was a warning for future generations as to the terrible consequences that can emerge from hatred among Jews. It is true that the results here were decreed by Hashem, but the fact that they occurred through the hatred of the brothers is a moral lesson to us as to the connection between cause and effect.

In *She'iltos D'Rebbi Achai Gaon* on our *parashah*, we are told: "Because of the hatred that his brothers hated Yosef... matters followed one another and our fathers went down to Egypt." In his *HaAmek She'elah*, *Netziv* explains that the matters followed one another as they did because of the decree of "You shall surely know." In any event the Torah did not tell us, without any reason, the way in which events led to our fathers going down to Egypt. Rather, it was to teach us a moral lesson, that it is possible for hatred itself to bring about such an evil.

Similar ideas are found among both *rishonim* and *acharonim*. According to *Maharal* in his *Gur Aryeh*, anyone who is superior to others causes feelings of jealousy and hatred, and that was why Yaakov was hated and why Yosef was hated. After all, Yosef was the *nazir* — the "separate one" — of his brothers. But even though we understand the causes of the hatred, the fact that the Torah tells us this as an introduction to the exile in Egypt is to teach us that there is a certain link between the two, and this must serve as a moral lesson for future generations.

⋐ "And a Man Found Him" — That Was Gavriel

The way to Egypt led through all types of convoluted twists and turns, and only the arrival at the final destination clarified everything that had come before. According to *Chazal*, the identity of the person who told Yosef where his brothers were fits into the remarkable pattern that emerged, which led directly to Egypt. And thus we are told that the "man" was in reality an angel, who, as part of his mission, prepared "iron chains," as it were, to drag Yaakov down to Egypt. This interpretation is in keeping with the spirit of the verses, that it was not all coincidence, but was with "the guidance of that old one."

The commentators seek for hints in the Torah for *Chazal's* interpretation. *Mizrachi* finds this in the fact that Yosef said to the man with assurance: "Please tell me where they are pasturing." And the possibility of him not knowing never even occurred to him.

Maharal finds this in the duplication of the word איש — "a man." "And a man found him, and the man asked him." *Chazal* therefore explained that this refers to "the" well-known man, as we see in the verse, "And the man Gavriel."

Levush Orah suggests this meaning for the word וַיִּמְצָאֵהוּ — "and he found him" — as if the Torah is telling us that the "man" was sent to find Yosef and to send him along the road that had been decided in advance. Other commentators, such as *Kli Yakar*, *Malbim*, and *HaAmek Davar* and others, also follow along these lines, for, according to them, the Torah should have written, "and he met him."

But *Ramban* finds this view of *Chazal* from the content and the spirit of the verses themselves. And these are his words:

> This is to teach us that [Hashem's] decree is true and [one's] diligence is worthless. Hashem prepared for him a guide who, without him being aware of it, brought him into their hands. And it is this that *Chazal* meant when they said that these people were angels; for this story does not appear without a purpose, but to teach us that Hashem's will is fulfilled.

The appearance of the "man" stresses the supernatural development of the events. Under natural conditions, Yosef would have escaped his fate after having gotten lost on the way, but here an angel appeared and directed him to the right place.

It is interesting that even *Rambam* in *Moreh Nevuchim* (2:42) takes the word אִישׁ out of its natural meaning in this case. It is true that *Rambam* places this event on a low level of miracles. According to him, Yosef did not speak to an angel directly, but to a בַּת קוֹל — a "Divine Voice" — which emanated from his soul. An angel that actually appeared would be a *prophetic* event, and Yosef was not yet ready for prophecy at that young age. According to *Rambam*, this appearance was like that of the angel who appeared to Hagar. In both cases, the Torah says, "and he found," an unusual term for prophetic appearances. Hagar was not ready for prophecy spiritually, and that was why all she saw was a vision. In any event, this event was out of the ordinary, and is part of the sequence leading to the fulfillment of the decree given at the *bris bein habesarim*.

But those who interpret the Torah according to *p'shat*, such as Ibn Ezra and *Rashbam*, explain the verses according to their plain meaning. According to Ibn Ezra, it was a wayfarer who directed Yosef to his brothers. Ibn Ezra adds to Yosef's question, "Where are they tending the flock" the words, "do you know?" This addition is characteristic of the way Ibn Ezra uses *p'shat*, where it is better to add words than to enter into the celestial spheres of *d'rush* or kabbalah.

Rashbam explains the purpose of the story as follows:

> This was written to tell us the importance of Yosef, who did not

want to return to his father when he did not find [his brothers] in Shechem, but looked for them until he found them. And even though he knew they envied him, he went and looked for them, as his father had told him, "Bring me back word."

But even those who explain the Torah according to *p'shat* do not deny the lofty secrets inside these events, which were finally revealed at the very end of the sequence, for the Torah itself tells us that Yosef told his brothers, "You wanted it to be bad, but *Elokim* wanted it to be good."

Akeidah tells us beautifully on this: "The overall plans of Hashem will not be diverted in any fashion; even if people try to combat them with all their might, they will not be able to, for even the contrary actions (which they take) will aid in accomplishing these plans.".

✍§ They Traveled Beyond This — From Brotherhood

The *p'shat* and the *d'rush* here are almost identical, namely that the other brothers "traveled" from their original status to another one. According to a number of *rishonim* and the Midrash, the man hinted to Yosef that the other brothers were planning to kill him. They did not want "this" (זֶה), which in *gematria* is 12; but were willing to kill Yosef and have only eleven tribes. They traveled, say *Chazal*, away from "the attribute of the *Makom*" (literally, "the place," meaning Hashem, in that Hashem is in every place), for they had moved away from Hashem's attribute of mercy.

Chanukas HaTorah has a sharp observation in the form of *d'rush*. *Chazal* say that the other brothers wanted to kill Yosef because they had seen that in the future Yeravam ben Nevat would be his descendant. That means that they wanted to kill him right then because of סוֹפוֹ — "his end" — based on how his descendants would turn out in the end. Judging a person based on his "end" is not the way Hashem works, because He judged Yishmael as he was then — when he and Hagar were wandering in the desert — and not how he later became. That was what the man meant when he told Yosef that the brothers had traveled away from "the attribute of the *Makom*."

Similarly, when the brothers said, "Let us go to Dosan" — נֵלְכָה דֹּתָיְנָה — *Chazal* explain it as meaning נִכְלֵי דָתוֹת (note the similarities in the Hebrew letters of the two Hebrew phrases — trans.) — that they conspired to find a legal excuse to justify the murder.

Or HaChayim wonders why Yosef voluntarily entered into danger, after he had been warned of the situation. The different *d'rush sefarim* all discuss this. Yosef relied on the general assumption that "those who are on a mission to do a *mitzvah* are not harmed," and he was on a mission of *kibud av* — "honoring his father." As to why he was nevertheless harmed, the reason is, as *Chazal* tell us, that this principle does not apply where there is a high risk involved. Alternately, he was not involved in *kibud av* at the time, because his father had given him instructions to go to Shechem, not to Dosan.

Rabbenu Bachya, *Ramban*, *Tur*, *Or HaChayim*, and others, all have more profound explanations. The man did not tell Yosef specifically that he was in danger, but said it in an ambiguous fashion. Yosef did not understand the meaning, as Hashem wanted him to go to Dosan. Had that not been the case, he would indeed have understood the dual meaning. It appears from this explanation that the angel did not want Yosef to lose his free will, thus, he could choose either meaning. He chose to understand it the way he did, and went on the way which Hashem led him.

An interesting interpretation of "they traveled from the attribute of the *Makom*" is to be found in *Yalkut Eliezer*. He says "the *makom*" refers to Shechem, where Shimon and Levi had killed the people of Shechem, and had endangered their lives in order to rescue their sister's honor. Now, suddenly, the brothers decided to have nothing to do with Yosef, and to sentence him to death. They traveled from the attribute of *Shechem*, which implied brotherly love and concern for Dinah, and now they hated their brother Yosef.

R' Samson Raphael Hirsch sees a special meaning in the fact that they went to have their flocks graze in Shechem. It was just because this place was the one where they had shown family unity against a common external enemy, that they felt it was the proper place to discuss how to deal with an internal enemy. They saw danger to their future, based on Yosef's desire to be master over them. The brothers had still not lived in freedom and brotherly love, and what would their future be if they all had to be subject to Yosef's desires for glory?

►§ "I Will Pull His Son Before Him"

Chazal in *Bereishis Rabbah* 86 give an analogy: "This is like a cow that was being pulled by the reins, but refused to move. What did they do to her? They pulled her calf in front of her, and she followed after the calf against her will."

This dramatic example explains the words "against his will by [Hashem's] word." The *parashah* before us shows this in every single phrase. Yaakov used the words, "Go and I will send you," which is never found in the Torah, except for one time in regard to Moshe going to Pharaoh. This parallel verse reminds us of the same pulling effect, and of how Yosef's way was directed by Hashem. Even when Yosef lost his way, where that could have saved him from being sold into Egypt, there was intervention from Above which led him straight into exile.

The commentators seek to fathom the meaning of the different verses. *Ba'al HaTurim* says that the words "and bring me back word" were said by Yaakov with a spark of Divine Inspiration, indicating that Yosef would ultimately return.

According to the commentators, each word here is filled with Divine Inspiration. Nor is the fact that this event involved Shechem merely coincidental. *Chazal* noted that Shechem is a place where troubles occur to Jews, and that is the place where David's kingdom was divided into two. This place was also given later to the children of Yosef. It thus appears that the early roots of later historic events are revealed to us here, and whatever happened was bound to happen.

The *rishonim*, such as *Chizkuni*, R' Yosef Bechor Shor, and R' Yitzchak ben Yehudah Halevi, say that Yaakov sent Yosef to Shechem to see if his brothers were well, because he was afraid that the relatives of the people killed by Shimon and Levi might have come to take revenge. *Rashbam*, too, quotes this view. This is already clearly stated in *Targum Yehonasan*, in the following words: "Behold, your brothers are grazing their flocks in Shechem, and go there, for maybe others came and killed them for having killed Chamor and Shechem."

Torah Temimah quotes a manuscript of the Midrash that says the same thing. According to this interpretation, the sequence of events leading to the exile in Egypt started even earlier — with Shimon and Levi killing the people of Shechem. As a result of that, Yaakov sent Yosef to see if his brothers were well. According to this view, the verse quoted above is most appropriate, when we read, "Come and see the works of *Elokim*; He is awesome in His plans toward the children of men." History is filled with various plots, each linked to the other, and one causing the other. The victory over the people of Shechem eventually resulted in exile. Who can see the pattern in advance, except He who weaves it?

III.
Who Sold Yosef to Egypt?

The commentators discuss the identity of those who sold Yosef. As far as the verses in the Torah are concerned, they conceal more than they reveal, and they sometimes even seem to be contradictory. In *Bereishis* 37:25, we are told that after the brothers had thrown Yosef into the pit, they sat down to eat bread, "and they lifted their eyes and saw, and behold a caravan of Ishmaelites coming from Gilead ... going down to Egypt." Seeing this, Yehudah proposed: "Let us sell him to the Ishmaelites." The Torah concludes this proposal with the words, "and the brothers heard." According to *Rashi*, this "hearing" means that they accepted the idea. But the Torah immediately tells us, "And Midianite men who were merchants passed. And they drew him and brought Yosef up from the pit. And they sold Yosef to the Ishmaelites, for twenty pieces of silver. And they brought Yosef to Egypt." The sudden appearance of the Midianites is strange, after the brothers had already seen a caravan of Ishmaelites in the distance. It is also strange that the Midianites sold Yosef to the Ishmaelites, and it was not the brothers who sold him.

Also, we are told, "And they drew him." Who drew him? And who took Yosef out of the well? According to the verse, it appears that the Midianites drew him up. If that is so, why are the brothers considered to have sinned by selling Yosef? And why did Yosef say to them, "I am Yosef your brother, whom you sold to Egypt"?

By the same token, it appears that there is a contradiction in the Torah regarding the identity of those who sold Yosef. In *Bereishis* 37:36, the Torah says: "And the Madanites sold him to Egypt, to Potiphar ..." Yet in *Bereishis* 39:1, it states, "And Potiphar the officer of Pharaoh, captain of the guard, bought him from the Ishmaelites." Who then sold Yosef to Egypt: the Madanites, the Midianites, or the Ishmaelites?

Nor is it clear what the Torah means when it precedes the sale of Yosef with the verse, "And they sat down to eat bread." What do those words imply? Abarbanel says that the Torah stresses here the cruelty of Yosef's brothers, who sat down calmly to eat their bread after their attempt on Yosef's life. *S'forno*, though, holds that this story proves how convinced they were of their righteousness, to the extent that they felt no reason to miss a meal.

In the story of the *pilegesh* in Giv'ah, we find that after the tribes of

Israel had killed their brothers of the tribe of Binyamin, they were at least bothered by their consciences and did not eat, as it states, "and they sat until the evening before *Elokim*, and they raised their voices and cried a great cry." But here, the brothers felt no pangs of conscience after what they had done. They ruled that Yosef was a *rodef* — a person who is out to kill another person. And a *rodef* may be killed by any person if there is no other way to prevent him from killing. By telling us that they ate, the Torah wishes to tell us how pure their motive was, and how convinced they were that they were right. (*Malbim* uses a similar approach, but was preceded by *S'forno*.)

As opposed to this, R' Samson Raphael Hirsch sees a sign of their conscience bothering them in the expression, "and they lifted their eyes." This expression is always used for a specific search, and is never used to refer to seeing things purely by chance. They sat down to eat, but were bothered. They constantly looked toward the pit, and then they suddenly saw a caravan of Ishmaelites coming. According to *Sha'arei Simchah*, this stilled their conscience. They regarded it as a sign from Heaven that Yehudah's idea had been correct, and that it was better to sell Yosef to the Ishmaelites.

Be'er Mayim Chayim explains their eating along the lines of *d'rush*. They ate right then because they had finished with their judgment of Yosef. The whole day they had sat and judged Yosef and didn't eat anything, in accordance with what R' Akiva says in *Sanhedrin*: "How do we know that a *Sanhedrin* which kills a person is not permitted to eat the entire day? We learn it from 'You shall not eat on the blood.'" After they have rendered their verdict, though, the judges may eat.

HaChayim VeHaShalom, by the Munkacher Rebbi, has a beautiful Chassidic explanation. He quotes his grandfather, that when a *tzaddik* eats, he brings bountiful food to the world. One of the aims of the sale of Yosef was in order to have food for Yosef's family when the famine arrived. Therefore Hashem arranged matters in such a way that they continued eating when they sold Yosef. This, says the Munkacher, is hinted at in the Midrash on the verse, "And they sat down to eat bread." There the Midrash tells us, "R' Achva bar Zeira said, 'The passing of the wicked is good for the world, the eating of the righteous is hope for the world.'"

And if we are already dealing with Chassidic interpretations, it is worth mentioning here an engaging Chassidic explanation by *Or HaTorah*. It is stated in *Chazal* and in the Midrash that the entire exile in Egypt was caused by the sale of Yosef. Further, *Seder Olam* says that Israel were not enslaved by Egypt as long as Levi was alive, and from the death of Levi until they left Egypt was 117 years. *Or HaTorah* explains why the slavery lasted for 117 years. When Yosef was sold, nine of his brothers were present. [Reuven had gone home to serve Yaakov, and Binyamin had never left home.] After he was sold, Yosef was a slave for thirteen years. (He was seventeen when he was sold and thirty when he appeared before Pharaoh.) Thus the nine brothers each carried the sin of selling Yosef for thirteen years, and multiplying the two sums gives us a total of 117 years of the sin they carried collectively. That was the number of years of the slavery.

❧ One Sale after the Other

Let us return to what we started with, in clarifying the identity of those who sold Yosef and in reconciling the seeming contradictions in the verses. *Rashi*, following *Chazal*, says that Yosef was sold repeatedly. " 'And Midianite men passed' — that was another caravan." The brothers sold him to the Ishmaelites, as the Torah states, "And they drew Yosef up from the pit." The brothers took him out of the pit and sold him to the Ishmaelites. Later, the Ishmaelites sold him to the Midianites who were passing by. The Midianites brought him down to Egypt, where they sold him to Potiphar. That is the way *Rashi* reconciles the different verses, but he does not explain what we are told in *Bereishis* 39:1: "And Potiphar bought him ... from the Ishmaelites." Mizrachi finds this omission by *Rashi* to be astonishing. He explains *Rashi*'s view that the Midianites bought Yosef from the Ishmaelites, even though the Torah only says that the Midianites "passed." Here, *Rashi* relies on verse 36: "And the Madanites sold him to Egypt." If they didn't buy him, how could they have sold him? In other words, the Torah is being very concise here, and implies that the Midianites passed and bought Yosef from the Ishmaelites. And even though the Torah writes it as "Madanites," that is the same as "Midianites," both of which were sister-nations of Avraham's concubines.

Mizrachi then explains the sequence of events according to *Rashi*. The brothers sold Yosef to the Ishmaelites, and the Ishmaelites sold him to the Midianites. *Rashi* could also have explained it differently, namely that the Midianites who passed by pulled Yosef out of the pit and sold him to the Ishmaelites to bring him down to Egypt, and then the verse in *Bereishis* 39:1 would fit, for there it tells us that the Ishmaelites sold Yosef to Egypt. However, says Mizrachi, *Rashi* starts with the assumption that "And they drew him and brought Yosef up from the pit, and they sold Yosef to the Ishmaelites" refers to the brothers and not to anyone else, because the Torah tells us that they saw a caravan of Ishmaelites approaching, and according to the *p'shat* they sold Yosef to the caravan.

Da'as Zekeinim MiBa'alei HaTosafos also explains matters along these lines, but according to this view there were four sales, and not three as *Rashi* holds. And that is also what is stated in the Midrash. According to this view, the order of the sales was also different. The brothers indeed saw the Ishmaelites coming and discussed among themselves the idea of selling Yosef, but while they were still speaking, Midianite merchants came and the brothers sold Yosef to the Midianites. Afterwards, the Midianites sold him to the Ishmaelites who had arrived earlier. Then the Ishmaelites sold him to the Madanites, who in turn sold him to Egypt. As to the fact that the Torah says that the Ishmaelites sold him to Egypt, that is because Potiphar did not believe that the Madanites owned Yosef, and claimed that "A white person sells a black, but a black person does not sell a white." Therefore the Ishmaelites were forced to appear and testify that they had sold him to the Madanites, who were thus the legal owners and were permitted to sell him.

As opposed to this explanation of a number of sales, which is in accordance with the Midrash, Ibn Ezra and other commentators hold that "Midianites" and "Ishmaelites" are the same people, because we are told in *Tanach* that the kings of Midian were Ishmaelites. R' Yosef Bechor Shor expands on this explanation. The Midianites, Madanites and Ishmaelites are related, all being descended from Avraham's concubines, with Ishmael the son of Hagar, and Madan and Midian the sons of Keturah. The caravan that went down to Egypt included people from all three nations. The Torah always refers to them by a different name, but they are all the same, just as the Jews are called Jews, Hebrews and Israelites.

This is also the view of Abarbanel and *Ralbag*. It is interesting that *Maharal*, in his *Gur Aryeh* on *Rashi*, disagrees with *Rashi* about the sales, and agrees with Ibn Ezra that the Midianites and Ishmaelites were brothers. The Torah called them Ishmaelites because that was the main branch, as it states (*Bereishis* 16:12), "He will dwell in the presence of all his brothers." In reality, they were Midianites, but they were dressed as Ishmaelites. Thus the brothers and Potiphar thought they were Ishmaelites, but the Torah tells us they were Midianites. Alternately, this was a mixed caravan. The group as a whole was known as Ishmaelites, but this particular group was of Midianites.

◆§ The Brothers Did Not Sell Yosef

Rashbam has a revolutionary *chiddush* about the sale of Yosef. It is true that the brothers consulted about selling Yosef, but as they were waiting for the Ishmaelites to come, a caravan of Midianites passed by and heard Yosef crying out from the pit. It was they who took Yosef out of the pit and sold him to the Ishmaelites, who then sold him to Potiphar, and it is possible that the brothers didn't even know about it. As to what Yosef said, "That you sold me," he meant to say that it was they who caused him to be sold, and not that they actually sold him. *Rashbam* says this is the *p'shat* of the verse, where we see that it says "and Midianite men passed," implying that it happened by chance, and it was they who sold Yosef to the Ishmaelites. And even if one wishes to say that the brothers sold Yosef to the Ishmaelites, it was the Midianites who had him pulled out of the pit. Otherwise, why are the Midianites mentioned here at all?

Rabbenu Bachya also holds that it was the Midianites who pulled Yosef out and sold him, and not the brothers. It was considered to be a sin by the brothers, for it was as if they had sold him.

HaKesav VeHaKabalah sees this as the *p'shat* of the Torah. The verse, "Come let us sell him," does not mean buying and selling as such, but a transfer to someone else, as we are told, "And Hashem sold Israel into the hands of Yavin." Yehudah only wanted to transfer Yosef to someone else, namely that he should be a slave, and that way he would not be conceited any longer and would not try to lord it over his brothers. Afterwards, the Torah tells us that Yehudah's plan did not work out either. And it was through Hashem that events turned out as they did. There happened to be Midianite merchants passing by, who pulled Yosef from the pit and sold him to the Ishmaelites. That is the *p'shat* of the verses. Later on, in *Bereishis* 45:4, *HaKesav VeHaKabalah* explains more clearly the sequence of events. The brothers were waiting for the Ishmaelites who were coming from one direction, but the Midianites came first from the opposite direction. The brothers thus did not sell him, but caused him to be sold. *HaKesav VeHaKabalah* adds that, even according to the commentators who hold that the brothers sold him, the sale to Egypt was a complicated business. The brothers wanted to sell Yosef to the Ishmaelites, who are desert people, and thought that the Ishmaelites would take Yosef into the desert, where he would not be found. They would not have sold him to merchants who would sell him to Egypt, because Egypt was a place where many people passed through, and their deed might become known. One should not therefore explain the words "that you sold me to Egypt" as a direct and planned action.

R' Samson Raphael Hirsch, too, says that the Ishmaelites were a tribe that lived near them. The brothers thus thought that after the Ishmaelites would sell their goods, they would take Yosef with them to Arabia, and they might indeed have planned to do that. But Hashem planned it differently and Midianite merchants passed by, and it was they who bought Yosef from the Ishmaelites so that they could resell him. If the Torah says later that Yosef was sold by the Ishmaelites to Potiphar, it really means by the Midianites. The Torah mentions the Ishmaelites so as to show the error of the brothers, who never thought that Yosef would be sold to Egypt. They thought that he was in Arabia, after they had sold him to the Ishmaelites. In spite of this, the brothers were blamed for the sale, because they indirectly caused Yosef to be brought to Egypt.

Based on the view that the other brothers did not sell Yosef directly, *Binah L'Itim* explains Yehudah's proposal. He saw the Ishmaelites coming from far away and therefore suggested to the other brothers: "Let us go," namely that they should move far away. This way, the Ishmaelites would find Yosef and take him with them, and the brothers would not be involved. This interpretation is found in *Malbim* as well.

⋄§ Camel Owners and Merchants

Ramban has a unique interpretation of the verses. According to him, in those days, the people that used camels were generally the Ishmaelites, whereas the Midianites were merchants. The brothers looked up and saw people coming from Gilead riding camels, and assumed it was an Ishmaelite caravan. As it was coming from Gilead, they presumed the members of the caravan were going to Egypt to sell the myrrh and balm they had brought from Gilead. Yehudah then suggested that Yosef be sold to them. When the caravan drew near, the brothers found out that the people were Midianites, who had rented the camels from the Ishmaelites. Thus the brothers sold Yosef to the Midianites. When the Torah says that the Ishmaelites brought Yosef down to Egypt, it is correct, in that the camels belonged to the Ishmaelites. By the same token, it is correct to say that the Midianites sold Yosef.

S'forno, too, explains that the owners of the camels were Ishmaelites. He adds that the brothers didn't want to negotiate with the merchants, because they were afraid they would recognize them the next time they met. Instead, they chose to speak to the owners of the camels, who served as middlemen, while the true buyers were the Midianites. *S'forno* also sees this sale as symbolic of what happened to our fathers in the Second *Beis HaMikdash*. At that time, when the different kings of the Chashmona'im quarreled, they sold their brother-Jews to the Romans, and this sale was what eventually led to the exile, just as the sale of Yosef by his brothers led to the exile in Egypt.

Avnei Shoham also sees this *parashah* as a symbol for the First *Beis*

HaMikdash. Reuven wanted to save Yosef completely, while Yehudah suggested that he be sold to the Ishmaelites. The children of Yosef were a thorn in the flesh of the sons of Yehudah when the House of David split up, while the tribe of Reuven took its portion across the Jordan, and did not stand at Yehudah's side during the fray.

R' Chayim of Volozhin has a beautiful discussion about Reuven and Yehudah. *Chazal* in *Sanhedrin* 6 said that one who blesses Yehudah (for his role in this episode) is really blaspheming. Yet it would appear that Yehudah's proposal, namely to sell Yosef to the Ishmaelites, was good in itself, as compared to that of the other brothers who wanted to kill him, and was certainly better than that of Reuven, which was to throw Yosef into a pit filled with snakes and scorpions. The reason why *Chazal* said what they did, explains R' Chayim, is that Reuven wanted to throw Yosef into a pit in *Eretz Yisrael,* while Yehudah wanted to sell him and have him taken out of the country. The scorpion pit of *Eretz Yisrael* is better than a royal crown outside of *Eretz Yisrael*.

IV.
"For I Know All Thoughts"

The interruption of the story of Yosef's sale by that of Yehudah and Tamar is the source for a comment by *Chazal* in Bereishis Rabbah 85:

> R' Shmuel bar Nachman commenced with (*Yirmiyahu* 29:11), "For I know the thoughts." The [other brothers] were involved in the sale of Yosef. Reuven was involved in sackcloth and fasting. Yehudah was involved in taking himself a wife. And Hashem was creating the light of the *Mashiach.*

This *d'rash* unifies all of the events into a single whole. Each individual only knows his own thoughts, but Hashem knows the purpose of all the deeds, and He weaves all of them into *Mashiach's* robe.

Tosefes Brachah uses this to explain the connection between the two *parashiyos.* He is preceded in this by the *rishonim,* who take the Midrash and expand on it.

Chizkuni says that even before the Jews were enslaved for the first time, the last redeemer was born. Peretz was born, from whom *Mashiach* would be descended, and only afterwards was Yosef taken down to Egypt, leading to the first enslavement of Israel.

HaAmek Davar quotes the verse (*Yeshayahu* 66:7), "Before she labored, she gave birth." From this vantage point, we can understand the words of *S'forno* on the verse (*Bereishis* 38:16), "For he did not know that she was his daughter-in-law," where he says, "Hashem planned this all, so that the seed would come from Yehudah, who was more perfect and more fitting than his son Shiloh, and from him our righteous *Mashiach* will come."

What one can ask, of course, is what the relationship should be between the last redeemer and the first enslavement. I have not found anyone to discuss this, except for *Sefas Emes*. He brings a statement by *Chazal*, that *Mashiach* will come at a time when people are distracted (*hesech ha'da'as*). According to him, both the birth of the redeemer and the appearance of the redemption will come in a concealed manner. Israel will have two redeemers — *Mashiach* ben Yosef and *Mashiach* ben David. The two of them will appear when people are distracted — when they are too occupied with their troubles to realize it. In our *parashah*, we see the light shine forth from both redeemers, through the clouds of the suffering of so many people.

It may be appropriate to add the following: Without a doubt the location here of the *parashah* of Yehudah and Tamar is intended to shed the light of redemption on the periods that followed. The presence of the *parashah* here indicates that Yehudah was compensated for Yosef's having ascended to royalty ahead of him. It was on account of this that the confrontation between Yosef's descendants, the tribe of Ephraim, and those of Yehudah developed later on. Ephraim did not want to relinquish his primacy. The Torah, however, inserted this *parashah* specifically at this point, as it tells of the unfolding of the kingdom of the House of David before the kingdom of Yosef. This teaches us that while everything has a beginning and an end, it was Hashem's design to commence with the crowning of Yehudah before his brothers. Neither deeds nor events make the difference, but rather Hashem's design. As we see from the Torah, it is Yehudah who, from the beginning, was part of that design.

The kabbalists deal with explanations of the fact that the light of redemption shines in hidden places, such as the cases of Yehudah and Tamar, and Boaz and Ruth. *Sifsei Kohen*, who was one of the disciples of *Ari*, explains the view of the kabbalists, that only a birth which takes place in concealment can preserve the soul of *Mashiach*, and can enable it to reach perfection and bring about the redemption.

This concealment prevents the forces of evil from interfering. Satan cannot discern the light hidden within these events.

To what is this analogous, asks the Dubno Magid? To a person who is trying to smuggle goods across a frontier. He dirties them and creases them, so that the border guards won't realize what they really are.

Or HaChayim in *Vayechi*, referring to the verse (*Bereishis* 49:9), "Yehudah is a lion's whelp," expands on the kabbalistic motif of elevated souls that are imprisoned in the *k'lipos* — "hard shells of darkness" — and which *kedoshei elyon* — "the saintly" — must elevate and return to their Divine source. Among these great souls he includes Avraham and Sarah, Ruth, Shemayah and Avtalyon, and others like them. Thus, Yehudah by his actions produced a great and elevated soul. That is what Yaakov our father indicated in his blessing: "From the prey, my son, you have gone up." In other words, you have rescued a great soul from the prey of outer forces. This motif appears frequently in kabbalistic literature in various ways. It is known that the downfall of those who entered the "garden" of kabbalah and did not emerge unscathed was caused by their inability to understand this concept. Not every mind can endure it. But the *kedoshei elyon* were not afraid to descend to the depths of the *k'lipos* in order to raise up from there a hidden treasure. With regard to Yehudah it is written (*Bereishis* 38:1), "And he went down." Thereafter, it is written (*Bereishis* 38:13), "And it was told to Tamar, behold your father-in-law is gone up ..." In fact, *Be'er Mayim Chayim* explains that "it was told," means that *Ru'ach HaKodesh* spoke to her. This was the *Shechinah* announcing that descent is a necessity in order to go up for the purpose of creating the light of *Mashiach* that radiates forth here from between the *parshiyos*.

Actually, it is not possible to understand the *parashah* of Yehudah and Tamar literally without the assistance of kabbalah. What does the Torah intend to tell us in this *parashah*? Why does this *parashah* interrupt the account of Yosef's ordeal? But, as we noted, the light of *Mashiach* shines forth here, as grasped by *Chazal* and the kabbalists. The latter provide a further dimension to this *parashah* by citing the verse (*Bereishis* 38:17), where Tamar asks Yehudah for a pledge "until you send שָׁלְחֶךָ — "a kid of the goats from the flock." The numerical value of שָׁלְחֶךָ is the same as that of *Mashiach*.

Rabbenu Bachya notes that the first letters of the words (וַיֹּאמֶר) יְהוּדָה הוֹצִיאוּהָ וְתִשָּׂרֵף הִיא (מוּצֵאת) — "and Yehudah said, 'Take her out and she will be burned,' and she was taken out" — spell out Hashem's four-letter name, showing us that this action was done for the sake of Heaven and for a predetermined purpose.

Chafetz Chaim also explains the words of *Chazal*:

"'And he turned to her' — against his will" — this was the beginning of the kingdom of the House of David. And the purpose of the story is to tell us that in the greatest of matters Satan intervenes, and there is no other solution but to go in a roundabout way, because on the straight path Satan intervenes, and goals cannot be attained.

In accordance with the above, R' Meir of Premishlan explained the verse, when Yehudah wanted to pay his debt, where he was told, "There was no harlot here." The *Ru'ach HaKodesh* announced, "*chas veshalom* that a harlot should have been here, but these are the sparks of the redemption, which pierce the dark."

The Magid of Dubno, though, holds — unlike the kabbalists — that the purpose of the Torah was not to hide the light from Satan, but was rather a punishment of measure for measure to Yehudah. This is analogous to a rich man who married off his son, and then sent a friend word of it on a letter which was all torn and dirty. His friend paid him back by sending him his present in an ugly wrapping. It is true that Yehudah saved Yosef by suggesting he be sold as a slave, but he told his father, "A bad animal ate him." As measure for measure, although the kingdom would still come from his sons, it would come in a devious way rather than in a straight path, as we see in the story of Tamar.

Michtam LeDavid deduces a practical lesson from this *parashah*. According to him, the Sages of each generation must study every new inspiration, in whatever form in which it may emerge, in order to recognize and utilize the positive element embedded in it. Below are his words. One who studies them carefully will know exactly how he related to the concept of a return to *Eretz Yisrael*. And this is the quotation:

> And behold all the movements and awakenings in the world, especially the major ones, in every fashion and every shade that they appear, are not empty matters. A wise man will be able to see where they are leading, from where and to where. In this generation, we see that many of our people wish to return to *Eretz Yisrael*. It is true that because of our many sins many of them are doing this in a perverse way, and these are not of the portion of Yaakov. Nevertheless, this means that the time of redemption is drawing nearer, and that there is a strong emergence of a longing for the *Mashiach* — if not because of our merits then as a result of our persecutions, for the pain of *galus* grows greater as more and more times goes by . . . [so did Tamar's pain increase, and therefore] "She removed the garments of her widowhood." She could no

longer endure the yoke of her personal exile, "For she had seen that Shelah [Judah's] had grown up" — the word Shelah is an allusion to *Mashiach*, who is referred to as "Shiloh."

It is known that *Michtam LeDavid* was among the early devoutly religious lovers of *Eretz Yisrael*, and that he urged religious farmers to move from Marmorosh to *Eretz Yisrael*. In his *halachic* work, there are a number of *t'shuvos* about living in *Eretz Yisrael* in accordance with the Torah. After the Holocaust he was able to move to *Eretz Yisrael*, and took an active part in the Torah and public life of the country.

⋘ Morals in Those Days

In the *parashah*, we find a number of moral practices which characterized that era. The *mitzvah* of *yibum*, where a man died without child, included not only the man's brother, but other relatives as well (in our case, the dead man's father). A woman who violated these laws was liable to be burned to death.

Rambam in *Moreh Nevuchim* 3:49 explains the morals in those days. Yehudah's action was not a sin before the giving of the Torah. Having intercourse with a harlot was considered to be marriage, while the payment given her was the equivalent of the *kesubah* of our times. There is no *chiddush* in the story as such, but it was only written to teach us certain lessons in the field of *bein adam lechaveiro* — how man should act with his fellow man. One can learn important ethical *halachos* from it. For example, we learn from it that one must keep his word; that everyone should be paid in full whatever is coming to him; that one should not hold onto money that belongs to another person, whether this is a wage, a *kesubah*, a loan or a pledge. There is no difference halachically between a person withholding the wages of his employee and a husband not paying the dowry owed his wife.

R' Samson Raphael Hirsch also discusses in this *parashah* the ethical behavior of that time. From the *parashah*, we can see the pure life of our forefathers, even before the giving of the Torah. Yehudah only took one wife. Only when she died did he falter. Marriage was solely for the purpose of establishing a family and having children. Marriages which didn't achieve this aim were not considered to be desirable. The father was the one who decided matters for the family, and he educated it. All the members of the family worked together in the building of a fortress of purity and morals. If the marriage did not achieve its aim and the husband died childless, then another member of the family had to carry on the family name, and had to marry the wife of his deceased brother or relative. These ethical concepts are close to the idea of *yibum*, where, after the Torah was given, Hashem restricted this to the brothers of the deceased. Because of the fact that the widow in such a case had to marry a relative of her deceased husband, she was considered to be a married woman, and if she had relations with any other man it was considered to be adultery, and was punished very severely.

R' Hirsch here is following in the path of *Ramban* who also sees *yibum* as a major axis of this *parashah*. Before the giving of the Torah they were very strict about this matter, and the requirement of *yibum* applied to every relative. Whoever refused to do so was breaking the law, and his house was given a derogatory name: "The one with the cast-off shoe." In the time of Boaz, *yibum* was practiced by all relatives (not forbidden by Torah law), and the action was known as *ge'ulah* — "redemption."

Chazal said that Yehudah was the first person to practice *yibum*. In other words, they acknowledge the legality of this form of *yibum* at that time. Given this background, we can see the actions of Tamar as an unusual effort to fulfill a family obligation. Yehudah thought she was a woman who had violated the moral laws and had become pregnant by adultery, at a time when she was forbidden to marry and had to wait for *yibum*. After he found out that she had done what she did only because she wanted to fulfill her obligation, he admitted without shame, "She is more righteous than I." It was I who wanted to commit a sin, whereas she wanted to fulfill a moral duty.

The Torah even gives a reason to explain why Tamar took this unconventional step, "Because she saw that Shelah had grown." The commentators discuss the meaning of this statement. *S'forno* holds that the Torah is trying to tell us that Tamar did not plan in advance to do what she did, but that she took off her widow's garments in order for Yehudah to be astonished at the step and to ask her why she had done so. Then she planned to tell him that Shelah had grown and should perform *yibum*, and that was why she was not willing to wait any longer. As Yehudah didn't recognize her because of her veil and offered her what he offered, she wanted him to hear her voice and said to him, "What will you give me?" This way, she hoped he would finally recognize who she was by her voice. But things developed differently. She only wanted him to give her a pledge as proof, and not a harlot's pay. If she would have received a payment and nothing else, she would not have been able to prove who the father was. Her intention was purely *l'shem Shamayim* — "for the sake of Heaven" — so that she would build her family from Yehudah. She only asked for those items that would be clearly identifiable as belonging to Yehudah: his staff, his seal and the special cord that he had. She wanted, by this means, to prove to Yehudah that all she wanted was to continue the family name, and not because she was a wanton woman. She then did what she did. *Chazal* refer to this action as an *aveirah li'shmah* — a sin for the sake of Heaven (*Nazir* 57).

Akeidah proves Tamar's virtue from various details of the story. She removed her widow's clothing so as to draw Yehudah's attention, because the time had come for her to be married. She covered her face, as was the custom of pious Jewish women in those days. She thought that Yehudah, or one of his servants, would come and ask her, "What is happening?" and then she would petition them to arrange for her *yibum*. But Hashem planned things differently, because Yehudah thought she was a wanton woman. She then realized that she had found a way to solve her problem, one that she hadn't even thought about. She would have *yibum* without Yehudah's knowledge, after Yehudah had delayed the *yibum* of his son Shelah all this time. She exploited the opportunity to the fullest, and in the end Yehudah too agreed, "She is more righteous than I."

It is interesting that the elders who blessed Boaz in almost similar circumstances mentioned the story of Yehudah and said, "May your house be as the house of Peretz, whom Tamar bore to Yehudah." The proposal that Ruth made to Boaz, "And spread your wings on your maidservant, because you are the redeemer," also referred back to the case of Yehudah, because after the Torah was given, according to *halachah* Boaz was not required to perform *yibum*, that law only applying to the husband's brother.

The commentators deal with the story of Yehudah and Tamar at great length. I would like to add a gem from the world of *d'rush*, which sheds light on the story of Tamar, in terms of everything being directed by Hashem and not being merely a coincidence. Had that not been the case, the Torah would not have devoted a whole *parashah* to this story. *Tzror HaMor* says that when the Torah tells us וַתִּתְעַלָּף (which most commentators explain to mean that she covered her face with a veil), it means exactly what the word normally means — that Tamar fainted, after realizing that she had to go through with this action. She knew that if Yehudah would not admit that he was the father, she would be sentenced to death; she nevertheless did what she did, for according to her, this step was essential for the building of the monarchy of the House of David. *Chazal* learn from here that "it is better for a person to throw himself into a furnace, rather than to shame another person in public." Tamar did not mention Yehudah's name, but merely said, "To the man to whom these belong."

R' A. Z. Werner of Tiberias learns from here that one is even forbidden to embarrass a person who is totally wicked. Had Yehudah not admitted it, she would have been burned to death with the two infants growing in her. Is there then anyone more wicked than a person who would allow three people to be killed just because of his lust? Yet she still remained silent and did not mention Yehudah by name, until he himself admitted it.

☙ Burning Alive — Why and for What Purpose?

The commentators are surprised at the severity of the sentence of burning, for at the most Tamar was no more than a *shomeres yabam* — a woman who had to marry her deceased husband's relative. *Rashi* quotes "Ephraim of Kasha'ah, a disciple of R' Meir," who explains that Tamar was the daughter of Shem, who was a *kohen* to Hashem, and the law is that if the daughter of a *kohen* commits adultery, she is burned to death.

Ramban is not content with that explanation. It is true that she was the daughter of a *kohen*, but even the daughter of a *kohen* is only burned if she committed adultery, and not if she is a *shomeres yabam*. Therefore *Ramban* says that Yehudah was the ruler of the area, and he sentenced her for disgracing his position. In addition, *Ramban* says that it was the custom in those days that if a woman committed adultery, her husband decreed what punishment she was to receive. Tamar was still considered like a married woman because she was supposed to be taken by Shelah, and that was why Yehudah sentenced her to death.

Da'as Zekeinim MiBa'alei HaTosafos maintains that this severe punishment was not in accordance with *halachah*, and especially before the giving of the Torah. This, though, was a generation of people who committed all types of sins, and in such a situation the *beis din* has the right to impose all types of punishments, even those that are not in accordance with the *halachah*, just as we see that Yehoshua killed Achan, not in accordance with *halachah*, but for the purpose of deterring others from sin.

The Lubavitcher Rebbi, in his *Likutei Sichos* on *Rashi*, explains *Rashi* based on the Midrash. He asks a number of questions: (a) The law regarding the burning of the daughter of a *kohen* is only mentioned in *Parashas Emor*, and was not in effect even after the Torah was given, until Hashem proclaimed it. How then could Yehudah have acted in this way? (b) Even after the Torah was given, the law only applies when the woman committed adultery after she was betrothed (*arusah*) or married (*nesu'ah*), and not in the case of a widow who is a *shomeres yabam*. The Lubavitcher Rebbi proves conclusively in the latter case that the woman is not considered to be married. After discussing the matter at length, he reaches the conclusion that the order that she was "to be burned" was a *hora'as sha'ah* — "one-time ruling" — just as in the case of Shimon and Levi killing the people of Shechem. It is reasonable to assume that the other nations also had laws to prevent adultery, and that was why Yehudah ruled as he did, and that Shimon and Levi did what they did. Such a tradition is considered to be binding even if one received the tradition from a single person, (as we see when Reuven said to his father: "You may kill my two sons"). This law of the other nations, though, only applied to a wanton woman, as where *Rashi* explains on the verse, " 'Shall our sister then be made a harlot?' — namely a wanton act." After it became clear that Tamar was not a wanton woman, her punishment automatically lapsed.

Malbim has an interesting note in his *Eretz Chemdah*. He asks why *Rashi* and the Midrash relate that R' Ephraim, who said that Tamar was the daughter of Shem, was a disciple of R' Meir. *Malbim* answers that when Tamar did what she did, her father, Shem, was no longer alive. Now, if the Torah's reason for the rule of burning the daughter of a *kohen* is because "she is defiling her father," that only applies as long as he is alive, but not after he dies. According to R' Meir, though, the reason for burning the woman is because people say, "Cursed be he who raised her; cursed be he who bore her," and that applies equally after the father is dead. Thus, by mentioning that R' Ephraim was a disciple of R' Meir, we understand why Tamar could be condemned to death even though Shem was not alive.

Ba'al HaTurim, quoting R' Yehudah HaChassid, has a special interpretation of the word שְׂרֵפָה — "burning." According to him, it referred to branding on the forehead with a burning iron, to let everyone know she was a harlot. *Rosh* in his *She'elos u'Teshuvos* 18:13 mentions that this practice still applied in his days.

I also saw that commentators mention that the rule of burning for adultery appears three times in the Torah: (a) here; (b) at the end of *Parashas Kedoshim*; (c) in *Parashas Emor* in regard to the daughter of a *kohen*. In the latter two cases, the Torah stresses, "she shall be burned with fire," whereas here it simply says, "she shall be burned." R' Yehudah HaChassid therefore maintains that this is in accordance with what *Chazal* tell us in *Shabbos*, regarding a verse in *Yeshayahu* (3:24), "Thus instead of beauty," where the word "thus" — כִּי — is translated by *Chazal* as meaning the same as כְּוִיָּה — "burning." Others quote a verse in *Yechezkel* (23:25), referring to an adulterous woman, "They will take away your nose and your ears." *Radak* says that that is what is done to a woman who commits adultery, where they make a mark on her by removing her nose and her ear. Here, too, Yehudah meant that type of mark.

Though the above provide a novel explanation, it would appear that the meaning of the Torah was for Tamar actually to be burned, as we see where we are told, "She was taken out," namely to be burned. In addition, *Chazal* conclude from Tamar's actions, "It is better for a person to throw himself into a furnace, rather than to shame another person in public." If so, the words must be taken literally. In general, though, it is difficult to understand why it was necessary for the commentators to investigate the practices prevalent before the Torah was given, when we don't know either the form or the reason for these practices.

Mikeitz – מקץ

I.
Miracles and Natural Events in Man's Actions

The chain of events leading to the exodus from Egypt finds its expression, both at the end of the previous *parashah* and the beginning of this *parashah*, in a series of incidents which appear to be coincidental.

Yosef interprets the dream of the royal cup-bearer, and asks that when Pharaoh returns the cup-bearer to his post, he should ask the king to free him. The cup-bearer promises, but promptly forgets his promise. Only two years later, when Pharaoh dreams and no one can interpret his dream, does the cup-bearer remember the young Hebrew who had interpreted his dream for him in prison. Why was there a gap of two years? And why does the Torah tell us that the cup-bearer forgot his promise?

The Torah does not give us any answer about this. We are told in *Bereishis Rabbah* (89), though, that "Yosef had been given a specific time to spend in the darkness of the prison." But then the question arises as to why two years? Apparently, this period of time fits into the unfolding of the events in a way that is known only to Hashem who planned them. But the Midrash does add another detail: "As Yosef said (two words) to the cup-bearer, זְכַרְתַּנִי — 'Remember me' — and וְהִזְכַּרְתַּנִי — 'Mention me' — two years were added to him." In other words, each superfluous word on the part of Yosef cost him a year of his freedom. In this way, two superfluous words resulted in his being incarcerated for two extra years.

Tosefes Brachah explains how the figure was calculated. We know that the span of one's memory is for a year, as the *gemara* tells us (*Berachos* 58): "The dead one is forgotten from the heart only after twelve months." Yosef mentioned the idea of remembering twice, and since the span of every memory is a year, he was sentenced to be forgotten for two years.

The Midrash adds one other element, the meaning of which is discussed by the commentators. " 'Happy is the man that has made Hashem his trust' (*Tehillim* 40:5) — that refers to Yosef. 'And did not turn to the arrogant' — because he said to the cup-bearer, 'remember me' and 'mention me,' he was given two more years of suffering."

This statement seems to have a built-in contradiction. At first, it says that Yosef trusted Hashem, and afterwards, that he placed his trust in the arrogant, asking for man's help. We also need to explain why he was punished. After all, isn't a person permitted to take whatever means available to get out of trouble in which he finds himself, even if he does trust Hashem? We are told on numerous occasions by *Chazal* that a person should do whatever he can to help himself, and should not rely on miracles.

When, then, is one permitted, or even required, according to Jewish belief, to take steps by himself, and when is this forbidden?

✥ Two Types of Believers

Most commentators explain the Midrash as coming to stress the greatness of Yosef's *bitachon* (confidence in Hashem), to the extent that Hashem even punished him for saying more than necessary in the circumstances. This was because, as we know, ה' מְדַקְדֵּק עִם צַדִּיקִים כְּחוּט הַשַּׂעֲרָה — literally, "Hashem is scrupulous with *tzaddikim* even to a single hair" — Hashem demands perfection of *tzaddikim*.

Rabbenu Bachya, though, in listing different degrees of *bitachon*, which he analyzes in great detail, sees a flaw in Yosef's behavior, namely, he placed his hopes on being saved in the specific intervention of Pharaoh's cup-bearer. Of course a person must try to do whatever possible in order to be saved, but he is forbidden to believe that it is only the specific method which he chose to try to save himself that delivered him. Hashem has many avenues open to Him and countless ways to arrange to save a person from distress. Each person, on his part, must do whatever he can, but must believe that Hashem will help him either through the measures he himself has taken or by another way. Yosef, though, placed all his trust in the royal cup-bearer, stressing to him, "remember me" and "mention me" as if trying to dictate to Hashem how he was to be rescued. For a person such as Yosef, this was a flaw in his *emunah* (faith).

We see, for example, that Eliyahu, when he was in the desert, also went looking for food, but hoped for Hashem to deliver him. In the end,

Hashem saved him by sending him ravens with food — a method he would never have dreamed of. Therefore, even though one is required to do whatever possible to help himself, his *emunah* must be only in Hashem, the One who directs the entire world, and who is the One who will determine how the person will ultimately be saved, in the most fitting and decisive manner.

The Dubno Magid sees Yosef's flaw as even worse than that. Yosef relied on man, at a time that he knew that man is a creature of free will, who is capable of changing his mind and desires. There was nothing wrong in searching for a way to be rescued, but another human being was the weakest way to do so. To what is this analogous? To a king who told a close friend, "You can live in any city in my kingdom, without having to pay any taxes." The friend then went and settled in a city where the king had promised all the city taxes to a certain person, and had promised not to intervene in that person's affairs. Shouldn't the person realize that in such circumstances the king's promise to his friend did not apply?

Toldos, in the name of *Besht*, says that there are two kinds of people, each with his own way of *emunah* and *bitachon*. If a simple person is in trouble, one must try to save him by natural means, as in the words of *Chazal*, "Many (who were not up to his level) did as R' Shimon bar Yochai (trying to rely on Hashem's miracles to support them) and were not successful" (*Berachos* 35). If such people act as R' Shimon bar Yochai, they leave their normal order of things before having entered into another, and they thus annul the way Hashem deals with them customarily. R' Shimon bar Yochai, though, was a *tzaddik*, of whom we are told, "A *tzaddik* will live by his faith." He was among the few who did not know the natural ways, and never lived in a natural way. The same is true for Yosef. These unique individuals, if they ever leave their customary way, cannot function according to the natural way of things. Attempting to do something by the natural way harms rather than helps them.

Based on that assumption, R' Baruch Epstein explains the verse: "Happy is the man who trusts in Hashem." There is a kind of man for whom all that is needed is trust in Hashem, but at the same time he carries out a natural action to help himself. But there is a higher level than that, and that is one where "Hashem is his trust." Hashem is not only the basis for his faith, but He is also the One who implements his deliverance. Such a person not only puts his faith in Hashem, but Hashem is his only faith. That was what Hashem demanded of Yosef.

One can also say that what the Midrash wants to tell us is not to disparage Yosef for having told the royal cup-bearer to remember him, but on the contrary, "Happy is the man who has made Hashem his trust" refers to Yosef. "And did not turn to the arrogant" also refers to Yosef. If one then asks why he said, "Remember me" and "Mention me," the Midrash answers that this came from Hashem, so that he would have to remain in prison for two more years. It was there that he stayed until Pharaoh dreamed, for it was when Yosef interpreted these dreams that he ascended to royalty. His remarks were involuntary so that events could take their predestined course. In reality, Yosef did not turn "to the arrogant," and did not trust in man for his salvation. He placed his trust only in Hashem and in none other.

∗§ Measure for Measure

R' Y. Z. Dushinski does not see Yosef as being punished, but rather that here we have a case of מִדָּה כְּנֶגֶד מִדָּה — "measure for measure." A person is permitted to do everything possible to save himself, but the person is treated by Hashem in accordance with the way he acted. Had Yosef chosen a supernatural way to try to save himself, he would have been saved supernaturally. Since he tried to be saved through natural means, he had to wait for two years until the time came to interpret Pharaoh's dream. According to this view, Yosef was not punished for the course that he chose, but what happened was the natural consequence of his course. A person is led by Hashem along the path that he chooses for himself.

This interpretation is found frequently in Chassidic and *mussar* works, and is based on our *hashkafah*. There is no difference between salvation by natural means or by supernatural means, for both come from Hashem. The difference depends only on the quality of the person. A person who serves Hashem through natural means is open to Hashem's influence through natural means, while a person who serves Hashem with *mesirus nefesh* — "total dedication of his life" — is open to Hashem's influence even through supernatural means.

In line with this view, *Ramban* writes in *Parashas Bechukosai* that a true *tzaddik* does not need natural medicines, for these were only created for ordinary people. *Taz* in *Yoreh De'ah* 336, though, disagrees with this view. But we find evidence of this view among both *rishonim* and *acharonim*. Many great Sages hold that a superior person does not need natural means to fulfill his material needs. This view is followed especially by the *mussar* works.

R' Chaim of Volozhin uses this to explain the views of R' Shimon bar Yochai and R' Yishmael ben R' Yose, where, according to R' Chaim, the former advocates supernatural intervention by Hashem and the latter natural intervention. In reality, R' Chaim says, there is no substantial argument between the two. Both hold that Hashem's benevolence from above depends on one's behavior below, but each describes a different part of that benevolence. R' Shimon refers to those whose entire behavior is supernatural, and therefore benevolence from Above comes in this form. R' Yishmael ben Yose, on the other hand, refers to those whose behavior is based on "And I will bless you in all that you do."

R' Dessler, in *Michtav Me'Eliyahu* (3:246), explains the idea of "measure for measure" in regard to Yosef in a similar fashion to R' Dushinski. As Yosef attempted to be saved by natural means, the royal cup-bearer, who was subject to natural human forgetfulness, forgot all about him. But after Yosef became more firm in his *emunah*, he emerged from his natural framework and was saved in an unexpected manner.

Other commentators, especially *Netziv* of Volozhin, see a flaw specifically in Yosef's attempting to be saved by natural means. Yosef, who had seen how event after event affecting him had had a supernatural component, had no right to attempt to be saved by natural means, but should have left Hashem to save him when the time came.

Ramban uses a similar concept in *Parashas Shelach*, in explaining why Hashem had reservations about the sending of spies into Canaan. The Jewish people, who had seen personally how their entire course of history had been miraculous, had no right to undertake natural steps to accomplish their aim, even if such actions were permitted to others. They had the obligation to trust solely in Hashem, knowing that He would lead them in the best possible way to the land, without any natural action on their part.

I have explained the Midrash brought above in accordance with the words of R' Moshe Chaim Luzzatto in *Mesilas Yesharim* 21, that even though a person must try to obtain what he needs by natural means, that is purely a result of the sin of Adam. Because of that sin we were sentenced to (*Bereishis* 3:19), "By the sweat of your brow you will eat bread." Before Adam's sin, the plan was that each person would obtain whatever he needed without having to work. However, Adam's sin imposed physical work upon man, but not that this should become one's purpose in life. When one works, whether a lot or a little, he has fulfilled the obligation of working as a punishment for the sin of Adam. After that work, each person should trust only in Hashem to supply him with what he needs. According to this introduction, one can say that Yosef's punishment came because he exaggerated in his efforts, saying, "Remember me," and "Mention me." It would have been enough for him to have said, "Mention me." It was not necessary for Yosef to ask the cup-bearer to "remember" him. That was why the cup-bearer forgot about him, until two years later, when the time came to "mention" him to Pharaoh — and then Yosef was saved. Thus we are told in the Midrash that too much effort on one's part can bring an opposite result: "As Yosef said to the cup-bearer, 'Remember me' and 'Mention me,' two years were added to him."

∽§ An Open Miracle and the Natural Within the Miracle of Chanukah

The miracle of Chanukah has all the characteristics of both the miraculous and the natural, as defined by the different commentators we brought above. *Kedushas Levi* says that there are two kinds of miracles. There are miracles which take place through man's actions, and these are referred to as "the miracles that are with us each day": "with us" — it is through us and with our participation that they take place. On the other hand, there are miracles that are defined as "Your wonders, every evening and morning." These are miracles in which Hashem's doing is clearly visible, without the aid of man.

The miracles which took place on Chanukah were natural miracles, and therefore we say after lighting them: ". . . וִיהִי נֹעַם (*Tehillim* 90:17), May the beauty of Hashem our God be upon us; and establish the work of our hands upon us." In other words, we ask that Hashem should have the miracles which we created by our hands continue to exist. As the commentators tell us, we need some minimal action on our parts to fulfill the requirement of having to try to help ourselves. When the Greeks were conquered, it was a case of "the many into the hands of the few." The "few" were necessary because a blessing from Hashem must have something on which to take effect. Even the miracle of the oil, which is a lofty and heavenly miracle, needed to have a little oil upon which the blessing would fall.

There is a famous question as to why we light the Chanukah candles eight days, when the miracle was only for seven, for there was enough oil for one day. Various answers are given, but that of *Taz* is in keeping with what we saw in the previous paragraph. According to *Taz*, we light the candles for eight days because it was the oil of the first day which caused the miracle to take place. Had it not been for that first bit of oil, there would not have been anything upon which the miracle could take place. By the same token, without man's taking some type of action, there cannot be any supernatural and miraculous salvation. The natural and the miraculous were bound together in Yosef's salvation.

It was from the miracles within nature that supernatural miracles grew, in accordance with the interpretation of some of the giants of Chassidus: "You have given a banner (or "miracle" — נֵס) to wave (לְהִתְנוֹסֵס) for those that fear you" (*Tehillim* 60:6). In other words, the first נֵס brings others in its wake. The other miracles grow out of the first.

The punishment of the Chashmona'im was similar to that of Yosef. They too placed their faith in "the arrogant," trusting in the Roman Empire. This is explained by *Ramban* at the beginning of *Parashas Vayishlach*: "They began to fall before Edom, because the kings of the Chashmona'im made a treaty with Edom." In the verse before this, *Ramban* explains that each person must try to use every possible natural method available to him, but at the same time must place his trust in Hashem, and must not trust only in man.

The miracles on Chanukah were encased in a natural wrapping, and they appeared to be *natural* events, except for the miracle of the oil. The other miracles dealt with the war and the victory of the few. This is explained by *Techeiles Mordechai*: "And for Your people Israel You made a great and holy name as this day" (from the עַל הַנִּסִּים prayer). In other words, the miracles were like the miracles which appear daily in the renewal of the act of creation each day, which too are wrapped in a natural covering.

There are two forces in creation, says the Lubavitcher Rebbi. There is the natural force, which also is dependent on the performing of *mitzvos*, as we see in, "And I will give your rains at their appointed times." Then there is the supernatural force, which is above our everyday reality, which comes through *mesirus nefesh*, and that is the force of מְהַדְרִין מִן הַמְּהַדְרִין — "the most scrupulous and pious." On Chanukah, each person can draw these forces down based on the way he acts and behaves. That was exactly the case with Yosef. Natural efforts bring, as measure for measure, natural salvation, while supernatural *emunah* brings about supernatural redemption.

Whoever has a sharp eye, says *Techeiles Mordechai*, sees within the depths of nature the outstretched arm of Hashem, which renews daily the act of creation. Hashem's hand acts in history, just as it did in the creation. This we refer to when we pray on Chanukah: "And for Your people Israel You made a great salvation as this day." The salvation of our people was also wrapped in the natural garb of wars — it also works through nature, as the renewal of the creation each day.

Bnei Yisaschar deals at length with the concealed miracles of Chanukah and Purim, and he explains why these were such and what they were. The time when these miracles occurred was at the transition period between open miracles and concealed miracles. Thus these miracles were half open and half concealed. Externally, the miracles were natural, but one can readily see in them Hashem "peeking from the cracks." Just as in nature there is a thing which is between the inanimate and animate, as is scientifically known, so too are there miracles which are between open and concealed miracles. The purpose of these is to prove that even the concealed miracles of our time are in reality open miracles if one can but read them correctly.

With this introduction, *Techeiles Mordechai* explains the meaning of the prayer, "and for Your people Israel You made a great salvation (תְּשׁוּעָה) and deliverance (פּוּרְקָן)." The last word in the phrase, פּוּרְקָן, is the Aramaic equivalent of the Hebrew תְּשׁוּעָה, and denotes the natural garb of the salvation. Chanukah teaches us that the different forms of תְּשׁוּעָה are really one, and are both from Hashem, and the reason they come in two forms is in order to bridge between the different periods and to raise all up in *emunah*.

II.
Yosef Interprets Dreams

Yosef's success in interpreting dreams was based, according to various commentators, on the principle that dreams often contain prophetic material. Pharaoh's sorcerers were unable to decipher the prophetic element in Pharaoh's dream, because in order to be able to do so one needs to be aided by Hashem.

According to *Rashbam*, Abarbanel, *S'forno*, *Akeidah* and other commentators, Yosef stressed this fact when he explained to Pharaoh the nature of his solution. In their first meeting, Pharaoh told Yosef, "I have heard that you listen to a dream to interpret it," namely that he saw him as a run-of-the-mill interpreter of dreams, of the kind of Pharaoh's sorcerers, except that Yosef was better than the others, as proven by the cup-bearer's testimony. But Yosef immediately told Pharaoh that he was wrong. It wasn't just a question of being more talented than the sorcerers, but a difference in substance and in content. Thus, Yosef stressed: "Only God will explain Pharaoh's dream." Yosef was saying, "I do not interpret dreams, but perform the mission from Hashem" in deciphering the prophetic message in Pharaoh's dream.

While the Torah alludes to this in vague terms, the Midrash on the verse, "And Yosef said to Pharaoh saying: 'It is not from me. God will answer the peace of Pharaoh,' " is more specific, when it states (*Bereishis Rabbah* 89), "[Yosef] gave credit to the One to whom it was due." Yosef repeated a number of times his mission from Hashem in interpreting dreams. Thus later, in *Bereishis* 41:25, Yosef said, "That which God wished to tell Pharaoh," and again in verse 32, "For this matter is truly from God, and God is hastening to do it."

Already in the previous *parashah*, *Rashi*, quoting the Midrash, sensed Yosef's pure intentions (see *Rashi* on *Bereishis* 39:3). It appears that Pharaoh clearly understood what Yosef was saying, for after hearing his interpretation, he said: "Is there then any other man like this with the spirit of God in him?" And again: "After God told you all this." Yosef achieved his aim in instilling the recognition that it is not he who was interpreting Pharaoh's dreams, but he was a messenger from Hashem. He continued in the ways of his fathers, in calling upon Hashem.

A second purpose in interpreting the dream was one which was unknown to Yosef at the time, that being to have him installed as second only to Pharaoh, and to bring Yosef's father and family down to Egypt in accordance with Hashem's wishes. This purpose was achieved by Yosef's accurate and correct interpretation of Pharaoh's dream, and his proposal of a complete program to fend off the problems of the future famine.

The commentators dwell at length on the explanation of the dream and its interpretation. Some of them also discuss the differences between the way the dream actually appeared, and the way it was reported by Pharaoh. For example, Pharaoh left out the fact that the lean cows stood next to the fat cows by the river, but added his own comment, "I have never seen such as these in all the land of Egypt for ugliness." So too did he add, "And they came within them and it was not visible that they had come within them, and their appearance was ugly as at first." There are other differences as well. The commentators wonder about the significance of the differences and analyze the symbols in these words, in terms of the interpretation of the dream. They also are surprised that Yosef, who was not an advisor to Pharaoh, should offer advice which was not part of the interpretation of the dream proper.

We will explain this *parashah*, utilizing *rishonim* and *acharonim*, according to the simple meaning of the text. We will unfortunately have to be brief in this, because there is a great amount of material on the entire *parashah*.

☙ The Dream and Its Interpretation

Ramban explains the dream as containing within itself the seeds of its interpretation. Egypt lives off the Nile River, its main source of water, and thus the Nile is the main source of plenty or want. Pharaoh saw healthy-looking cows coming out of the river, and that symbolized plowing. He saw the full grains of wheat, and that symbolized the reaping of the grain. Thus, on the basis of these two, Yosef understood that they represented seven years of plenty. Again, Pharaoh saw lean and ugly cows, and that the river rose very little, so Yosef understood that meant that there would be no plowing; whereas the lean and wind-blown ears of wheat symbolized that there would be no harvest. Yosef interpreted the dream to mean that the years of plenty would affect only Egypt, while the famine would apply to all the countries. Thus the explanation was really readily discernible.

According to *Ramban*, when Pharaoh saw the second group of cows standing next to the first, he realized that there would not be a break between the years of plenty and the years of famine (although, according to *S'forno*, the proximity of both varieties of cows was an indication that the years of famine and plenty would coincide. The years of plenty would be in Egypt, while the famine would be in other countries). It is possible, says *Ramban*, that Pharaoh didn't tell Yosef that he saw the different cows standing side-by-side, but Yosef interpreted it in accordance with Pharaoh's dream. Also, the vision that Pharaoh saw and the way he reported it may have been the same. Even though there are differences in the Torah between the two, the Torah didn't mention all the details of what Pharaoh actually told Yosef. Similarly, we see that the Torah alludes to details that Pharaoh mentioned on his own: "And it could not be discerned that they had come into them." This part of the dream indicated that the years of famine would swallow up the years of plenty, and it was in accordance with this that Yosef suggested the laying aside of food for that time, that too being part of the interpretation of the dream.

In his explanation, Yosef stressed the years of famine (see *Bereishis* 31:26-28), for years of plenty were nothing new in Egypt. In addition, the whole purpose of the dream was to know how to support the country during the years of famine. Yosef also found a reason for the fact that the theme appeared in two dreams, for "God is hastening to do it," even though this repetition was also meant to refer to the plowing and harvesting (cows are a symbol of plowing, while wheat is a symbol of the harvest). In reality, everything could have been included in a

254 / *Yosef Interprets Dreams*

single dream. The repetition of the dream, but not of the actual subjects, came to tell Pharaoh that the dream would soon be realized. This is the dream and its interpretation according to *Ramban*. Many other commentators follow in this path.

R' Samson Raphael Hirsch also follows in the path of *Ramban*, but expands on the interpretation of the pictures and symbols in the dream. Seven times the river produced healthy-looking cows, and seven times lean and ugly cows. As the river brings forth its blessings only once each year, this is a clear indication that the dreams of cows and sheaves of wheat are two different symbols. Pharaoh stood at the river engrossed in thought. He understood that the cows and the wheat were the gifts of the river. In addition, when the healthy-looking cows came up from the river, they found grazing land and went to graze there. By the time the lean cows arose from the river, the healthy-looking cows had already finished grazing and had returned to the river bank. The lean cows were not animals of prey. They would not have eaten the healthy-looking cows if the latter had left them grass to graze. But the healthy-looking cows had eaten everything there was. This was a clear indication, says Hirsch, not to use up all the grain in the years of plenty, and that was why Yosef interpreted the dream as he did. Below we will discuss the views of other commentators on this topic.

Hashem spoke to Pharaoh in images. Pharaoh did not understand that every thing he saw symbolized something, and that was why he was not totally accurate in relating what he had seen. That was why his sorcerers were unable to interpret his dream. Pharaoh dreamed that he was standing by the river engrossed in his thoughts. According to Hirsch, then, the key to understanding his dream was the proper evaluation of the importance of the river. Yet, when Pharaoh told of his dream, he said that he was standing by the banks of the river, and that small change made all the difference in the interpretation of the dream. In Pharaoh's dream, the cows were "pleasing of appearance and healthy of flesh," thus symbolizing the importance of the cows to man as food. But when he told the dream, he only mentioned that they were "pleasing of appearance," thus implying that these cows had nothing to do with food, and would be of interest only to a painter or sculptor. And that, according to *Chazal* in *Bereishis Rabbah* 89, was how the sorcerers interpreted the dream — dealing with seven daughters or seven provinces. Similarly, in regard to the other cows, Pharaoh saw them in his dream as being "ugly-looking and lean," implying that they had little food value to man, and were thus of little use to him. In telling the dream, though, Pharaoh said that they were "emaciated and ugly-looking," implying only a description of how they looked, and not how this would affect man's needs. Nor did Pharaoh mention that the ugly-looking ones had stood next to the healthy-looking ones by the river, from which one could have deduced that the lean ones ate the healthy-looking ones only because they were starving, and not instead of pasture.

Thus, by not giving an accurate report of what he had dreamed and by changing matters, Pharaoh led his sorcerers astray, but Yosef pointed out the correct interpretation to him, and that was another remarkable thing about his explanation.

⇜§ Differences Between the Dream and Its Narration

Pa'aneach Raza holds that Pharaoh deliberately changed the content of his dream, in order to test Yosef's ability to interpret dreams. But Yosef pointed out to him where he had changed things, and then proceeded to interpret the dream according to its actual content. *Pa'aneach Raza* also interprets the words וְעַל הִשָּׁנוֹת הַחֲלוֹם, which is normally taken to mean "and that the dream was repeated," as a hint to the effect that Yosef told Pharaoh that he had changed (שִׁינָה) the original content of the dream, and that he, Yosef, had interpreted it based on the actual content. That in itself, Yosef told him, was one proof that his interpretation was correct. As for the element that the dream was repeated in different forms twice, that was the indication that "the thing is established by God, and God is hurrying to bring it to pass."

HaKesav VeHaKabalah follows along similar lines, and it would appear that R' Samson Raphael Hirsch was influenced by his explanation as to how Yosef interpreted the dream. According to *HaKesav VeHaKabalah*, the Torah gives us the story of Pharaoh's dream at length, in order to emphasize Yosef's wisdom in not allowing Pharaoh to distort the dream. Pharaoh saw cows which were "pleasing of appearance and healthy of flesh," which symbolized plenty. Then he saw them standing by the river, indicating that the years of plenty would be followed by years of famine. But Pharaoh did not mention that the lean-looking ones had stood next to the healthy-looking ones. On the contrary, he added that "it was not known that [the healthy-looking cows] had come into them and their appearance was bad as at first." Thus it would have been very easy for Pharaoh to deceive one into thinking that there was no link between the years of plenty and the years of want, and there was no hint at having the years of plenty take care of the years of want. The same was true with the sheaves. Pharaoh dreamed of sheaves which were "healthy" (בְּרִיאוֹת), which would be a symbol of plenty, but in telling of his dream, he spoke of "full" sheaves (מְלֵאוֹת), which simply meant that they were ripe, without any hint at plenty. There are other such examples of differences between the two.

In relating his dream, Pharaoh mixed up the dream and its interpretation. But Hashem enabled Yosef to interpret Yosef's dream as it was, without any changes. Then Pharaoh remembered all the details of his dream, and realized that Yosef was "a man with whom the spirit of God dwells." Not only had Yosef been able to interpret the dream, but he also knew the dream itself, just as it had been.

HaKesav VeHaKabalah quotes as proof of his explanation the words of *Midrash Tanchuma*:

> When Pharaoh came to tell him his dream, he wanted to test him, and turned the dream around. Yosef said to him, "That was not the way you saw it, but 'pleasing of appearance' and 'full and good.' Not 'withered,' but 'empty and blasted with the east wind.'"

Thus we see that according to *Chazal*, Pharaoh told Yosef his dream with certain changes, and when Yosef saw through these changes, Pharaoh was amazed at his wisdom.

Yosef's advice as to how to store the crops of the good years was also embedded in the dream. Pharaoh saw in his dream that he was standing "by the river," namely standing and thinking about what to do with the extra grain, but in telling his story, he merely stated that he was standing "by the banks of the river," as if he was looking about him without any clear goal. "By the river" meant that Pharaoh was standing by the river and trying to think of how to control it, and how to arrange for the plenty of the good years to be used for the later years. Yosef's words, "And now let Pharaoh appoint," were the answer to Pharaoh's question on controlling the river.

Meshech Chochmah says that this solution came to Yosef based on what Pharaoh had dreamed: "And behold seven other cows . . . and they stood next to the cows." Yosef realized that this implied there was an action that Pharaoh had to take. When the seven lean cows stood next to the seven healthy ones, that indicated that Pharaoh had to collect grain for the lean years. The reason why the idea of standing next to one another only occurred in the dream about the cows and not in the dream about the sheaves was because this was not something that Hashem would do (unlike the other aspects of both dreams), but something that Pharaoh himself had to take care of. Pharaoh left out that detail in telling Yosef of his dream, but when he saw that Yosef used that detail in his interpretation when he suggested that grain be collected, Pharaoh realized that Yosef had Divine wisdom. (This idea is also found in *Michtam LeDavid*.)

Kli Yakar also sees the differences between the dream and its narration as important, and explains them in his own way. Pharaoh considered the river to be a god, and that was why he did not tell Yosef that he was standing "by the river" to pay his respects to his god. That was also the reason he didn't want to say that the lean cows came "out of the river," as he had seen in his dream, because he thought the river could only be a source of good, and not of bad. He might even have thought that there was a different god who acted evilly. He did not tell Yosef that the two groups of cows stood next to one another, because that would have implied that the two gods had quarreled and the bad one had emerged victorious, defeating his god. He therefore indicated that the good cows "came inside" the bad ones, as if to indicate that they did so of their own free will.

Abarbanel says, as does *Ramban* elsewhere, that the discrepancies in Pharaoh's narration have no significance, but were the way he briefly summarized the major points of his dream.

∾ Who Made Yosef Pharaoh's Advisor?

Ramban asks who it was that made Yosef into Pharaoh's advisor. In this section, we have already brought the views of a number of commentators that Yosef's advice to Pharaoh was part of the interpretation of Pharaoh's dream.

Abarbanel holds that Yosef's advice was given though *Ru'ach HaKodesh* — "Divine Inspiration." A prophet is not permitted to suppress his prophecy, just as Yirmiyahu said (*Yirmiyahu* 20:9), "His word was in my heart as a burning fire shut up in my bones, and I was afraid to bear it, but I could not stop."

Ramban, though, as we mentioned, holds that the advice that Yosef gave was implicit in the dream itself, in the words, "And the ugly-looking ... cows ate the seven cows that were pleasing of appearance." This sentence includes within itself the principle that the surplus from the years of plenty should be used to supply food for the years of famine. One can also see from the fact that the seven lean cows did not change appearance even after swallowing the seven healthy-looking cows, that the surplus from the seven good years would be only enough to meet the bare necessities in the years of famine.

The above explanation by *Ramban* is different from that of *Rashi*, who explains that the meaning of the dream of the lean cows eating the healthy-looking cows was that the entire joy of the seven good years would be forgotten in the seven lean years.

Mizrachi and *Gur Aryeh* clarify the argument between *Rashi* and *Ramban*. The two *rishonim* differ as to whether eating the seven healthy-looking cows was meant to provide food for the seven lean cows, or whether this act simply symbolized the destruction of food. According to *Rashi*, the meaning of this act was the destruction of food. Proof of this can be seen in the poor sheaves consuming the good sheaves, an action which did not feed the poor sheaves, but simply destroyed the good ones. *Ramban*, though, does not consider the two acts as identical, and explains the case of the cows as a sign that the years of plenty would supply the necessary food for the years of want.

HaKesav VeHaKabalah gives an interesting explanation for how Yosef was able to give the advice he did based on the dream. According to him, Yosef deduced this from "and Pharaoh awoke." Pharaoh too told Yosef that he had woken up from his dream. All of this seems to be superfluous, for what difference does it make if he woke up or not? Rather, this teaches us that Pharaoh needed to wake up and take immediate steps because of the evil that was going to befall his country, and to prepare while there was still time. Not only does waking up imply arising from sleep, but it also implies awakening to take action.

S'forno and *Rivash* give a simple explanation of Yosef's advice. Yosef told Pharaoh that when Hashem had shown him the interpretation of Pharaoh's dream, He had also shown him that steps were necessary to prevent a calamity from befalling the land during the years of famine.

Akeidah sees this in the verse, "that which God will do, He has shown *to* Pharaoh." This is not a simple dream with a simple solution, as the sorcerers suggested, but the dream and its solution refer directly to the throne, to Pharaoh.

Ma'asei Hashem explains the verse: "There was none to interpret them to Pharaoh" in a similar way. The interpretations of the sorcerers did not refer to Pharaoh, to the throne. These were personal interpretations, as we see above in *Chazal*, whereas Yosef's interpretation was meant to save the kingdom.

Abarbanel and other commentators stress the word "them" in the verse, "There was none to interpret them to Pharaoh," quoted above. Pharaoh thought that his two dreams were one. "And he told them his dream." But his sorcerers interpreted it as meaning two things, as it states, "and none were able to interpret them for Pharaoh." The interpretation of two dreams did not appeal to Pharaoh, and that is why he immediately accepted Yosef's interpretation that the two were in reality a single dream.

BEREISHIS — MIKEITZ

All of these together — mentioning the changes that Pharaoh had introduced in telling the story, the correct advice which the commentators see as showing Yosef's worldly intelligence and knowledge of nature, engineering and mathematics (see *Ramban*, *Rashbam*, Ibn Ezra, *Or HaChayim*, *HaKesav VeHaKabalah*, Hirsch and others) — persuaded Pharaoh that before him stood a remarkable man in every sense of the word. *Kesav Sofer* expresses this in a few words: " 'Is there then to be found a man with the spirit of God in him?' Can one then find such a combination of a practical person on the one hand, with the spirit of God in him on the other?" And that was why he decided to make Yosef his deputy.

III.
The Purpose of the False Allegations and Punishments

Yaakov saw that there was grain (שֶׁבֶר) in Egypt, and he said to his sons, "Why do you look at one another?" The Midrash in *Bereishis Rabbah* 91 tells us that Yaakov sensed what his sons did not — that there were both disaster (also שֶׁבֶר) and hope (סֵבֶר) in Egypt, when he sent them there to purchase food in that country. The disaster lay in the exile, and the hope in Yosef. This is faithful to the view that when we are told וַיַּרְא יַעֲקֹב — "Yaakov saw" — it was not a physical act of seeing, for immediately afterwards he told his sons "for I have heard." Thus, according to *Chazal*, Yaakov's "seeing" was a supernatural one. This interpretation fits in well with the *Targum Yehonasan*, for when the Torah tells us that Yaakov said to his sons, "Why do you look at one another?" the Targum states, "Why do you fear to go down to Egypt?" Yaakov saw by *Ru'ach HaKodesh* that Yosef was in Egypt, and he sensed why the brothers were afraid to go there to buy grain. They were afraid of what might happen if they went to Egypt, and that was why he told them not to fear. It is as if the Torah had written לָמָּה תִּתְיָרְאוּ — "Why do you fear?" — rather than the actual text of לָמָּה תִּתְרָאוּ — "Why do you look at one another?"

Some of the commentators who rely on *p'shat*, such as *Chizkuni* and Ibn Ezra, though, say that "Yaakov saw" is meant to be understood metaphorically, and not as an actual physical act of seeing. According to

Ibn Ezra, *Tanach* often interchanges the physical and the metaphorical, as all are derived from the same source. He brings examples of this, such as (*Bereishis* 27:27), "See the fragrance of my son," and, "The light is sweet." *Chizkuni* brings proof from (*Shemos* 20:15), "And all the people saw the sounds." This interpretation is not meant to deny that Yaakov might have seen through prophecy the two hundred and ten years that the Jewish people would spend in Egypt. It is simply meant to make the Torah verses more intelligible to those who are not familiar with kabbalah, etc. One must admit, though, that there are many places in this *parashah* where it is very difficult to interpret the events according to *p'shat* alone. The entire *parashah*, as it were, is surrounded by wonder and *sod* — a hidden kabbalistic meaning.

According to the commentators who rely on *p'shat*, the words לָמָּה תִּתְרָאוּ are a form of rebuke. *Rosh* explains this sentence in terms of הַתְרָאָה — "a warning" — "Why are you waiting for me to warn you or rebuke you?" as Yaakov adds later: "that we may live and not die," when he places the responsibility for the family's future on them.

Ramban uses a similar approach, but with certain differences. Yaakov rebuked his sons because there were still to be seen (מִתְרָאִים) in Canaan, when they should have been on their way to Egypt to buy grain.

Tosafos HaRosh and Ibn Ezra explain the word תִּתְרָאוּ in terms of לְכוּ וְנִתְרָאֶה פָּנִים — namely that they were not to show their wealth, or that they were not to quarrel with one another. *S'forno* sees these words as a rebuke for the fact that each brother tried to delegate the mission to the others. לָמָּה תִּתְרָאוּ — "Why do you look at one another" like "a pot belonging to partners which is neither cold nor hot" (*Eiruvin* 3a), while, because of internal disputes as to who should act, the deed remains undone?

There are innumerable interpretations along such lines among various *rishonim* and *acharonim*, but there are two original explanations in *Ralbag* and in *HaKesav VeHaKabalah*. *Ralbag* holds that the words לָמָּה תִּתְרָאוּ express Yaakov's great fear of the brothers' wandering about in the cities of Canaan, for there might still be "avengers of the blood" of the inhabitants of Shechem that Shimon and Levi had killed. *HaKesav VeHaKabalah*, on the other hand, explains the word תִּתְרָאוּ as being derived from the word תּוֹר — "time," and the meaning of this phrase is: "Why are you delaying and thereby losing your turn to buy grain?"

According to these explanations, the children of Yaakov had no grain reserves left. Yaakov spurred them on to go to Egypt and to buy grain, for there it could be bought easily and cheaply, while in Canaan this was a much more difficult task.

BEREISHIS — MIKEITZ / 261

According to *Rashi*, on the other hand, basing himself on *Chazal*, they still had reserves of grain, but Yaakov taught them a basic lesson in life — not to appear to be full when others were hungering. Yitzchak too behaved humbly when he met with his brother Esav, as *Rashi* explains at the beginning of *Parashas Vayishlach*. Yaakov then explained: "That we should live and not die," as if to stress that it was this lesson that could lead to life or, *chas veshalom*, to death.

●§ "A Person Attempts to Minimize His Wealth"

Chazal in *Sanhedrin* 29 state a legal principle, based on the common tendency of people, that "a person attempts to minimize his wealth." Based on this principle, a person is not held responsible to pay a debt he admitted to (where there is no other evidence of such a debt), if he later chooses to retract his announcement. It is assumed that he only admitted he owed various debts in order to appear less wealthy than he really is. According to *Rashi*, people act this way in order to keep away the *ayin hara* (evil eye), while according to *Ramah* they do so to prevent people from being jealous.

Revid HaZahav notes that the source for this *halachah* is in our *parashah*, the way *Chazal* explain the phrase לָמָּה תִּתְרָאוּ when Yaakov instructed his sons not to show off their wealth to the children of Yishmael and Esav. *Torah Temimah* also gives this as the source, although here he does not quote *Revid HaZahav*.

This rule, that "a person attempts to minimize his wealth," is also applied by the *poskim* in reference to one's children. *Chazal* in *Sanhedrin* 30 tell us that:

> If [children] saw their father burying money and he said to them, "it belongs to so-and-so," or, "this is *ma'aser sheni* money" ... if his statement was made as an evasion (e.g., as a way of hiding his wealth so that his sons don't squander his money — *Rashi*), it is as if he has said nothing.

Thus we see that a person conceals his financial condition even from his own children.

According to *Ridvaz* in his *teshuvos*, that rule does not apply to *hekdesh*; namely, if a person bought a house for *hekdesh* — i.e., to be consecrated for the *Beis HaMikdash* — and then claims that he really bought it for himself but was trying to minimize his wealth to everyone else, that claim is dismissed. Other commentators, though, argue against the ruling by *Ridvaz* from the *gemara* we quoted above, where if a person claimed he was burying *ma'aser sheni* money and later says that he was trying to minimize his wealth, he is believed. *Ketzos HaChoshen*, though, says that the *gemara* in *Sanhedrin* is no proof against *Ridvaz*, because *ma'aser sheni* belongs to the person himself, and even according to those who say it is *hekdesh*, all agree that the person himself has the right to eat it in Yerushalayim, and no other person has any right to it. That is why when a person claims money he is burying is *ma'aser sheni*, he may later claim that he had stated this in order to avoid his children squandering his money, but he cannot make such an assertion in regard to money he claimed was *hekdesh*.

The above rule is based on a commonly accepted principle in daily life. *Ketzos HaChoshen* 81 regards this as a widely used practice. As we mentioned, the source for this is to be seen from Yaakov's instructions to his sons not to appear to be sated in the presence of the children of Esav and those of Yishmael. *Ramban*, though, finds the above somewhat surprising, for after all, neither the children of Esav nor the children of Yishmael were in Canaan. *Ramban* wishes to answer that the children of Yishmael were in the habit of passing through Canaan on the way to buy grain in Egypt. *Mizrachi*, though, does not understand that statement either, for Edom is to the south of *Eretz Yisrael*, and there is no need to go through *Eretz Yisrael* when traveling to Egypt.

Maharsha in *Ta'anis* 10 holds that *Chazal* deliberately referred to "Esav and Yishmael," because they were related to the children of Yaakov; when people are related to one another, they help one another in their troubles. Those that are not related have no cause to expect anything, and therefore there was no reason to worry about such people being jealous. Thus, according to *Maharsha*, the idea of Yaakov's sons not flaunting their food had nothing to do with the rule that a person tries to minimize his wealth, but was simply advice as to how to act in the presence of such relatives as Esav and Yishmael.

One can use this logic to answer a question posed by *Taz* in *Divrei David*. *Taz* asks how *Rashi* stated that the reason for the sons' conduct was in order not to appear sated before others, when *Rashi* himself, in *Parashas Devarim*, says, "'For Hashem your God has blessed you' — therefore do not be ungrateful and do not act as if you are poor, but show yourselves to be wealthy." According to *Maharasha*, though, our *parashah* is only referring to jealousy in times of distress, whereas one should not otherwise avoid appearing well off.

Nachalas Yaakov Yehoshua explains the question posed by *Taz* along *d'rush* lines. *Ramban* in *Parashas Toldos* on the verse, "And Esav scorned the birthright," quotes *Koheles* 8:14:

BEREISHIS — MIKEITZ / 263

"There are the righteous who receive according to the work of the wicked." This refers to wealth (i.e., there are righteous people who, in spite of their righteousness, are still poor). But that does not apply to those who were blessed directly by Hashem, because (*Mishle* 10:22), "The blessing of Hashem makes rich, and He adds no sorrow with it."

Therefore in *Parashas Devarim*, where the Torah tells us about Israel, "Hashem, your God, has blessed you," *Rashi* had no hesitation in saying that one must display his wealth, and not be afraid of an *ayin hara* — "He adds no sorrow to it."

One may add that even if a person is forbidden to be ostentatious with his wealth because of לָמָּה תִּתְרָאוּ, that does not refer to the nation as a whole, which can benefit in prestige by displaying its wealth and might. Yaakov and his sons were living among non-Jews, and for them the rule of לָמָּה תִּתְרָאוּ certainly applied. In *Parashas Devarim*, though, the reference was to the entire nation, which was trying to persuade Edom to allow it to pass through Edom's borders. Edom did not have to fear that the Jews would eat food without paying for it, for the nation was wealthy. Thus, in that case, *Rashi* could say that the principle of לָמָּה תִּתְרָאוּ did not apply. On the contrary, there was benefit to be derived from showing off Israel's wealth.

It is interesting to quote in this context the words of *Kli Yakar* in *Parashas Devarim* on the verse, "Now turn to the north," where he says:

> The idea of "to the north" (צָפוֹנָה), it appears to me, is that if any Jew finds any small amount of success, he should bury and hide it (וְיִצְפִּינֶנָּה) from Esav, for there is no nation which is so jealous of Israel as is Esav. In their opinion everything was stolen from them, from the blessing of our father Yaakov that took Esav's blessings with shrewdness. So too did Yaakov command his sons, לָמָּה תִּתְרָאוּ, which, as *Rashi* explains, refers to the children of Yishmael and Esav: (Do not act) as if you are sated. For both Esav and Yishmael believe that Yaakov stole Esav's success by his actions. That was why it is specifically commanded in reference to Esav, "Now turn to the north," so that he should not be jealous of them. And that is the opposite of what Israel does in these times in the lands of their enemies, for whoever has a hundred (coins of the realm) shows himself off in the finest clothes and with a distinguished-looking home, as if he had thousands; and they incite the other nations against them, and (thereby) violate "turn to the north." This practice is the curse of the

members of our people, and that is what causes all the troubles that have befallen us.

☙ False Accusations: Atonement or Punishment?

Chazal in *Bereishis Rabbah* 91 explain לָמָּה תִּתְרָאוּ as an instruction by Yaakov to his sons not to enter the city together, and not to provoke attention by the sudden appearance together of tall, strong men. Yosef's claim, "You are spies!" was based on the fact that the brothers came in through ten different gates. In this way, Yaakov became a party to the false accusations that were leveled later on, for it was he who had told his sons, לָמָּה תִּתְרָאוּ.

We can understand this better from *Ramban's* explanation, that these false accusations were not meant as punishments for the brothers. This view contradicts that of Abarbanel who says that Yosef wanted to punish his brothers and make them suffer for having wanted to kill him, even though they failed to do so. Such sinful intent requires retribution and penance.

According to *Ramban*, Yosef did not want to punish his brothers, but wanted to ensure that his dreams would be fulfilled in full. Similarly, with the case of the goblet, he wanted to see to what extent the other brothers loved Binyamin.

R' Samson Raphael Hirsch goes into this in depth in his commentary on the Torah. Yosef did not want to stand before his brothers as an important minister and ruler, but as a faithful member of the family. That was why he wanted to have the brothers test him, while he would test them. Earlier, they had been afraid of his dreams, and he therefore wanted to show them that even though his dreams were being fulfilled, he still remained the same Yosef. On the other hand, he wanted to see how they behaved, and to test to see if they had changed their ways. Indeed, by his schemes and the way he acted toward them, he succeeded in unifying the family members.

According to this interpretation, Yosef's schemes were a means to test the hearts of his brothers. This test did not have to be carried out in the way it was, and there could have been other ways to test the brothers.

Kli Yakar and other commentators, though, who follow in the footsteps of Abarbanel, see an inseparable link between the schemes and the aim. The punishment which the brothers received was measure for measure. The accusation that the brothers were spies was against the fact that they had suspected Yosef of bearing tales against them. The imprisonment of Shimon came about because the brothers had thrown Yosef into the pit. Finally, the accusation that Binyamin had stolen

Yosef's cup was meant to have the brothers declare their readiness to be slaves, and that way to atone for the fact that they had sold Yosef to be a slave. Abarbanel adds that the money returned in the brothers' sacks (and the fear that this caused) was meant to atone for their selling Yosef for twenty pieces of silver.

This is a beautiful interpretation, but from the *p'shat* of the verses it appears that Yosef wanted to discover his brothers' inner feelings, and as soon as he succeeded in doing so, he revealed himself to them.

There are four "confessions" implied on the part of the brothers in this *parashah*, and each of them comes after another "scheme" of Yosef's. After the brothers were accused of being spies, they indirectly admitted to the existence of Yosef, when they said, "Twelve are your servants, who are brothers, the sons of one man in Canaan. The youngest is with our father now, and the one is not." This was an indirect confession, and the beginning of their stock-taking. After Yosef told them to bring Binyamin, they admitted openly, "But we are guilty for our brother, in that we saw the distress of his soul when he pleaded to us and we did not listen. That is why this trouble has come upon us." When their money was found in their sacks, again they take stock, as we see in the verse, "And each man trembled with his brother saying: 'What did God do to us?'" This statement shows their recognition of their sin, and their knowledge that Hashem was punishing them. Finally, after Yosef's cup was found, Yehudah confessed openly to Yosef and said: "What can we say to my lord? What can we speak and how can we justify ourselves? God has found the sin of your servants." Yosef, who knew that they had not sinned with the cup, saw in this full regret in terms of confession of the sin. This sequence of confessions at different points clarifies to us that Yosef's schemes were meant to have the brothers confess and regret their actions. After Yosef had accomplished this and revealed himself to his brothers, we can see that, as *Chazal* tell us, his father was also a party to the aim of having the brothers confess, by means of his first command to the brothers: לָמָּה תִּתְרָאוּ. By having the brothers enter Egypt by different gates, Yaakov ensured that Yosef was able to accuse them of being spies.

Vayigash – ויגש

I.
Yosef Reveals Himself to His Brothers

The scene in which Yosef reveals himself to his brothers is a dramatic one, which touches the heart. Everything that had been bottled up in Yosef's heart burst forth. He was no longer able to maintain the disguise he had been using until then. He could no longer hold himself back. Until then, says *Rashbam*, he had acted with restraint, but now he was no longer able to do so. When we are told, "and Yosef was no longer able לְהִתְאַפֵּק," *Rashbam* says (and in this he echoes *Targum Onkelos*) that the word לְהִתְאַפֵּק (normally translated as "to restrain himself") means to be strong and stand firm.

Abarbanel explains that Yosef was no longer able to hold back the tears that welled forth from within him. Nor could he retire to a side room to cry, because of "all those who were standing by him" — there were people who were blocking his way. He therefore ordered all the other people to leave the room. In order not to have it appear to be as if he was ashamed of his brothers, he then cried aloud. That is what we see when the Torah tells us, "And he lifted his voice and cried." In this, the Torah meant to stress that when he revealed himself to his brothers, he did so in a demonstrative way. He had everyone else leave, not because he was ashamed of his brothers, but on the contrary, so that his brothers would not be ashamed. That is what *Rashi* says when he explains that לְהִתְאַפֵּק means "to tolerate." Yosef was not able to tolerate having the Egyptians stand around and see his brothers ashamed, when he identified himself to them.

S'forno explains that as the ruler, Yosef had numerous people who were waiting for him, to hear his decisions on various issues. Now he was unable to restrain himself until he could take care of all the issues of the people standing around him, and was forced to ask them to leave and to return at a later time.

Or HaChayim also holds that the *p'shat* of the verse is that Yosef was unable to restrain himself until those about him would leave the room, and began to shout that they should leave immediately.

Why was Yosef suddenly not able to restrain himself, after having been patient for so long a time? *Ramban* says that the reason was that many people became involved in Yosef's dispute with his brothers, and asked that he return Binyamin to the brothers. The Torah tells us that Yosef was unable to withstand the pleading of all those about him. His spirit broke when he was faced with this universal plea, and he ordered that everyone be sent out.

Abarbanel does not agree with *Ramban*. One cannot imagine that Yosef would reveal himself to his brothers only because strangers pleaded with him. Yosef had planned his moves in advance, so as to repay his brothers "measure for measure," and he had no need for other people to move him to take pity on his brothers.

HaKesav VeHaKabalah, though, contests Abarbanel's interpretation. Yosef did not act toward his brothers as a stranger because he sought revenge, but because, as the Torah says, "He remembered the dreams." He was waiting for all the dreams to be fulfilled completely. Until now, only the "stars" (i.e., his brothers) had bowed down to him. Had the Egyptians not begged him, he would have restrained himself until Hashem's decree had been carried out in full. However, after others pressed him, he was forced to content himself with only partial fulfillment of the dream.

HaKesav VeHaKabalah, after defending *Ramban* against Abarbanel's argument, nevertheless offers an alternate interpretation, for he feels that most of what *Ramban* says cannot be seen in the verses themselves. Thus *HaKesav VeHaKabalah* states that, had the literal meaning of the Torah indeed been in accordance with *Ramban's* interpretation, it should have said "all who were standing by him to plead with him." Because of this, *HaKesav VeHaKabalah* explains the word לְהִתְאַפֵּק as being derived from the root פוק, which means to bring forth, as various examples in *Tanach* show us. Thus, what the verse means is that Yosef was unable to "bring forth" his words when everyone was standing about him. That is why he called for their removal.

Further, *HaKesav VeHaKabalah* adds *Ramban's* comment that Yosef did not want the Egyptians to hear of how he had been sold into slavery, because the Egyptians would have reacted by saying, "There is no place for such betrayers in our land." He did not want to have the Egyptians hear him say the words, "whom you sold to Egypt."

Pardes Yosef quotes the Gerer Rebbi to the effect that Yosef was not willing to reveal himself until his brothers totally accepted his authority, for he remembered how they had been angry, exclaiming, "Will you then rule over us?" When Yehudah, the leader of the brothers, accepted Yosef's authority and referred to himself as "your servant," Yosef was no longer able to restrain himself, and identified himself to them.

Shem MiShmuel explains this in a similar fashion. In all his stratagems, Yosef wanted to bring his brothers to repent for having sold him into slavery. When he heard Yehudah say: "And now let your servant remain instead of the lad," he realized that Yehudah had indeed repented, and was even willing to accept the humiliation and suffering of a slave, as long as this would atone for his sin. It was then that he announced, "I am Yosef."

When he made that declaration, *Chafetz Chaim* tells us, the darkness before the brothers' eyes was lifted, and they suddenly had answers to all the questions that had been bothering them. What had Hashem done to them? Why had He done it? The simple declaration, "I am Yosef," clarified everything. In the future, says *Chafetz Chaim*, when Hashem appears before all and announces, "I am Hashem," that will explain everything that has happened until that time.

⋑§ Is My Father Still Alive?

Chazal in *Chagigah* 2 remark that the brothers were so overwhelmed that they were unable to answer Yosef.

> R' Eliezer, when he reached this verse, would cry. He would say, "If when one is rebuked by flesh and blood, the verse states, 'And his brothers could not answer him because they were afraid before him,' then how much more so is this true with the rebuke of Hashem."

A number of *acharonim* wonder what rebuke there was in Yosef's words, for at that time he did not mention anything about their selling him to Egypt; all he did was to ask how his father was. *Malbim* says that the words "Is my father still alive?" include a great deal of rebuke. How could you not have been concerned about our father? Weren't you afraid that he might not withstand this great sorrow?

Beis HaLevi expands further in explaining the meaning of this rebuke. It was an answer to Yehudah, who asked for mercy for his father's sake. It was as if Yosef said to him: "Are you asking for mercy? How then were you not concerned about [Yaakov's] life when you sold me?" That was something that the brothers couldn't answer, for they feared Yosef. (This idea is also cited in *Torah Temimah*.)

Kli Yakar goes even further in explaining the rebuke and the reason why the brothers were taken aback. Yosef stressed "my father" and not "our father," as if to say, "My father is not your father after what you did to me." At first, he also said to them, "I am Yosef," and did not add "your brother." They were afraid that he would not treat them like brothers, and that was the source of their great anxiety. Only after he added, "I am Yosef, your brother whom you sold," did they begin to feel less fearful. He stressed that he was their brother even though they had sold him. The first words he spoke, though, were a hidden rebuke to them; they understood this and were afraid. Thus we understand what *Chazal* mean when they say: "How much more so is this true with the rebuke of Hashem."

According to *Rashi*, the brothers were taken aback after Yosef's first words, not because of fear, but because of shame. *Mizrachi* and other commentators on *Rashi* explain that *Rashi* holds that after Yosef ordered everyone to leave the room so that no one else could hear, and after the brothers heard him crying, there was no reason to fear. That was why *Rashi* explained that they were ashamed. One could nevertheless venture to say that *Rashi* bases himself on the words of *Chazal*, who said that Yosef rebuked them, and that their conscience bothered them. That is also the view of *Chizkuni*, who says, "They were concerned and regretted what they had done."

R' Simcha Zisl of Kelm, in *Or Rashaz*, says that in order to remove this shame from the brothers' hearts once and for all, Yosef immediately attacked them with the strong charge, "I am Yosef, your brother whom you sold." This was a psychological approach. He started by firing a shot from the largest cannon, and after that there was nothing for them to fear. Yosef had already told the brothers everything there was to say, and yet he still related to them as a brother.

Or HaChayim explains that when Yosef saw that the brothers remained silent, he could not understand what the silence meant. He attributed it to one of two causes: (a) Either the brothers were mortified for what they had done; or (b) they were still in doubt whether he was really their brother. He reacted to both their shame and doubts. In regard to their shame, he told them, "I am Yosef, your brother. You have nothing to be ashamed of before me. I have always been your brother." As to their doubt, he proved that he was Yosef by adding "whom you sold to Egypt." That was clear proof, because no other person knew of that incident, not even a prophet.

Pa'aneach Raza also holds like *Ramban*, that it was in order to reveal this to his brothers that Yosef had everyone else leave him. He was not ashamed of having Pharaoh's servants hear of the sale. It was rather because the brothers had determined that anyone who would reveal what they had done to Yosef would be excommunicated. Yosef too obeyed that ban, and did not want to mention the sale except before his brothers alone.

S'forno and other commentators add that when Yosef told the brothers, "Please come to me," that too was meant to conceal the fact that the brothers had sold him. He wanted to say what he had to say quietly, so that no one else would hear, neither the servants of Pharaoh nor even Binyamin. It was not his plan to blame his brothers, but merely to rebuke them and to persuade them that he was indeed Yosef. What he said later, "whom you sold," was merely to verify that he was indeed Yosef as he had stated.

Sefas Emes has a beautiful interpretation of "whom you sold." When Hashem talked to Moshe about the two tablets "which you broke," *Chazal* tell us that He said to Moshe, "I thank you for having broken them." Here too, when Yosef said to his brothers, "Whom you sold," he was implying "I thank you for having sold me. The result of that action was good for both me and you, because 'God has sent me for sustenance before you.'"

◆§ And Now Do Not Be Sad

In order to allay their fears and make them feel better, Yosef told his brothers that this had not been a sale, but a mission. "And let it not be evil in your eyes that you sold me here, for God has sent me for sustenance before you." You did not send me here, God did.

The *rishonim*, such as Abarbanel, *Rivash*, *S'forno* and others, explain at length the persuasive words that were used here by Yosef. What Yosef stressed was that the brothers were not to think that everything was coincidental, for they were but tools in Hashem's hands to fulfill His aim, "To preserve you a remainder in the earth, and to save your lives by a great deliverance." Therefore, says Abarbanel, there is no mention that Hashem punished the brothers for selling Yosef, or that Yaakov rebuked the brothers for what they had done. It is true that man is a creature of free will, but Hashem sometimes turns man's free will to accomplish one of His goals. The brothers chose to hate Yosef, and as a result Yosef wound up being sold. Yet the aim of that sale was to have Yosef fulfill a mission.

Akeidah, though, explains Yosef's words differently. Yosef did not absolve his brothers of their guilt for selling him, but placed the stress on the Hebrew word *heinah* (הֵנָּה) — "to this place." It is true that you sold me, but the way things worked out, I was sold specifically "to this place." Later, too, Yosef added, "It was not you that sent me to this place." It was Hashem who arranged that that action should be part of the overall chain of events. "I arrived here, and as a result your sale turned into a mission."

Some commentators see in the words, וְעַתָּה אַל תֵּעָצְבוּ — "and now, do not be sad" — a hint that this would only be a temporary salvation. "Now you have no reason to be sad, for I will support you, but in the end there will be reason to be concerned. The exile in Egypt will soon be here." Yaakov deserved to be taken down to Egypt in iron chains, but things worked out differently, so that he came down in terms of "God has sent me as sustenance before you."

Sifsei Kohen sees other hints in Yosef's words. "For sustenance" (לְמִחְיָה) is made up of למ, which adds up to seventy in *gematria*, and the word חָיָה, which means, in this context, "people," thus alluding to the seventy people that came down to Egypt with Yaakov. "That a posterity shall remain for you" — here, in Egypt, you will survive as a people. The Egyptians detest you, and as a result you will not be assimilated among them. In addition, I was sent so that Hashem will "save your lives by a great deliverance" — in the end, a large multitude of you will go out to freedom.

✽ Hasten and Go Up to My Father

The main aim now was to have Yaakov go down to Egypt. After Yosef revealed himself to his brothers, he urged them to persuade their father that he, Yosef, was alive and well, and that Yaakov had to come down to Egypt. Yosef then provided them with various signs to persuade his father. On the verse, "And behold, your eyes see, and the eyes of my brother Binyamin," *Oznayim LaTorah* says that Yosef told his brothers that Yaakov might not believe them because they had already told him once of his son's death. "But now," Yosef continues, "Binyamin has seen me and he is convinced that I am alive and well, so that our father will at least believe him."

Chizkuni, using *d'rush*, explains that Yosef told his brothers that they might not be in a position to bring the news to Yaakov, since they had all sworn not to divulge what had really happened. Binyamin, however, was not in their company when they took their oath. "He therefore can tell father that I am alive," Yosef said.

Rivash, though, has a simple explanation of the verse quoted above. Yosef told his brothers: "Both you and Binyamin are convinced that I am Yosef whom you sold, since no one else other than myself knew of your deed. Moreover, Binyamin is convinced that I am alive and well, and not dead, as he was disposed to believe until today, because of what you had told him."

Rashbam says that Yosef gave another proof, in that "the mouth of the speaker is to you." Yosef said: "It is not hearsay that I am alive, but I myself that am telling you."

Rivash states that what Yosef meant to say, in order to persuade his father, was that it was not the ruler of Egypt who wanted him to come down to Egypt, but "the mouth of the speaker is to you" — that of a son who only wanted his father's welfare.

In the Midrash we are told that Yosef spoke to his brothers in Hebrew, and that too was meant to be proof that he was indeed Yosef. The commentators on the Midrash ask on this: "Weren't there then Canaanites who spoke Hebrew?" *Matnos Kehunah* answers that even though the people of Canaan spoke Hebrew, they did not use the pure language used by Yaakov and his children. Similarly, *Chazal* tell us that even though Bilaam spoke Hebrew, he spoke a corrupted version of it.

Gan Raveh has an interesting interpretation. Yosef told them that until that time the brothers had been unable to recognize his voice, because he had been speaking a foreign language, but now that he was speaking Hebrew, they would be able to recognize his voice.

Ramban, though, holds that knowledge of Hebrew was no proof. The people of Canaan knew Hebrew, and it was not surprising that it would be known by the ruler of Egypt. Nebuchadnezzar also knew Hebrew. Rather, what the meaning of the words, "the mouth of the speaker is to you," is that Yosef asked his brothers to persuade Yaakov that Yosef was able to support him, for he was the ruler of Egypt, and whatever he said, he was able to fulfill.

Chasam Sofer has a beautiful explanation of this matter. Yosef was afraid that his brothers would not believe him, but would think that he was some type of sorcerer or astrologer, just as they thought when they saw him seating the brothers according to their ages. Yosef therefore tried to persuade them that he was a schemer and not an astrologer, for he spoke a good Hebrew, and why then had he always placed an interpreter between them? That showed that he knew everything that was going on, but it had all been part of his stratagem.

Chasam Sofer also says that by showing them that he knew Hebrew, Yosef wanted to persuade his brothers and his father that he had remained a Jew. One only retains the Hebrew language if he makes an effort to do so. When the Jews were exiled to Babylon, they began speaking Chaldean because they did not preserve their sanctity.

Oznayim LaTorah adds that Yosef persuaded his brothers not only by the fact that he spoke Hebrew, but by the content of what he said.

He constantly referred to Hashem. He said, "God has sent me as sustenance before you;" "And God has sent me before you;" "God has made me the master." This holy tongue was the most persuasive proof that he was their brother, the son of Yaakov.

II.
The First "Ghetto" in Jewish History

Goshen was the first "ghetto" in Jewish history. Historians say that in every place and every time, it was the Jews who created the ghettos, as a way to keep apart from the people among whom they lived and so that they could live in a Jewish atmosphere among themselves. The non-Jews only erected the walls and gates to the ghettos, in order to prevent the Jews from leaving the quarters which they themselves had set up. Sometimes, the Jews were shut up in ghettos ostensibly for their own protection, but in most cases it was done to prevent them from forming any close ties with their neighbors.

The first voluntary ghetto of this kind was in Goshen. *Kli Yakar* says Yosef's brothers deliberately said, "Your servants are shepherds," so that Pharaoh would move them away from the Egyptians, for "all shepherds are detestable to Egypt." Various *acharonim* take this idea further.

HaAmek Davar says that, in spite of the fact that living apart from the Egyptians would make the Egyptians detest them, Yosef nevertheless wanted to have his brothers live in isolation, in order to preserve their purity as Jews.

R' Samson Raphael Hirsch takes this idea, and adds:

> As long as the ethical dawn of the other nations had not yet come, it was the partitions which the other nations erected which preserved Israel from being infected by the corruption of the people among whom it dwelled for hundreds of years. That is why [Yosef] immediately stressed here a step which would arouse Egyptian loathing, with the clear intention of thereby having set aside for [his brothers] a special place for their dwellings.

Various *rishonim*, though, give different explanations for Yosef's advice to his brothers to have them tell Pharaoh that they were shepherds. Yosef wanted to involve them in productive and creative work, in which they would be able to support themselves without excessive effort. It is true, says, Abarbanel, that Yosef could have made his brothers government officials, but he did not want them to assume positions of authority, preferring to have them engage in easy and clean work.

Rabbenu Bachya lays great stress on the ethical value of working as a shepherd. He lists two advantages of this type of work: (a) One earns money from the wool, the lambs and the milk; (b) as "all shepherds are detestable to Egypt," the brothers would not have any competition, and would have this work entirely to themselves. This way they would find satisfaction and sustenance in their work. This type of work, adds Rabbenu Bachya, also brings about spiritual elevation. Shepherds live in the midst of nature, and not with other people — and people are full of lies, talebearing and other evil practices. The isolation which shepherds experience is a necessary condition for prophecy. The greatest prophets, such as Eliyahu and Elisha, isolated themselves in the desert. Other shepherds were Hevel (Abel), Moshe, Shmuel, David, and Shaul.

Sifsei Kohen explains this in a similar fashion. Living in the city involves the acquiring of more and more possessions and luxuries, whereas Yosef wanted to enable his brothers to live a more simple life.

Sha'ar Bas Rabim expands on this idea and explains that Yosef wanted to instill in his brothers the characteristic of compassion, and that was why he made them shepherds. A shepherd is compassionate toward his flock, and all the more so toward people. That was also the reason that Pharaoh did not take them into his army. A person who was taught to be compassionate could not serve in Pharaoh's army, because being in the army meant being cruel and shedding blood.

R' Shlomo Kluger says that even before Pharaoh knew that Yosef's brothers were shepherds, Yosef had a message sent to Pharaoh that "My father and my father's house... have come to me." He stressed that they had come, with the idea that they would be of use to Pharaoh, just as Yosef himself was. However, after hearing that Yosef's brothers were shepherds, Pharaoh had no further interest in them, and said, "Your father and brothers have come to you." He decided that he had no need for them.

Yosef achieved the goal which he wanted, to separate his brothers from the Egyptians, and to enable them to live an ethical life in which they would support themselves from their work. Yaakov and his sons became shepherds, settled in Goshen, and had no contacts with the Egyptians.

⊷§ How Many Went Down to Egypt?

There are numerous questions about the number of people who went down to Egypt. The Torah tells us that the number of the descendants of Leah was "thirty-three," but the listing shows only thirty-two. Similarly, we are told that seventy people went down to Egypt, but the listing only shows sixty-nine. Almost all *rishonim* discuss how these figures can be reconciled.

Chazal in *Bava Basra* 123 reconcile the question of seventy people. They say that Yocheved was conceived on the trip, and was born as they entered the walls of Egypt. In other words, sixty-nine people left Canaan, but seventy arrived in Egypt.

Rosh has a simpler explanation. The Torah will normally round off to the nearest ten when a number ends with a nine. This we see in, "He will receive forty lashes," whereas the number is really thirty-nine. The other commentators, though, ask on *Rosh*: If what he says is correct, how does he explain that we are told the descendants of Leah were thirty-three, when the actual number was thirty-two?

As a result, *Rashbam*, *Baalei HaTosafos* and other commentators explain that Yaakov too was included in the number. Together with him, the descendants of Leah totaled thirty-three people, and by the same token, we have seventy people who went down to Egypt.

Tur says that Dinah gave birth to a child from Shechem, and that child was included in the number, even though the Torah doesn't mention the child.

According to *HaKesav VeHaKabalah*, Osnas, Yosef's wife, was included in the figure. He holds that the name אָסְנַת is derived from נֶאֱנָסָה — "violated" — for she was the daughter of Dinah, who had been violated. While the wives of Yaakov's sons were not included, Osnas was.

HaDrush VeHaIyun has a beautiful interpretation. According to him, the number of those who went down included Yaakov and his three wives. They bring the number up to seventy. At first, the numbering included only those "who came forth from his loins," which added up to sixty-six people (Yosef and his two sons had preceded Yaakov to Egypt), but in the end the Torah stresses, "all the people who came to Egypt." All of them were included in the seventy.

Ibn Ezra expresses wonder at the fact that *Rashi* quotes *Chazal* to the effect that Yocheved was born between the walls, and that brought the number to seventy. He asks, "If Yocheved was born between the walls, it would mean that she gave birth to Moshe at the age of one hundred and thirty, and that is more remarkable even than Sarah, who gave birth at ninety! Why then is there no hint at this in the Torah?" Furthermore, says Ibn Ezra, the authors of various *piyutim* note that Yocheved died after Moshe's death, which would mean that she was more than two hundred and fifty years old when she died! Because of these questions, Ibn Ezra concurs with the commentators cited above — that Yaakov was

276 / The First "Ghetto" in Jewish History

included in the number. Together with him, the number was seventy. And if we include him with the descendants of Leah, that number then becomes thirty-three.

According to Ibn Ezra, there is no special significance in the fact that the Torah says that "all those who came forth from his loins were seventy." The Torah does not give exact details. We find something similar to this when the Torah states "whom Yaakov bore in Padan Aram," even though Binyamin had not yet been born. So too does the Torah mention "all the souls who came with Yaakov to Egypt," even though Menasheh and Ephraim were born in Egypt, and did not go down to it. Thus we see that the Torah does not go into exact details, and even though it specifies "who came forth from his loins," it includes Yaakov in that number.

◆§ Daughters or Granddaughters?

Ramban has a different view. When *Chazal* tell us that Yocheved was born between the walls, that is definitive. As to why the Torah does not mention the wonder of Yocheved giving birth at one hundred and thirty, he adds that the Torah only mentions miracles that were announced through a prophet, and not other miracles. The entire Torah is one long account of miracles. All of the Torah revolves around supernatural events. This includes such occurrences as *kares* (premature death) or the *tochechah* (warning and admonition in *parashas Bechukosai*). But the Torah does not mention miracles which are not an open change from the laws of nature. From the time that Israel arrived in its land until David was born, a period of three hundred and seventy years passed. If we divide this time period into the four generations between the two events, namely Salmon, Boaz, Oved and Yishai, it works out that each gave birth after the age of ninety, which was almost as old as Avraham's age when he had Yitzchak, and yet this wonder is not mentioned anywhere. There is nothing remarkable about the fact that Avraham had a son in his old age, for thereafter he lived another seventy-five years. That means that when Yitzchak was born, Avraham had lived less than two thirds of his total life span. What was then so wondrous about that? After all, people generally have children until three-quarters of their lives have passed, or even later.

The wonder in the case of Avraham and Sarah was something different. They were by their natures barren, and only gave birth in their old age, when Sarah no longer had her monthly periods. That was a miracle which diverged from the rules of nature. But the fact that Yocheved gave birth at one hundred and thirty was nothing remarkable.

BEREISHIS — VAYIGASH

Hashem delayed the birth of Moshe until the time came for the end of the slavery. Therefore, says *Ramban*, Yocheved was indeed born between the walls, and if we include her together with Yosef and his sons, we receive a total of seventy people.

The Torah lists among those who came, "his daughters and his granddaughters with him, and all his seed." *Rashi* says this refers to his sons' daughters, namely "Serach, daughter of Asher, and Yocheved, daughter of Levi."

Sifsei Chachamim finds the verse surprising, for the Torah mentions "his daughters," and Yaakov only had a single daughter, Dinah. One cannot say that this refers to the daughters that were the twin sisters of every son born to Yaakov, for *Rashi* later says that they all died before they came to Egypt. Nor can one say that this refers to Yaakov's daughters-in-law, because the Torah says that these were all "who came forth from [Yaakov's] loins." *Sifsei Chachamim* then notes that the Torah often uses a plural for the singular, such as "and the sons of Dan were Chushim." Therefore the word "his daughters" refers to Dinah alone. On the other hand, in regard to "his sons' daughters," there were indeed two, and that was why *Rashi* mentioned their names. It is interesting that *Ramban* says almost the same thing in similar language.

Ibn Ezra, though, holds that "his daughters" refers to the young maidservants that grew up with Dinah, daughter of Yaakov; we thus find in another place in *Tanach* that children that one takes care of are referred to as one's own children, such as "and the sons of Michal." In regard to "and the sons of Dan were Chushim," Ibn Ezra says that Dan had had two sons, but one had died.

Ba'alei HaTosafos have a different view. After a long discussion, they conclude that "his daughters" refers to Yaakov's daughters-in-law. They then discuss the meaning of the verse, "All the souls, his sons and daughters were thirty-three," which one cannot say refers to his daughters-in-law, for the Torah immediately adds: "besides the wives of the sons of Yaakov." They therefore explain that "his daughters" in this verse refers to his sons' daughters, who are also considered to be daughters.

HaAmek Davar has his own *chiddush* — novel interpretation — of this. According to him, Yaakov's sons had many daughters, and not only the two that *Rashi* mentioned, but these were not included in the calculation of the seventy. So too did Yaakov have other daughters besides Dinah, as we see in the verse: "And his sons and daughters arose to comfort him." None of these daughters, though, are mentioned by name, because they had nothing to do with our history as a people. The only exception is Dinah, who is mentioned because of the incident with

Shechem. And there is no reason to be surprised about this, because *Chazal* said that Avraham also had a daughter, and her name is not mentioned, because it had no relevance to our history.

HaAmek Davar remarks on the difference between what the Torah says in regard to the coming of Yaakov's sons and sons' sons to Egypt, and the coming of his daughters and his sons' daughters. In the case of the latter, we are told, "he brought with him," which implies against their will. His sons and sons' sons came of their own free will, because they had been commanded to go down to Egypt, but his daughters did not want to go down, and he brought them forcibly.

This idea is cited by *Or HaChayim* who says that the term "with him" (אִתּוֹ) separates his sons and sons' sons from his daughters and sons' daughters. His sons and sons' sons came "with him" of their own free will, whereas he brought his daughters and sons' daughters with him to Egypt against their will.

This distinction also explains what *Chazal* tell us, that as long as any of those who came to Egypt were alive, the slavery did not begin. Yet we know that Yocheved and Serach, who had both come to Egypt, were still alive when the slavery began. However, says *Or HaChayim*, *Chazal* refer to those who came of their own free will, and the women came against their will. Those who accepted the servitude and came to Egypt of their own free will were not made to endure slavery, whereas those who came against their wills were affected by the slavery.

Divrei Shaul explains the words of *Chazal* quoted by *Rashi*, that in regard to Esav, we are told that there were six נְפָשׁוֹת (literally, "souls"), while with Yaakov it states there were seventy נֶפֶשׁ (literally, "a soul"). A Jew, says *Divrei Shaul*, is not an individual soul. He combines with other Jews for *bircas hamazon* and for a *minyan*. All Jews are responsible for one another. Therefore the entire community is referred to as a single soul. It is considered like a single person. That is not true for the other nations, where there is no mutual responsibility and whose unity crumbles. Each of their individuals appears as a separate soul.

Ya'aros D'vash explains a certain comment by *Chazal* along similar lines. The *gemara* in *Yoma* 22 quotes a verse (*Hoshea* 2:1): "The number of the Children of Israel will be as the sand at the seashore, which cannot be measured or counted." On this, *Chazal* tell us that one part of this verse ("cannot be measured or counted") refers to when *Bnei Yisrael* do Hashem's will, for that is how large the Jewish people will be. The other part of the verse ("the 'number' of the Children of Israel"), on the other hand, refers to when they do not do His will. In such a case, while the Jewish people will still be large, it will not be so large that it cannot be counted.

Chazal teach: "A person should never exclude himself from the community." In general, most members of the community are good, and therefore it is good to join the community and not to appear as a separate unit. However, if a person knows that the majority of the people are bad, one must separate himself from them and maintain an independent existence. That is what *Chazal* meant when they said that when the Jews do the will of Hashem, they will all be part of the whole, which "cannot be measured or counted." However, if they do not do Hashem's will, then it is "the number of the Children of Israel." In such a case, it is better to be counted separately, and not as a part of the whole.

◆§ The Establishment of a Yeshivah in Goshen

We are told in *Midrash Rabbah* (95), on the verse (*Bereishis* 46:28), "And he (i.e., Yaakov) sent Yehudah before him to Yosef to direct him to Goshen," that "he sent him to prepare for him a *beis midrash* from where Torah would come forth." Various *d'rush* works deal with explaining this quotation from *Chazal*, which carries an eternal message for us: the importance of setting up *batei midrash* wherever Jews may find themselves.

Chasam Sofer says that Yaakov wanted by this gesture to ensure that the monarchy would go to Yehudah, after the material monarchy had been given to Yosef temporarily. Thus we are told in *Asarah Ma'amaros* (4:12) that when, at the time of the Chashmona'im, *Chazal* saw that the monarchy had been taken from Yehudah, they made the head of the *Beis Din* a member of the house of Hillel (who was descended from Yehudah), so that Yehudah would still maintain a certain degree of rule. And that was what Yaakov did in our *parashah*, in fulfillment of the verse (*Bereishis* 49:10), "The scepter shall not depart from Yehudah."

Oznayim LaTorah says that Yaakov wanted to teach his sons, "*Talmud Torah* is more important than saving lives" (*Megillah* 15). Yosef told his brothers (*Bereishis* 45:13), "And you shall tell my father of all my glory in Egypt and all that you saw," namely that he was feeding the hungry and was engaged in *hatzalas nefashos* — saving lives. People think that that *mitzvah* is greater than any other and absolves one from learning Torah. Yaakov therefore sent Yehudah to set up a *beis midrash* and to demonstrate to all that *hatzalas nefashos* does not exempt one from setting aside times for Torah study.

Tzofnas Pa'aneach holds that Yehudah's mission was a "type of battle." He quotes *Yerushalmi Horiyos* (ch. 3), that Yehudah is always the one to go out to war first. *Chazal* (*Avodah Zarah* 25) also say that Yehudah must be the first to go out to fight. We cannot say that Yaakov sent Yehudah to determine *halachah*, for *Chazal* tell us that "we only find *talmidei chachamim* that rule on *halachah* in the tribes of Levi or Yisachar." That excludes the tribe of Yehudah. Thus, *Tzofnas Pa'aneach* says that when *Chazal* tell us that Yehudah was sent "to set up a *beis midrash* from where Torah would come forth," this was meant to show that the *Sanhedrin* would be located in his tribe's territory. And indeed we see in *Zevachim* 118 that both during the time the *Mishkan* was in Shiloh and during the time of the *Beis HaMikdash*, the *Sanhedrin* was in either the territory of Yosef or of Yehudah.

The Lubavitcher Rebbi sees contemporary significance in this quotation by *Chazal*. It seems difficult to understand why Yosef waited until Yehudah established a *beis midrash* in Egypt, and why he himself did not do so first. After all, *Chazal* say there was never a time that there was no *yeshivah* among our fathers. Yosef must surely have founded a *yeshivah* as did his fathers, especially when *Chazal* tell us that "the wagons (עֲגָלוֹת) that Yosef sent" were a sign from Yosef to his father about the laws of the *eglah arufah* (which we will define below) that they had been studying together. If so, why was there need for another *yeshivah*?

According to the Lubavitcher Rebbi, *Chazal* intend to convey a deep meaning in this statement. There was a difference between Yosef's level and that of his father and brothers. The latter were removed from worldly concerns, and that was why they chose to be shepherds who remain removed from the everyday affairs of the world. Yosef, though, had not been a shepherd from his youth. Once he was sold to Egypt, he became involved in Potiphar's business ventures, for, as Onkelos explains on the verse, "and he came to his house to do his work," Yosef was assigned "to examine his accounting books." Afterwards Yosef became the ruler over all of Egypt. It was true that Yosef himself was not affected by the world about him so as to forget about the eternal life, for to him this world was irrelevant. But all these daily concerns could affect his Torah learning. One who learns the life-giving Torah must be linked only to the Torah itself, without any division of any kind, as in the expression, "his profession is Torah." Thus we see that the *Levi'im* were not given any portion or inheritance in the land, as *Rambam* says at the end of the laws of *Shemittah* and *Yovel*: "Levi was set aside to serve Hashem, and therefore they were separated from those who reside in the world. And that does not only apply to Levi, but to every human who so desires it." Yaakov therefore sent Yehudah to set up a *yeshivah*, as a person who had no ties to this world, rather than contenting himself with learning the Torah of Yosef, which was Torah involved with daily life.

III.
The Wagons Which Yosef Sent

After Yosef revealed himself to his brothers, he instructed them to complete the task by bringing Yaakov to Egypt. In his words, we can see how generous and how psychologically aware he was. He was worried about his brothers' peace of mind on the way, as well as how Yaakov would accept the news.

According to *Rashi*, when he told his brothers, "Do not be angry — תִּרְגְּזוּ — (or "delay") along the way," he wanted them not to quarrel about the circumstances of his sale. Onkelos too translates this as "do not argue along the road."

Rashbam, Ramban, Chizkuni and *Ba'alei HaTosafos*, though, do not explain this as an order or as advice, but simply as a way to reassure the brothers. Do not be afraid either on the way to Canaan or on your way back, even though you are carrying much merchandise with you, because you have the ruler's personal protection.

R' Samson Raphael Hirsch, too, explains the word רוגֶז in terms of fear. Yosef reassured his brothers not to be afraid of what would happen in the future, but to do what he told them, with complete confidence.

Abarbanel sees Yosef's words as a blessing and wish for success. Yosef blessed his brothers that no evil should befall them on the way, for *sh'luchei mitzvah* — those on a *mitzvah* errand — are not harmed.

Ba'al HaTurim says that Yosef directed his brothers not to go through any plowed fields, or the like, so that they would not become involved in confrontations with others. The phrase אַל תִּרְגְּזוּ is taken here to mean אַל תַּרְגִּזוּ — "do not provoke others."

Most commentators see the words of Yosef as urging the brothers to come back as soon as possible, and not to delay on the way for any reason. *Si'ach Sarfei Kodesh*, though, brings a Chassidic commentary, quoting the Kotzker Rebbi, with the exact opposite meaning. Yosef told his brothers not to be too hasty, and not to rush things unnecessarily, for in any event everything is arranged from Above by a "clock" that never loses a second. If they were too fast, something would happen that would delay them on the way, in accordance with Hashem's intent. A time had been set for the commencement of the *galus* — "exile" — and it could not vary.

Chasam Sofer hears in these words the clanging of iron chains. The root of the word תִּרְגְּזוּ appears in the Blessings and the Curses in *Devarim* (28:65) in the form of "And Hashem will give you there לֵב רַגָּז — a faint heart," which *Chazal* explain as referring to the Babylonian exile, and is therefore not applicable to *Eretz Yisrael*. Yosef was afraid that his brothers might become faint of heart now that they were getting ready for the exile in Egypt. He therefore warned them אַל תִּרְגְּזוּ — "do not become faint of heart."

R' Sa'adiah Gaon has an interesting explanation of this verse, based on an Arabic word root: "Do not walk slowly while singing long songs on the way."

◆§ Do Not Engage in Halachic Questions

In *Ta'anis* 10b, *Chazal* explain Yosef's words as an order not to engage in any halachic discussions on the way. Various works discuss this comment by *Chazal*. This explanation is not in keeping with one in the *Bereishis Rabbah* 94, which explains this in the opposite way: "Do not refrain from studying Torah." It is also not in keeping with the words of *Chazal* on the verse in *Shema*, וּבְלֶכְתְּךָ בַדֶּרֶךְ — "And when you walk on the way," that one is required to study Torah even when walking along the way.

Chazal in *Ta'anis* ask a question from the words of R' Ila'i, who says, "Two who walk by the way and have no words of Torah between them deserve to be burned to death." The Talmud explains that the first applies to reciting matters by heart, which one is required to do, and the second to intensive study, which is forbidden, because one may become oblivious to danger on the way.

Taz in *Divrei David* and other commentators say that the prohibition against intensive study only applies to *pilpul* — intense discussion. *Vayosef Avraham* on *Revid HaZahav* expands on this. According to him, the *gemara* knew that one must differentiate between intensive study and *pilpul*, and that is why it does not ask any question from the verse, "and when you walk by the way." It only has a question from the words of R' Ila'i who says, "Two ... who have no words of Torah between them," which can also be understood to refer to either *pilpul* or reciting matters from memory. In its conclusion, the *gemara* states that the words of R' Ila'i refer only to reciting matters from memory. Thus there is no contradiction between *Chazal* in *Ta'anis* and in the Midrash, who say that one should not stop studying Torah, for all are of the opinion that one is not excused from Torah study that is not intensive when traveling on the road.

Vayosef Avraham brings an interesting view by *Ba'alei Tosafos*, that Yosef ordered his brothers not to be too stringent in their observance of certain *halachos* on their trip, so as not to quarrel with innkeepers on the way, for, as *Chazal* tell us, "One is permitted to feed the poor and innkeepers *demai*" (fruits and vegetables about which there is doubt as to whether *terumos* and *ma'aseros* were taken).

Kli Yakar has a beautiful interpretation. *Chazal* were not afraid of a person being harmed by learning Torah on the way, but of *the halachah* being harmed, because one cannot concentrate sufficiently in such circumstances. And indeed *Rashi* adds, "The way may be רָגֵז for you" — namely that you will become confused, and will err in a question of *halachah*.

It appears that *Chazal* based this on the words of Yosef, as the word "on the way" (בַּדֶּרֶךְ) refers, in other places in *Chazal*, to *halachah*, as seen in the verse, "And when you walk on the way" (וּבְלֶכְתְּךָ בַדֶּרֶךְ). Yosef warned his brothers to be careful in this matter, either because of the dangers to themselves, or for the sake of the *halachah*. *Chazal* also derived other rules of walking on the way from this verse. Among these are: "Do not take over-large steps," and, "One should enter the city during the daylight."

Various *d'rush* works throughout the ages have found sources here for actual life situations. It is worth mentioning here a penetrating observation of R' Moshe Avigdor Amiel, which has implications for our generation as well. Yosef gave his brothers several essential rules in the laws related to exile and redemption. "Do not become involved in halachic questions" — do not waste your time on a theoretical and ideological argument, rather than doing something constructive. "Do not take over-large steps" — do not switch from one moment to the next from one extreme to the other, but always follow the golden mean. "And enter the city during the daylight" — as long as the sun of success is shining for you, prepare yourself, and not when you have no alternatives and are in trouble.

⋞§ And the Spirit of Their Father Yaakov Revived

After his instructions concerning his father, Yosef was concerned about how his father would take the news. After all, Yaakov was convinced that Yosef had been torn to shreds. He had seen Yosef's coat dipped in blood. How would he now believe that Yosef was still alive? How would he deal with the fact that Yosef had been sold by his brothers? *Ramban* says that Yaakov was never told that Yosef had been sold, for the brothers did not want to incriminate themselves. Instead, they claimed that Yosef had become lost, and those who found him had taken and sold him. Now he had been found to be alive. In the Torah, we see two things that were done in order to convince Yaakov that that was what had happened: (a) The brothers conveyed to Yaakov the words of Yosef, and (b) they showed him the wagons.

How could these two be persuasive? The Torah does not explain this. Various commentators attempt to decipher what the Torah meant with these words. *Rashbam* explains that "all the words of Yosef" referred to all the details of how he revealed himself to his brothers, and how he had cried to them and demonstrated his brotherly love for them. As to the wagons, they were hitched to oxen, and oxen could not be exported from Egypt without permission of the ruler. Other commentators also say that the wagons sent by Yosef were meant to persuade his father.

Ramban says that Yaakov fainted when he suddenly heard the news. His sons raised their voices to get his attention. They showed him the wagons in order to make him happy, and he gradually recovered and understood what they had told him.

According to *S'forno*, the phrase "all the words of Yosef" refers to evil tidings: "For another five years there will be famine." These evil tidings diminished the joy, and that way Yaakov was able to modify his emotions and understand what he had been told.

Chizkuni sees a convincing proof in the wagons which were sent "by Pharaoh" specially. In general, only castrated animals were permitted to be exported from Egypt, in accordance with the *Chazal* mentioned above. As even non-Jews are forbidden to castrate animals, Yosef did not want to bring the non-Jews to commit a sin, and that was why this act was done by the special orders of Pharaoh.

Many commentators discuss the differences in the Torah in the words of Pharaoh to Yosef, in regard to the sending of the wagons. *Chazal* in *Bereishis Rabbah* ask on the verse, "And he saw the wagons which Yosef sent," where were the wagons sent by Pharaoh? "Those wagons which Pharaoh sent to carry them had *avodah zarah* — 'idols' — engraved on them, so Yehudah went and burned them." A difficult question is asked on these words of *Chazal*, for we are told later, "And *Bnei Yisrael* carried Yaakov their father and their young ones and their wives in the wagons which Pharaoh had sent to carry them." I have not found an answer to this question, but R' Wolf of Strikov has a striking idea. The wagons which were meant to take Yaakov out of *Eretz Yisrael* were idolatrous, for whoever lives outside *Eretz Yisrael* is as if he has no God. Yaakov did not want to travel in wagons sent by Pharaoh, because they were idolatrous by leaving *Eretz Yisrael*. After Hashem appeared to him and told him, "I will go down with you to Egypt and I will bring you up," he understood that he could not evade traveling in these wagons.

These wagons had been sent by Pharaoh, says *Igra D'Kala*, to begin the exile. This we see in the words of Pharaoh: "And thus I have commanded, do the following." There is no choice here. You must carry out my orders. You are already enslaved to Egypt now.

~§ The Parashah of Eglah Arufah

Chazal in the Midrash say that the "wagons" (עֲגָלוֹת) which Yosef sent were as a symbol of the laws of *eglah arufah* (עֶגְלָה עֲרוּפָה), which Yosef had been studying with his father just before leaving to look for his brothers in Shechem. (The law of *eglah arufah* applies when a murdered body is found outside city limits. The *halachah* in such a case is that the elders of the community closest to where the body was found must take a calf, break its neck and proclaim: "Our hands have not shed this blood." — see *Devarim* 21.) After Yaakov saw this sign, he believed that Yosef was alive, and his spirits were lifted.

The simplest explanation for the link between the "wagons" and the *eglah arufah* is that the Hebrew letters of the word Pharaoh — פַּרְעֹה — when rearranged, form the word *arufah* — עֲרוּפָה. Thus עֶגְלוֹת פַּרְעֹה — the wagons of Pharaoh — are read as עֶגְלָה עֲרוּפָה — *eglah arufah*, which Yosef sent as a sign to his father. This explanation fits in well with the events in this *parashah*, for the "elders of the community" are a link in the chain of events, and are indirect accomplices to the murder that has occurred. By the same token, Yaakov was to an extent an accomplice in what happened to Yosef, because of the coat of many colors which he gave to Yosef. The symbolism in the *parashah* combines with the tragic events.

There are commentators, though, who are surprised at the above interpretation, for the word עֶגְלָה in *eglah arufah* has entirely different vowels than the word עֲגָלָה — *agalah* — a wagon. *Tur* says that both the letters as they are written and the way the words are pronounced can be used for interpretation.

Others give various difficult explanations, but in truth one can say that the *d'rush* is a valid one, for in the plural both words are identical — *agalos*. The only question is what connection *eglah arufah* can have to this *parashah*. It would appear that *Chazal* wished to link the father and the son by some type of Torah tie, and to find an explanation as to why Yaakov's spirits were revived in the fact that Yosef was still involved in Torah, and remembered what he had learned.

HaDrush VeHaIyun sees this as a clear indication of Yosef's *yiras shamayim* (fear of Heaven), in accordance with a saying of *Chazal*: "Whoever's fear of sin precedes his wisdom, his wisdom will endure" (*Avos* 3). If we see that Yosef's wisdom had been preserved, it was proof that he was indeed God-fearing.

There are innumerable explanations among both *rishonim* and *acharonim* on the words by *Chazal* about the *agalos*. *Ba'al HaTurim*, for example, uses his customary method of explaining this with *gematria*. וַיַּרְא אֶת הָעֲגָלוֹת — "And he saw the wagons" — is equivalent in *gematria* to רָאָה בְּהִלְכוֹת עֶגְלָה עֲרוּפָה — "He saw the laws of *eglah arufah*."

Those involved in *pilpul* see in this a debate between Yosef and his father as to who should go to whom. The question boiled down to one dealing with *eglah arufah*, in a case when a dead body is found equidistant from two cities. In such a case, there is a question as to whether the city to which the head is closest must bring the *eglah arufah*, or whether the city to which the body is closest must do so. Here, the question was whether the head (Yaakov) must follow the body (Yosef), in which case Yaakov would have to come to Yosef, or whether the body must follow the head, in which case Yosef would have to come to Yaakov. The *gemara* in *Sotah* 45 discusses the question of the *eglah arufah*, and concludes that the head follows the body. This meant that Yaakov had to come to Yosef.

Techeiles Mordechai finds a remarkable lesson to be deduced here from *Chazal*, namely that a person should seek natural solutions to his doubts, and not wait for miraculous solutions. The purpose of the *eglah arufah*, according to *Rambam* in *Moreh Nevuchim*, is to publicize the fact that a murder was committed so that all will talk about it, and the murderer may be traced. The Torah tells us that we must use natural means to attempt to find the murderer, even though Hashem can reveal the murderer by supernatural means. The same was true then with Yosef. Hashem manipulated various natural means and events to bring about a situation where Yosef provided sustenance to his family, even though Hashem could have arranged matters in another fashion. If Yaakov would find it difficult to believe in such an intricate unfolding of events, the *parashah* of *eglah arufah* would demonstrate for him that Hashem's *hashgachah* works through natural means.

There are, as we mentioned, countless explanations of this. The major point is that the Torah was and remains the content of the life of our forefathers and their sons, and it was Torah which linked the ruler of Egypt to his father in Canaan. In his talks on *Parashas Vayigash*, the Lubavitcher Rebbi adds that Yaakov was not content to learn Yosef's Torah, which was based on clinging to Hashem while being involved in worldly matters, but instead sent Yehudah before him to Goshen, to prepare a *beis midrash* for him, from which Torah would emanate, a place where those who studied Torah would not have any dealings with other matters, but would engage only in the study of Torah.

IV.
Going Down to Egyptian Exile

The time had come for Hashem's decree of the *bris bein habesarim* to be implemented. In its first stage, it was "sugar-coated." Yaakov was taken down to Egypt to meet his lost son, Yosef. He went of his own accord, saying, "I will go and see him before I die," but had he not gone voluntarily, he would have been dragged down — in iron chains if necessary.

Yaakov went down to Egypt. On the way, just as he reached the Egyptian border, he was suddenly gripped by fear, without understanding what it was he was fearing. Subconsciously, though, he realized into what he was headed, and drew back. He offered sacrifices, but these were *shelamim* — peace offerings, and not *olos* — burnt offerings, and *shelamim* were not the norm in his days. What was the "*shalom*" that he sought with his *shelamim*?

Everything was unclear and obscure. He offered his sacrifices "to the God of his father Yitzchak." Why only Yitzchak, and not "the God of his fathers?"

Hashem appeared to him at night, and that too was symbolic. Why only in the dark and not during the day?

Hashem comforted him and said, "Yaakov, Yaakov." Hashem did not use the name that Yaakov had been given earlier by the angel, namely "Yisrael." Instead He reverted to his original name, Yaakov. And Hashem even told him: "Do not fear to go down to Egypt, for I will make you into a great nation." This is a clear indication that Yaakov was afraid. But the Torah doesn't tell us why he was afraid.

Hashem promised him, "I will go down with you to Egypt, and I will surely bring you up again." This promise shows us what Yaakov feared. But Hashem's promise also needs an explanation. Was this meant as a personal promise to Yaakov, or a communal one to all his descendants? And further, the rest of the promise is also bewildering: "And Yosef will put his hands on your eyes." What does this mean? And how was this meant to reassure Yaakov?

According to *Rashi*, the reference to "my father Yitzchak" has nothing but halachic significance. A person is required to show greater respect for his father than for his grandfather. That was why Yaakov mentioned his father when he brought the sacrifices.

Ramban is not content with that explanation. Why did Yaakov change the text here? He should have prayed to "the God of his fathers," just as he did on other occasions. *Ramban* therefore gives a kabbalistic interpretation, as he does in other places. "Yitzchak" symbolizes Hashem's attribute of strict justice — מִדַּת הַדִּין. Yaakov saw with *Ru'ach HaKodesh* — "Divine Inspiration" — that the exile in Egypt was beginning now, with this journey. He was afraid and wanted to appease Hashem's מִדַּת הַדִּין. That was why he offered *shelamim* rather than the *olos* which had been brought from the time of Noach until that time, in order to "make peace" with all Hashem's attributes. Thus, according to *Ramban*, Yaakov had a very specific fear, namely, a fear of the *galus* that was about to begin. It was for this reason that Hashem appeared to him and called him "Yaakov." That name had not been used since Yaakov's struggle with the angel, and by reverting to it, Hashem told Yaakov that he would no longer contend with God and man (the phrase used by the angel when he renamed him Yisrael), but would be in bondage to another nation.

Chizkuni, too, holds that the fear that gripped Yaakov was the fear of the *galus* which was approaching. Hashem then reassured him and told him not to fear, for just as the *galus* was approaching, as told to Avraham at the *bris bein habesarim*, the other part of Hashem's promise to Avraham, "And I will make you into a great nation," would also be fulfilled, and לְפוּם צַעֲרָא אַגְרָא — "the greater the suffering, the greater the reward."

With this background, *HaAmek Davar* explains why the vision appeared to Yaakov when it did: בְּמַרְאֹת הַלַּיְלָה (which is usually translated, "in visions of the night"). According to *HaAmek Davar*, the vision occurred in the middle of the day, but what he saw was a vision of the night of *galus* descending. The purpose of the vision was to let Yaakov realize that the time had come for him to accept the *galus*, which is compared to night. Both physical and spiritual darkness was about to descend on the world. Hashem's *Ru'ach HaKodesh* would now appear only at rare intervals, as a lightning flash which lights up the darkness of the night.

Meshech Chochmah has a different explanation. Hashem appeared to Yaakov בְּמַרְאֹת הַלַּיְלָה, unlike the way He appeared to Avraham and Yitzchak, in order to hint to him that he was now going into a long *galus*. Yet even there the *Shechinah* would accompany him and be with him, as *Chazal* tell us in *Megillah* 29: "Wherever they were exiled, the *Shechinah* was exiled with them." And indeed, Hashem told him afterwards, "I will go down with you to Egypt."

Rabbenu Bachya has a beautiful comment on the words here. In regard to going down to Egypt, Hashem tells Yaakov: "I will go down with you," whereas in regard to coming up from Egypt afterwards, Hashem says simply, "I will surely bring you up again," but mentions nothing about coming up with him. The difference between the two is that the first refers to the Jews going into exile; here Hashem promises Yaakov that He will go down with them. The second case refers only to the fact that Hashem will ensure that Yaakov's body will be brought back to *Eretz Yisrael*, but the *Shechinah* will remain in Egypt with the Jewish people.

Derashos El Ami explains this concept further: When the Jews are in *galus*, the *Shechinah* too is, as it were, in decline, for, as R' Yehudah tells us, "All the prophets only prophesied in [*Eretz Yisrael*] or about it," and *Chazal* tell us that there is no prophecy outside *Eretz Yisrael*.

The Gaon of Brizhan adds a further concept in regard to going down to exile. It is known that there are two ways to serve Hashem: (a) by investigation, as Avraham did, until he reached the most sublime heights of understanding; (b) simple faith, which was the way of Yitzchak, who was bound upon the altar without questioning Hashem. When Yaakov was on the verge of entering *galus*, he offered sacrifices to "the God of my father Yitzchak," implying: "This is the proper method for those in *galus* to adopt, rather than that of Avraham." We know from the great Sages of Spain that those Jews who based their belief on simple faith were willing to offer their lives for their faith, whereas those who followed a philosophical course were often unable to withstand the terrible test.

↫§ Fear of Leaving Eretz Yisrael

Rashi, quoting *Chazal*, says that Yaakov was distressed because he had to leave *Eretz Yisrael*. *S'forno* explains this concept, as does Abarbanel in greater depth. According to *S'forno*, the reason that Yaakov prayed "to the God of his father Yitzchak" was because Hashem had commanded Yitzchak, "Do not go down to Egypt."

Abarbanel also asks why Yaakov was suddenly afraid, after having left of his own free will, saying, "I will go and see him before I die." Abarbanel answers that Yaakov was afraid to leave *Eretz Yisrael* after Yitzchak had been offered as a sacrifice at the *Akeidah*, where his spiritual qualities had been bound specifically to *Eretz Yisrael*. Earlier, when Yaakov had gone from Beersheva to Charan to seek a wife, he had received permission from Hashem to do so. Hashem had promised him, "And I will return you to this land." Now, that he was again leaving *Eretz Yisrael*, he arrived in Beersheva, where he came to receive permission for his journey from "the God of my father Yitzchak," for it was Yitzchak who had been bound on the altar and whose soul had become attached to *Eretz Yisrael*. In addition, says Abarbanel, Yaakov feared four things in regard to leaving *Eretz Yisrael*: (a) His descendants might be killed in Egypt, and might not become a nation; (b) Egypt was full of idolatry, and Hashem might therefore not watch over him; (c) he might die in Egypt and be buried there, rather than in *Eretz Yisrael*; (d) Yosef might die before Yaakov, and then there would be no one to take care of him and his family. It was against these fears that Hashem gave him four promises. On the first fear, Hashem told him, "Do not fear to go down to Egypt, for I will make you a great nation there." As to the second, he was told, "I will go down with you." In regard to the third hesitation, "And I will surely bring you up." And finally, with the fourth, Hashem told him, "And Yosef will put his hands on your eyes." Thus Hashem removed all Yaakov's fears, and with them the obstacles which impeded him from going to Egypt.

Radak has a similar approach. The reason that Yaakov prayed to "the God of my father Yitzchak" was because Yitzchak had been commanded not to leave *Eretz Yisrael*. Yaakov offered sacrifices at the edge of *Eretz Yisrael*, in Beersheva, so that Hashem's prophecy might rest on him, and he would be given answers to his concerns. Indeed, Hashem's prophecy did rest on him. When Hashem called to him, "Yaakov, Yaakov!" that was to make him realize that Hashem was speaking to him through prophecy. The promise was a communal one, even though it was addressed to him individually. "I will make you" meant, "I will make your descendants," and so too, "I will surely bring you up." Hashem promised, "Yosef will put his hands on your eyes" and would support Yaakov's children and descendants as long as Yosef remained alive.

HaAmek Davar, on the other hand, holds that Yaakov was afraid that his descendants would be assimilated among the Egyptians and would remain there. "The Jewish flame," thought Yaakov, "can only be preserved in *Eretz Yisrael*." But Hashem promised him that He would make him into a great nation, and that his descendants would not be assimilated among the Egyptians.

S'forno has a different view. Hashem told Yaakov, "Do not fear," for only in *Eretz Yisrael* was there reason to be afraid that his descendants would be assimilated among the other nations living there. In Egypt, though, the Jews were hated, "For the Egyptians could not eat with them, because they were Hebrews," and it was that hatred which would prevent them from assimilating. One of the aims of the *galus* was to form the sons of Yaakov into a national group, so that they would not be assimilated among the other nations.

Meshech Chochmah inserts a new element regarding Yaakov's fear. Now that Yaakov was going to his son and would need to be supported by him, he remembered that he had not honored his father for twenty-two years when he was away from home. That was the reason that he offered sacrifices to "the God of my father Yitzchak." He wanted to atone for this sin, so that he would not be punished "measure for measure" by not having his son Yosef honor him as a son honors his father.

܀§ I Am with Him in Distress

The concept of "the *Shechinah* in *galus*" appears in kabbalistic literature, in regard to going down to Egypt. Hashem said to Yaakov, "I will go down to Egypt," and according to the kabbalists, this means that Hashem, as it were, would personally accompany Yaakov into Egypt. Onkelos also translates this phrase literally.

Rambam in *Moreh Nevuchim* 27 wishes to prove from Onkelos that בְּמַרְאֹת הַלַּיְלָה means that everything that Yaakov saw was in a dream. Had that not been the case, he asks, how could Onkelos explain Hashem's going down as being tangible, for Onkelos usually explains any terms indicating movement by Hashem as being symbolic of Hashem's revealing Himself. If Onkelos explained matters differently here, it was because the sight which Yaakov saw was only in a dream. Therefore, when Yaakov reported on his dream, the way he saw Hashem's going down in his dream was indeed tangible.

The way *Rambam* explains Onkelos arouses a sharp response from *Ramban*. He tries to prove, using innumerable examples, that Onkelos explains many verses as the appearance of Heavenly forces in physical guise. On the other hand, he proves that sometimes, even in the case of dreams, Onkelos takes explanations out of the *p'shat*, and interprets them by *Ru'ach HaKodesh*. This is clear evidence that Onkelos is not a philosopher, as *Rambam* would have it, but is rather a commentator. That was why he interpreted the verse, "And I will go down with you," as meaning exactly that, namely, "They were exiled to Egypt, and the *Shechinah* was exiled with them."

Following *Ramban's* disagreement with *Moreh Nevuchim*, Abarbanel and Shem Tov, in their commentaries on *Moreh Nevuchim*, come to *Rambam's* defense. *Abarbanel* answers each question of *Ramban* at length. On the other hand, *Akeidah* justifies *Ramban's* approach, even though he chooses a different path. His view is that there was no dream here, but rather prophecy, although the word "I will go down" refers to special Divine supervision and protection.

R' Chisdai Crescas also follows this path. He says that *Rambam's* words are indeed "the words of the living God," but the meaning of the verse is that Hashem's supervision over Yaakov and his sons would be greater than before in Egypt. As opposed to this, Rabbenu Bachya holds with *Ramban* that Onkelos changed from his normal style here, specifically because he wished to explain the word "I will go down" in its simple meaning, namely, "the *Shechinah* went into exile with them."

Abarbanel, as mentioned, is opposed to references which impart human qualities to Hashem, and he therefore explains the verse about Hashem going down to Egypt in terms of *Kiddush Hashem* and *Chilul Hashem*. When it is good for Israel, Hashem's name is sanctified and His glory is proclaimed throughout the world. On the other hand, when it is bad for Israel, Hashem's name is brought low, as in "Why should the nations say . . ." Many other commentators follow along these lines.

Of course, if the verse "and I will go down with you" is explained in terms of "the *Shechinah* in *galus*," one must explain the rest of the verse, "and I will surely bring you up," in a similar fashion. *Beis HaLevi* says that the second half of the verse was the greatest promise to Israel; that their going up is linked to the *Shechinah's* esteem increasing. This idea is expanded on in many Chassidic works.

Sefas Emes has an incisive explanation. "I" in the verse, "I will go down with you," refers to the Torah. All of Israel's exile and redemption is influenced by the Torah. In exile, the Torah is concealed and limited, as a type of descent, while in *Eretz Yisrael* it is in ascent. Nevertheless, in every place there is the "I." At all times and in all circumstances, whether in descent or ascent, the Torah, as embodied in the word "I," is with us. That is our consolation in our distress.

Other commentators explain the promise, "I will surely bring you up," in a physical sense. *Rashi*, Ibn Ezra and others see a promise here that Yaakov will be buried in *Eretz Yisrael*. *Da'as Zekeinim MiBa'alei HaTosafos* explains that the promise is that the people of Israel will be great even in Egypt itself.

S'forno explains the seeming redundancy in the words אַעַלְךָ גַם עָלֹה (which is usually translated, "I will surely bring you up") as meaning that this is a promise to the entire community, that when they go up from Egypt, they will be at a greater level than when they went down. Other commentators see here a promise of elevation both materially and spiritually, to the receiving of the Torah, and to the hearing of "I [am Hashem your God]" at Sinai. All see these promises as hints and symbols of matters that will later be fulfilled. They are said here in a cryptic type of format, as is usual for prophecy.

✦ Yosef Will Put His Hands on Your Eyes

This last promise is also the object of much discussion among the commentators. Ibn Ezra says simply that they had a custom that the living would shut the eyes of the dead. In this, he echoes *Zohar* in *Parashas Vayechi*, on the verse (*Bereishis* 47:31), "Swear to me," which states that there is a kabbalistic meaning in the fact that the son must shut his father's eyes after the father dies. Based on this, *Elya Rabbah* 311 rules, in the name of *Tosafos Yom Tov*, that even on *Shabbos*, when one is forbidden to move the limbs of the dead, one is permitted to close his father's eyes.

Rashbam and *S'forno*, though, explain that Hashem told Yaakov that Yosef would take care of all of his needs in Egypt and would support him and his family until his death. On the other hand, in *Bava Basra* 108, *Rashbam* rules that it is a blessing for a person to have his son bury him, and there he derives it from this same verse: "Yosef will put his hands on your eyes."

One of the *acharonim* explained that Hashem said to Yaakov, "The way things evolved regarding Yosef will be a sign for you that good will yet come out from this bad. Yosef was sold as a slave and became a ruler. Similarly, the *galus* which you are now entering will also turn out for the good, and from the slaves in Egypt, a kingdom of priests and a holy nation will emerge."

Abarbanel finds a symbolic and actual significance to the verse, based on his own experiences. Throughout our history, the "Yosefs" — who have achieved success and gained the recognition of gentile rulers — hide from us the tragic reality of our exile. One may add that in the darkness of our exile, one "Yosef" or another shines brilliantly from time to time, whether his name is Abarbanel in Spain, or *lehavdil*, Walter Rathenau in Germany. These give the illusion that the Jews can find peace and can develop normally while in exile. They hide from us the truth of our terrible condition, until a yawning abyss suddenly opens up under our feet and swallows up masses of Jews together with the "Yosefs." In these words of Jacob, there is a serious warning to the Jewish people not to be misled by illusions. *Galus* spells doom for our people, and one should, therefore, always bear in mind the one and only certain promise: "I will surely bring you up."

Vayechi – ויחי

I.
Rejection of the Firstborn Cult

When Yaakov placed his right hand on Ephraim, the younger of Yosef's sons, the commentators tell us that that was another blow against the status of the firstborn, until finally the entire concept of the importance of the firstborn as a spiritual and ethical value disappeared from Israel. We have already discussed this in the section where Yaakov bought the birthright from Esav, but there we were discussing the evil Esav, whereas in our *parashah* we are dealing with the two sons of Yosef, who were without vice.

The preference given to the younger over the older is explained as a vision for the future. But according to Judaism, a person is judged by his condition at the present, and if in this situation Yaakov displayed a special relationship to the younger son, there was obviously a conceptual message that accompanied the reason for his behavior.

Among the various commentators, almost all of whom discuss this cryptic *parashah* in the Torah, *Kli Yakar*, especially, goes into this question at great length. According to him, the Torah wished to stress that Hashem chooses the weak and the downtrodden, as opposed to the cult of strength and might associated at the time with the status of the firstborn. Hashem lifts up those who possess an element of smallness in them, as it is written (*Devarim* 7:7), "Hashem did not desire you, or choose you, because you were more numerous than any people; for you are the fewest of all people." So too do we see (*Yeshayahu* 60:22), "A little one shall become a thousand, and a small one a strong nation." In a similar vein, *Kli Yakar* demonstrates how this idea unfolded in Avraham's family. Yishmael was the firstborn, and Yitzchak was chosen. Esav was the firstborn, and Yaakov was chosen. Reuven was the firstborn, and Yosef was chosen. Menasheh was the firstborn, and Ephraim was chosen. *Kli Yakar* concludes by saying, "This is a clear hint, and the wise will understand it."

R' Samson Raphael Hirsch delves into this concept at length in his commentary on the Torah. This tendency began even before Avraham and continued after our forefathers. Already in the very first generation, Hevel was chosen over Cain. With Shem, Cham and Yefes, we are not told who was the firstborn, but it appears that it was not Shem. After the forefathers, Moshe was chosen, even though he was the younger brother, and the same was true for David. In the end, the firstborn were replaced by the Levites. The aim behind all this, says R' Samson Raphael Hirsch, is to stress that there is no ethical or spiritual superiority that derives from one's birth, but, on the contrary, "the older will serve the younger" if the younger is ethically superior to the older. The only advantage the firstborn has is his material inheritance. In the spiritual world, no one enjoys superiority as the result of inheritance. Only the one chosen by Hashem, because of his spiritual qualities, merits the lofty status that accompanies holiness.

In the pagan world, the firstborn was not only the head of the family, but also acted as the priest and the one closest to the gods. *Chazal* stress Yaakov's protest against this sort of arrangement regarding basic inheritance, as well as his refusal to come to terms with the possibility that his wicked brother Esav would be the one to perform the service to Hashem. Of course, that example bears no comparison to our case. Menasheh was no less fitting than his brother, yet Yaakov preferred his younger brother over him in an area which had no bearing on the inheritance of property. In Yaakov's blessing, the firstborn enjoys no special privilege where there is a brother who is spiritually superior. The seed of Ephraim would be superior spiritually to that of Menasheh, since fathers are the root from which their offspring emanate. *Or HaChayim* tells us that Yaakov did not hesitate to stress this superiority in his blessing, which alluded to the future.

Other commentators go even further. *Pa'aneach Raza* compares what was said about Yaakov: "And Israel's eyes became heavy from old age," to what was said about Yitzchak: "And when Yitzchak became old ..." There is a distinct similarity here in events, and in the two forefathers' evaluations of their sons. In both cases, the father had wanted to favor the firstborn, but Heaven intervened and the situation was reversed. This is one of the boldest of commentaries on this *parashah*. There is no hint in the Torah of an attempt to take away the birthright from Menasheh. On the contrary, the Torah stresses that Menasheh was the firstborn. So, too, in *Yehoshua*, in regard to the inheritance of Menasheh the Torah stresses that he was the firstborn of Yosef.

There are those who wish to rely on the lamentation of *Yirmiyahu* (ch. 31) regarding the exile of Ephraim, where Yirmiyahu refers to him as "Ephraim, My firstborn," but one who examines the matter thoroughly will see that that term was only used as a sign of affection, as in the expression, "My son, My firstborn, Israel." Alternatively, the expression in *Yirmiyahu* might be referring back to Yosef, who was indeed considered to be a firstborn.

In any event, the fact that Yaakov placed his right hand on Ephraim is a source for contemplation, and it was not for nothing that Yosef was shaken and exclaimed, "Not so, my father," a form of speech upon which most commentators remark.

Pesikta Rabbasi 3 says clearly that Yosef was shaken, because he was afraid that Yaakov wanted to deprive Menasheh of the birthright. One can understand his fear, given the background of Yosef's own life and the fact that he had been sold, all this tracing back to the fact that his father had shown preference to him. He thought that Yaakov was not aware of his having been sold by the brothers, and was therefore not careful about the effects of this action. Yaakov's answer, as explained by *Chazal*, fits in well with this: " 'I know, my son, I know' — I know of your being sold" (*Pesikta Rabbasi* 3). If Yaakov knew, and nevertheless did what he did, that allayed Yosef's fears and he accepted his father's actions.

⇜§ He Crossed His Hands for Menasheh Was the Firstborn

There have been hundreds of explanations on the verse, "He crossed his hands for Menasheh was the firstborn." Most *rishonim* state that Yaakov knew that Menasheh was the firstborn, and he nevertheless did what he did deliberately and intentionally. Thus the second part of the verse is understood to mean "even though Menasheh was the firstborn." Yosef did not know that his father was doing this deliberately, and therefore he was disturbed.

Pa'aneach Raza explains this in an original fashion. He adds a question mark to the words: "Is this not so, my father?" Wasn't I correct in placing the firstborn to your right? To this, Yaakov replied, "I know my son, I know." What you did was undoubtedly correct, and in spite of that I have placed my right hand on Ephraim, as a sign of what will occur in the future.

Other commentators see the fact that Yaakov placed his right hand on Ephraim as a sign of the wisdom of Yaakov, who wished to emphasize Ephraim's superiority, but not in a way that would shame Menasheh the firstborn. Had Yaakov switched the sons and placed

Ephraim to his right, say *Chizkuni*, *Shaloh* and others, he would have rejected Menasheh, and Yaakov did not want to do that. He therefore "crossed his hands," doing what he did only with his hands, "for Menaṣheh was the firstborn," and he did not want to impugn his honor. By placing his right hand on Ephraim, Yaakov added honor to him, without in any way diminishing from that of Menasheh.

The Dubno Magid in *Ohel Yaakov* expands on this topic. We find in *Bamidbar Rabbah* on the verse (*Bamidbar* 3:12), "And I have taken the Levites instead of every firstborn," that *Chazal* tell us, "I am adding to My love of them." What *Chazal* mean is that there is no rejection of the firstborn, but an addition of love to the Levites. Hashem gives to people, and does not take away from them. The firstborn remain holy and must be redeemed. The same was true with the sons of Yosef. "For Menasheh was the firstborn" — and no one wanted to change that fact. By placing his right hand on Ephraim, Yaakov was simply adding to Ephraim, by giving his seed added strength and power.

It is interesting that *HaKesav VeHaKabalah* explains the verse before this one — "And he blessed Yosef" — as meaning that Yaakov blessed Yosef's sons with Yosef, namely that Yosef joined into the blessings delivered by Yaakov. This explanation answers a question asked by various commentators as to why there was no special blessing of Yosef, and only blessings for his two sons. In reality, the verse just quoted should belong after the disagreement between Yaakov and Yosef, but the Torah placed it at this spot.

It is possible that the meaning of this verse relates to the beginning of the *parashah*. Yaakov tells Yosef that (*Bereishis* 48:5) "Ephraim and Menasheh will be to me as Reuven and Shimon." Later too, he says (*Bereishis* 48:22), "I have given you a portion above your brothers," which most commentators explain as an additional portion in the inheritance of the land. This portion traces back to the birthright which was taken from Reuven and given to Yosef. This birthright must apply to the right of the firstborn in inheriting, and not to the birthright which Yaakov bought from Esav, for that referred to the right to serve Hashem. We never find any allusion of *kehunah* — "priesthood" — with Yosef.

Other commentators explain that Yaakov indeed bequeathed the *kehunah* to Yosef in his days, for at that time that was linked to the birthright; but one cannot ignore what the Torah states clearly, that Yosef received an additional tribe, based on what Yaakov had given him.

Many commentators discuss the halachic basis for this gift by Yaakov at the expense of the other brothers, and especially at the expense of Reuven the firstborn. This discussion is generally to be found on the verse (*Bereishis* 48:22), "Which I took from the Emorite with my sword and with my bow."

In any event, it is a fact that two tribes arose from Yosef, based on the blessing they received from their father. This means that both should enjoy full equality, without one being given the status of a firstborn over the other, for both of them derived their status from the right of the firstborn which was transferred directly to them. The rights of the firstborn were granted to "the sons of Yosef," and not to Yosef. This idea is explained beautifully by *Meshech Chochmah*. It is thus possible that by crossing his hands, Yaakov wished deliberately to mix the two together, and to stress that they were as a single unit. Thus, the meaning of the verse, "He crossed his hands for Menasheh was the firstborn," would mean that Yaakov deliberately crossed his hands because Menasheh was the firstborn, and might err and think that he was also to be considered the firstborn in regard to the inheritance of the land. Yaakov therefore took an action to clarify and demonstrate that the right of the firstborn included both sons. Only after Yosef had reacted and claimed that this action might harm Menasheh's right as a firstborn, did Yaakov explain his action as a prophetic intimation of what lay ahead for both tribes in the future. Legally, as a result of Yaakov's blessing, both sons enjoyed equal rights in the inheritance of the land, and the very fact that they were entitled to be treated as two tribes stemmed from the right of the firstborn. Yaakov's blessing was a single one for both of them in regard to inheriting the land.

There are yet other cryptic aspects of the *parashah* that are worth exploring. Ephraim appears later in Jewish history in the monarchy named after him, the kingdom of Israel. The sons of Rachel, whether from Binyamin or Ephraim, contended with the House of David over the monarchy. Ephraim continued in its opposition to the House of David, even after Binyamin joined Yehudah.

According to Ibn Ezra, the words of the blessing (*Bereishis* 48:16), "And let my name be named on them, and the name of my fathers Abraham and Isaac," also refer to a later event, where all of Israel was known as Ephraim.

Ibn Ezra discusses the desire of Yaakov on this matter, and says:

> All of Israel will be called Ephraim. So too does the verse state, "Rachel cries for her children," for she was the main one in his mind. That is why the verse says, "The children of Rachel, the wife of Yaakov." And when Rachel gave birth, [Yaakov] immediately said to Lavan, "Send me away." He also gave Yosef

the right of the firstborn, for he was the first of his thought. As Reuven was not fitting for the birthright, Yosef took his place, as the firstborn to his mother, and not Dan and not Gad for they were the sons of maidservants. The right is more honored than the left and is more powerful.

◆§ Ephraim and Menasheh as Symbols and as Approaches

In addition to the commentaries on the *parashah*, there are also *d'rush* and other views, which express various ideas and concepts over which there are differences of opinion. *Be'er Moshe* clarifies an idea, which is found often in the Chassidic works, that Yaakov preferred one outlook over another. Menasheh helped his father in his administration of affairs, and was involved in worldly matters, as we are told by *Chazal*, "and the interpreter was between them" — that was Menasheh. So too are we told on, "And he did as Yosef commanded" — that was Menasheh. Menasheh symbolized political control and being involved in the world. Ephraim, on the other hand, sat in the Torah academy, as *Chazal* tell us that he studied Torah with Yosef.

Yaakov gave precedence to Ephraim to show that his was the correct approach. Yaakov did not reject Menasheh's way, for "he too will grow," but in Yaakov's opinion, Ephraim's approach was the greater.

Another idea is brought in various *d'rush* works, one of which has relevance to our times. Menasheh symbolizes being cut off from one's roots, as in Yosef's declaration when giving him his name (*Bereishis* 41:51), "For God has made me forget (נַשַּׁנִי) all my toil, and all my father's house," whereas Ephraim reminded one that when a person is away from his home and birthplace, he is a stranger, as when Yosef said in reference to Ephraim's name (*Bereishis* 41:52), "For God has caused me to be fruitful (הִפְרַנִי) in the land of my affliction." Yaakov wanted to stress the symbolism contained in the name "Ephraim," and he therefore placed his right hand on him.

It is interesting that the preceding "modern" interpretation by R' Amiel is to be found in *Chasam Sofer* on our *parashah*, and these are his words:

> Yosef sinned when he was a slave in the home of Potiphar, combed his hair and forgot the distress of his father, before Hashem saved him and seated him on the ruler's throne. It was in accordance with this that he gave his firstborn his name based on, "For God has made me forget." And indeed, he was forbidden

300 / Rejection of the Firstborn Cult

(*Hoshea* 9:1) to forget his father's house: "Rejoice not, O Israel, for joy, as other people: for you have gone astray from your God." Therefore [Yaakov] hinted to him, "In you will Israel be blessed," in placing Ephraim before Menasheh, not to rejoice over having gone astray from Hashem in *galus*.

If even seemingly clear matters in our *parashah* are explained symbolically, how much more is this true for those matters which are obscure, such as when Yaakov said about Menasheh that he would "grow to a people," and his words about Ephraim, that "his offspring['s fame] will fill the nations." Except for *Rashi*, who follows the Midrash, no commentator has revealed the *p'shat* of these allusions. [Which "people" and "nations" did Yaakov mean?] There is no doubt that this refers to chapters of history which have not yet been written. For example, the commentators attempt to explain what Yaakov meant when he said, "Which I took from the Emorite with my sword and with my bow." Only one of the early commentators, R' Yosef Bechor Shor, says that "this certainly means that [Yaakov] took it in war, but we do not know when." The eternity of the Torah rests also in this: The symbols provide an ethical lesson for all generations even where the historical narrative is not available.

II.

Do Not Bury Me in Egypt

In our *parashah*, we find the longing of our fathers to be buried only in *Eretz Yisrael*, if they were unable to be there during their lives. This has had a decisive influence on all generations. *Midrash Rabbah* 96 says: "Why did the forefathers demand to be buried in *Eretz Yisrael*? R' Yehoshua ben Levi said, 'I shall walk before Hashem in the land of the living'" (i.e., in *Eretz Yisrael*).

We also find in *Chazal* (*Sanhedrin* 111) a negative opinion of those who wish to be brought to be buried in *Eretz Yisrael* after their deaths. R' Eleazar referred this verse to them (*Yirmiyahu* 2:7), "And you came and contaminated My land, and you have made My inheritance an abomination." And he adds, "In your lives you did not go up, shall you then in death come and contaminate My land?" This negative view seems to conflict with Yaakov's last will and testament, although it was by Hashem's decree that he was unable to leave Egypt.

Abarbanel at the end of *Parashas Vayechi* discusses this topic at length. In order to appreciate his interesting view, I will quote it directly:

> There are many people who spend their lives in comfort, with Torah and good deeds, and always follow in "the light of Hashem in the Land of the Living." Because of their uprightness and perfection in life they deserve to be brought in death to *Eretz Yisrael* and to be buried there. Those people do not contaminate the land, because their bodies were holy instruments, pure and clean, and they will in the future see the resurrection of the dead. These deserve to be buried in "the Land of the Living" and will arise without having to roll [under their graves to *Eretz Yisrael* at the time of the resurrection of the dead], and without distress.
>
> There are very many other people who spend their lives on vanity and run after material lusts, and it is these who even in life are called dead. When they die, they command their children to give charity and gifts to the poor, which they did not do when they were alive. There are those of this group who command that they be buried in *tallis* and *tefillin*, while in their lives they wore wool and linen (*sha'atnez*). And there are those who command that their bones be taken to be buried in *Eretz Yisrael*, while in their lives they rejected and detested it. It is as if in their lives they were wicked, and when they died they become righteous people who keep the *mitzvos*. It is known that this is an invalid view, because one performs *mitzvos* when alive, and not after one is dead. *Chazal* have already said, what is meant by (*Iyov* 3:19), "And a slave free of his master"? When a person dies, he is free of the *mitzvos*. It is about these that R' Eleazar said, "In your lives you did not go up, shall you then in death come and contaminate My land?"

A logical reason for Yaakov's wish to be buried in *Eretz Yisrael* is given by R' Samson Raphael Hirsch. He bases himself on the conditions of his generation. Yaakov lived in Egypt for seventeen years. He already knew the results of slavery, "And they took hold of it," and of the emotional and spiritual condition of his sons and descendants. They had begun to look to the Nile rather than to the Jordan, and to regard Egypt as their homeland. That was the basic reason why Yaakov asked not to be buried in Egypt. He wanted to show his sons that he did not recognize Egypt as a permanent home for the Jews. He did not even want to be buried there, and it was all the more true that his children should not want to live there.

⌘§ When Should a Person Write His Will?

Abarbanel learns a lesson for us and for our children for all generations from our *parashah*. A person should not delay in making his will until close to his death, because then his flesh aches and he mourns for himself, and he does not have the strength and presence of mind — because of his illness — to will as is proper. Rather, before that time, he should command his household, just as [with Yaakov, who] before he became ill called Yosef to command him about his burial.

In Abarbanel's view, Yaakov was not yet ill, but felt that his strength was ebbing. He thus summoned his son Yosef, knowing that the latter had the ability to fulfill his wishes, as *Rashi* explains. Abarbanel notes the view of *Chazal* that as Yosef was the one who had caused his father to come to Egypt, Yaakov imposed on him the obligation to bring his body out of that country to *Eretz Yisrael*.

Chizkuni says that Yaakov called Yosef after Hashem had told him, "And Yosef will put his hands on your eyes." Other commentators also hold that Yaakov called Yosef even before he became ill. Abarbanel follows *Ramban* in this, where *Ramban* explains the verse, "And the days of Yaakov to die drew close" — that Yaakov felt his strength was ebbing. This was the last year of his life. He felt weaker, but was not yet feeble. He knew that he would not live much longer and therefore called Yosef. The same is true for the meaning of the verse, "And the days of David to die drew near" — that David felt his life was coming to an end. That was why he said, "I am going in the way of all the land."

Rashi, though, holds that "drawing close to die" refers to a person who will not attain the age of his fathers. Yitzchak lived 180 years, while Yaakov lived only 147 years. David, too, did not live as long as his father Yishai. "Drawing near" therefore means that one's life is drawing to a close before one's time, based on the life of one's fathers.

According to *Divrei David* by *Taz*, what the Torah meant was that there was a reason for this "drawing near." When the people about whom this phrase was written were first born, they were meant to live longer, but their deaths took place prematurely. The Torah, though, does not explain the reason for this.

The Torah also does not explain the basis for the dispute between Yaakov and his son. Yaakov asked Yosef, from the very first instant, to promise with an oath to fulfill his father's will, exclaiming, "Place your hand under my thigh." In his answer, Yosef committed himself to doing so, but without an oath, and said, "I will do as you say." But Yaakov was not content with that statement, and again demanded that Yosef swear to this. Only after Yaakov's second request did Yosef swear to fulfill his father's request.

Targum Yehonasan says that Yosef was not opposed to the oath itself, but did not want to put his hand under Yaakov's thigh, for that is not respect for one's father. Yaakov accepted Yosef's refusal, and agreed that he should swear in another manner. It was then that Yosef fulfilled his father's wish.

Abarbanel and *S'forno*, though, explain that in his answer, "I will do as you say," Yosef did not obligate himself completely, especially in terms of taking an oath to that effect. He merely said that he would do what he could. It all depended on whether Pharaoh would give him permission. "I," to the extent that it depends on me, "will do as you say."

Or HaChayim also explains that Yosef's words were a rejection of the oath. As we see, though, Yaakov was insistent that Yosef swear to him. The reason for this insistence, according to *Ramban* and other commentators, was because Yaakov was afraid that Pharaoh would prevent the mission from being carried out, should there only be an assurance without an oath. He therefore wanted to strengthen the assurance with an oath.

Indeed, according to *Rashi*, Pharaoh later told Yosef that it was only because of the oath that he would give him permission to go and bury his father, and he said: "Go up and bury your father as he had you swear."

Pa'aneach Raza wonders at Yaakov's concern about the burial, for Hashem had promised him, "I will surely bring you up." He answers that Yaakov was afraid that only his bones would be brought back to *Eretz Yisrael*, just as happened later with Yosef's bones.

Tiferes Yehonasan holds that Yaakov was afraid, in accordance with what *Chazal* say in the Midrash, that when Yosef said, "I will do as you say," Yosef would do exactly what his father had done, and just as Yaakov had asked him to bring his bones up to Canaan, Yosef would ask others to bring Yaakov's bones up to Canaan. Yaakov then became afraid that his bones would only be brought up together with those of Yosef. He therefore asked Yosef to swear that his body be brought up immediately, while the body was still whole.

Rashi, in *Parashas Shemos*, says that a sign had been transmitted from Yaakov to Yosef, that with the words "פָּקֹד יִפְקֹד — he will surely remember" *Bnei Yisrael* would be redeemed. This is unusual, for where do we see that Yaakov transmitted this sign to Yosef? *Da'as Zekeinim* explains *Rashi's* comment, on the basis of the Midrash quoted in the previous paragraph, that Yosef answered his father that "just as you are commanding me, I will command my brothers when I die." Indeed, we find that Yosef told his brothers, פָּקֹד יִפְקֹד, and as Yosef had told his father that he would do as Yaakov had said, and would command his brothers with the same words his father had commanded him, we understand that Yaakov used the same words, even though this is not stated specifically in the Torah.

⚜ Do Not Bury Me in Egypt

Abarbanel and *S'forno* explain, as quoted in *Pa'aneach Raza* above, that Yaakov's will was to have his body brought up to *Eretz Yisrael* immediately, without any temporary interment in Egypt.

According to *Rashi* quoting the Midrash, Yaakov had three reasons for this: (a) The earth of Egypt would eventually turn into vermin (כִּנִּים); (b) those who die outside *Eretz Yisrael* are not revived at the time of *tchiyas ha'meisim* (the resurrection of the dead) until their bodies have rolled underground through tunnels to *Eretz Yisrael*; and that (c) the Egyptians should not deify him after his death.

Kli Yakar explains that the three reasons given by *Rashi* are dependent on one another. Yaakov was not afraid that vermin would infest his body, because the bodies of the righteous are not affected by worms, but was afraid that when the Egyptians saw that his body did not decay, they would begin to worship him. These two reasons, though, only explain why Yaakov should not be buried in Egypt, but not why he should be buried in *Eretz Yisrael*. The latter is because of the concern over the necessity to roll underground to *Eretz Yisrael*.

Divrei David explains the need for these three reasons. He says that the reason that the earth of Egypt would turn into vermin was insufficient, because Yaakov could be buried in Goshen, where the Jews lived, and the Ten Plagues did not affect Goshen.

Avnei Shoham, though, is surprised at the words of *Divrei David*, for *Rambam* on *Avos* 5:4 says clearly that the vermin affected the Jews in Goshen, but did not cause them distress. If that is the case, the reason of the earth turning to vermin should be a sufficient one for Yaakov to ask to be buried in Canaan, and the other two reasons should be unnecessary. *Avnei Shoham* leaves the question unanswered.

Oznayim LaTorah brings proof to the words of *Rambam* that the vermin did affect Goshen, for we are told in *Tehillim* 105:32, "Vermin 'in all' their borders."

Chizkuni is puzzled by the statement of most commentators that Yaakov's main wish was not to be buried even temporarily in Egypt, for *Chazal* in *Nazir* 65 imply that Yaakov was indeed buried there temporarily. There *Chazal* in the Mishnah tell us: "One who finds a dead body lying in the normal burial position (implying that it had once been buried) may take it and the soil it occupies (for reburial elsewhere)." The *gemara* then asks what is considered "the soil that it occupies," to which R' Yehudah answers that we have a verse where Yaakov said (*Bereishis* 47:30), "And you shall carry me from Egypt," which means "And you shall carry me (along with some earth taken) from Egypt." The *gemara* continues, "And how much is the soil which is occupied? It is a depth of three fingers." From this we see that Yaakov was indeed buried in Egypt, and when they took his body for reburial in Canaan, they also took the soil occupied by the body.

Tosafos Yom Tov and other commentators on *Shas* discuss the apparent contradiction between Yaakov's request not to be buried even temporarily in Egypt and the fact that his body was taken together with the soil it occupied. *Chizkuni's* view, though, is that Yaakov was indeed buried in Egypt.

A number of *acharonim* also discuss this question. *Tzofnas Pa'aneach* has an original interpretation. They placed his body in a stone coffin, which according to *Ra'avad* (*Hil. Tumas Meis* 6:8) is considered to be the same thing as burial. The command not to have him buried in Egypt was observed, and yet the fact that Yaakov was placed in such a coffin was considered as if he had been buried in Egypt.

Revid HaZahav holds that Yaakov's body was placed in a coffin which had holes in it, so that the fluids which exuded from his body mixed with the earth, and that was why they also had to take along the soil occupied by the body. According to *Revid HaZahav*, Yaakov had ordered that he was not to be buried in the ground of Egypt, namely with soil beneath and above him.

Vayosef Avraham brings the question raised by R' Yeshaya in *Hadar Zekeinim* on the words of *Chazal* in *Nazir*: Can it be that they did not obey Yaakov's last will? R' Chaim, though, answers the question beautifully. Yaakov told Yosef, "Do not bury me in Egypt," not even temporarily, so that you will not have to take along the soil of Egypt which the body occupies. On this basis, *Chazal* concluded that in the case of reburial one is required to take along the soil that the body occupied in its previous resting place. In reality, though, Yaakov was not buried in Egypt, and there was no need to take any Egyptian soil.

Ramban on *Bereishis* 48:7 makes a number of comments, from which it appears that Yaakov was indeed first buried outside *Eretz Yisrael*. He explains the verse there, "and I, when I came from Padan," as being an apology by Yaakov for not having buried Rachel at *Me'aras HaMachpelah*. She died suddenly on the road, and he was unable to leave his children and flocks and take Rachel to be buried there. Nor were there any doctors present who might embalm her. *Ramban* then adds the following sentence: "He therefore said that she died in the Land of Canaan and was not buried outside it, as would happen if Yaakov were buried in Egypt." One can explain the words, "as would happen" as a fact, as *Chazal* tell us in *Nazir*. But what Yaakov meant was that he had buried Rachel in *Eretz Yisrael*, and not as he would be buried, should Yosef not fulfill his will, thereby requiring him to remain buried outside of *Eretz Yisrael*. The purpose of Yaakov's account of Rachel's burial outside of *Me'aras HaMachpelah* was to remind Yosef that he had buried his mother in *Eretz Yisrael*.

Rashi, though, quoting Midrash, as well as *Rashbam*, Ibn Ezra and other commentators, clarifies the words of Yaakov: "And I, when I came from Padan," as Yaakov justifying the fact that he had not buried Rachel in *Me'aras HaMachpelah*. *Rashi* says that Rachel was buried where she was by Divine order, so that she would be able to help her descendants after Nevuzradan exiled them, as we see in (*Yirmiyahu* 31:14), "A voice is heard on high, with lamentation and bitter weeping; Rachel weeping for her children." *Rashi* also adds that, "I did not even take her to Beis Lechem to bring her into the land."

Ramban, whom we quoted above, is surprised at *Rashi's* words. Does that mean that Rachel was buried outside *Eretz Yisrael*? After all, the verse says clearly (*Bereishis* 48:7), "Rachel died by me in the land of Canaan in the way." *Chasam Sofer*, though, has a novel explanation, that even though *Eretz Yisrael* has been ours by right since the days of our forefathers, it was never sanctified until the time of Yehoshua bin Nun, and as long as it was not sanctified, it was considered to be outside *Eretz Yisrael*. The only exception to this were *Me'aras HaMachpelah*, which was bought by Avraham, and the place that Yaakov bought in Shechem for an altar. Had Yaakov bought the place where Rachel was buried in Beis Lechem, it too would have been sanctified with the sanctity of *Eretz Yisrael*, but as Yaakov buried Rachel in an ownerless place, it was considered to be outside *Eretz Yisrael*, until Yehoshua later sanctified it.

Based on this idea, we can understand the importance which Yaakov attached at the end of chapter 49 to being buried specifically in *Me'aras HaMachpelah*, and the stress on the fact that "Avraham bought the field." It was this purchase which consecrated the Cave as part of *Eretz Yisrael*. By being buried there, Yaakov would ensure that he was indeed buried in *Eretz Yisrael*.

Abarbanel explains that Yaakov strengthened his claim to *Me'aras HaMachpelah* when he stated, "There they buried Avraham and his wife Sarah" — Yishmael has no claim to the Cave. "There they buried

Yitzchak and Rivkah his wife" — and Esav has no claim to the Cave, because "there I buried Leah." I have performed an act of *chazakah* — of taking possession — and therefore the Cave is now *mine*, and no one else has any claim to it.

Akeidah, though, as well as *S'forno*, *Or HaChayim*, and others, explain that when Yaakov said, "and I, when I came from Padan, Rachel died on me," he was not trying to justify himself for not having buried her in *Me'aras HaMachpelah*. Rather he was explaining how he knew that the "multitude of nations" promised him referred to Menasheh and Ephraim.

Leah had already stopped giving birth, and the maidservants came to Yaakov only on behalf of their mistresses. [Thus, if their mistresses could no longer live with Yaakov, he would not live with the maidservants.] Rachel, however, had just begun to give birth, and she had died on the way, and thus the prophecy applied only to Yosef [who was Rachel's continuation].

III.
To Whom Was Yaakov's Will Told?

Parashas *Vayechi* deals overwhelmingly with a description of Yaakov's last days and his bequests. If we ignore the blessings to his children and pay attention only to those things which he commands them to do, we find three points in his will: (a) He commands Yosef not to bury him in Egypt, but to bring his body to *Eretz Yisrael* and to bury it there with the bodies of his fathers; (b) he promises Yosef, and reinforces this by hints in his will, that he will be considered the firstborn and that his sons will be two tribes, as if they had been his own sons; (c) he orders in his will that Yehudah is to be the ruler of his brothers and hints that he will be given the monarchy.

The first of these three is stated specifically, while the second and third are only implied, in that we are told about Reuven (*Bereishis* 49:6), "Unstable as water, you shall not excel," implying that Reuven is unsuitable. (It is true that earlier, in *Bereishis* 48:22, Yaakov said to Yosef, "I have given you one portion above your brothers," but that did not necessarily mean that Reuven was to lose the birthright.) In *Divrei HaYamim* 5:1-2, though, this is stated clearly: "Now the sons of Reuven the firstborn of Israel . . . as he defiled his father's bed, his birthright was given to the sons of Joseph. For Yehudah prevailed over his brothers, and from him came the chief ruler; but the birthright was Yosef's."

In our *parashah* too we read, "Ephraim and Menasheh shall be to me as Reuven and Shimon."

✎§ The Command to Yosef

Yaakov's request to be buried in *Eretz Yisrael* was addressed to Yosef. It appears that this matter required legal permission, which depended on the king. The proof of this is that Yaakov did not accept Yosef's word, "I will do as you say," but insisted on receiving an oath from him that the will would be carried out.

Ramban and other commentators, though, state that Yaakov never suspected Yosef of not fulfilling his wishes, but rather wanted him to swear in order to make his position stronger when he came to request permission from Pharaoh. This way, Yosef could claim that he had been bound by an oath to fulfill his father's will. Indeed, Pharaoh only gave Yosef permission because of that oath, as it states, "Go up and bury your father as he had you swear." As *Rashi* states on this verse, had there not been an oath, Pharaoh would have prevented Yosef from going, because he wanted to bury Yaakov as a "prophet" on Egyptian soil, or, as *Ramban* explains, because he would have told Yosef that it was not necessary for him to accompany the body, since he could leave this task to his brothers or servants.

From the outset, Yosef realized that there might be problems with Pharaoh, and that was why, according to Abarbanel and *S'forno*, he attempted to avoid swearing to his father, saying merely, "I will do as you say," namely, "I will do as much as I am able to do of what you say." Yaakov, though, wanted a greater commitment than that, and also wanted to ensure that Yosef would be able to claim to Pharaoh that he is forced to fulfill his oath to his father.

In order to be sure that Pharaoh would grant him permission, we see that Yosef diverged somewhat from his father's words, suiting them to the situation. Yaakov ordered Yosef not only to bring his body up to *Eretz Yisrael*, but also not to bury him in Egypt. In fact, as *S'forno* points out, Yaakov did not even allow Yosef to have him buried in Egypt for even a short time, although that was later the case with Yosef. When speaking to Pharaoh, though, Yosef did not mention his father's negative attitude toward burial in Egypt, and only mentioned that his father wished to be buried "in my grave which I dug for myself in the Land of Canaan." Yosef did not tell him that his father did not wish to be buried in an impure land, but merely that he had already dug a grave for himself in a certain place, and by custom he had to be buried there.

BEREISHIS — VAYECHI / 309

In this, Yaakov continued the tradition of Avraham and Yitzchak. Avraham said, "Guard yourself that you do not return my son there," while Yitzchak never even left *Eretz Yisrael*. So too did Yaakov want to be returned to *Eretz Yisrael*, and to be buried in *Me'aras HaMachpelah*, where his forefathers were buried.

Ramban, Rashbam, Ibn Ezra and others hold that when Yaakov exclaimed later, "And I, when I came from Padan, Rachel died by me in the land of Canaan on the way," was also referring to his request to be buried with his fathers. Yaakov came to placate Yosef for the fact that he had not done the same with Rachel. He apologized for this, explaining that he had buried Rachel near Beis Lechem, because she had died when they were on the way.

Ramban explains Yaakov's words that Rachel had "died by me," as an attempt to explain to Yosef that when Rachel died, he, Yaakov, was all alone. Even though it was not that great a distance to *Me'aras HaMachpelah*, he could not abandon his flocks. He was thus forced to bury Rachel where she had died. He nevertheless consoled Yosef by telling him that "Rachel died by me in the land of Canaan" — that Rachel was buried in the Land of Canaan, whereas if Yosef did not bring Yaakov's body up, it would remain in the Land of Egypt.

Rashi, though, says that Yaakov told Yosef: "Even though I am imposing on you to bring me to be buried in the Land of Canaan, and I did not do the same for your mother . . ." Afterwards, on the words, "and I buried her there," *Rashi* comments, "And I did not even bring her to Beis Lechem to bury her in the land." Thus it appears from *Rashi* that Yaakov is apologizing for not having buried Rachel in *Eretz Yisrael*. It is not surprising that various commentators are surprised at *Rashi*, for the Torah states clearly, "Rachel died by me in the land of Canaan." They therefore are forced to explain that when *Rashi* says that "I did not even bring her . . . to bury her in the land," refers to settled land. *Rashi* nevertheless deserves further study, for in the previous section he states, "And even though I am imposing on you to bring me to be buried in the Land of Canaan, and I did not do the same for your mother . . ."

Rosh, on the other hand, states that the phrase, "and I, when I came from Padan," has nothing to do with the question of the burial place, for Yaakov interrupts himself in the middle and promises Yosef that Ephraim and Menasheh will be as Reuven and Shimon to him. *Rosh* therefore says that the statement about Rachel's burial relates to the inheritance. After Yaakov promises Yosef a double inheritance, he tells him that he deliberately did not bury Rachel in *Me'aras HaMachpelah*, so that she should rest between the portion of Binyamin and of

Ephraim, her children. Thus, when Yaakov says, "On the way to Efras," he is referring to the fact that this is on the way to Ephraim's portion.

The *gaon* of Dvinsk deduces from Yaakov's words, "Ephraim and Menasheh shall be to me as Reuven and Shimon," that Yaakov wished to say that Menasheh's inheritance was to be equal to that of Ephraim, and he was not to be considered the firstborn for inheritance when compared to his brother Ephraim. This explanation is also understandable logically. If Ephraim and Menasheh were to be two tribes because Yosef was to be considered the firstborn, then both had to be considered as a single unit. There could not be an additional firstborn; for there can only be a single firstborn among brothers (see *Ramban* on 48:6).

The reason why the birthright was transferred from Reuven to Yosef is stated clearly in *Divrei HaYamim*, "As he defiled his father's bed." *Ramban* sees this as a punishment of "measure for measure." Reuven defiled his father's bed as he did not want to have his father have any other children, for that would decrease his share as the firstborn. As a punishment, the rights of the firstborn were taken from him. These were given to Yosef as a reward for having supported his father and brothers in Egypt, or as compensation for the fact that Yaakov had shamed his mother by not burying her in *Me'aras HaMachpelah*, as stated by a number of commentators.

Zohar, though, holds that the rights of the firstborn were given to Yosef because in thought he was indeed the firstborn, as Yaakov had thought that Leah was Rachel.

Meshech Chochmah, on the other hand, explains this according to *p'shat*. Yaakov favored Ephraim over Menasheh in order to demonstrate that he gave priority to quality over quantity. He did this even before he had transferred the status of the firstborn from Reuven to Yosef. His intention in establishing the precedent that quality is all-important was to ensure that people would not think that it was due to Yaakov's love for Rachel that he was giving the birthright to her son. He chose Yosef over Reuven because of Yosef's personal merit.

Various commentators ask how it was possible for Yaakov to violate a specific law of the Torah (*Devarim* 21:16), "He may not make the son of the beloved the firstborn." According to *Rashi*, *Eretz Yisrael* was divided up *per capita*, so there was no favoring of one tribe over another in material terms. The fact that Menasheh and Ephraim were considered as two separate tribes did not affect the way the land was divided up, and Yaakov's choice was simply an ethical one.

Ibn Ezra has a beautiful explanation of why the rights of the firstborn were transferred from Reuven to Yosef. The rights of the firstborn are dependent on the opening of the womb. Reuven was rejected, as we saw

BEREISHIS — VAYECHI

earlier. The two other firstborn were the sons of maidservants. It was thus natural for the rights of the firstborn to apply to Yosef, who was the firstborn to his mother who was Yaakov's wife.

In any event, not only Yaakov was considered the father of all the tribes, but Yosef was a partner in this, for his two sons, too, became tribes of Israel. It is possible that that is what the Torah means when it states, "These are the descendants of Yaakov, Yosef..." The tribes are the descendants of two people: both Yaakov and Yosef, and from now on we are told what happened to them. Yosef thus becomes one of the forefathers, while the other brothers are the sons.

↭§ The Kehunah to Levi and the Monarchy to Yehudah

Chazal explain the three attributes of Reuven: (a) my firstborn, my might; (b) excessive rank; (c) excessive strength. In specifying these three, Yaakov was depriving Reuven of the three special roles normally reserved for the firstborn, these being: (a) the rights of the firstborn; (b) the *kehunah* (priesthood); (c) the monarchy. The first was taken from Reuven and given to Yosef; the second to the tribe of Levi, when it came to the defense of Hashem's glory with the Golden Calf; and the third was given to Yehudah. Here, in Yaakov's blessing, only the first and third were taken from Reuven. Levi was still considered to be Shimon's partner, and was not worthy of receiving the priestly crown. Only when Moshe blessed the Jewish people was Levi mentioned as "Your faithful one," for the tribe's loyalty during the Golden Calf. As opposed to this, not only did the tribe of Shimon not improve during Moshe's time, but on the contrary, it deteriorated in the case of Kozbi bas Tzur, to the extent that Moshe did not even mention Shimon in his blessings. The Midrash tells us that Moshe did draw Reuven close to him, but did not return to him that which had been taken away.

We also find that at the time of Moshe, Dasan and Aviram, both of the tribe of Reuven, protested about the *kehunah*. In fact, *Ramban* at the beginning of *Parashas Korach* explains that the revolt broke out when the firstborn were replaced by the tribe of Levi. The firstborn were annoyed and Dasan, Aviram and others of the Tribe of Reuven used this opportunity to protest the expropriation of the *kehunah* from their tribe, which was the firstborn, and its transfer to Levi. After this rebellion had failed, we never again find in Jewish history any attempt by Reuven to regain any of the birthright. On the other hand, we find a continual quarrel between Yehudah and Menasheh, Yosef's son, over the monarchy.

Tosefta on *Berachos* lists the qualities for which Yehudah was chosen to assume the monarchy. He confessed in regard to Tamar. He was very humble. His tribe sanctified Hashem in public. Thus, *S'forno* explains that the verse, "Yehudah, your brothers will acknowledge you," means that all the other tribes agreed that Yehudah was fitting for the monarchy.

Yaakov not only approved Yehudah's receiving the monarchy, but promised him that, for eternity, "the scepter will not depart from Yehudah." During the Second Temple period too, they prayed, "דְּלָא יַעֲדֵי שָׁלְטָן מִדְּבֵית יְהוּדָה — That the rule should not depart from the house of Yehudah."

Many wonder why this prayer was said in Aramaic. *Rambam's* version of the prayer is in the Biblical Hebrew. Some say that the reason that the prayer was said in Aramaic was that the word שֵׁבֶט can be ambiguous; it can mean not only the scepter of a ruler, but also the "staff of wickedness," or the staff which is used to beat a person, thus having a negative connotation. Since the staffs of evil were common in that era, they preferred to translate its correct sense in Aramaic.

IV.
Blessing or Prophecy?

The commentators clarify Yaakov's blessings to his sons. Ibn Ezra states that these verses are not blessings but prophecy for the future. If these were meant to be blessings, asks Ibn Ezra, where do we see Reuven, Shimon and Levi being blessed? *Rashi*, too, says later that at first Yaakov said what he had to say to each son, and only afterwards did he bless them all with a single communal blessing. The nature of that blessing is not explained. *Rashi* explains on the verse, "Each according to his blessing he blessed them," that each blessing said to any individual person applied to all of them. Thus, when Yaakov attributed to Yehudah the strength of a lion, to Binyamin the voraciousness of a wolf, and to Naftali the swiftness of a deer, one might imagine that they might not then be included in the general blessing. It therefore states, "He blessed them." This means that every blessing was a general one, even though it was said individually.

What is unique about this section of blessings? What was their purpose and nature? Why were words of criticism said to some, while others were praised? Why was an individual blessing pronounced for each, when in the end Yaakov included all together?

Except for Abarbanel, who links all the blessings into a unified whole, there is no comprehensive explanation of this entire *parashah* by any of the *rishonim* or *acharonim*.

❧ Why Superiority for Yehudah?

Abarbanel explains that what Yaakov wished to do was to clarify who was to be the king over his sons, and who would be given the monarchy. Yaakov saw through prophecy that his children would increase greatly, and it was only proper that they have a king to lead them. He thus examined all his sons to see who was worthy of this great mission. He mentioned the qualities of each brother, not in terms of a blessing or rebuke nor to foretell their future, but to determine who among them was worthy of ruling.

Only in Yehudah did he find all the necessary qualifications, and that for four reasons: (a) "Yehudah, your brothers will acknowledge you" — all acknowledged his superiority and were not jealous of him; (b) "Your hand is on the neck of your enemies" — he was so strong in battle that all his enemies turned their backs and fled; (c) "From the prey, my son, you have arisen" — he was superior to his brothers spiritually and ethically. He was not unstable as Reuven, nor were instruments of battle in his hands, as they were in the hands of Shimon and Levi; here Yaakov hinted that Yehudah's hands were not blood stained, on the contrary, it was he who had saved Yosef from being killed, when he had said, "What gain is there if we kill our brother?"; (d) "He crouches as a lion, and as an old lion; who shall rouse him up?" — he had the required strength and the persistence; he remained in his place like a crouching lion, and there was no one who dared to move him. These four reasons were enough to determine that "the scepter shall not depart from Yehudah, nor the ruler's staff from between his feet."

Indeed, Yehudah was always at the head of everything. In regard to selling Yosef, his brothers listened to his advice. When they met with Yosef as the ruler of Egypt, it was he who spoke first. When Yaakov did not want to allow Binyamin to go down to Egypt, it was Yehudah who persuaded his father to change his mind. When Yaakov went down to Egypt, he sent Yehudah before him. When *Bnei Yisrael* camped in the desert, the tribe of Yehudah camped in the east, and was the first to travel. When the altar was consecrated, Nachshon ben Aminadav of the tribe of Yehudah was the first to bring his sacrifice. When the Torah mentions the names of those who would inherit the land with Eleazar the *kohen* and Yehoshua bin Nun, the first to be mentioned was Kalev ben Yefuneh, of the tribe of Yehudah. In war, Hashem commanded, "Yehudah shall go up first." When the land was divided up, the tribe of Yehudah was the first to receive its portion. At the time of Shaul, when he counted the people in order to have them go out to save Yavesh Gilad, all of Israel together numbered three hundred thousand people, while Yehudah was counted separately. The same was true when they counted the people to go out against Amalek. Afterwards, David became king, and from that time the monarchy has always belonged to Yehudah, until *Mashiach* comes.

Even when the Jews were in exile, Yehudah maintained its rule, its members serving as the Exilarchs (*Resh Galusa*). At the time of the Second *Beis HaMikdash*, the head of the *Sanhedrin* was from the tribe of Yehudah. Abarbanel concludes by noting that even in his time, there was no doubt that the leaders of the Jewish people in France and Spain were from the House of David, in keeping with the verse, "The scepter shall not depart from Yehudah, nor the ruler's staff from between his feet."

Why indeed was Yehudah superior to the other brothers? Abarbanel goes on to explain this. It was true that Reuven was the firstborn, but his "instability" made him lose the kingdom. This instability was visible when he "defiled his father's bed," and when his tribe later chose to settle in Transjordan, abandoning *Eretz Yisrael*. Shimon and Levi were unfitting, because "their anger was strong, and their wrath was fierce." They killed Shechem and utterly destroyed the city, not leaving a single person alive. They had also taken part in the sale of Yosef. Abarbanel also finds a hint of Shimon's involvement in the incident of Shittim, and the sin of Levi with Korach. From all of these, Yaakov concluded that neither Shimon nor Levi was suited for the monarchy, for "instruments of battle are in their habitations." A king must set up his monarchy based on justice. In addition, both tribes would be scattered among the others, with Shimon living amidst Yehudah, while Levi would not receive any inheritance in *Eretz Yisrael*, and therefore the monarchy was not suitable for either.

Similarly, Yaakov rejected the other tribes from the monarchy, not because they had sinned, but because of other logical reasons. Zevulun would dwell at the seashore, and would trade with Sidon. They would thus be a tribe of traders, and tradesmen should not become rulers. Yisachar was also not fit to rule, because most of the tribe were farmers. The members of the tribe would "pay a servant's tribute" in order to be exempted from going out to battle. As such, it was not fit to rule. While the tribe of Dan would be one of warriors, its battles would be fought stealthily, "as a serpent by the way," and not with the bravery of a lion. Yaakov stressed that this was not the type of deliverance he sought, but "for Your deliverance I wait, O Lord."

Gad would be prey for the enemy forces, which would attack it. It would always follow behind its enemies, but never before them, and as such it could not be a tribe which would rule and be a model of valor in battle. Asher would do well materially, and would supply the needs of the king and his servants. Naftali would be exemplary in strength, in doing the king's bidding. Its sons would also be known for their sharp minds. As such, they would be excellent as servants of the king, but not as rulers.

Yaakov praised Yosef for two great qualities: (a) Although he was so handsome that "women climb up" to see him, nevertheless "his bow remained strong" and he conquered his passions; (b) he was generous even to his brothers; though they had caused him such grief, he supported them during the famine. Because of these great qualities, Yaakov pronounced lofty blessings on him, but nevertheless did not give him the monarchy, for in spite of his qualities, he did not attain Yehudah's status of being "acknowledged by his brothers." They were jealous of him and even feared him, so he was not fit to rule over them.

Binyamin, too, was not fit to be king, for he was symbolized as being "ravenous as a wolf," which is improper for a king. Furthermore, Yaakov says of him, "In the evening he divides the spoils," and it is improper for a king to build his kingdom on the basis of spoils. This alludes to Shaul, who "swept down on the spoils" at the time of the war against Amalek. Thus the only one left was Yehudah, who was destined to rule because of his strength, generosity and justice.

At the end of his words, Yaakov tied all together. He referred to them as "the tribes of Israel," and compared them to branches coming out of the same root. He blessed all of them with a single blessing, "And this is what their father spoke to them and blessed them." But he had already decided that Yehudah should be the ruler, and that all would be subservient to him, and all accepted this for all future generations.

◆§ The Scepter Shall Not Depart from Yehudah — A Decree or a Promise?

The commentators disagree whether "the scepter shall not depart from Yehudah" was a decree by Hashem or simply a promise. *Ramban* holds that this is not to be explained as a promise, for we are told, "Hashem will lead you and your king whom you will set up over you to a nation which you did not know, you and your fathers," and if the Jews went into exile, there would obviously be no ruler from the tribe of Yehudah. He therefore explains that what the Torah means is that we are forbidden to have any other tribe rule until *Mashiach* comes. Shaul was made king because the people asked Hashem improperly, but even that episode was only a temporary one. Of it we are told, "I will give you a king in My anger and I will take in My wrath." This monarchy was against Hashem's wishes, and that was why Shaul and his sons were killed in battle.

By the same token, when the ten tribes set up their own monarchy, it was against Yaakov's wishes, and on it Hoshea said (*Hoshea* 8:4), "They have set up kings, but not by Me." It is true that the ten tribes relied on the words of Achiya the Shiloni, who told Yeravam (*I Melachim* 11:39), "And I will for this afflict the seed of David, but not forever." They, though, wanted their kingdom to last forever, and thus violated Yaakov's will. That was why their kingdom perished.

Ramban then moves on to discuss the kingdom of the Chashmona'im. The kings of the Chashmona'im were righteous men, and were it not for them, Torah and *mitzvos* would have been forgotten by Israel. They were nevertheless punished very severely, for four of the mighty sons of Matisyahu fell at the hands of their enemies. Their monarchy eventually reached the stage that *Chazal* tell us, "Whoever is from the house of the Chashmona'im is a slave." Some of them were *Tziddukim*, but most of them were righteous, and the only reason they were punished was because they had taken the monarchy from the House of David. Their punishment was "measure for measure," with their slaves ruling in their place, and it was these slaves who destroyed the entire family. Another possibility is that they were punished because they were *kohanim*, who were charged with doing the *avodah* — "sacrificial service" — in the *Beis HaMikdash*, and not to rule.

Yerushalmi Horiyos says: "One does not anoint *kohanim* to be kings." All the more so is this true for other tribes, who are never anointed (*kohanim* at least are anointed for their duties) and who certainly cannot be kings. For *kohanim*, there is a double violation, in that they should not be anointed as kings, and that they should serve in the *Beis HaMikdash*. That was why the Chashmona'im were totally wiped out, without leaving a trace.

Abarbanel, though, disagrees with *Ramban*. According to him, "the scepter shall not depart from Yehudah" is a promise and not a decree. If there were times when the tribes placed kings over themselves who were from other tribes, they were simply annulling Yaakov's promise. Only during the time of David and Shlomo was all of Israel under Yehudah, for during the days of Rechavam they had already violated this promise. It is impossible to say that Yaakov's prophecy only applied to that short a time period.

Abarbanel cites *Ran's* view that Yaakov's promise was not that there would not be any other rulers over Israel, but that from the time that David became king, the scepter of rulers would not depart from his house. There would always be descendants of the house of Yehudah. According to *Ran*, the Chashmona'im were not considered to be a monarchy, because they were always subservient to foreign rulers.

At the end, though, Abarbanel rejects this view as well. It is impossible to say that all that Yaakov promised was that there would always be descendants of the House of David. Rather, the promise was that eventually the monarchy would revert to Yehudah. There was indeed a time that the Chashmona'im ruled without being dependent on outside force. Similarly, they signed treaties with Rome of their own free will, and were not subservient to them. Abarbanel therefore explains that what the Torah meant was not necessarily a reference to the monarchy, but to ruling and authority. Yaakov promised that every type of rule would come from the tribe of Yehudah, both in *Eretz Yisrael* and outside it. It is interesting that in the *tochechah* — "rebuke" — in *Parashas Ki Savo*, Abarbanel says that the period of the Second *Beis HaMikdash* was not a time of redemption, because the Jews were initially subservient to the Greeks and later to the Romans.

∽§ Until Shiloh Comes

Hundreds of explanations have been given of the word "Shiloh." There are some who say that it is the name of a city, while others say it is the name of *Mashiach*. Each commentator follows his own path. Ibn Ezra brings a number of explanations, and tends to say that the verse means "until the *Mishkan* comes to Shiloh," and the meaning of the verse will then be that the scepter would not depart from Yehudah until David appeared as the first king from Yehudah.

On the other hand, *Rashbam's* view is the exact opposite. The scepter would not depart from Yehudah until Rechavam came to Shechem, for it was there that the kingdoms were divided. Shechem is next to Shiloh, or may even be identical with it, as we see in *Yehoshua* 24:1, "And Yehoshua gathered all the tribes of Israel to Shechem," and later it says, "All these matters were in Shiloh before Hashem."

Chasam Sofer also explains it in a similar fashion to *Rashbam*, but according to him Shiloh is a reference to Achiya the Shiloni, who tore the kingdom of Rechavam to shreds and gave the lion's share to Yeravam. "And unto him the people will gather" — he would smash the unified kingdom of Israel, and make of it two nations.

Rabbenu Bachya has an interesting interpretation. What the verse means is that *Mashiach* will be born of a woman, coming from her placenta (שִׁלְיָה — *shilya*), like any other creature. Rabbenu Bachya brings the words of *Rashba* in response to various Christians. The latter said to him that since the Torah says that the scepter will not depart from Yehudah until Shiloh — i.e., *Mashiach* — comes, and since the Jewish monarchy ended at the time of Yeshu, that was surely a sign that *Mashiach* has already come. *Rashba* answered that the meaning of the verse is that the scepter will not depart from Yehudah forever — for *Mashiach* will come. (This is a play on words, where *Rashba* took the verse, לֹא יָסוּר שֵׁבֶט מִיהוּדָה, עַד כִּי יָבֹא שִׁילֹה, and changed the punctuation to read לֹא יָסוּר שֵׁבֶט מִיהוּדָה עַד — כִּי יָבֹא שִׁילֹה). This debate with Christians brings Rabbenu Bachya to explain that *Mashiach* will be born naturally, out of a placenta, and not through the "Holy Spirit." Rabbenu Bachya also adds that Yehudah's name is mentioned here three times, unlike the other brothers, to hint at three periods of monarchy: Yehudah son of Yaakov, David son of Yishai, and *Mashiach*.

Rabbenu Bachya has another interesting comment. In blessing Yehudah, Yaakov used all the letters of the Hebrew alphabet, except for the letter ז. This is a hint that the future Jewish monarchy will not be based on weapons (כְּלֵי זַיִן), and the land will not be taken by the sword. Instead, it will be based on truth and justice. This we see in (*Zecharyah* 4:6): "'Not by might, nor by power, but by My spirit,' says Hashem, Lord of hosts."